# 80 READINGS

## FOR COMPOSITION

### Second Edition

*David Munger*

**PEARSON**
**Longman**

New York    Boston   San Francisco
London   Toronto   Sydney   Tokyo   Singapore   Madrid
Mexico City   Munich   Paris   Cape Town   Hong Kong   Montreal

Publisher: Joseph Opiela
Senior Sponsoring Editor: Virginia L. Blanford
Book Design: DTC
Electronic Page Makeup: Alison Barth Burgoyne
Cover Designer/Manager: John Callahan
Cover Image: Courtesy of Photodisc, Inc.
Manufacturing Buyer: Mary Fischer
Printer and Binder: Courier-Westford
Cover Printer: Coral Graphic Services

ISBN: 0-321-41991-X

1 2 3 4 5 6 7 8 9 10 – CRW – 08 07 06 05

# CONTENTS

# 1 WRITERS ON WRITING   1

# 2 NATURE   53

# 3 WOMEN AND MEN   115

# 4 CUSTOMS AND HABITS   175

# 5 POLITICS AND BELIEF   201

# 6 RIGHTS AND OBLIGATIONS   233

# 7 COMING OF AGE   305

# Rhetorical Contents

## EXAMPLE

## CLASSIFICATION

## COMPARISON AND CONTRAST

## ANALOGY

# PROCESS ANALYSIS

# CAUSE AND EFFECT

# DEFINITION

# DESCRIPTION

# NARRATION

# Argument Contents

# Writing About the Disciplines Contents

## NATURAL SCIENCES/GEOLOGY, BIOLOGY

# POLITICAL SCIENCE/HISTORY

# PSYCHOLOGY

# RELIGION

# SOCIOLOGY/ANTHROPOLOGY

# LITERATURE

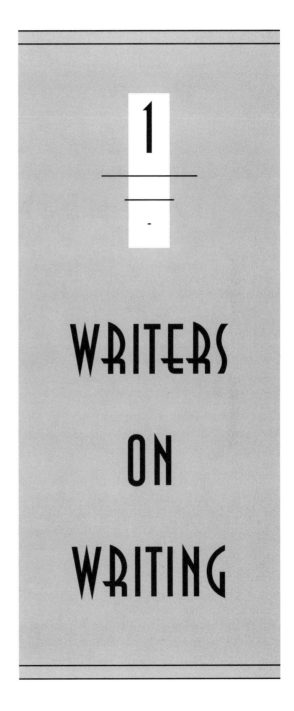

1

WRITERS

ON

WRITING

# JOAN DIDION

# On Keeping a Notebook

Joan Didion (b. 1934) got her first big break in 1956 when she won a writing contest sponsored by *Vogue* magazine. The prize was her choice of a trip to Paris or a job on *Vogue*'s editorial staff. She took the job, and since then has become one of our nation's most acclaimed essayists and novelists. She continues to produce novels, essays, magazine articles, movie screenplays, and recollections, most notably the novels *Salvador*, in 1983, and *The Last Thing He Wanted*, in 1996. In "On Keeping A Notebook," Didion explores the desires and feelings of guilt that make it necessary for her to keep a notebook.

"'THAT WOMAN ESTELLE,'" THE NOTE READS, "'IS PARTLY THE REASON why George Sharp and I are separated today.' *Dirty crêpe-de-Chine wrapper, hotel bar, Wilmington RR, 9:45* A.M. August Monday morning."

Since the note is in my notebook, it presumably has some meaning to me. I study it for a long while. At first I have only the most general notion of what I was doing on an August Monday morning in the bar of the hotel across from the Pennsylvania Railroad station in Wilmington, Delaware (waiting for a train? missing one? 1960? 1961? why Wilmington?), but I do remember being there. The woman in the dirty crêpe-de-Chine wrapper had come down from her room for a beer, and the bartender had heard before the reason why George Sharp and she were separated today. "Sure," he said, and went on mopping the floor. "You told me." At the other end of the bar is a girl. She is talking, pointedly, not to the man beside her but to a cat lying in the triangle of sunlight cast through the open door. She is wearing a plaid silk dress from Peck & Peck, and the hem is coming down.

Here is what it is: the girl has been on the Eastern Shore, and now she is going back to the city, leaving the man beside her, and all she can see ahead are the viscous summer sidewalks and the 3 A.M. long-distance calls that will make her lie awake and then sleep drugged through all the steaming mornings left in August (1960? 1961?). Because she must go directly from the train to lunch in New York, she wishes that she had a safety pin for the hem of the plaid silk dress, and she also wishes that she could forget about the hem and the lunch and stay in the cool bar that smells of disinfectant and malt and make friends with the woman in the crêpe-de-Chine wrapper. She is afflicted by a little self-pity, and she wants to compare Estelles. That is what that was all about.

Why did I write it down? In order to remember, of course, but exactly what was it I wanted to remember? How much of it actually happened? Did any of it? Why do I keep a notebook at all? It is easy to deceive oneself on all those scores. The impulse to write things down is a peculiarly compulsive one, inexplicable to those who do not share it, useful only accidentally, only secondarily, in the way that any compulsion tries to justify itself. I suppose that it begins or does not begin in the cradle. Although I have felt compelled to write things down since I was five years old, I doubt that my daughter ever will, for she is a singularly blessed and accepting child, delighted with life exactly as life presents itself to her, unafraid to go to sleep and unafraid to wake up. Keepers of private notebooks are a different breed altogether, lonely and resistant rearrangers of things, anxious malcontents, children afflicted apparently at birth with some presentiment of loss.

My first notebook was a Big Five tablet, given to me by my mother with the sensible suggestion that I stop whining and learn to amuse myself by writing down my thoughts. She returned the tablet to me a few years ago; the first entry is an account of a woman who believed herself to be freezing to death in the Arctic night, only to find, when day broke, that she had stumbled onto the Sahara Desert, where she would die of the heat before lunch. I have no idea what turn of a five-year-old's mind could have prompted so insistently "ironic" and exotic a story, but it does reveal a certain predilection for the extreme which has dogged me into adult life; perhaps if I were analytically inclined I would find it a truer story than any I might have told about Donald Johnson's birthday party or the day my cousin Brenda put Kitty Litter in the aquarium.

So the point of my keeping a notebook has never been, nor is it now, to have an accurate factual record of what I have been doing or thinking. That would be a different impulse entirely, an instinct for reality which I sometimes envy but do not possess. At no point have I ever been able successfully to keep a diary; my approach to daily life ranges from the grossly negligent to the merely absent, and on those few occasions when I have tried dutifully to record a day's events, boredom has so overcome me that the results are mysterious at best. What is this business about "shopping, typing piece, dinner with E, depressed"? Shopping for what? Typing what piece? Who is E? Was this "E" depressed, or was I depressed? Who cares?

In fact I have abandoned altogether that kind of pointless entry; instead I tell what some would call lies. "That's simply not true," the members of my family frequently tell me when they come up against my memory of a shared event. "The party was *not* for you, the spider was *not* a black widow, *it wasn't that way at all.*" Very likely they are right, for not only have I always had trouble distinguishing between what happened and what merely might have happened, but I remain unconvinced that the distinction, for my purposes, matters. The cracked crab that I recall having for lunch the day my father came home from Detroit in 1945 must certainly be embroidery, worked into the day's pattern to lend verisimilitude; I was ten years old and would not now remember the cracked crab. The day's events did not turn on cracked crab. And yet it is precisely that fictitious crab that makes me see the afternoon all over again, a home movie run all too often, the father bearing gifts, the child weeping, an exercise in family love and guilt. Or that is what it was to me. Similarly, perhaps it never did snow that August in Vermont; perhaps there never were flurries in the night wind, and maybe no one else felt the ground hardening and summer already dead even as we pretended to bask in it, but that was how it felt to me, and it might as well have snowed, could have snowed, did snow.

*How it felt to me:* that is getting closer to the truth about a notebook. I sometimes delude myself about why I keep a notebook, imagine that some thrifty virtue derives from preserving everything observed. See enough and write it down, I tell myself, and then some morning when the world seems drained of wonder, some day when I am only going through the motions of doing what I am supposed to do, which is write—on that bankrupt morning I will simply open my notebook and there it will all be, a forgotten account with accumulated interest, paid passage back to the world out there: dialogue overheard in hotels and elevators and at the hat-check counter in Pavillon (one middle-aged man shows his hat check to another and says, "That's my old football number"); impressions of Bettina Aptheker and Benjamin Sonnenberg and Teddy ("Mr. Acapulco") Stauffer; careful *aperçus* about tennis bums and failed fashion models and Greek shipping heiresses, one of whom taught me a significant lesson (a lesson I could have learned from F. Scott Fitzgerald, but perhaps we must meet the very rich for ourselves) by asking, when I arrived to interview her in her orchid-filled sitting room on the second day of a paralyzing New York blizzard, whether it was snowing outside.

I imagine, in other words, that the notebook is about other people. But of course it is not. I have no real business with what one stranger said to another at the hat-check counter in Pavillon; in fact I suspect that the line "That's my old football number" touched not my own imagination at all, but merely some memory of something once read, probably "The Eighty-Yard Run." Nor is my concern with a woman in a dirty crêpe-de-Chine wrapper in a Wilmington bar. My stake is always, of course, in the unmentioned girl in the plaid silk dress. *Remember what it was to be me:* that is always the point.

It is a difficult point to admit. We are brought up in the ethic that others, any others, all others, are by definition more interesting than ourselves; taught to be diffident, just this side of self-effacing. ("You're the least important person in the room and don't forget it," Jessica Mitford's governess would hiss in her ear on the advent of any social occasion; I copied that into my notebook because it is only recently that I have been able to enter a room without hearing some such phrase in my inner ear.) Only the very young and the very old may recount their dreams at breakfast, dwell upon self, interrupt with memories of beach picnics and favorite Liberty lawn dresses and the rainbow trout in a creek near Colorado Springs. The rest of us are expected, rightly, to affect absorption in other people's favorite dresses, other people's trout.

And so we do. But our notebooks give us away, for however dutifully we record what we see around us, the common denominator of all we see is always, transparently, shamelessly, the implacable "I." We are not talking here about the kind of notebook that is patently for public consumption, a structural conceit for binding together a series of graceful *pensées;* we are talking about something private, about bits of the mind's string too short to use, an indiscriminate and erratic assemblage with meaning only for its maker.

And sometimes even the maker has difficulty with the meaning. There does not seem to be, for example, any point in my knowing for the rest of my life that, during 1964, 720 tons of soot fell on every square mile of New York City, yet there it is in my notebook, labeled "FACT." Nor do I really need to remember that Ambrose Bierce liked to spell Leland Stanford's name "£eland $tanford" or that "smart women almost always wear black in Cuba," a fashion hint without much potential for practical application. And does not the relevance of these notes seem marginal at best?:

> In the basement museum of the Inyo County Courthouse in Independence, California, sign pinned to a mandarin coat: "This MANDARIN COAT was often worn by Mrs. Minnie S. Brooks when giving lectures on her TEAPOT COLLECTION."

> Redhead getting out of car in front of Beverly Wilshire Hotel, chinchilla stole, Vuitton bags with tags reading:

> MRS LOU FOX
> HOTEL SAHARA
>
> VEGAS

Well, perhaps not entirely marginal. As a matter of fact, Mrs. Minnie S. Brooks and her MANDARIN COAT pull me back into my own childhood, for although I never knew Mrs. Brooks and did not visit Inyo County until I was thirty, I grew up in just such a world, in houses cluttered with Indian relics and bits of gold ore and ambergris and the souvenirs my Aunt Mercy Farnsworth brought back from the Orient. It is a long way from that world to Mrs. Lou Fox's world, where we all live now, and is it not just as well to remember that? Might not Mrs. Minnie S. Brooks help me to remember what I am? Might not Mrs. Lou Fox help me to remember what I am not?

But sometimes the point is harder to discern. What exactly did I have in mind when I noted down that it cost the father of someone I know $650 a month to light the place on the Hudson in which he lived before the Crash? What use was I planning to make of this line by Jimmy Hoffa: "I may have my faults, but being wrong ain't one of them"? And although I think it interesting to know where the girls who travel with the Syndicate have their hair done when they find themselves on the West coast, will I ever make suitable use of it? Might I not be better off just passing it on to John O'Hara? What is a recipe for sauerkraut doing in my notebook? What kind of magpie keeps this notebook? *"He was born the night the Titanic went down."* That seems a nice enough line, and I even recall who said it, but is it not really a better line in life than it could ever be in fiction?

But of course that is exactly it: not that I should ever use the line, but that I should remember the woman who said it and the afternoon I heard it. We were on her terrace by the sea, and we were finishing the wine left from lunch, trying to get what sun there was, a California winter sun. The woman whose husband was born the night the *Titanic* went down wanted to rent her house, wanted to go back to her children in Paris. I remember wishing that I could afford the house, which cost $1,000 a month. "Someday you will," she said lazily. "Someday it all comes." There in the sun on her terrace it seemed easy to believe in someday, but later I had a low-grade afternoon hangover and ran over a black snake on the way to the supermarket and was flooded with inexplicable fear when I heard the checkout clerk explaining to the man ahead of me why she was finally divorcing her husband. "He left me no choice," she said over and over as she punched the register. "He has a little seven-month-old baby by her, he left me no choice." I would like to believe that my dread then was for the human condition, but of course it was for me, because I wanted a baby and did not then have one and because I wanted to own the house that cost $1,000 a month to rent and because I had a hangover.

It all comes back. Perhaps it is difficult to see the value in having one's self back in that kind of mood, but I do see it; I think we are well advised to keep on nodding terms with the people we used to be, whether we find them attractive company or not. Otherwise they turn up unannounced and surprise us, come hammering on the mind's door at 4 A.M. of a bad night and demand to know who deserted them, who betrayed them, who is going to make amends. We forget all too soon the things we thought we could never forget. We forget the loves and the betrayals alike, forget what we whispered and what we screamed, forget who we were. I have already lost touch with a couple of people I used to be; one of them, a seven-teen-year-old, presents little threat, although it would be of some interest to me to know again what it feels like to sit on a river levee drinking vodka-and-orange-juice and listening to Les Paul and Mary Ford and their echoes sing "How High the Moon" on the car radio. (You see I still have the scenes, but I no longer perceive myself among those present, no longer could even improvise the dialogue.) The other one, a twenty-three-year-old, bothers me more. She was always a good deal of trouble, and I suspect she will reappear when I least want to see her, skirts too long, shy to the point of aggrava-tion, always the injured party, full of recriminations and little hurts and stories I do not want to hear again, at once saddening me and angering me with her vulnerability and ignorance, an apparition all the more insistent for being so long banished.

It is a good idea, then, to keep in touch, and I suppose that keeping in touch is what notebooks are all about. And we are all on our own when it comes to keeping those lines open to ourselves: your notebook will never help me, nor mine you. *"So what's new in the whiskey business?"* What could that possibly mean to you? To me it means a blonde in a Pucci bathing suit sitting with a couple of fat men by the pool at the Beverly Hills Hotel. Another man ap-proaches, and they all regard one another in silence for a while. "So what's new in the whiskey business?" one of the fat men finally says by way of welcome, and the blonde stands up, arches one foot and dips it in the pool, looking all the while at the cabaña where Baby Pignatari is talking on the telephone. That is all there is to that, except that several years later I saw the blonde coming out of Saks Fifth Avenue in New York with her California complexion and a voluminous mink coat. In the harsh wind that day she looked old and irrevocably tired to me, and even the skins in the mink coat were not worked the way they were doing them that year, not the way she would have wanted them done, and there is the point of the story. For a while after that I did not like to look in the mirror, and my eyes would skim the newspapers and pick out only the deaths, the cancer victims, the premature coronaries, the suicides, and I stopped riding the Lexington Avenue IRT because I noticed for the first time that all the strangers I had seen for years—the man with the seeing-eye dog, the spinster who read the classified pages every day, the fat girl who always got off with me at Grand Central—looked older than they once had.

It all comes back. Even that recipe for sauerkraut: even that brings it back. I was on Fire Island when I first made that sauerkraut, and it was raining, and we drank a lot of bourbon and ate the sauerkraut and went to bed at ten, and I listened to the rain and the Atlantic and felt safe. I made the sauerkraut again last night and it did not make me feel any safer, but that is, as they say, another story.

*Student Essay*

# ANNE JOHNSON

# *On "On Keeping a Notebook"*

Anne's essay in response to Didion's essay is an excellent response to the difficult task of writing about writing.

GREEN COUCH, BURNT ORANGE CARPETING, BRIGHT-ORANGE LAMP, *ginger ale. Late night. A boy I love reads me an essay that shows me the limitless possibility of subjective prose. I love him even more for doing this.*
In Joan Didion's essay "On Keeping a Notebook," she reminds us of the fragility of memory and the difficulty of recording history or "fact." While she writes down snippets of bar conversation or words written on display cards at museums, she manages to address also the difficulty of choosing what to remember and what to dispose of in memory. What she retains is preserved and what she jettisons becomes lost to time and space. (However, Didion suggests that what she wants to remember is what her notes suggest: the presence of the writer—herself—in a bar, on a train, at an interview.)
As an essayist, Didion must listen carefully to every word, whether told directly to her or overheard. What she records, however, is not necessarily what "really" happening but "How it felt to me." On the surface, she describes "exactly" what she sees, but it is

impossible for her to remove herself from her vision. In fact, it is impossible for any writer, even those who go by such titles as "journalist" or "historian" to remove themselves from the scene. Didion acknowledges that in describing what she sees, it is impossible for her to remove herself from the scene; describing makes the describer part of the action.

Didion cites Jessica Mitford's governess as saying "You're the least important person in the room and don't you forget it" on any social occasion. Didion sympathizes with Mitford and rebels against this and other ways of playing down her presence—or anyone else's. For her, the notebook allows her to live out that rebellion; she can make herself the center of scenes that were important to her without failing to defer politely to another's point of view. She is the most important person in the notebook.

The occasions and conversations she notes down allow her to recall and recount moments of her life, which is in turn her reason for writing. The point of her keeping notebooks is not that she should note all the interesting parts and people of the world, but that she can relive her own life. Writing is, for her, both an act of selfishly pleasing herself and, indirectly, pleasing the world with her bright and cogent observations.

*Rereading Didion, I relive my own life. A long time ago, I heard of Estelle from a boy I loved. Exact words fade, but the ideas remain clear, and that moment will stick with me forever. My subjective experience of the subjective experience of Joan Didion . . .*

*Student Essay*

## SUSAN SCARBEK

# Monkey See, Monkey Do

Though this essay seems mostly to complain about writing instructors, it also has a good point to make about writing: there is no one way to write well. Sometimes "I am going bananas" is just the right sentence for the situation.

DURING A RECENT WORKSHOP ON GRAMMAR, A SENTENCE—"I AM going bananas"—was introduced for comment. A short poll of this class has rendered some suggestions about the kinds of responses a teacher would give if a student dared to write such a sentence.

"I am going bananas." The teacher will write "Slang. Please rewrite" in the margin. The student will obviously know what's slangy about the sentence, so no further comment is needed. This approach avoids the sticky question of verbs altogether and especially avoids discussion of intransitive, transitive, and linking verbs.

The teacher will probably get "I am going crazy" as the rewritten sentence. If this does indeed occur, the teacher can choose between two attacks: (1) Ignore it and go on, or (2) Mark "Too colloquial for Standard English models. Please rewrite." The latter is the more common, and certainly the preferred teacher response, since it affords her the opportunity to explain what colloquialisms are and why Standard English is *so* much better. After she has explained how "crazy" can be improved upon, she'll probably get the following rewrite: "I am losing my mind."

This sentence will really allow the teacher to deliver the *coup de grace* to the student! She'll simply write "Idiom" next to the sentence. After all, everyone knows you don't *really* lose your mind unless you have a particularly leaky cranium. If people really could lose their minds, others of us would find them lying around, wouldn't we? The student, of course, will believe this to be another error, and take one of two courses. He'll either give up, or produce an unsolicited rewrite.

The result might look like this: "As a response to certain unfavorable stimuli in an increasingly complex and hostile environment, this subject is developing a labile personality and is rapidly approaching an irrational state of mind." This, fellow writers, is a teacher's gold mine. She might begin with wordiness and jargon, but the majority of students polled (99.9%) felt that the following teacher comment would be most fitting and would help the student understand the intricacies of the English language more fully: "Jargon. Be concise and clear. Why don't you just write, 'I'm going bananas'?"

# MARY WOLLSTONECRAFT SHELLEY

# Introduction to Frankenstein

Mary Wollstonecraft Shelley (1797–1851), herself a great novelist, spent her life in the company of other great literary figures. Her mother, Mary Wollstonecraft (who died in childbirth), was a pioneer feminist; her husband, Percy Bysshe Shelley, a renowned poet. Though in this preface she is quite modest about the accomplishment of writing Frankenstein, giving much credit to her husband, the novel she wrote is today regarded as one of the greatest of all time. Here she describes the moment of inspiration that produced Frankenstein.

THE PUBLISHERS OF THE STANDARD NOVELS, IN SELECTING "Frankenstein" for one of their series, expressed a wish that I should furnish them with some account of the origin of the story. I am the more willing to comply, because I shall thus give a general answer to the question, so very frequently asked me—"How I, then a young girl, came to think of, and to dilate upon, so very hideous an idea?" It is true that I am very averse to bringing myself forward in print; but as my account will only appear as an appendage to a former production, and as it will be confined to such topics as have connection with my authorship alone, I can scarcely accuse myself of a personal intrusion.

It is not singular that, as the daughter of two persons of distinguished literary celebrity, I should very early in life have thought of writing. As a child I scribbled; and my favourite pastime, during the hours given me for recreation, was to "write stories." Still I had a dearer pleasure than this, which was the formation of castles in the air—the indulging in waking dreams—the following up trains of thought, which had for their subject the formation of a succession of imaginary incidents. My dreams were at once more fantastic and agreeable than my writings. In the latter I was a close imitator—rather doing as others had done, than putting down the suggestions of my own mind. What I wrote was intended at least for one other eye—my childhood's companion and friend; but my dreams were all my own; I accounted for them to nobody; they were my refuge when annoyed—my dearest pleasure when free.

I lived principally in the country as a girl, and passed a considerable time in Scotland. I made occasional visits to the more picturesque parts; but my habitual residence was on the blank and dreary northern shores of the Tay, near Dundee. Blank and dreary on retrospection I call them; they were not so to me then. They were the eyry of freedom, and the pleasant region where unheeded I could commune with the creatures of my fancy. I wrote then—but in a most common-place style. It was beneath the trees of the grounds belonging to our house, or on the bleak sides of the woodless mountains near, that my true compositions, the airy flights of my imagination, were born and fostered. I did not make myself the heroine of my tales. Life appeared to me too common-place an affair as regarded myself. I could not figure to myself that romantic woes or wonderful events would ever be my lot; but I was not confined to my own identity; and I could people the hours with creations far more interesting to me at that age, than my own sensations.

After this my life became busier, and reality stood in place of fiction. My husband, however, was, from the first, very anxious that I should prove myself worthy of my parentage, and enrol myself on the page of fame. He was for ever inciting me to obtain literary reputation, which even on my own part I cared for then, though since I have become infinitely indifferent to it. At this time he desired that I should write, not so much with the idea that I could produce any thing worthy of notice, but that he might himself judge how far I possessed the promise of better things hereafter. Still I did nothing. Travelling, and the cares of a family, occupied my time; and study, in the way of reading, or improving my ideas in communication with his far more cultivated mind, was all of literary employment that engaged my attention.

In the summer of 1816, we visited Switzerland, and became the neighbours of Lord Byron. At first we spent our pleasant hours on the lake, or wandering on its shores; and Lord Byron, who was writing the third canto of Childe Harold, was the only one among us who put his thoughts upon paper. These, as he brought them successively to us, clothed in all the light and harmony of poetry, seemed to stamp as divine the glories of heaven and earth, whose influences we partook with him.

But it proved a wet, ungenial summer, and incessant rain often confined us for days to the house. Some volumes of ghost stories, translated from the German into French, fell into our hands. There was the History of the Inconstant Lover, who, when he thought to clasp the bride to whom he had pledged his vows, found himself in the arms of the pale ghost of her whom he had deserted. There was the tale of the sinful founder of his race, whose miserable doom it was to bestow the kiss of death on all the younger sons of his fated house, just when they reached the age of promise. His gigantic, shadowy form, clothed like the ghost in Hamlet, in complete armour, but with the beaver up, was seen at midnight, by the moon's fitful beams, to advance slowly along the gloomy avenue. The shape was lost beneath the shadow of the castle walls; but soon a gate swung back, a step was heard, the door of the chamber opened, and he advanced to the couch of the blooming youths, cradled in healthy sleep. Eternal sorrow sat upon his face as he bent down and kissed the forehead of the boys, who from that hour withered like flowers snapt upon the stalk. I have not seen these stories since then; but their incidents are as fresh in my mind as if I had read them yesterday.

"We will each write a ghost story," said Lord Byron; and his proposition was acceded to. There were four of us. The noble author began a tale, a fragment of which he printed at the end of his poem of Mazeppa. Shelley, more apt to embody ideas and sentiments in the radiance of brilliant imagery, and in the music of the most melodious verse that adorns our language, than to invent the machinery of a story, commenced one founded on the experiences of his early life. Poor Polidori had some terrible idea about a skull-headed lady, who was so punished for peeping through a key-hole—what to see I forget—something very shocking and wrong of course; but when she was reduced to a worse condition than the renowned Tom of Coventry, he did not know what to do with her, and was obliged to despatch her to the tomb of the Capulets, the only place for which she was fitted. The illustrious poets also, annoyed by the platitude of prose, speedily relinquished their uncongenial task.

I busied myself to *think of a story,*—a story to rival those which had excited us to this task. One which would speak to the mysterious fears of our nature, and awaken thrilling horror—one to make the reader dread to look round, to curdle the blood, and quicken the beatings of the heart. If I did not accomplish these things, my ghost story would be unworthy of its name. I thought and pondered—vainly. I felt that blank incapability of invention which is the greatest misery of authorship, when dull Nothing replies to our anxious invocations. *Have you thought of a story?* I was asked each morning, and each morning I was forced to reply with a mortifying negative.

Every thing must have a beginning, to speak in Sanchean phrase, and that beginning must be linked to something that went before. The Hindoos give the world an elephant to support it, but they make the elephant stand upon a tortoise. Invention, it must be humbly admitted, does not consist in creating out of void, but out of chaos; the materials must, in the first place, be afforded: it can give form to dark, shapeless substances, but cannot bring into being the substance itself. In all matters of discovery and invention, even of those that appertain to the imagination, we are continually reminded of the story of Columbus and his egg. Invention consists in the capacity of seizing on the capabilities of a subject, and in the power of moulding and fashioning ideas suggested to it.

Many and long were the conversations between Lord Byron and Shelley, to which I was a devout but nearly silent listener. During one of these, various philosophical doctrines were discussed, and among others the nature of the principle of life, and whether there was any probability of its ever being discovered and communicated. They talked of the experiments of Dr. Darwin, (I speak not of what the Doctor really did, or said that he did, but, as more to my purpose, of what was then spoken of as having been done by him,) who preserved a piece of vermicelli in a glass case, till by some extraordinary means it began to move with voluntary motion. Not thus, after all, would life be given. Perhaps a corpse would be reanimated; galvanism had given token of such things: perhaps the component parts of a creature might be manufactured, brought together, and endued with vital warmth.

Night waned upon this talk, and even the witching hour had gone by, before we retired to rest. When I placed my head on my pillow, I did not sleep, nor could I be said to think. My imagination, unbidden, possessed and guided me, gifting the successive images that arose in my mind with a vividness far beyond the usual bounds of reverie. I saw—with shut eyes, but acute mental vision,— I saw the pale student of unhallowed arts kneeling beside the thing he had put together. I saw the hideous phantasm of a man stretched

out, and then, on the working of some powerful engine, show signs
of life and stir with an uneasy, half vital motion. Frightful must it
be; for supremely frightful would be the effect of any human
endeavour to mock the stupendous mechanism of the Creator of
the world. His success would terrify the artist; he would rush away
from his odious handywork, horror-stricken. He would hope that,
left to itself, the slight spark of life which he had communicated
would fade; that this thing, which had received such imperfect animation, would subside into dead matter; and he might sleep in the
belief that the silence of the grave would quench for ever the transient existence of the hideous corpse which he had looked upon as
the cradle of life. He sleeps; but he is awakened; he opens his eyes;
behold the horrid thing stands at his bedside, opening his curtains,
and looking on him with yellow, watery, but speculative eyes.

I opened mine in terror. The idea so possessed my mind, that a
thrill of fear ran through me, and I wished to exchange the ghastly
image of my fancy for the realities around. I see them still; the very
room, the dark *parquet,* the closed shutters, with the moonlight
struggling through, and the sense I had that the glassy lake and
white high Alps were beyond. I could not so easily get rid of my
hideous phantom; still it haunted me. I must try to think of something else. I recurred to my ghost story,—my tiresome unlucky ghost
story! O! if I could only contrive one which would frighten my
reader as I myself had been frightened that night!

Swift as light and as cheering was the idea that broke in upon
me. "I have found it! What terrified me will terrify others; and I
need only describe the spectre which had haunted my midnight pillow." On the morrow I announced that I had *thought of a story.* I
began that day with the words, *It was on a dreary night of November,*
making only a transcript of the grim terrors of my waking dream.

At first I thought but of a few pages—of a short tale; but Shelley
urged me to develope the idea at greater length. I certainly did not
owe the suggestion of one incident, nor scarcely of one train of feeling, to my husband, and yet but for his incitement, it would never
have taken the form in which it was presented to the world. From
this declaration I must except the preface. As far as I can recollect,
it was entirely written by him.

And now, once again, I bid my hideous progeny go forth and
prosper. I have an affection for it, for it was the offspring of happy
days, when death and grief were but words, which found no true

echo in my heart. Its several pages speak of many a walk, many a drive, and many a conversation, when I was not alone; and my companion was one who, in this world, I shall never see more. But this is for myself; my readers have nothing to do with these associations.

# JOHN O'HAYRE

# A First Look at Gobbledygook

This essay is taken from a United States Department of the Interior, Bureau of Land Management, publication *Gobbledygook Has Gotta Go*. The author, John O'Hayre, is an employee of the Bureau. In his preface, O'Hayre says, "If we are to succeed in these times of new technologies, new demands, and new attitudes, we must improve our communications radically. We must abandon soggy formality and incoherence in favor of modern personal communications. No longer can gobbledygook be allowed to clog communication lines." This work was published in 1966. If we can believe what we read about the proliferation of "officialese," we can only conclude that O'Hayre's crusade has made little progress in more than thirty years.

A DISGRUNTLED STATE DIRECTOR TOSSED A COPY OF A MEMO ON OUR desk some time back. "Here's a lusty sample of what good writing ain't," he said. "Maybe you can use it to show some of our staff how not to write."

He picked up the memo and rattled it, saying: "All I did was write this solicitor a short memo. I told him I thought we could solve a nasty trespass case we'd both been working on. We suggested we give this trespasser a special-use permit and make him legal. That way we'd all get off the hook. All I asked the solicitor was, 'is this okay with you?'"

He threw the memo on the desk and scowled. "Cripes! All he had to do was say 'yes' or 'no.' But look what he sends me!"

Properly meek by this time, I asked: "Did the solicitor say 'yes' or 'no'?"

The state director whirled: "How the heck do I know! I've only read it twice!"

There was no doubt about it, that state director had a problem; he simply couldn't get readable writing out of his staff, or, more important this day, his solicitor.

Our distressed state director wasn't alone in his sweat over unreadable writing. Leaders in government, business, and industry have had the same feverish feeling for years. One chemical company executive put it this way: "If our antifreeze had the same quality as our writing, we'd rust out half the radiators in the country in six months."

A study showed executives in one company used 200 words to write 125-word memos, eight paragraphs for four-paragraph letters, and nearly 200 pages for 100-page reports. Another corporation finally got so frustrated it quit trying to hire writers and started training the ones it already had. Most big corporations are doing this now; they have to. This way they get good writing and save good money—lots of it. An average letter's cost varies from $6 for top executives to $2 at lower levels.

Let's read the memo that shook up the state director:

To: State Director
From: John Lawbook, Solicitor
Subject: Roland Occupancy Trespass

This responds to your memorandum dated February 21,1964, requesting that we review and comment concerning the subject Roland trespass on certain lands under reclamation withdrawal.

We appreciate your apprising us of this matter and we certainly concur that appropriate action is in order to protect the interests of the United States.

We readily recognize the difficult problem presented by this situation, and if it can be otherwise satisfactorily resolved, we would prefer to avoid trespass action. If you determine it permissible to legalize the Roland occupancy and hay production by issuance of a special use permit, as suggested in your memorandum, we have no objection to that procedure.

Any such permit should be subject to cancellation when the lands are actively required for reclamation purposes and should provide for the right of the officers, agents, and employees of the

United States at all times to have unrestricted access and ingress to, passage over, and egress from all said lands, to make investigations of all kinds, dig test pits and drill test holes, to survey for reclamation and irrigation works, and to perform any and all necessary soil and moisture conservation work.

If we can be of any further assistance in this matter, please advise. We would appreciate being informed of the disposition of this problem.

Before we edit the solicitor's memo, let's look at two of its weak points:

1. *False Opening:* The solicitor starts his memo by telling the state director: "This is my memo to you, answering your memo to me." Who could care less? Openings like this tell nobody nothing. Yet many memos and letters start in this word-wasteful manner.

2. *Writer's Grade:** The solicitor's memo has 217 words, 44 difficult words, 3 syllables or over, and a writer's grade of 53; it should grade out at 70 or above to be reasonably readable. A high grade means that, even if you're not saying what you mean, you're saying it readably well. Your sentences are short, your constructions simple, and your words are not painfully syllabic. A high writer's grade is a guarantee of readable writing. With it you're in business as a writer; without it you're in trouble with the reader.

A basic rule for all writing is: Have something to say; say it simply; quit! The next rule is: After you've quit, go over it again with a harsh pencil and a vengeance, crossing out everything that isn't necessary.

Let's see if the solicitor's memo takes well to the pencil. On our first trip through, in order to be fair to the solicitor, we won't change any of his words or word order.

Let's start penciling out:

~~This responds to your memorandum dated February 21,1964, requesting that we review and comment~~ concerning the ~~subject~~ Roland trespass ~~on certain lands under reclamation withdrawal.~~

~~We appreciate your apprising us of this matter and~~ we ~~certainly~~ concur that ~~appropriate~~ action is in order ~~to protect the interests of the United States.~~

---

*Refers to the Lensear Write Formula, a system for grading effective writing used by this author.

~~We readily recognize the difficult problem presented by this situa-~~ ~~tion, and if it can be otherwise satisfactorily resolved,~~ we would prefer to avoid trespass action. If you determine it permissible to legalize the Roland occupancy ~~and hay production~~ by issuance of a special use permit, ~~as suggested in your memorandum,~~ we have no objection ~~to that procedure.~~

Any such permit should be subject to cancellation ~~when the lands are actively required for reclamation purposes~~ and should provide for the right of ~~the officers, agents, and employees of the~~ United States at all times ~~to have unrestricted access and ingress to, passage over, and egress from all said lands, to make investigations of all kinds, dig test pits and drill test holes, to survey for reclamation and irrigation works, and~~ to perform any ~~and all~~ necessary ~~soil and moisture con-~~ ~~servation~~ work.

~~If we can be of any further assistance in this matter, please advise.~~ We would appreciate being informed of the disposition of this problem.

What did we accomplish in this quick trip? Well, let's see. We cut the number of words from 217 to 75, cut the difficult words from 44 to 10, and raised the writer's grade from 53 (difficult) to 60 (acceptable).

Can we cut more yet? Let's go over it again and see, still without changing the solicitor's words or word order.

First sentence: Concerning the Roland trespass case, we concur that action is in order.

We can throw this whole sentence out, because: (1) the subject heading of the memo clearly states what the memo concerns; and (2) both knew "action was in order." That's why they had been writing each other.

Second and third sentences: We would prefer to avoid trespass action. If you determine it permissible to legalize Roland's occupancy by issuance of a special use permit, we have no objection.

Let's leave this for now; it contains the essence of the memo; it's the answer.

Fourth sentence: Any such permit should be subject to cancellation and should provide for the right of the United States at all times to perform all necessary work.

Let's throw this out, too. The state director and his staff issue special use permits as a matter of routine. They know what cancellation clauses and special-use provisions these have to carry. Why tell them what they already know?

Fifth sentence: We would appreciate being informed of the disposition of this problem.

Let's leave this sentence as it is and see what we have left after two editings.

> We would prefer to avoid trespass action. If you determine it permissible to legalize Roland's occupancy by issuance of a special use permit, we have no objection.
>
> We would appreciate being informed of the disposition of the problem.

A recount shows we're now down to 38 words, 8 difficult words, and have a writer's grade of 68.

The question now is: Does the edited memo carry the essential message and does it read easily? It does both pretty well. However, it could have a little more clarity and a little less pretension if it said simply:

> We'd like to avoid trespass action, if possible. So, if you can settle this case by issuing Roland a special use permit, go ahead. Please keep us informed.

This is the way we would have written the memo had we been in the solicitor's seat. The memo now has 28 words, 2 difficult words, and a writer's grade of 70. That's good writing.

Let's go back to the original memo. What we did first was to concentrate on axing out empty words and phrases. Note how they strain to sound unnatural—and succeed. Note how they can be replaced with simple, direct words.

First and second sentences: This responds to your memorandum dated February 21, 1964, requesting that we review and comment concerning the subject Roland trespass on certain lands under reclamation withdrawal. We appreciate your apprising us of this matter, and we certainly concur that appropriate action is in order to protect the interests of the United States.

How much better had he said: "Got your memo on the Roland trespass case. You're right; action is needed."

Third sentence: We readily recognize the difficult problem pre-

sented by this situation, and if it can be otherwise satisfactorily resolved, we would prefer to avoid trespass action.

Why didn't he just say, "The problem is tough, and we'd like to
avoid trespass action if we can"?

Fourth sentence: If you determine it permissible to legalize
Roland's occupancy by issuance of a special use permit, as suggested in your memorandum, we have no objection to that procedure.

It's a lot clearer this way: "If you can solve this problem by issuing Roland a special use permit, go ahead."

Fifth sentence: Any such permit should be subject to cancellation
when the lands are actively required for reclamation purposes and
should provide for the right of officers, agents and employees of the
United States at all times to have unrestricted access and ingress to,
passage over, and egress from all said lands, to make investigations
of all kinds, dig test pits and drill test holes, to survey for reclamation
and irrigation works, and to perform any and all necessary soil and
moisture conservation work.

Such a lawyerish enumeration belongs, if it belongs at all, in a
legal contract, not in an inter-office memo. If the solicitor felt an
obligation to give the state director a reminder, he might have said:
"Please spell out the Government's cancellation rights and right-to-
use provisions in the permit."

Sixth and seventh sentences (adequate but somewhat high-
blown): If we can be of any further assistance in this matter, please
advise. We would appreciate being informed of the disposition of this
problem.

It's somewhat better, at least shorter, this way: "If we can be of
further help, please call. Keep us informed."

How does the whole, empty-word-less memo read now? Would
it, too, be satisfactory? Let's look:

> Got your memo on the Roland trespass case. You're right; action
> is needed. The problem *is* tough, and we'd like to avoid trespass
> action if we can. So, if you can settle this case by issuing Roland
> a special-use permit, go ahead. Please spell out the Government's
> cancellation rights and right-to-use provisions in the permit.
>
> If we can be of further help, please call. Keep us informed.

In this version we have 70 words, only four difficult words, and
a writer's grade of 69.

Moreover, we've said everything the solicitor said in his original memo, even the stuff that didn't need saying. The only difference is that we threw out the empty words, shortened the sentences, changed the passive to the active, and generally tried to say things simply, directly, and clearly. The gobbledygook is gone!

# VIRGINIA WOOLF

# *If Shakespeare Had Had a Sister*

Virginia Woolf (1882–1941) was a poet, essayist, editor, and most notably, a novelist. She was the focus of the "Bloomsbury Group," a gathering of important thinkers, including T. S. Eliot, John Maynard Keynes, and E. M. Forster, who had wide influence in the early part of this century. In this passage from *A Room of One's Own* (1929), she builds a convincing case that a woman in Elizabethan England would never have been allowed the opportunity to create works like Shakespeare's plays.

IT IS A PERENNIAL PUZZLE WHY NO WOMAN WROTE A WORD OF THAT extraordinary [Elizabethan] literature when every other man, it seemed, was capable of song or sonnet. What were the conditions in which women lived, I asked myself; for fiction, imaginative work that is, is not dropped like a pebble upon the ground, as science may be; fiction is like a spider's web, attached ever so lightly perhaps, but still attached to life at all four corners. Often the attachment is scarcely perceptible; Shakespeare's plays, for instance, seem to hang there complete by themselves. But when the web is pulled askew, hooked up at the edge, torn in the middle, one remembers that these webs are not spun in midair by incorporeal creatures, but are the work of suffering human beings, and are attached to grossly material things, like health and money and the houses we live in. . . .

But what I find . . . is that nothing is known about women before the eighteenth century. I have no model in my mind to turn about this way and that. Here am I asking why women did not write poetry in the Elizabethan age, and I am not sure how they were educated; whether they were taught to write; whether they had sitting-rooms to themselves; how many women had children before they were twenty-one; what, in short, they did from eight in the morning till eight at night. They had no money evidently; according to Professor Trevelyan they were married whether they liked it or not before they were out of the nursery, at fifteen or sixteen very likely. It would have been extremely odd, even upon this showing, had one of them suddenly written the plays of Shakespeare, I concluded, and I thought of that old gentleman, who is dead now, but was a bishop, I think, who declared that it was impossible for any woman, past, present, or to come, to have the genius of Shakespeare. He wrote to the papers about it. He also told a lady who applied to him for information that cats do not as a matter of fact go to heaven, though they have, he added, souls of a sort. How much thinking those old gentlemen used to save one! How the borders of ignorance shrank back at their approach! Cats do not go to heaven. Women cannot write the plays of Shakespeare.

Be that as it may, I could not help thinking, as I looked at the works of Shakespeare on the shelf, that the bishop was right at least in this; it would have been impossible, completely and entirely, for any woman to have written the plays of Shakespeare in the age of Shakespeare. Let me imagine, since facts are so hard to come by, what would have happened had Shakespeare had a wonderfully gifted sister, called Judith, let us say. Shakespeare himself went, very probably—his mother was an heiress—to the grammar school, where he may have learnt Latin—Ovid, Virgil and Horace—and the elements of grammar and logic. He was, it is well known, a wild boy who poached rabbits, perhaps shot a deer, and had, rather sooner than he should have done, to marry a woman in the neighbourhood, who bore him a child rather quicker than was right. That escapade sent him to seek his fortune in London. He had, it seemed, a taste for the theatre; he began by holding horses at the stage door. Very soon he got work in the theatre, became a successful actor, and lived at the hub of the universe, meeting everybody, knowing everybody, practising his art on the boards, exercising his wits in the streets, and even getting access to the palace of the queen. Meanwhile his extraordinarily gifted sister, let us suppose, remained at home. She was as adventurous, as imaginative, as agog to see the world as he was. But she was not sent to school. She had no chance of learning grammar and logic, let alone of reading Horace and Virgil. She picked up a book now and then, one of her brother's perhaps, and read a few pages. But then her parents came in and told her to mend the stockings or mind the stew and not moon about with books and papers. They would have spoken sharply but kindly, for they were substantial people who knew the conditions of life for a woman and loved their daughter—indeed, more likely than not she was the apple of her father's eye. Perhaps she scribbled some pages up in an apple loft on the sly, but was careful to hide them or set fire to them. Soon, however, before she was out of her teens, she was to be betrothed to the son of a neighbouring wool-stapler. She cried out that marriage was hateful to her, and for that she was severely beaten by her father. Then he ceased to scold her. He begged her instead not to hurt him, not to shame him in this matter of her marriage. He would give her a chain of beads or a fine petticoat, he said; and there were tears in his eyes. How could she disobey him? How could she break his heart? The force of her own gift alone drove her to it. She made up a small parcel of her belongings, let herself down by a rope one summer's night and took the road to London. She was not seventeen. The birds that sang in the hedge were not more musical than she was. She had the quickest fancy, a gift like her brother's, for the tune of words. Like him, she had a taste for the theatre. She stood at the stage door; she wanted to act, she said. Men laughed in her face. The manager—a fat, loose-lipped man—guffawed. He bellowed something about poodles dancing and women acting—no woman, he said, could possibly be an actress. He hinted—you can imagine what. She could get no training in her craft. Could she even seek her dinner in a tavern or roam the streets at midnight? Yet her genius was for fiction and lusted to feed abundantly upon the lives of men and women and the study of their ways. At last—for she was very young, oddly like Shakespeare the poet in her face, with the same grey eyes and rounded brows—at last Nick Greene the actor-manager took pity on her; she found herself with child by that gentleman and so— who shall measure the heat and violence of the poet's heart when caught and tangled in a woman's body?—killed herself one winter's night and lies buried at some cross-roads where the omnibuses now stop outside the Elephant and Castle.

That, more or less, is how the story would run, I think, if a woman in Shakespeare's day had had Shakespeare's genius. But for my part, I agree with the deceased bishop, if such he was—it is unthinkable that any woman in Shakespeare's day should have had Shakespeare's genius. For genius like Shakespeare's is not born among labouring, uneducated, servile people. It was not born in England among the Saxons and the Britons. It is not born today among the working classes. How, then, could it have been born among women whose work began, according to Professor Trevelyan, almost before they were out of the nursery, who were forced to it by their parents and held to it by all the power of law and custom?

# NATHANIEL HAWTHORNE

# *Journal Notes on Thoreau*

Following his graduation from Bowdoin College in 1825, Nathaniel Hawthorne (1804–1864) returned to live with his widowed mother and began his literary career. After sixteen years of producing work that was unsatisfactory to him, Hawthorne purchased a share in the transcendentalists' Brook Farm utopian community. In less than two years he found communal living unattractive; married his fiancee, Sophia Peabody; and purchased a home in West Roxbury, Massachusetts, once owned by Ralph Waldo Emerson. It was then that he abandoned his English Gothic style and began to write as an American about the American experience. When he lost his job in the Boston Customs House because of politics, he turned full-time to his writing and in the next five to six years produced the bulk of his total output—including *The Scarlet Letter, The House of the Seven Gables,* and *Twice-Told Tales.* In this passage we see a glimpse of a professional writer's personal journal.

MR. THOREAU DINED WITH US YESTERDAY. HE IS A SINGULAR CHAR-acter—a young man with much of wild original nature still re-maining in him; and so far as he is sophisticated, it is in a way and method of his own. He is as ugly as sin, long-nosed, queer-mouthed, and with uncouth and somewhat rustic, although courteous manners, corresponding very well with such an exterior. But his ugliness is of an honest and agreeable fashion, and becomes him much better than beauty. He was educated, I believe, at Cambridge, and formerly kept school in this town; but for two or three years back, he has repudiated all regular modes of getting a living, and seems inclined to lead a sort of Indian life among civilized men—an Indian life, I mean, as respects the absence of any systematic effort for a livelihood. He has been for sometime an inmate of Mr. Emerson's family; and, in requital, he labors in the garden, and performs such other offices as may suit him—being entertained by Mr. Emerson for the sake of what true manhood there is in him. Mr. Thoreau is a keen and delicate observer of nature—a genuine observer, which, I suspect, is almost as rare a character as even an original poet; and Nature, in return for his love, seems to adopt him as her especial child, and shows him secrets which few others are allowed to witness. He is familiar with beast, fish, fowl, and reptile, and has strange stories to tell of adventures, and friendly passages with these lower brethren of mortality. Herb and flower, likewise, wherever they grow, whether in garden or wild wood, are his familiar friends. He is also on intimate terms with the clouds, and can tell the portents of storms. It is a characteristic trait, that he has great regard for the memory of the Indian tribes, whose wild life would have suited him so well; and strange to say, he seldom walks over a ploughed field without picking up an arrow-point, a spear-head, or other relic of the red men—as if their spirits willed him to be the inheritor of their wealth.

With all this he has more than a tincture of literature—a deep and true taste for poetry, especially the elder poets, although more exclusive than is desirable, like all other Transcendentalists, so far as I am acquainted with them. He is a good writer—at least, he has written one good article, a rambling disquisition on Natural History, in the last *Dial*,—which, he says, was chiefly made up from journals of his own observations. Methinks this article gives a very fair image of his mind and character—so true, minute, and literal in observation, yet giving the spirit as well as the letter of what he sees, even as a lake reflects its wooded banks, showing every leaf, yet giving the wild beauty of the whole scene;—then there are passages in the article of cloudy and dreamy metaphysics, partly affected, and partly the natural exhalations of his intellect;—and also passages where his thoughts seem to measure and attune themselves into spontaneous verse, as they rightfully may, since there is real poetry in him. There is a basis of good sense and of moral truth, too, throughout the article, which also is a reflection of his character; for he is not unwise to think and feel, however imperfect is his own mode of action. On the whole, I find him a healthy and wholesome man to know.

After dinner (at which we cut the first water-melon and musk melon that our garden has ripened) Mr. Thoreau and I walked up the bank of the river; and, at a certain point, he shouted for his boat. Forthwith, a young man paddled it across the river, and Mr. Thoreau and I voyaged further up the stream, which soon became more beautiful than any picture, with its dark and quiet sheet of water, half shaded, half sunny, between high and wooded banks. The late rains have swollen the stream so much, that many trees are standing up to their knees, as it were, in the water; and boughs, which lately swung high in air, now dip and drink deep of the passing wave. As to the poor cardinals, which glowed upon the bank, a few days since, I could see only a few of their scarlet caps, peeping above the water. Mr. Thoreau managed the boat so perfectly, either with two paddles or with one, that it seemed instinct with his own will, and to require no physical effort to guide it. He said that, when some Indians visited Concord a few years since, he found that he had acquired, without a teacher, their precise method of propelling and steering a canoe. Nevertheless, being in want of money, the poor fellow was desirous of selling the boat, of which he was so fit a pilot, and which was built by his own hands; so I agreed to give him his price (only seven dollars) and accordingly became the possessor of the Musketaquid. I wish I could acquire the aquatic skill of its original owner at as reasonable a rate.

# TONI MORRISON

# Nobel Lecture 1993

Although now her list of novels is long, including *The Bluest Eye, Song of Solomon, Tar Baby, Beloved,* and *Jazz,* it wasn't until 1978 that Toni Morrison cut down her editorial work and decided to make a full commitment to writing. Born in 1931 into a poor but hard-working family in Cleveland, Ohio, Morrison was able to attend college and graduate school with the help of her parents. During her years as a professor at Howard University, she wrote in secret and did not let other people see her work. After divorcing her husband, she moved to New York and became an editor at Random House, where her gift as a writer was discovered. Morrison won the Pulitzer Prize for fiction in 1988, and in 1993 she won the Nobel Prize for literature, where she gave the speech reprinted here.

"ONCE UPON A TIME THERE WAS AN OLD WOMAN. BLIND BUT WISE." Or was it an old man? A guru, perhaps. Or a griot soothing restless children. I have heard this story, or one exactly like it, in the lore of several cultures.

"Once upon a time there was an old woman. Blind. Wise."

In the version I know the woman is the daughter of slaves, black, American, and lives alone in a small house outside of town. Her reputation for wisdom is without peer and without question. Among her people she is both the law and its transgression. The honor she is paid and the awe in which she is held reach beyond her neighborhood to places far away, to the city where the intelligence of rural prophets is the source of much amusement.

One day the woman is visited by some young people who seem to be bent on disproving her clairvoyance and showing her up for the fraud they believe she is. Their plan is simple: they enter her house and ask the one question the answer to which rides solely on her difference from them, a difference they regard as a profound disability: her blindness. They stand before her, and one of them says, "Old woman, I hold in my hand a bird. Tell me whether it is living or dead."

She does not answer, and the question is repeated. "Is the bird I am holding living or dead?"

Still she doesn't answer. She is blind and cannot see her visitors, let alone what is in their hands. She does not know their color, gender, or homeland. She only knows their motive.

The old woman's silence is so long, the young people have trouble holding their laughter.

Finally she speaks and her voice is soft but stern. "I don't know," she says. "I don't know whether the bird you are holding is dead or alive, but what I do know is that it is in your hands. It is in your hands."

Her answer can be taken to mean: if it is dead, you have either found it that way or you have killed it. If it is alive, you can still kill it. Whether it is to stay alive, it is your decision. Whatever the case, it is your responsibility.

For parading their power and her helplessness, the young visitors are reprimanded, told they are responsible not only for the act of mockery but also for the small bundle of life sacrificed to achieve its aims. The blind woman shifts attention away from assertions of power to the instrument through which that power is exercised.

Speculation on what (other than its own frail body) that bird-in-the-hand might signify has always been attractive to me, but especially so now, thinking, as I have been, about the work I do that has brought me to this company. So I choose to read the bird as language and the woman as a practiced writer. She is worried about how the language she dreams in, given to her at birth, is handled, put into service, even withheld from her for certain nefarious purposes. Being a writer, she thinks of language partly as a system, partly as a living thing over which one has control, but mostly as agency—as an act with consequences. So the question the children put to her—"Is it living or dead?"—is not unreal because she thinks of language as susceptible to death, erasure, certainly imperiled and salvageable only by an effort of the will. She believes that if the bird in the hands of her visitors is dead, the custodians are responsible for the corpse. For her a dead language is not only one no longer spoken or written; it is unyielding language content to admire its own paralysis. Like statist language, censored and censoring. Ruthless in its policing duties, it has no desire or purpose other than maintaining the free range of its own narcotic narcissism, its own exclusivity and dominance. However moribund, it is not without effect, for it actively thwarts the intellect, stalls conscience, suppresses human potential. Unreceptive to interrogation, it cannot form or tolerate new ideas, shape other thoughts, tell another story, fill baffling silences. Official language smitheryed to sanction ignorance and preserve privilege is a suit of armor, polished to shocking glitter, a husk from which the knight departed long ago. Yet there it is: dumb, predatory, sentimental. Exciting reverence in schoolchildren, providing shelter for despots, summoning false memories of stability, harmony among the public.

She is convinced that when language dies, out of carelessness, disuse, and absence of esteem, indifference or killed by fiat, not only she herself but all users and makers are accountable for its demise. In her country children have bitten their tongues off and use bullets instead to iterate the voice of speechlessness, of disabled and disabling language, of language adults have abandoned altogether as a device for grappling with meaning, providing guidance, or expressing love. But she knows tongue-suicide is not only the choice of children. It is common among the infantile heads of state and power merchants whose evacuated language leaves them with no access to what is left of their human instincts, for they speak only to those who obey, or in order to force obedience.

The systematic looting of language can be recognized by the tendency of its users to forgo its nuanced, complex, midwifery properties for menace and subjugation. Oppressive language does more than represent violence; it is violence; does more than represent the limits of knowledge; it limits knowledge. Whether it is obscuring state language or the faux-language of mindless media; whether it is the proud but calcified language of the academy or the commodity-driven language of science; whether it is the malign language of law-without-ethics, or language designed for the estrangement of minorities, hiding its racist plunder in its literary cheek—it must be rejected, altered, and exposed. It is the language that drinks blood, laps vulnerabilities, tucks its fascist boots under crinolines of respectability and patriotism as it moves relentlessly toward the bottom line and the bottomed-out mind. Sexist language, racist language, theistic language—all are typical of the policing languages of mastery, and cannot, do not permit new knowledge or encourage the mutual exchange of ideas.

The old woman is keenly aware that no intellectual mercenary, no insatiable dictator, no paid-for politician or demagogue, no counterfeit journalist would be persuaded by her thoughts. There is and will be rousing language to keep citizens armed and arming, slaughtered and slaughtering in the malls, courthouses, post offices, playgrounds, bedrooms, and boulevards; stirring, memorializing language to mask the pity and waste of needless death. There will be more diplomatic language to countenance rape, torture, assassination. There is and will be more seductive, mutant language designed to throttle women, to pack their throats like paté-producing geese with their own unsayable, transgressive words; there will be more of the language of surveillance disguised as research; of politics and history calculated to render the suffering of millions mute; of language glamorized to thrill the dissatisfied and bereft into assaulting their neighbors; arrogant, pseudoempirical language crafted to lock creative people into cages of inferiority and hopelessness.

Underneath the eloquence, the glamour, the scholarly associations, however stirring or seductive, the heart of such language is languishing, or perhaps not beating at all—if the bird is already dead.

She has thought about what could have been the intellectual history of any discipline if it had not insisted upon, or been forced into, the waste of time and life that rationalizations for and representations of dominance required—lethal discourses of exclusion blocking access to cognition for both the excluder and the excluded.

The conventional wisdom of the Tower of Babel story is that the collapse was a misfortune. That it was the distraction, or the weight of many languages that precipitated the tower's failed architecture. That one monolithic language would have expedited the building and heaven would have been reached. Whose heaven, she wonders? And what kind? Perhaps the achievement of Paradise was premature, a little hasty, if no one could take the time to understand other languages, other views, other narratives. Had they, the heaven they imagined might have been found at their feet. Complicated, demanding, yes, but a view of heaven as life, not heaven as postlife.

She would not want to leave her young visitors with the impression that language should be forced to stay alive merely to be. The vitality of language lies in its ability to limn the actual, imagined, and possible lives of its speakers, readers, writers. Although its poise is sometimes in displacing experience, it is not a substitute for it. It arcs toward the place where meaning may lie. When a President of the United States thought about the graveyard his country had become and said "The world will little note nor long remember what we say here. But it will never forget what they did here," his simple words were exhilarating in their life-sustaining properties because they refused to encapsulate the reality of 600,000 dead men in a cataclysmic race war. Refusing to monumentalize, disdaining the "final word," the precise "summing up," acknowledging their "poor power to add or detract," his words signal deference to the uncapturability of the life it mourns. It is the deference that moves her, that recognition that language can never live up to life once and for all. Nor should it. Language can never "pin down" slavery, genocide, war. Nor should it yearn for the arrogance to be able to do so. Its force, its felicity is in its reach toward the ineffable.

Be it grand or slender, burrowing, blasting, or refusing to sanctify, whether it laughs out loud or is a cry without an alphabet, the choice word, the chosen silence, unmolested language surges toward knowledge, not its destruction. But who does not know of literature banned because it is interrogative, discredited because it is critical, erased because alternate? And how many are outraged by the thought of a self-ravaged tongue?

Word-work is sublime, she thinks, because it is generative; it makes meaning that secures our difference, our human difference—the way in which we are like no other life.

We die. That may be the meaning of life. But we do language. That may be the measure of our lives.

"Once upon a time . . . ," visitors ask an old woman a question. Who are they, these children? What did they make of that encounter? What did they hear in those final words: "The bird is in your hands"? A sentence that gestures toward possibility or one that drops a latch? Perhaps what the children heard was "It's not my problem. I am old, female, black, blind. What wisdom I have now is in knowing I cannot help you. The future of language is yours."

They stand there. Suppose nothing was in their hands? Suppose the visit was only a ruse, a trick to get to be spoken to, taken seriously as they have not been before? A chance to interrupt, to violate the adult world, its miasma of discourse about them, for them, but never to them? Urgent questions are at stake, including the one they have asked: "Is the bird we hold living or dead?" Perhaps the question meant: "Could someone tell us what is life? What is death?" No trick at all; no silliness. A straightforward question worthy of the attention of a wise one. An old one. And if the old and wise who have lived life and faced death cannot describe either, who can?

But she does not; she keeps her secret, her good opinion of herself, her gnomic pronouncements, her art without commitment. She keeps her distance, enforces it, and retreats into the singularity of isolation, in sophisticated, privileged space.

Nothing, no word follows her declarations of transfer. That silence is deep, deeper than the meaning available in the words she has spoken. It shivers, this silence, and the children, annoyed, fill it with language invented on the spot.

"Is there no speech," they ask her, "no words you can give us that help us break through your dossier of failures? Through the education you have just given us that is no education at all because we are paying close attention to what you have done as well as to what you have said? To the barrier you have erected between generosity and wisdom?

"We have no bird in our hands, living or dead. We have only you and our important question. Is the nothing in our hands something you could not bear to contemplate, to even guess? Don't you remember being young when language was magic without meaning? When what you could say, could not mean? When the invisible was what imagination strove to see? When questions and demands for answers burned so brightly you trembled with fury at not knowing?

"Do we have to begin consciousness with a battle heroines and heroes like you have already fought and lost, leaving us with nothing in our hands except what you have imagined is there? Your answer is artful, but its artiness embarrasses us and ought to embarrass you. Your answer is indecent in its self-congratulation. A made-for-television script that makes no sense if there is nothing in our hands.

"Why didn't you reach out, touch us with your soft fingers, delay the sound bite, the lesson, until you knew who we were? Did you so despise our trick, our modus operandi, you could not see that we were baffled about how to get your attention? We are young. Unripe. We have heard all our short lives that we have to be responsible. What could that possibly mean in the catastrophe this world has become, where, as a poet said, 'nothing needs to be exposed since it is already barefaced.'? Our inheritance is an affront. You want us to have your old, blank eyes and see only cruelty and mediocrity. Do you think we are stupid enough to perjure ourselves again and again with the fiction of nationhood? How dare you talk to us of duty when we stand waist deep in the toxin of your past?

"You trivialize us and trivialize the bird that is not in our hands. Is there no context for our lives? No song, no literature, no poem full of vitamins, no history connected to experience that you can pass along to help us start strong? You are an adult. The old one, the wise one. Stop thinking about saving your face. Think of our lives and tell us your particularized world. Make up a story. Narrative is radical, creating us at the very moment it is being created. We will not blame you if your reach exceeds your grasp, if love so ignites your words they go down in flames and nothing is left but their scald. Or if, with the reticence of a surgeon's hands, your words suture only the places where blood might flow. We know you can never do it properly—once and for all. Passion is never enough; neither is skill. But try. For our sake and yours, forget your name in the street; tell us what the world has been to you in the dark places and in the light. Don't tell us what to believe, what to fear. Show us belief's wide skirt and the stitch that unravels fear's caul. You, old woman, blessed with blindness, can speak the language that tells us what only language can: how to see without pictures. Language alone protects us from the scariness of things with no names. Language alone is meditation.

"Tell us what it is to be a woman so that we may know what it is to be a man. What moves at the margin. What it is to have no home on this place. To be set adrift from the one you knew. What it is to live at the edge of towns that cannot bear your company.

"Tell us about ships turned away from shorelines at Easter, placenta in a field. Tell us about a wagonload of slaves, how they sang so softly their breath was indistinguishable from the falling snow. How they knew from the hunch of the nearest shoulder that the next stop would be their last. How, with hands prayered in their sex they thought of heat, then suns. Lifting their faces as though it was there for the taking. Turning as though there for the taking. They stop at an inn. The driver and his mate go in with the lamp, leaving them humming in the dark. The horse's void steams into the snow beneath its hooves, and its hiss and melt is the envy of the freezing slaves.

"The inn door opens: a girl and a boy step away from its light.

They climb into the wagon bed. The boy will have a gun in three years, but now he carries a lamp and a jug of warm cider. They pass it from mouth to mouth. The girl offers bread, pieces of meat, and something more: a glance into the eyes of the one she serves. One helping for each man, two for each woman. And a look. They look back. The next stop will be their last. But not this one. This one is warmed."

It's quiet again when the children finish speaking, until the woman breaks into the silence.

"Finally," she says, "I trust you now. I trust you with the bird that is not in your hands because you have truly caught it. Look. How lovely it is, this thing we have done—together."

*Stockholm, 8 December 1993*

# WILLIAM SAFIRE

# *The Perfect Paragraph*

Columnist, author, and former speechwriter for President Richard Nixon, William Safire (b. 1929) was known as a *"wunderkind"* from the days when he was copyboy for the famous New York *Herald Tribune* columnist Tex McCrary. Safire parlayed that job into a successful public relations business, and then into the Nixon White House—after he volunteered his services as a speechwriter during the 1968 election. He was credited with writing many of the "zingers and zappers" that set the tone for Vice President Spiro Agnew's campaign—lines like "nattering nabobs of nepotism" and "the hopeless, hysterical hypochondriacs of history." In 1973, Safire was hired by the *New York Times* to be its conservative columnist. He continues to write that column, as well as another column, *On Language*, for the *New York Times Magazine*. "The Perfect Paragraph" appeared in Safire's *On Language* column in 1995.

THE GREEK ORATOR DEMOSTHENES OWES ME A FAVOR.

His oration "On the Crown," ripping into one of his detractors in an early example of negative campaigning, is rated by many classicists and students of rhetoric as the greatest speech by the greatest public speaker of antiquity. However, in the translations I've seen, he goes on and on in massive blocks of type with no paragraphs.

Sensing that the poor guy needed a break, I broke the speech of Demosthenes into paragraphs when editing an anthology of great speeches. The oration is no great shakes in modern terms—just as the Wright Brothers' plane was not much compared to jetliners—but the broken-up version of his diatribe against that "accursed scribbler" Aeschines is now a lot easier to read.

That's the purpose of paragraphing: to give the reader a breather by sensibly breaking up the prose. A paragraph is to a writer what a quick intake of breath is to a singer—a little interruption that makes possible refreshed continuation.

Barbara Weber sends in this pertinent question from an air base overseas: "Where on earth do you start a new paragraph? I know the official rule is 'when there's a change of scene or subject,' but that's an awfully broad statement. I kind of have an idea about where to start and stop paragraphs, but (a Gallic shrug of the shoulders and hands) I have looked through several grammar books, and the best I could find is that vague definition. Can you help?"

Her note was like a message across the ages from Demosthenes. The first aid I can supply is to caution against the redundancy *shrug the shoulders*. A *shrug* is a hunching forward of the shoulders; only the shoulders can be shrugged; you don't shrug your knees or eyebrows or anything else. Period. Graph.

"Nobody talks in paragraphs," notes Bill Kretzschmar, at work on the Linguistic Atlas Project at the University of Georgia. (The indentation before the quotation marks signifies a paragraph, called for there because a useful prose-writing convention is to start all quotations of each person in dialogue with such an indentation, and I am creating the illusion of having a conversation with an expert on paragraphs.) "The paragraph is purely something written (throughout its history, beginning with little 'pointing hands' next to significant bits of the text in medieval manuscripts), and the tired, old saws about using paragraphs for completed ideas and about making paragraphs complete by including a beginning (topic), middle (evidence, argument) and end (conclusion, transition) seem to me to be good advice."

The trouble with that advice is the narrowness of most newspaper columns. If a reporter were to write a classic unitary paragraph, with its lede, meat and snapper, the prose—cramped into a column width of just over 12 picas, using the front page of The New York Times, for example—would stretch down the page in an uninviting way. Copy editors exist only to make reverse-P signs in the middle of such well-constructed units, introducing that little bit of white space at the start and end of every sentence or two that tempts the reader to keep going. It is like feeding a baby tiny spoonfuls of mashed banana, building an appetite between insertions of the spoon in the ready-to-squawl mouth. That bit-by-bit philosophy is at the heart of modern newspaper layout and accounts for the new ailment of hyper-paragraphication. In the paragraph you are reading, you were grabbed by a topic sentence ("The trouble with that advice . . ."), given the argumentation to support it (why some copy editors exist, then a symbol of prose-breaking as spoon-feeding) and presented with a conclusion ended by a heart-stopping neologism, "hyperpara-graphication." Now pretend you have not yet read this paragraph; hold the newspaper a little farther away, and look at this article as a whole. Would you read this paragraph? Of course not; it seems never to end, which would cause you to ask: Why should any cautious read-er plunge into a block of type from which he may never emerge? On the other hand, if you are into logo-masochism, then at this point you are undergoing the lung-bursting sensation of a swimmer who cannot quite make it up to the surface. To save you from the need for page-to-page resuscitation, the copy editor would first break this para-graph at the sentence beginning "Copy editors," and again at "Now pretend."

Why in those particular places? One reason is what linguists call *the lifeguard factor*, expressed by summer camp counselors as "O.K., you kids, everybody out of the water, you're all turning blue." In the same way, copy editors say, "A couple of inches is more than enough." Grammarians who find this arbitrary and capricious are directed to John F. Kennedy's "Life is unfair."

A second reason (an enumeration is always a good place to hit the graph key) is *the zag component*: any deviation from the march of argument is a good place to take a break. Thus, the sentence begin-ning "Copy editors exist" (recalling the Cartesian proofreader's "I edit, therefore I am")—with its slight delinkage from the previous thought—is a natural place for the medieval finger symbol. A third reason—excuse me. . . .

Thirdly, *the bank substitute*. Fast-leafing readers are being stopped and their attention snatched by "banks" of large type embedded in columns of small type. In that way, a provocative sentence is almost headlined, forcing the disintermediated reader to squint at the small type and search to see if that outrageous line could be true in context. Writers who do not trust the copy desk to jerk the right sentence out of context use the instant-paragraph device to set up their own mini-bank. The lead sentence of this piece, about some Greek character assassin's owing me a favor, is a topic sentence that should properly be followed within the same paragraph by the next two sentences. However, I have this lust to have it stand out, like a bank, and so I make it a paragraph by itself.

Finally (sentence adverbs are excellent graphing spots), there is the *not-so-fast element*. See that "However, I have this lust" sentence ending the previous paragraph? Any contrasting or contrary thought; a careful reservation beginning with *but*; a detour that acknowledges the opposing argument set up with the smarmy *to be sure*—all these are legitimate break points.

How to avoid hyperparagraphication? Consider the lowly ding-bat. If you want to set off items in a list, a range of typographical devices is available. "If you mean to write a paragraph," Professor Kretzschmar observes, "follow the handbooks; if you just want to emphasize something, you can add some additional sign, such as a dash (—) or bullet mark of some kind (e.g., •, > or *), so nobody mistakes your purpose."

# KURT VONNEGUT

# *How to Write with Style*

Kurt Vonnegut's writing has often focused on the conundrum of a technological world—the profusion of technology that makes it so much simpler for government propaganda machines to inject their version of reality into society. Perhaps it is ironic that his work, especially after the publication and subsequent film of his novel *Slaughterhouse Five*, has acquired something of a cult following, particularly among the technological elite: there are more references to Vonnegut on the Internet than to any of the other writers appearing in this book. What has Vonnegut himself to say about all this? "The Internet stuff is spooky," Vonnegut commented after someone sent him a printed copy of the Alt.books.kurt-vonnegut FAQ World Wide Web page. "I am of course not on line. I do remember ham radio operators though, usually in attics or basements, pallid, unsociable, and obsessed, inhabiting a spirit world, and harmless." A writer could do worse than imitate Vonnegut's highly readable, impeccably precise style.

NEWSPAPER REPORTERS AND TECHNICAL WRITERS ARE TRAINED TO reveal almost nothing about themselves in their writings. This makes them freaks in the world of writers, since almost all of the other ink-stained wretches in that world reveal a lot about themselves to readers. We call these revelations, accidental and intentional, elements of style.

These revelations tell us as readers what sort of person it is with whom we are spending time. Does the writer sound ignorant or informed, stupid or bright, crooked or honest, humorless or playful–? And on and on.

Why should you examine your writing style with the idea of improving it? Do so as a mark of respect for your readers, whatever you're writing. If you scribble your thoughts any which way, your readers will surely feel that you care nothing about them. They will mark you down as an egomaniac or a chowderhead—or worse, they will stop reading you.

The most damning revelation you can make about yourself is that you do not know what is interesting and what is not. Don't you yourself like or dislike writers mainly for what they choose to show you or make you think about? Did you ever admire an empty-headed writer for his or her mastery of the language? No.

So your own winning style must begin with ideas in your head.

## 1. Find a Subject You Care About

Find a subject you care about and which you in your heart feel others should care about. It is this genuine caring, and not your games with language, which will be the most compelling and seductive element in your style.

I am not urging you to write a novel, by the way—although I would not be sorry if you wrote one, provided you genuinely cared about something. A petition to the mayor about a pothole in front of your house or a love letter to the girl next door will do.

## 2. Do Not Ramble, Though

I won't ramble on about that.

## 3. Keep It Simple

As for your use of language: Remember that two great masters of language, William Shakespeare and James Joyce, wrote sentences which were almost childlike when their subjects were most profound. "To be or not to be?" asks Shakespeare's Hamlet. The longest word is three letters long. Joyce, when he was frisky, could put together a sentence as intricate and as glittering as a necklace for Cleopatra, but my favorite sentence in his short story "Eveline" is this one: "She was tired." At that point in the story, no other words could break the heart of a reader as those three words do.

Simplicity of language is not only reputable, but perhaps even sacred. The Bible opens with a sentence well within the writing skills of a lively fourteen-year-old: "In the beginning God created the heaven and the earth."

## 4. Have the Guts to Cut

It may be that you, too, are capable of making necklaces for Cleopatra, so to speak. But your eloquence should be the servant of the ideas in your head. Your rule might be this: If a sentence, no matter how excellent, does not illuminate your subject in some new and useful way, scratch it out.

## 5. Sound Like Yourself

The writing style which is most natural for you is bound to echo the speech you heard when a child. English was the novelist Joseph Conrad's third language, and much that seems piquant in his use of English was no doubt colored by his first language, which was Polish. And lucky indeed is the writer who has grown up in Ireland, for the English spoken there is so amusing and musical. I myself grew up in Indianapolis, where common speech sounds like a band saw cutting galvanized tin, and employs a vocabulary as unornamental as a monkey wrench.

In some of the more remote hollows of Appalachia, children still grow up hearing songs and locutions of Elizabethan times. Yes, and many Americans grow up hearing a language other than English, or an English dialect a majority of Americans cannot understand.

All these varieties of speech are beautiful, just as the varieties of butterflies are beautiful. No matter what your first language, you should treasure it all your life. If it happens not to be standard English, and if it shows itself when you write standard English, the result is usually delightful, like a very pretty girl with one eye that is green and one that is blue.

I myself find that I trust my own writing most, and others seem to trust it most, too, when I sound most like a person from Indianapolis, which is what I am. What alternatives do I have? The one most vehemently recommended by teachers has no doubt been pressed on you, as well: to write like cultivated Englishmen of a century or more ago.

### 6. Say What You Mean to Say

I used to be exasperated by such teachers, but am no more. I understand now that all those antique essays and stories with which I was to compare my own work were not magnificent for their datedness or foreignness, but for saying precisely what their authors meant them to say. My teachers wished me to write accurately, always selecting the most effective words, and relating the words to one another unambiguously, rigidly, like parts of a machine. The teachers did not want to turn me into an Englishman after all. They hoped that I would become understandable—and therefore understood. And there went my dream of doing with words what Pablo Picasso did with paint or what any number of jazz idols did with music. If I broke all the rules of punctuation, had words mean whatever I wanted them to mean, and strung them together higgledy-piggledy, I would simply not be understood. So you, too, had better avoid Picasso-style or jazz-style writing, if you have something worth saying and wish to be understood.

Readers want our pages to look very much like pages they have seen before. Why? This is because they themselves have a tough job to do, and they need all the help they can get from us.

### 7. Pity the Readers

They have to identify thousands of little marks on paper, and make sense of them immediately. They have to *read*, an art so difficult that most people don't really master it even after having studied it all through grade school and high school—twelve long years.

So this discussion must finally acknowledge that our stylistic options as writers are neither numerous nor glamorous, since our readers are bound to be such imperfect artists. Our audience requires us to be sympathetic and patient teachers, even willing to simplify and clarify—whereas we would rather soar high above the crowd, singing like nightingales.

That is the bad news. The good news is that we Americans are governed under a unique Constitution, which allows us to write whatever we please without fear of punishment. So the most meaningful aspect of our styles, which is what we choose to write about, is utterly unlimited.

## 8. For Really Detailed Advice

For a discussion of literary style in a narrower sense, in a more technical sense, I commend to your attention *The Elements of Style,* by William Strunk Jr., and E. B. White (Macmillan, 1979). E. B. White is, of course, one of the most admirable literary stylists this country has so far produced.

You should realize, too, that no one would care how well or badly Mr. White expressed himself, if he did not have perfectly enchanting things to say.

## DONALD M. MURRAY

# The Maker's Eye: Revising Your Own Manuscript

"My writing day begins about eleven-thirty in the morning when I turn off the computer and go out to lunch," says Donald Murray about his means of inspiration. "I have written and now I will allow the well to refill." He hasn't stopped writing—at least 500 words a day—since he got his first job at the *Boston Herald* in 1948. In the interim he's won the Pulitzer Prize, published two novels, and written a number of books about writing. He also founded the journalism program at the University of New Hampshire, where he is professor emeritus of English. In this essay, which first appeared in *The Writer* and was then rewritten for a different anthology, he analyzes the processes he and other great writers use to revise their work.

WHEN STUDENTS COMPLETE A FIRST DRAFT, THEY CONSIDER THE JOB of writing done—and their teachers too often agree. When professional writers complete a first draft, they usually feel that they are at the start of the writing process. When a draft is completed, the job of writing can begin.

That difference in attitude is the difference between amateur and professional, inexperience and experience, journeyman and craftsman. Peter F. Drucker, the prolific business writer, calls his first draft the "zero draft"—after that he can start counting. Most writers share the feeling that the first draft, and all of those which follow, are opportunities to discover what they have to say and how best they can say it.

To produce a progression of drafts, each of which says more and says it more clearly, the writer has to develop a special kind of reading skill. In school we are taught to decode what appears on the page as finished writing. Writers, however, face a different category of possibility and responsibility when they read their own drafts. To them the words on the page are never finished. Each can be changed and rearranged, can set off a chain reaction of confusion or clarified meaning. This is a different kind of reading which is possibly more difficult and certainly more exciting.

Writers must learn to be their own best enemy. They must accept the criticism of others and be suspicious of it; they must accept the praise of others and be even more suspicious of it. Writers cannot depend on others. They must detach themselves from their own pages so that they can apply both their caring and their craft to their own work.

Such detachment is not easy. Science fiction writer Ray Bradbury supposedly puts each manuscript away for a year to the day and then rereads it as a stranger. Not many writers have the discipline or the time to do this. We must read when our judgment may be at its worst, when we are close to the euphoric moment of creation.

Then the writer, counsels novelist Nancy Hale, "should be critical of everything that seems to him most delightful in his style. He should excise what he most admires, because he wouldn't thus admire it if he weren't . . . in a sense protecting it from criticism." John Ciardi, the poet, adds, "The last act of the writing must be to become one's own reader. It is, I suppose, a schizophrenic process, to begin passionately and to end critically, to begin hot and to end cold; and, more important, to be passion-hot and critic-cold at the same time."

Most people think that the principal problem is that writers are too proud of what they have written. Actually, a greater problem for most professional writers is one shared by the majority of students. They are overly critical, think everything is dreadful, tear up page after page, never complete a draft, see the task as hopeless.

The writer must learn to read critically but constructively, to cut what is bad, to reveal what is good. Eleanor Estes, the children's book author, explains: "The writer must survey his work critically, coolly, as though he were a stranger to it. He must be willing to prune, expertly and hard-heartedly. At the end of each revision, a manuscript may look . . . worked over, torn apart, pinned together, added to, deleted from, words changed and words changed back. Yet the book must maintain its original freshness and spontaneity."

Most readers underestimate the amount of rewriting it usually takes to produce spontaneous reading. This is a great disadvantage to the student writer, who sees only a finished product and never watches the craftsman who takes the necessary step back, studies the work carefully, returns to the task, steps back, returns, steps back, again and again. Anthony Burgess, one of the most prolific writers in the English-speaking world, admits, "I might revise a page twenty times." Roald Dahl, the popular children's writer, states, "By the time I'm nearing the end of a story, the first part will have been reread and altered and corrected at least 150 times. . . . Good writing is essentially rewriting. I am positive of this."

Rewriting isn't virtuous. It isn't something that ought to be done. It is simply something that most writers find they have to do to discover what they have to say and how to say it. It is a condition of the writer's life.

There are, however, a few writers who do little formal rewriting, primarily because they have the capacity and experience to create and review a large number of invisible drafts in their minds before they approach the page. And some writers slowly produce finished pages, performing all the tasks of revision simultaneously, page by page, rather than draft by draft. But it is still possible to see the sequence followed by most writers most of the time in rereading their own work.

Most writers scan their drafts first, reading as quickly as possible to catch the larger problems of subject and form, then move in closer and closer as they read and write, reread and rewrite.

The first thing writers look for in their drafts is *information*. They know that a good piece of writing is built from specific, accurate, and interesting information. The writer must have an abundance of information from which to construct a readable piece of writing.

Next writers look for *meaning* in the information. The specifics must build to a pattern of significance. Each piece of specific information must carry the reader toward meaning.

Writers reading their own drafts are aware of *audience*. They put themselves in the reader's situation and make sure that they deliver information which a reader wants to know or needs to know in a manner which is easily digested. Writers try to be sure that they anticipate and answer the questions a critical reader will ask when reading the piece of writing.

Writers make sure that the *form* is appropriate to the subject and the audience. Form, or genre, is the vehicle which carries meaning to the reader, but form cannot be selected until the writer has adequate information to discover its significance and an audience which needs or wants that meaning.

Once writers are sure the form is appropriate, they must then look at the *structure*, the order of what they have written. Good writing is built on a solid framework of logic, argument, narrative, or motivation which runs through the entire piece of writing and holds it together. This is the time when many writers find it most effective to outline as a way of visualizing the hidden spine on which the piece of writing is supported.

The element on which writers may spend a majority of their time is *development*. Each section of a piece of writing must be adequately developed. It must give readers enough information so that they are satisfied. How much information is enough? That's as difficult as asking how much garlic belongs in a salad. It must be done to taste, but most beginning writers underdevelop, underestimating the reader's hunger for information.

As writers solve development problems, they often have to consider questions of *dimension*. There must be a pleasing and effective proportion among all the parts of the piece of writing. There is a continual process of subtracting and adding to keep the piece of writing in balance.

Finally, writers have to listen to their own voices. *Voice* is the force which drives a piece of writing forward. It is an expression of the writer's authority and concern. It is what is between the words on the page, what glues the piece of writing together. A good piece of writing is always marked by a consistent, individual voice.

As writers read and reread, write and rewrite, they move closer and closer to the page until they are doing line-by-line editing. Writers read their own pages with infinite care. Each sentence, each line, each clause, each phrase, each word, each mark of punctuation, each section of white space between the type has to contribute to the clarification of meaning.

Slowly the writer moves from word to word, looking through language to see the subject. As a word is changed, cut, or added, as a construction is rearranged, all the words used before that moment and all those that follow that moment must be considered and reconsidered.

Writers often read aloud at this stage of the editing process muttering or whispering to themselves, calling on the ear's experience with language. Does this sound right—or that? Writers edit, shifting back and forth from eye to page to ear to page. I find I must do this careful editing in short runs, no more than fifteen or twenty minutes at a stretch, or I become too kind with myself. I begin to see what I hope is on the page, not what actually is on the page.

This sounds tedious if you haven't done it, but actually it is fun. Making something right is immensely satisfying, for writers begin to learn what they are writing about by writing. Language leads them to meaning, and there is the joy of discovery, of understanding, of making meaning clear as the writer employs the technical skills of language.

Words have double meanings, even triple and quadruple meanings. Each word has its own potential for connotation and denotation. And when writers rub one word against the other, they are often rewarded with a sudden insight, an unexpected clarification.

The maker's eye moves back and forth from word to phrase to sentence to paragraph to sentence to phrase to word. The maker's eye sees the need for variety and balance, for a firmer structure, for a more appropriate form. It peers into the interior of the paragraph, looking for coherence, unity, and emphasis, which make meaning clear.

I learned something about this process when my first bifocals were prescribed. I had ordered a larger section of the reading portion of the glass because of my work, but even so, I could not contain my eyes within this new limit of vision. And I still find myself taking off my glasses and bending my nose towards the page, for my eyes unconsciously flick back and forth across the page, back to another page, forward to still another, as I try to see each evolving line in relation to every other line.

When does this process end? Most writers agree with the great Russian writer Tolstoy, who said, "I scarcely ever reread my published writing. If by chance I come across a page, it always strikes me: all this must be rewritten; this is how I should have written it."

The maker's eye is never satisfied, for each word has the potential to ignite new meaning. This article has been twice written all the way through the writing process, and it was published four years ago. Now it is to be republished in a book. The editors made a few small suggestions, and then I read it with my maker's eye. Now it has been re-edited, revised, re-read, re-re-edited, for each piece of writing is to the writer full of potential and alternatives.

A piece of writing is never finished. It is delivered to a deadline, torn out of the typewriter on demand, sent off with a sense of accomplishment and shame and pride and frustration. If only there were a couple more days, time for just another run at it, perhaps then . . .

# JOHN KEATS

# When I Have Fears That I May Cease to Be

In his short life, John Keats (1795–1821) became a master of the poetic form. His life was punctuated by illness; he watched both his mother and brother die of tuberculosis and was not reluctant to prophesy the same end for himself. In "When I Have Fears," as George Schimmel notes in the essay following this poem, Keats expresses his fear that he would die before he was able to write the works he had in his head. Ironically, it was during periods of illness that Keats produced some of his best work.

When I have fears that I may cease to be
  Before my pen has glean'd my teeming brain,
Before high piled books, in charactry,
  Hold like rich garners the full ripen'd grain;
When I behold, upon the night's starr'd face,
  Huge cloudy symbols of a high romance,
And think that I may never live to trace
  Their shadows, with the magic hand of chance;
And when I feel, fair creature of an hour,
  That I shall never look upon thee more,
Never have relish in the fairy power
  Of unreflecting love;—then on the shore
Of the wide world I stand alone, and think
Till love and fame to nothingness do sink.

*Student Essay*

## GEORGE SCHIMMEL

# Redaction in Keats' "When I Have Fears That I May Cease to Be"

George Schimmel's essay is the result of a close comparison of "When I Have Fears" to another work of Keats, "Sleep and Poetry." Notice how Schimmel supports the assertions he makes, either with a passage from the relevant poem, or the known details of Keats's life.

OF JOHN KEATS WE KNOW A NUMBER OF THINGS: THAT HE WAS BORN son of a stableman, that he trained first at Edmonton and later at Guy's Hospital, London, as a surgeon, and that he died relatively early, at the age of twenty-six, having written by the time of his death more poems than either Chaucer, Shakespeare, or Milton had written by the same age. As Susan Wolfson describes in her essay "Feminizing Keats" and as Professor James Najarian has shrewdly observed, we know, more specifically, that Keats had a sense of his own early death, and because of this set about his own poetry with an unmatched urgency. Keats' urgency is readily observable in many of his poems. Specifically, "Sleep and Poetry," or certain portions of it, prefigures Keats' sonnet "When I Have Fears That I May Cease To Be" because of this urgent sense, and the latter, in effect, redacts or rereads the selections from the earlier poem.

Two themes of "Sleep and Poetry" parallel similar themes of "When I have fears": the charioteer riding his "steeds with streamy manes" among the clouds, and at the poem's end, the fleeing vision and the "sense of real things [that] comes doubly strong." The first, the charioteer, appears in line 125:

> For lo! I see afar,
> O'er sailing the blue cragginess, a car
> And steeds with streamy mains—the charioteer
> Looks out upon the winds with glorious fear:
> And now numerous tramplings quiver lightly
> Along a huge cloud's ridge.

Perhaps the most telling aspect of this equestrian is his artifice: not only is the charioteer an artificial construct, a product of Keats' poetically-oriented imagination, but he *represents* artifice; the charioteer is a symbol of the more majestic forms of poetry. One easily imagines the genesis of the image: staring at shapes in the clouds until one shape yields an actual figure, here a charioteer, and the figure's attendant romance and grandeur. Of course, this immediately recalls the second movement of Keats' sonnet in which the speaker laments what seems his foredoom, his foreshortened experience. The speaker wants to live, to trace romantic images in the clouds:

> When I behold, upon the night's starr'd face,
> Huge cloudy symbols of a high romance,

> And think that I may never live to trace
>    Their shadows, with the magic hand of chance.

Here is the same idea expressed in "Sleep and Poetry." The clouds in both poems naturally pair, not merely for the fact that both concern identical aspects of the weather, but for what the clouds represent. They stand for, at least in part, invention and artifice. The charioteer riding among clouds is an *imagined* charioteer, in very much the same way the speaker of the sonnet fancies romance, "huge cloudy symbols." Similarly, the idea of nothingness is prevalent in both, though perhaps more explicitly in "Sleep and Poetry":

> And in their stead
> A sense of real things comes doubly strong,
> And, like a muddy stream, would bear along
> My soul to nothingness: but I will strive
> Against all doubtings, and will keep alive
> The thought of that same chariot, and the strange
> Journey it went.

The "nothingness" described here exists antithetically to the charioteer, which reveals quite a bit about the speaker's "soul." When the fancy departs, a sense of "real things" supplants it, which threatens to bear away the speaker's soul in the much same way it banishes the visions. The speaker's soul, therefore, is invention, and artifice, and poetic fancy and creation; the nothingness then is reality as *opposed to these things.* But the fact is not apparent in the sonnet until the final three lines:

> —then on the shore
> Of the wide world I stand alone, and think
> Till love and fame to nothingness do sink.

Keats works in the mode of the English sonnet, keenly utilizing each quatrain to express a particular thought, all of which culminate in the couplet, the fulcrum upon which the meaning of the sonnet turns. "Love and fame" also are evident: fame refers to the first stanza, to the books Keats would like to write, and love to the two quatrains following, the romance in the clouds and the "fair creature of an hour." What, though, is this nothingness? Not considering read "Sleep and Poetry" one might well assume that it is mere absence, the physical state of nothing, and while this reading is not incorrect it is certainly not complete. The earlier poem, though, helps us understand nothingness to be that which is induced by doubt, an antithesis to poetry and its faith-built structure, and that which is not the soul; thus it is not absence alone, for it has, paradoxically, a negative value. In light of "Sleep and Poetry," then, the speaker of the sonnet stands on the edge of the world, and thinks, until the things which comprise his concern leave him— the act is one of de-poeticism, of removing the *thingness* from those realities which cause anguish.

The ultimate irony, of course, is that the poet accomplishes this act by his poem; that is, the poet escapes from poetry *through* the poem itself. Although this interpretation seems at first somewhat rarefied, it is really quite simple: though the speaker would enjoy romance, especially one which could be traced and chiselled into poetic shapes (as are the clouds) and though the speaker would like to see the "full-ripen'd grain" of his poetic labors transcribed in "high piled books," these things all describe anguish, especially to the one who has not a full life to live—whose body, as it were, were failing. Thus the poem offers itself as strategy, a means for coping with the anguish of early death, of bodily cessation, and provides an escape  from the *effects* of the poem, and how they bear in upon the physical person—to the physical fact of the poem itself.

# 2

NATURE

# CHIEF SEATTLE

# Address

Chief Seattle (1786?–1866) was chief of the Duwamish and other tribes when the United States took possession of what are now the states of Washington and Oregon. His tribes' situation when he made this speech was similar to what had already been the fate of hundreds of tribes across America: faced with the overwhelming might and numbers of Americans, they were forced into signing disadvantageous treaties—eventually losing almost everything they had. Seattle's speech was made in response to Governor Isaac Stevens' offer to purchase two million acres of Duwampo territory. As Seattle's speech implies, his tribe in fact had little choice in the matter. There has been specu-lation in recent years that the text of this speech was largely fabricated, that Seattle's words were appropriated by white men after the fact. Nonetheless, whatever the source of these words, they remain a profound statement of Native American philosophy, which has been used by whites and Indians alike to better understand the Indian world.

THE GOVERNOR MADE A FINE SPEECH, BUT HE WAS OUTRANGED AND outclassed that day. Chief Seattle, who answered on behalf of the Indians, towered a foot above the Governor. He wore his blanket like the toga of a Roman senator, and he did not have to strain his famous voice, which everyone agreed was audible and distinct at a distance of half a mile. Seattle's oration was in Duwamish. Doctor Smith, who had learned the language, wrote it down; under the flowery garlands of his translation the speech rolls like an articulate iron engine, grim with meanings that outlasted his generation and may outlast all the generations of men. As the amiable follies of the

54

white race become less amiable, the iron rumble of old Seattle's speech sounds louder and more ominous. Standing in front of Doctor Maynard's office in the stumpy clearing, with his hand on the little Governor's head, the white invaders about him and his people before him, Chief Seattle said:

"Yonder sky that has wept tears of compassion upon my people for centuries untold, and which to us appears changeless and eternal, may change. Today is fair. Tomorrow may be overcast with clouds. My words are like the stars that never change. Whatever Seattle says the great chief at Washington can rely upon with as much certainty as he can upon the return of the sun or the seasons. The White Chief says that Big Chief at Washington sends us greetings of friendship and goodwill. That is kind of him for we know he has little need of our friendship in return. His people are many. They are like the grass that covers vast prairies. My people are few. They resemble the scattering trees of a storm-swept plain. The great, and—I presume—good, White Chief sends us word that he wishes to buy our lands but is willing to allow us enough to live comfortably. This indeed appears just, even generous, for the Red Man no longer has rights that he need respect, and the offer may be wise also, as we are no longer in need of an extensive country. . . . I will not dwell on, nor mourn over, our untimely decay, nor reproach our paleface brothers with hastening it, as we too may have been somewhat to blame.

"Youth is impulsive. When our young men grow angry at some real or imaginary wrong, and disfigure their faces with black paint, it denotes that their hearts are black, and then they are often cruel and relentless, and our old men and old women are unable to restrain them. Thus it has ever been. Thus it was when the white men first began to push our forefathers further westward. But let us hope that the hostilities between us may never return. We would have everything to lose and nothing to gain. Revenge by young men is considered gain, even at the cost of their own lives, but old men who stay at home in times of war, and mothers who have sons to lose, know better.

"Our good father at Washington—for I presume he is now our father as well as yours, since King George has moved his boundaries further north—our great good father, I say, sends us word that if we do as he desires he will protect us. His brave warriors will be to us a bristling wall of strength, and his wonderful ships of war will fill our harbors so that our ancient enemies far to the northward—the

Hydas and Tsimpsians—will cease to frighten our women, children, and old men. Then in reality will he be our father and we his children. But can that ever be? Your God is not our God! Your God loves your people and hates mine. He folds his strong and protecting arms lovingly about the paleface and leads him by the hand as a father leads his infant son—but He has forsaken His red children—if they really are his. Our God, the Great Spirit, seems also to have forsaken us. Your God makes your people wax strong every day. Soon they will fill the land. Our people are ebbing away like a rapidly receding tide that will never return. The white man's God cannot love our people or He would protect them. They seem to be orphans who can look nowhere for help. How then can we be brothers? How can your God become our God and renew our prosperity and awaken in us dreams of returning greatness? If we have a common heavenly father He must be partial—for He came to his paleface children. We never saw Him. He gave you laws but He had no word for His red children whose teeming multitudes once filled this vast continent as stars fill the firmament. No; we are two distinct races with separate origins and separate destinies. There is little in common between us.

"To us the ashes of our ancestors are sacred and their resting place is hallowed ground. You wander far from the graves of your ancestors and seemingly without regret. Your religion was written upon tables of stone by the iron finger of your God so that you could not forget. The Red Man could never comprehend nor remember it. Our religion is the traditions of our ancestors—the dreams of our old men, given them in solemn hours of night by the Great Spirit; and the visions of our sachems; and it is written in the hearts of our people.

"Your dead cease to love you and the land of their nativity as soon as they pass the portals of the tomb and wander way beyond the stars. They are soon forgotten and never return. Our dead never forget the beautiful world that gave them being.

"Day and night cannot dwell together. The Red Man has ever fled the approach of the White Man, as the morning mist flees before the morning sun. However, your proposition seems fair and I think that my people will accept it and will retire to the reservation you offer them. Then we will dwell apart in peace, for the words of the Great White Chief seem to be the words of nature speaking to my people out of dense darkness.

"It matters little where we pass the remnant of our days. They will not be many. A few more moons; a few more winters—and not one of the descendants of the mighty hosts that once moved over this broad land or lived in happy homes, protected by the Great Spirit, will remain to mourn over the graves of a people once more powerful and hopeful than yours. But why should I mourn at the untimely fate of my people? Tribe follows tribe, and nation follows nation, like the waves of the sea. It is the order of nature, and regret is useless. Your time of decay may be distant, but it will surely come, for even the White Man whose God walked and talked with him as friend with friend, cannot be exempt from the common destiny. We may be brothers after all. We will see.

"We will ponder your proposition, and when we decide we will let you know. But should we accept it, I here and now make this condition that we will not be denied the privilege without molestation of visiting at any time the tombs of our ancestors, friends and children. Every part of this soil is sacred in the estimation of my people. Every hillside, every valley, every plain and grove, has been hallowed by some sad or happy event in days long vanished. . . . The very dust upon which you now stand responds more lovingly to their footsteps than to yours, because it is rich with the blood of our ancestors and our bare feet are conscious of the sympathetic touch. . . . Even the little children who lived here and rejoiced here for a brief season will love these somber solitudes and at eventide they greet shadowy returning spirits. And when the last Red Man shall have perished, and the memory of my tribe shall have become a myth among the White Men, these shores will swarm with the invisible dead of my tribe, and when your children's children think themselves alone in the field, the store, the shop, upon the highway, or in the silence of the pathless woods, they will not be alone. . . . At night when the streets of your cities and villages are silent and you think them deserted, they will throng with the returning hosts that once filled and still love this beautiful land. The White Man will never be alone.

"Let him be just and deal kindly with my people, for the dead are not powerless."

*Student Essay*

# ALLISON HOBGOOD

# Sioux Sun Dance Ceremony

Here's what Allison Hobgood has to say about the composition of her essay:

The purpose of this paper is to combine a completely fictional, unconscious narrative with factual evidence concerning the Sioux Native American Sun Dance Ceremony. The first person narrator, Strong Bull's younger brother, seeks to honor his dead brother and also to find his own courage and identity. He explains the logistics of the Sun Dance Ceremony while also allowing the reader into his internal thoughts before and during his entire experience.

The alternating narrative between factual, historically based information and fictional insights displays the interconnected nature of the two—the dance itself is inseparable from the mental and physical preparations that precede it. The narrator's thoughts are dream-like and surreal as he has been fasting for many days and is enduring great pain. These unconscious thoughts digress and become stream-of-consciousness as the dance progresses and his fatigue increases.

There are general themes which invade the mind of the narrator as he dances. Initially, he fluidly and coherently recollects the Sioux myth concerning the origin of the Sun and its power. He then begins to chant the Sioux song of the sun, which is taught to a dreamer in order to derive power from this heavenly body. He describes how his physical body feels in its dancing rhythm while also convincing himself of his ability to mentally master the ceremony.

As the narrator becomes fatigued, his thoughts become disjointed and muddled. He looks to his power animal, the red fox, for support and guidance and dreams of the moment when he will see only the white light of unconsciousness, the symbol of his ultimate success. In his stupor, the narrator begins to hallucinate. He imagines that he sees White Buffalo Woman, the mythological creator of the Sioux Sun Dance Ceremony, and dreams that she caresses his body and dances seductively along with him.

The final thoughts of the narrator are completely incoherent and vaguely related. He knows that he is approaching the end of his dance and acknowledges the white light of the unconsciousness. His thanks to the Great Spirit are not only for the obvious, tangible objects which give him strength but also for his belief that he has been successful in honoring his brother.

My paper attempts to relate the major historical aspects of the Sioux Sun Dance Ceremony through a personal, internal and external narrative. We watch as the narrator of this piece works through his fears and insecurities, finding strength and courage within himself. The paper utilizes an ironic end, for the narrator's state of physical unconsciousness implies that he has achieved superior mental clarity. The end of his dance symbolizes the ultimate purpose of the ceremony; not only is honor properly bestowed upon his brother, but the narrator has come of age, gaining strength, confidence, and a personal identity as well.

MY OLDEST BROTHER, STRONG BULL, DIED DURING THE COLD WINTER moons. He had raided on the White Man's camp and had come home an entirely different man. He had seen Death, felt its icy grasp, and had lost his hope and courage. He returned to camp, bringing with him the White Scabs Disease and poison in his heart. As I saw this powerful evil consume him, I knew I must pledge a sacrifice in honor of his bravery.

I approached Lone Bird, the Many-Faces-Man of our tribe, and told him how I longed to honor my brother's spirit; I explained to him my desire to sacrifice my body to the Wakan Tanka, Big Holy. Lone Bird took me to the mountaintop and announced to the Great Spirit that I wished to make this sacrifice. When we returned to the tribe, I told my family of my decision. They supported my participation in a summer Sun Dance Ceremony and my same-age cousin, Runs-With-the-Deer, pledged that he too would make this sacrifice.

*At that moment of creation time, Sun called out to the Great Spirit, Wakan Tanka, and he arrived in a flourish of hot mist and secret power, a shadow speaking with lightning and with thunder. Upon the Great Spirit's arrival, the Sun began to move faster than even the light. He released his life-giving warmth while Wakan Tanka, the Sun's seventh shadow, stood nearby, watching. Some say that they both began to whirl furiously through space and time, uniting in a bolt of lightning and becoming one* (Erdoes and Ortiz, 129-139).

When my people heard that there was to be a Sun Dance, they began at once to prepare. The women crafted ornate decorations for the warriors, head-dresses with porcupine quill work and smooth, buckskin skirts. The chiefs selected a site for the dance and sent word to other neighboring tribes. Lone Bird spoke to me about the importance of my undertaking and began at once to mentally prepare me for my quest.

As the ceremony approached, I became increasingly anxious. What if I was to dishonor the spirit of my brave brother, Strong Bull? I was a young warrior with no real experience and I had witnessed only one other Sun Dance. I remembered how I had marveled at the strength of the fluid dancers. They moved with passion and intensity even as their warm blood coursed down their chests. I also remembered how I had looked away as their skin snagged and tore from the rough sarvisberry sticks and they sank to their knees, too fatigued to stand any longer. I wondered if perhaps I had overestimated my own power, been overconfident concerning my strength. But these fears I shared with no one.

> Wakan tan han he ya u we lo
> Wakan tan han he ya u we lo
> Mita we cohan topa wan la ka nun we
> He ya u we lo anpewi kin he ya
> He ya u we lo e ya ya yo

Coming from above saying, coming from above saying, you will see my deeds, that is what the Sun says, as it comes down (Standing Bear, 216).

There sounds a constant pulse in my head–the solitary throbbing, beat of a drum . . . or of my own swollen heart. An eagle-bone whistle is clasped in my grinding, white teeth and my chest is torn by the bear claw. Torn through, a claw beneath my skin, an attempt to tear out my courage, bleed it from my chest. I defy you, great black bear. My power burns too hotly for your sharp claw–it melts your touch. I yield to nothing but weave with the dawn and the light and the rattle in my head.

Our tribe moved to the selected ceremonial spot, four moons before the Sun Dance was to occur. We paraded to the site on elegant war-ponies, clothed in our best ceremonial dress. Much work still had to be done upon our arrival but our group settled and waited as other tribes joined ours. Together, we formed a camp that was fairly scattered and covered more than mile of land. Within this area were over a hundred tipis, five which were strictly for the dancers and filled with food and drink. I feasted, along with the other chosen warriors, from these tipis for just two moons. Then I began my purification.

On the second dawn before the ceremony, all of the tribes met at the center of camp. Scouts were chosen and sent out to select the cottonwood tree which would be used as the center pole to which the dancers would be tied. In what seemed like only moments, the scouts had picked the appropriate tree and had chopped it down. Twenty or so men were then responsible for carrying the sacred tree back to the center of camp.

During the trek back to the site, the men were permitted four times to stop and rest. At each of the first three stops, Lone Bird or one of the other Many-Faces-Men would call out, WO-O-E-E-E, W-O-O-E-E-E, the cry of the wolf. At the final stop, the men and boys who followed behind the pole procession raced back to camp, vying to be the first to touch the wooden effigy erected at the center of camp, a temporary placeholder for the cottonwood tree.

Once the men arrived with the pole, over twenty other braves joined their forces. Together, these forty men pushed, pulled, and prodded the cottonwood pole into its designated hole and up to a standing position. Laugh Dreamer, our tribe's virtuous Sacred-Vow-Woman, chanted silently through all of this, not wanting to disgrace her family and plague her people if the pole did not stand tall on this first try.

And then the pole was upright. With its bare cottonwood body and raw, white skin, it was beautifully ominous. I stood beneath its majesty, clenching my fists to calm the tremors of my fingers. Only two moons and I would become part of this tree, a human branch, a writhing, sacrificial limb, twisted around its base and twined within its inescapable grasp.

> *Wakan tan han he ya u we lo*
> *Wakan tan han he ya u we lo*
> *Mita we cohan topa wan la ka nun we . . .*

*As I walk with you my Red Fox, your power guides my lame feet. Your cunning is my strength and courage. You call to the sun as it rises to meet the morning and I move to your rhythm. You scamper onto the horizon, melting into the red dawn. Its light fills my hungry mouth and streams into my aching stomach as I dream only of white brightness.*

*Wi wamjano wacipi, wi wamjano wacipi—I dance for the Sun, I dance for the Sun* (Standing Bear, 224).

*There approaches the Holy Woman, she who taught my great people this dance. Dressed in white buffalo skin, she moves with the grace of a waterfall. She walks in haze of white smog, the nectar of the sun. Your hands caress my bare chest, making it pulse with the sweet pain of life. Your eyes flicker to the music of the dawn and dance in my raw heartbeat.*

During my fasting time, I missed much of the before-dance festivities. I waited two moons in the sacred, medicine tipi, taking my sweat baths, abstaining from food or drink, and fulfilling my purification. Outside, I heard the sounds of the owanka ona sto wacipi—the smoothing of the floor dance (Standing Bear, 223). All of the braves and young men not participating in the ceremony were in lines, marching like soldiers, sometimes fifteen abreast, preparing the ground beneath the pole. They placed sagebrush upon the earth and rhythmically trampled it down to smooth out the grass beneath.

The moon was almost in hiding when I was finally ready. The morning was quickly approaching and with it, the start of the ceremony. All of the dancers stood silent at the base of the cottonwood, awaiting the sunrise. Embedded in my chest were two sarvisberry sticks. From these extended two rawhide ropes connecting to the top of the pole. My face and body were adorned in bright paint and my wrists were bound with sagebrush. I wore a piece of rawhide around my neck, cut in the shape of a sunflower, for the sunflower is the only flower to follow the orbit of the sun, always facing it as it moves from dawn to dusk.

As the sun rose in the east, I heard a loud wail from one of the women behind me and then the thundering beat of a drum. I began to move my feet almost instinctively. My fear vanished as I backed away from the pole and I smiled at the pain. My head contained only clarity and I feasted hungrily on my own blood and sweat. I welcomed the dawn and with it, the tearing of my flesh. I embraced my body and my spirit as one, knowing nothing but the music of the Sun, commanding me to dance.

>    *Wakan tan han he ya u we lo*
>    *Wakan tan han . . .*

*I live in the house of the Sun. I dance for you Great Spirit. Praising you for the buffalo, the Red Fox, and the rains—for the Holy White Buffalo Woman, brave Strong Bull—for the light—the black—for this whiteness . . .*

## Works Cited

Erdoes, R. and Alfonso Ortiz. ed. *American Indian Myths and Legends.* New York: Pantheon Books, 1984.

Standing Bear, L. *Land of the Spotted Eagle.* New York: Houghton Mifflin Co., 1933.

*Student Essay*

# DIANA PECK

# *The Shellfish of Arey's Pond*

The quintessential *bad* essay topic is "What I did during my summer vacation." It has acquired such a negative reputation that few students are even assigned it anymore, leaving elementary school teachers across the nation struggling to come up with adequate lesson plans for the first day of school. Yet even topics like this one can be turned into great essays if the recollections are described with a fond realism and the whole piece makes a good point. Diana Peck does precisely that in this essay, progressing in a careful manner from descriptions of the most common shellfish of her pond to the most coveted. A simple description becomes a quest, and in the end becomes a comment on the relationship of humanity and nature.

THE ATLANTIC OCEAN POUNDING THE CAPE COD SHORELINE FINDS a break in the dunes just north of Monomoy Point. Here, it can enter the calm, shallow waters of Pleasant Bay, separated from the ocean's surf by the outsized sand dune named Nauset. Continuing a tidal journey, some ocean water finds its way to the northern reaches of the bay and sidetracks into a small channel called Namequoit. Twice a day, every day, ocean water completes its journey down this channel and fills Arey's Pond, one of the many ponds that terminate similar channels. Nursed by this fresh supply of nutrient-rich waters, Arey's Pond, small though it is, has until recently provided the spawning grounds for a rich variety of marine fauna. When I was a child, many a summer day's activities revolved around the shellfish life of the pond.

The periwinkle was both the most common and the most useless shellfish in the pond. Hundreds of these small black snails, the size of lima beans, littered our tiny beach at low tide. As we stepped on them, unable to avoid them, they squashed into the wet sand, emerging undaunted a moment later. Although edible, they were useless as food since it would have taken a dozen of their soft black insides to produce a thimbleful of escargots. Adults ignored periwinkles, and even children quickly tired of picking them up, waiting for them to stick their bodies out of the shells, then poking them to watch them disappear inside their shells. Sometimes, picking up these shells, we were surprised to find the tiniest fiddler crab had made an empty shell its home. Struggling to pull its right claw, equal in size to the rest of its body, inside the borrowed shell, the crab entertained us for a few moments. We enjoyed it far more, however, when an adult fiddler crab, accidentally shell-less, would run frantically around the beach, terrorized by its vulnerability.

Less common were the horseshoe crabs which the tide brought to our beach. Often they were paired, the male glued to the back of the female, and it thrilled us to pick up one spiny tail and lift up the two helpless, heavy bodies, their dozens of small underlegs thrashing in the air. The dark brown armored semicircles of their bodies, often about ten inches in width, were too heavy for us to hold for long, and so they would usually be freed within a half-minute. Meatless, they had only one use: sometimes my father split a female horseshoe crab with one blow of his axe, put each of her halves in an eel pot, and attracted eels for miles around with her roe.

An animal which was not particularly common but could be found accidentally was the blue crab. The big brother of the Maryland soft-shell crab, this species offered little meat and was therefore usually ignored except at a clambake where the joy of cracking open the shells excused the meager store of meat. The only aggressive variety of shellfish we encountered, this type of crab would endlessly surprise us, pinching our toes as we waded in the water, gripping our drop lines as we pulled up what we thought was a flounder, staring at us through the wires as we hauled up our eel pots.

But hiding in the mud of the pond were the rare bivalves with edible meat, especially sought-after by adults who, aided by curious children, spent whole afternoons searching for them, spurred on by my father's enthusiasm. The most common of the bivalves were clams, called soft-shell clams by the tourists but just plain clams by Cape Codders. My father led the expeditions at dead-low tide, armed with a shovel and a bucket. In the sand near the water, he looked for telltale air holes, then dug a shovelful of mud and dumped it out on the beach. The children, responsible for combing the mud with their fingers to find the smooth, oval bodies of the clams, usually squeezed each clam, watching it squirt a last stream of water through its long, thick neck, then tossed it unceremoniously into the waiting bucket. We worked our way down the shoreline until, as the tide started in, we stood in a few inches of water. Over and over, my father dug into the muck, sending swirls of black grit into the water, raising the pungent smell of disturbed compost, dumping shovelfuls of oozing mud into the shallow water for us to search. Over and over we gushed the mud through our fingers, plucked out the clams, and moved on to the next shovelful, often stepping into the soft warm muck up to our ankles, hearing the "pop" of the suction as we pulled out our feet. The clams, hard-won from the mud, would provide a feast of steamers for all the relatives, as well as bait for the next day's fishing.

More difficult to find were the quahogs, and not until we were older did my father teach us, one by one, how to find them. Adults considered them more of a delicacy than the clams and either ate the meat raw or ground it for chowder. A hard-shelled clam, quahogs have no necks and keep their mantles inside their tightly closed shells. They, too, burrow in the mud, but they keep a ridge of shell just above the surface. To find quahogs, my father, in goggles and bathing suit, floated face down along the shoreline where the water was about a foot deep. The water being too murky to see through, he pulled himself along, feeling the mud with his hands for the telltale ridge. When he found one, he loosened the surrounding mud with his fingers and pulled the quahog out of its hiding place. This was a slow, arduous process, demanding too much patience for most of us children. But my father was motivated by his love for the result of his labors, especially enjoying the sweet flavor of the small quahogs' meat, called cherrystones, as he swallowed them raw.

Even more treasured than quahogs and more difficult to find were the jewels of Arey's Pond: the oysters. Even my father, experienced shellfisherman as he was, had a special smile as he emerged from the water with an oyster. Hiding in their sharp, blotchy, irregularly shaped shells amidst the roots of the eel grass at the shore's edge, oysters were impossible to see. Feeling for them was difficult, because the edges of the eel grass felt similar to the layered edges of the oyster's shell. The grass eventually yielded to pressure, while the oyster remained firm, but anyone pressing hard enough to distinguish the difference was sure to cut his fingers on the reedy edge of the grass or the sharp edge of a shell. Wearing gloves made the hands too clumsy to detect the difference. For my father it was a labor of love. The scores of tiny cuts on his fingers were small payment for the joy of eating a raw oyster, captured only minutes before. Children were never offered oysters, and those adults fortunate enough to be present when my father caught some usually mirrored his sublime expression as they swallowed the fresh meat. Even the oyster's shell had value, serving as bureau-top catchalls, ash trays, or a decorative border for the garden.

We still visit Arey's Pond whenever we can, my father still digging for clams and searching for quahogs. But some years ago, the channel to the bay was deepened to provide access for pleasure boats. The shellfish never recovered. After two or three years some of the clams came back and a few quahogs can still be found, but the oysters are gone and none of the crabs can negotiate the channel. Only the periwinkles remain in abundance to remind us of how it once was.

# MARK TWAIN

# *Two Views of the Mississippi*

Mark Twain was born in 1835, the year of the appearance of Halley's comet, and foresaw his own death with the return of that comet in 1910. Like the comet that framed his life, Mark Twain's writing lurks as a shadow behind all of American literature, and then occasionally, inevitably, bursts onto the scene in a fire of relevance. This unusual essay, excerpted from *Life on the Mississippi,* reveals none of the wry wit usually associated with Mark Twain. It is, instead, a lyrical, pensive reflection on his view of the river before and after he was trained as a riverboat pilot.

THE FACE OF THE WATER, IN TIME, BECAME A WONDERFUL BOOK—A book that was a dead language to the uneducated passenger, but which told its mind to me without reserve, delivering its most cherished secrets as clearly as if it uttered them with a voice. And it was not a book to be read once and thrown aside, for it had a new story to tell every day. Throughout the long twelve hundred miles there was never a page that was void of interest, never one that you could leave unread without loss, never one that you would want to skip, thinking you could find higher enjoyment in some other thing. There never was so wonderful a book written by man; never one whose interest was so absorbing, so unflagging, so sparklingly renewed with every reperusal. The passenger who could not read it was charmed with a peculiar sort of faint dimple on its surface (on the rare occasions when he did not overlook it altogether); but to the pilot that was an *italicized* passage; indeed, it was more than that, it was a legend of the largest capitals, with a string of shouting exclamation points at the end of it; for it meant that a wreck or a rock was buried there that could tear the life out of the strongest vessel that ever floated. It is the faintest and simplest expression the water ever makes, and the most hideous to a pilot's eye. In truth, the passenger who could not read this book saw nothing but all manner of pretty pictures in it, painted by the sun and shaded by the clouds, whereas to the trained eye these were not pictures at all, but the grimmest and most dead-earnest of reading matter.

Now when I had mastered the language of this water and had come to know every trifling feature that bordered the great river as familiarly as I knew the letters of the alphabet, I had made a valuable acquisition. But I had lost something, too. I had lost something which could never be restored to me while I lived. All the grace, the beauty, the poetry had gone out of the majestic river! I still keep in mind a certain wonderful sunset which I witnessed when steamboating was new to me. A broad expanse of the river was turned to blood; in the middle distance the red hue brightened into gold, through which a solitary log came floating, black and conspicuous; in one place a long, slanting mark lay sparkling upon the water; in another the surface was broken by boiling, tumbling rings, that were as many-tinted as an opal; where the ruddy flush was faintest, was a smooth spot that was covered with graceful circles and radiating lines, ever so delicately traced; the shore on our left was densely wooded, and the somber shadow that fell from this forest was broken in one place by a long, ruffled trail that shone like silver; and high above the forest wall a clean-stemmed dead tree waved a single leafy bough that glowed like a flame in the unobstructed splendor that was flowing from the sun. There were graceful curves, reflected images, woody heights, soft distances; and over the whole scene, far and near, the dissolving lights drifted steadily, enriching it, every passing moment, with new marvels of coloring.

I stood like one bewitched. I drank it in, in a speechless rapture. The world was new to me, and I had never seen anything like this at home. But as I have said, a day came when I began to cease from noting the glories and the charms which the moon and the sun and the twilight wrought upon the river's face; another day came when I ceased altogether to note them. Then, if that sunset scene had been repeated, I should have looked upon it without rapture, and should have commented upon it, inwardly, after this fashion: This sun means that we are going to have wind tomorrow; that floating log means that the river is rising, small thanks to it; that slanting mark on the water refers to a bluff reef which is going to kill somebody's steamboat one of these nights, if it keeps on stretching out like that; those tumbling "boils" show a dissolving bar and a changing channel there; the lines and circles in the slick water over yonder are a warning that that troublesome place is shoaling up dangerously; that silver streak in the shadow of the forest is the "break" from a new snag, and he has located himself in the very best place he could have found to fish for steamboats; that tall dead tree, with a single living branch, is not going to last long, and then how is a body ever going to get through this blind place at night without the friendly landmark?

No, the romance and the beauty were all gone from the river. All the value any feature of it had for me now was the amount of usefulness it could furnish toward compassing the safe piloting of a steamboat. Since those days, I have pitied doctors from my heart. What does the lovely flush in a beauty's cheek mean to a doctor but a "break" that rippled above some deadly disease? Are not all her visible charms sown thick with what are to him the signs and symbols of hidden decay? Does he ever see her beauty at all, or doesn't he simply view her professionally, and comment upon her unwholesome condition all to himself? And doesn't he sometimes wonder whether he had gained most or lost most by learning his trade?

# JOHN MUIR

# A Wind-Storm in the Forests

John Muir (1838–1914) has had so many mountains, trails, creeks, and lakes named for him that the U.S. Geological Survey has said it would refuse to approve naming any more landmarks after Muir, to avoid confusion on maps. In his zeal to see the great natural sites of North America, he has been burned by sulfur vents on Mt. Shasta (to avoid being frozen in a blizzard), lived on a crust of bread while hiking through the Alaskan wilderness (so as to see more, while traveling lightly), and survived bouts of malaria and typhoid fever in the swamps of Florida. A founder of the Sierra Club, which has been credited with preserving much of California's wilderness, Muir later in life began to write about some of the spectacular wilderness he so loved—the better for the rest of us to appreciate it. Though we may never experience a severe windstorm in an expansive forest, Muir can relate that experience from his own unconventional viewpoint, painting a picture so vivid that we almost feel like we *are* there, experiencing the storm with Muir.

THE MOUNTAIN WINDS, LIKE THE DEW AND RAIN, SUNSHINE AND snow, are measured and bestowed with love on the forests to develop their strength and beauty. However restricted the scope of other forest influences, that of the winds is universal. The snow bends and trims the upper forests every winter, the lightning strikes a single tree here and there, while avalanches mow down thousands at a swoop as a gardener trims out a bed of flowers. But the winds go to every tree, fingering every leaf and branch and furrowed bole; not one is forgotten; the Mountain Pine towering with outstretched arms on the rugged buttresses of the icy peaks, the lowliest and most retiring tenant of the dells; they seek and find them all, caressing them tenderly, bending them in lusty exercise, stimulating their growth, plucking off a leaf or limb as required, or removing an entire tree or grove, now whispering and cooing through the branches like a sleepy child, now roaring like the ocean; the winds blessing the forests, the forests the winds, with ineffable beauty and harmony as the sure result.

After one has seen pines six feet in diameter bending like grasses before a mountain gale, and ever and anon some giant falling with a crash that shakes the hills, it seems astonishing that any, save the lowest thickset trees, could ever have found a period sufficiently stormless to establish themselves; or, once established, that they should not, sooner or later, have been blown down. But when the storm is over, and we behold the same forests tranquil again, towering fresh and unscathed in erect majesty, and consider what centuries of storms have fallen upon them since they were first planted,—hail, to break the tender seedlings; lightning, to scorch and shatter; snow, winds, and avalanches, to crush and overwhelm,—while the manifest result of all this wild storm-culture is the glorious perfection we behold; then faith in Nature's forestry is established, and we cease to deplore the violence of her most destructive gales, or of any other storm-implement whatsoever.

There are two trees in the Sierra forests that are never blown down, so long as they continue in sound health. These are the Juniper and the Dwarf Pine of the summit peaks. Their stiff, crooked roots grip the storm-beaten ledges like eagles' claws, while their lithe, cord-like branches bend round compliantly, offering but slight holds for winds, however violent. The other alpine conifers— the Needle Pine, Mountain Pine, Two-leaved Pine, and Hemlock Spruce—are never thinned out by this agent to any destructive extent, on account of their admirable toughness and the closeness of their growth. In general the same is true of the giants of the lower zones. The kingly Sugar Pine, towering aloft to a height of more than 200 feet, offers a fine mark to storm-winds; but it is not densely foliaged, and its long, horizontal arms swing round compliantly in the blast, like tresses of green, fluent algae in a brook; while the Silver Firs in most places keep their ranks well together in united strength. The Yellow or Silver Pine is more frequently overturned than any other tree on the Sierra, because its leaves and branches form a larger mass in proportion to its height, while in many places it is planted sparsely, leaving open lanes through which storms may enter with full force. Furthermore, because it is distributed along the lower portion of the range, which was the first to be left bare on the breaking up of the ice-sheet at the close of the glacial winter, the soil it is growing upon has been longer exposed to post-glacial weathering, and consequently is in a more crumbling, decayed condition than the fresher soils farther up the range, and therefore offers a less secure anchorage for the roots.

While exploring the forest zones of Mount Shasta, I discovered the path of a hurricane strewn with thousands of pines of this species. Great and small had been uprooted or wrenched off by sheer force, making a clean gap, like that made by a snow avalanche. But hurricanes capable of doing this class of work are rare in the Sierra, and when we have explored the forests from one extremity of the range to the other, we are compelled to believe that they are the most beautiful on the face of the earth, however we may regard the agents that have made them so.

There is always something deeply exciting, not only in the sounds of winds in the woods, which exert more or less influence over every mind, but in their varied waterlike flow as manifested by the movements of the trees, especially those of the conifers. By no other trees are they rendered so extensively and impressively visible, not even by the lordly tropic palms or tree-ferns responsive to the gentlest breeze. The waving of a forest of the giant Sequoias is indescribably impressive and sublime, but the pines seem to me the best interpreters of winds. They are mighty waving goldenrods, ever in tune, singing and writing wind-music all their long century lives. Little, however, of this noble tree-waving and tree-music will you see or hear in the strictly alpine portion of the forests. The burly Juniper, whose girth sometimes more than equals its height, is about as rigid as the rocks on which it grows. The slender lash-like sprays of the Dwarf Pine stream out in wavering ripples, but the tallest and slenderest are far too unyielding to wave even in the heaviest gales. They only shake in quick, short vibrations. The Hemlock Spruce, however, and the Mountain Pine, and some of the tallest thickets of the Two-leaved species bow in storms with considerable scope and gracefulness. But it is only in the lower and middle zones that the meeting of winds and woods is to be seen in all its grandeur.

One of the most beautiful and exhilarating storms I ever enjoyed in the Sierra occurred in December, 1874, when I happened
to be exploring one of the tributary valleys of the Yuba River. The
sky and the ground and the trees had been thoroughly rain-washed
and were dry again. The day was intensely pure, one of those incom-
parable bits of California winter, warm and balmy and full of white
sparkling sunshine, redolent of all the purest influences of the
spring, and at the same time enlivened with one of the most brac-
ing wind-storms conceivable. Instead of camping out, as I usually
do, I then chanced to be stopping at the house of a friend. But
when the storm began to sound, I lost no time in pushing out into
the woods to enjoy it. For on such occasions Nature has always
something rare to show us, and the danger to life and limb is hardly
greater than one would experience crouching deprecatingly beneath
a roof.

It was still early morning when I found myself fairly adrift.
Delicious sunshine came pouring over the hills, lighting the tops of
the pines, and setting free a steam of summery fragrance that con-
trasted strangely with the wild tones of the storm. The air was mot-
tled with pine-tassels and bright green plumes, that went flashing
past in the sunlight like birds pursued. But there was not the slightest dustiness, nothing less pure than leaves, and ripe pollen, and
flecks of withered bracken and moss. I heard trees falling for hours
at the rate of one every two or three minutes; some uprooted, partly
on account of the loose, water-soaked condition of the ground;
others broken straight across, where some weakness caused by fire
had determined the spot. The gestures of the various trees made a
delightful study. Young Sugar Pines, light and feathery as squirrel-
tails, were bowing almost to the ground; while the grand old patri-
archs, whose massive boles had been tried in a hundred storms,
waved solemnly above them, their long, arching branches streaming
fluently on the gale, and every needle thrilling and ringing and
shedding off keen lances of light like a diamond. The Douglas
Spruces, with long sprays drawn out in level tresses, and needles
massed in a gray, shimmering glow, presented a most striking
appearance as they stood in bold relief along the hilltops. The
madroños in the dells, with their red bark and large glossy leaves
tilted every way, reflected the sunshine in throbbing spangles like
those one so often sees on the rippled surface of a glacier lake. But
the Silver Pines were now the most impressively beautiful of all.

Colossal spires 200 feet in height waved like supple goldenrods chanting and bowing low as if in worship, while the whole mass of their long, tremulous foliage was kindled into one continuous blaze of white sun-fire. The force of the gale was such that the most stead-fast monarch of them all rocked down to its roots with a motion plainly perceptible when one leaned against it. Nature was holding high festival, and every fiber of the most rigid giants thrilled with glad excitement.

I drifted on through the midst of this passionate music and motion, across many a glen, from ridge to ridge; often halting in the lee of a rock for shelter, or to gaze and listen. Even when the grand anthem had swelled to its highest pitch, I could distinctly hear the varying tones of individual trees;—Spruce, and Fir, and Pine, and leafless Oak,—and even the infinitely gentle rustle of the withered grasses at my feet. Each was expressing itself in its own way,—singing its own song, and making its own peculiar gestures,—manifesting a richness of variety to be found in no other forest I have yet seen. The coniferous woods of Canada, and the Carolinas, and Florida, are made up of trees that resemble one another about as nearly as blades of grass, and grow close together in much the same way. Coniferous trees, in general, seldom possess individual character, such as is manifest among Oaks and Elms. But the California forests are made up of a greater number of distinct species than any other in the world. And in them we find, not only a marked differentiation into special groups, but also a marked individuality in almost every tree, giving rise to storm effects indescribably glorious.

Toward midday, after a long, tingling scramble through copses of hazel and ceanothus, I gained the summit of the highest ridge in the neighborhood; and then it occurred to me that it would be a fine thing to climb one of the trees to obtain a wider outlook and get my ear close to the Æolian music of its topmost needles. But under the circumstances the choice of a tree was a serious matter. One whose instep was not very strong seemed in danger of being blown down, or of being struck by others in case they should fall; another was branchless to a considerable height above the ground, and at the same time too large to be grasped with arms and legs in climbing; while others were not favorably situated for clear views. After cautiously casting about, I made choice of the tallest of a group of Douglas Spruces that were growing close together like a tuft of grass, no one of which seemed likely to fall unless all the rest fell with it.

Though comparatively young, they were about 100 feet high, and their lithe, brushy tops were rocking and swirling in wild ecstasy. Being accustomed to climb trees in making botanical studies, I experienced no difficulty in reaching the top of this one, and never before did I enjoy so noble an exhilaration of motion. The slender tops fairly flapped and swished in the passionate torrent, bending and swirling backward and forward, round and round, tracing indescribable combinations of vertical and horizontal curves, while I clung with muscles firm braced, like a bobolink on a reed.

In its widest sweeps my tree-top described an arc of from twenty to thirty degrees, but I felt sure of its elastic temper, having seen others of the same species still more severely tried—bent almost to the ground indeed, in heavy snows—without breaking a fiber. I was therefore safe, and free to take the wind into my pulses and enjoy the excited forest from my superb outlook. The view from here must be extremely beautiful in any weather. Now my eye roved over the piny hills and dales as over fields of waving grain, and felt the light running in ripples and broad swelling undulations across the valleys from ridge to ridge, as the shining foliage was stirred by corresponding waves of air. Oftentimes these waves of reflected light would break up suddenly into a kind of beaten foam, and again, after chasing one another in regular order, they would seem to bend forward in concentric curves, and disappear on some hill-side, like sea-waves on a shelving shore. The quantity of light reflected from the bent needles was so great as to make whole groves appear as if covered with snow, while the black shadows beneath the trees greatly enhanced the effect of the silvery splendor.

Excepting only the shadows there was nothing somber in all this wild sea of pines. On the contrary, notwithstanding this was the winter season, the colors were remarkably beautiful. The shafts of the pine and libocedrus were brown and purple, and most of the foliage was well tinged with yellow; the laurel groves, with the pale undersides of their leaves turned upward, made masses of gray; and then there was many a dash of chocolate color from clumps of manzanita, and jet of vivid crimson from the bark of the madroños, while the ground on the hillsides, appearing here and there through openings between the groves, displayed masses of pale purple and brown.

The sounds of the storm corresponded gloriously with this wild exuberance of light and motion. The profound bass of the naked branches and boles booming like waterfalls; the quick, tense vibrations of the pine-needles, now rising to a shrill, whistling hiss, now falling to a silky murmur; the rustling of laurel groves in the dells, and the keen metallic click of leaf on leaf—all this was heard in easy analysis when the attention was calmly bent.

The varied gestures of the multitude were seen to fine advantage, so that one could recognize the different species at a distance of several miles by this means alone, as well as by their forms and colors, and the way they reflected the light. All seemed strong and comfortable, as if really enjoying the storm, while responding to its most enthusiastic greetings. We hear much nowadays concerning the universal struggle for existence, but no struggle in the common meaning of the word was manifest here; no recognition of danger by any tree; no deprecation; but rather an invincible gladness as remote from exultation as from fear.

I kept my lofty perch for hours, frequently closing my eyes to enjoy the music by itself, or to feast quietly on the delicious fragrance that was streaming past. The fragrance of the woods was less marked than that produced during warm rain, when so many balsamic buds and leaves are steeped like tea; but, from the chafing of resiny branches against each other, and the incessant attrition of myriads of needles, the gale was spiced to a very tonic degree. And besides the fragrance from these local sources there were traces of scents brought from afar. For this wind came first from the sea, rubbing against its fresh, briny waves, then distilled through the redwoods, threading rich ferny gulches, and spreading itself in broad undulating currents over many a flower-enameled ridge of the coast mountains, then across the golden plains, up the purple foot-hills, and into these piny woods with the varied incense gathered by the way.

Winds are advertisements of all they touch, however much or little we may be able to read them; telling their wanderings even by their scents alone. Mariners detect the flowery perfume of land-winds far at sea, and sea-winds carry the fragrance of dulse and tangle far inland, where it is quickly recognized, though mingled with the scents of a thousand land-flowers. As an illustration of this, I may tell here that I breathed sea-air on the Firth of Forth, in Scotland, while a boy; then was taken to Wisconsin, where I remained nineteen years; then, without in all this time having breathed one breath of the sea, I walked quietly, alone, from the middle of the Mississippi Valley to the Gulf of Mexico, on a botanical excursion, and while in Florida, far from the coast, my attention wholly bent on the splendid tropical vegetation about me, I suddenly recognized a sea-breeze, as it came sifting through the palmettos and blooming vine-tangles, which at once awakened and set free a thousand dormant associations, and made me a boy again in Scotland, as if all the intervening years had been annihilated.

Most people like to look at mountain rivers, and bear them in mind; but few care to look at the winds, though far more beautiful and sublime, and though they become at times about as visible as flowing water. When the north winds in winter are making upward sweeps over the curving summits of the High Sierra, the fact is sometimes published with flying snow-banners a mile long. Those portions of the winds thus embodied can scarce be wholly invisible, even to the darkest imagination. And when we look around over an agitated forest, we may see something of the wind that stirs it, by its effects upon the trees. Yonder it descends in a rush of water-like ripples, and sweeps over the bending pines from hill to hill. Nearer, we see detached plumes and leaves, now speeding by on level currents, now whirling in eddies, or, escaping over the edges of the whirls, soaring aloft on grand, upswelling domes of air, or tossing on flame-like crests. Smooth, deep currents, cascades, falls, and swirling eddies, sing around every tree and leaf, and over all the varied topography of the region with telling changes of form, like mountain rivers conforming to the features of their channels.

After tracing the Sierra streams from their fountains to the plains, marking where they bloom white in falls, glide in crystal plumes, surge gray and foam-filled in boulder-choked gorges, and slip through the woods in long, tranquil reaches—after thus learning their language and forms in detail, we may at length hear them chanting all together in one grand anthem, and comprehend them all in clear inner vision, covering the range like lace. But even this spectacle is far less sublime and not a whit more substantial than what we may behold of these storm-streams of air in the mountain woods.

We all travel the milky way together, trees and men; but it never occurred to me until this storm-day, while swinging in the wind, that trees are travelers, in the ordinary sense. They make many journeys, not extensive ones, it is true; but our own little journeys, away and back again, are only little more than tree-wavings—many of them not so much.

When the storm began to abate, I dismounted and sauntered down through the calming woods. The storm-tones died away, and, turning toward the east, I beheld the countless hosts of the forests hushed and tranquil, towering above one another on the slopes of the hills like a devout audience. The setting sun filled them with amber light, and seemed to say, while they listened, "My peace I give unto you."

As I gazed on the impressive scene, all the so-called ruin of the storm was forgotten, and never before did these noble woods appear so fresh, so joyous, so immortal.

*Student Essay*

# ANDREW CAMPBELL

# *Night in the Woods*

Good nature writing requires incredibly precise observation about the environment. But precision is not all that is required, because the best nature writing also involves the selection of a worthwhile topic, and the appropriate framing of the subject. In this essay, the frame is a Boy Scout gathering, but the subject is something more profound: the simple beauty of a night in the forest.

MANY THINGS CAN HAPPEN ON A CLEAR MAY NIGHT. I, FOR ONE, WAS stumbling through woods with an indian pump towards the fire-lay I had erected earlier that day. At least I hoped I was; in truth, I was lost. And more than lost, through seven years of Scout campouts, bonfires, and ghost stories, I had camouflaged my fear of the dark.

The responsibility devolved upon me, as the Vigil committee chairman and member of the ceremonies team, to prepare the site of the ceremony. The Vigil candidates, who had risen through the ranks of Boy Scouts and the Order of the Arrow, were to come before me, as Chief of the Fire, for their final preparation before spending their night alone. And now I was lost.

Would I wander forever through the forests of the Southern Appalachians, joining the ranks of the ghosts and bogeymen of the Tuesday night campfire? Or could I live down the story of my returning to the brightly lit circle of friends and organizing a search party for a site I had secretly created myself? As I lugged the increasingly heavy water tank uphill, my wish list began to grow.

I wish I had a bigger flashlight.

I wish a capote was easier to walk in.

I wish water wasn't so dense.

I wish I knew where I was.

I wish I had a friend along.

One wish came true; I found my modest collection of tinder and kindling and awaited the arrival of my other wishes.

Even though I was on the ceremonial team, I had neither the time nor the money to invest in the elaborate American Indian outfits some of my friends made for their ceremonial roles. Therefore I made a capote, a reservation-period Sioux coat, out of an old army blanket—the US was on the inside—to keep myself warm and somewhat authentic. My capote, with its deep, army green folds swathing me from head to mid-calf, was not overly commodious—seated or ambulant. It also itched of government-issue wool. I took it off.

Now more comfortable, I was still alone, and in the dark. Perhaps those earlier ceremony chairmen hadn't found their fires and haunted those who did. Perhaps the storied mountain troglodytes with wild hair, jagged fingernails, and an antipathy for interlopers such as myself had some basis in fact. Perhaps the vicious dogs and shotguns protecting the illegal distilleries and illicit fields of truer tales had migrated into my vicinity. Maybe the spider that just ran down my collar was as large as my frenetic nervous system estimated it to be.

Flipping on my flashlight, a solitary bright white-yellow light, I reviewed my part in the ceremony. A sudden crashing in the branches directly above shattered my feeble concentration as the flashlight fell from my trembling hand; my blood pressure doubled, and my mind's eye rushed to keep pace with my imagination's phantasmagoric deluge. Discovering of a pair of flying squirrels sporting about among the overhanging branches reduced my imaginative possibilities but did nothing to alleviate my pounding heart.

I sat back down in the dark, hoping that the others in camp would not mistake the rapid tattoo for an overexuberant ceremonies drummer and come rescue me. As the buffeting diminished, I began to gauge my surroundings: a common wood, a fire-lay, some underbrush. Certainly, I said to my skeptical self, this was no different than the innumerable forest locales I had safely enjoyed before. Then I saw the fire flies. Too concerned elsewhere, I had not noticed their presence earlier except when, in desperation, I mistook one for a flashlight-equipped companion and hailed him. But now, they began to glide into my world.

I had never seen this type before. Glowing with a warm bluish light with a touch of green, they remained lambent for minutes on end. Now, in the increasingly silent glimmer, they spread back throughout their forest sanctum, each a king of his coleopteran realm. Always two feet above the crisp brown leaves, their soft aura diffused through the trees. Each followed the gently undulating and ever flowing plane, a more orderly reflection of the stars high above the forest canopy. Their cool soothing glow lifted my imagination above myself, into a higher, natural wonder. Where did they come from? Where were they going? Why did they share this moment with me? They each had what I had wished for, light, companionship, orientation, and the stillness of the night.

A few brief hours later, I remained awake, awaiting the dawn. I lay—my capote protecting me against the cool night air—and watched the silver stars churn their silent wakes across the sable sea. A dazzling white-green meteor clove a sudden blazing trail, briefly surpassing its fellow celestial mariners. Alone, I quietly rejoiced in this brilliant display of wonder, framed perfectly across the gloriously dark sky.

# MARY AUSTIN

# *Water Trails of the Ceriso*

Though her books sometimes barely covered their own expenses, Mary Austin's fame in the West was made secure by her intense personality and her association with the literary and cultural elite of the region: she had ties with Jack London, Bret Harte, Ansel Adams, and Willa Cather, to name a few. Her many books, including *Land of Little Rain*, *Earth Horizon*, and *Taos Pueblo*, were recognized as great works by the literary community of the time. Yet her work has only recently begun to be accepted into the larger "canon" of American literature. In "Water Trails of the Ceriso," which originally appeared in *Land of Little Rain*, Mary Austin (1868–1934) offers a unique perspective on the lives of the inhabitants of the desert.

BY THE END OF THE DRY SEASON THE WATER TRAILS OF THE CERISO are worn to a white ribbon in the leaning grass, spread out faint and fanwise toward the homes of gopher and ground rat and squirrel. But however faint to man-sight, they are sufficiently plain to the furred and feathered folk who travel them. Getting down to the eye level of rat and squirrel kind, one perceives what might easily be wide and winding roads to us if they occurred in thick plantations of trees three times the height of a man. It needs but a slender thread of barrenness to make a mouse trail in the forest of the sod. To the little people the water trails are as country roads, with scents as signboards.

It seems that man-height is the least fortunate of all heights from which to study trails. It is better to go up the front of some tall hill, say the spur of Black Mountain, looking back and down across the hollow of the Ceriso. Strange how long the soil keeps the impression of any continuous treading, even after grass has overgrown it. Twenty years since, a brief heyday of mining at Black Mountain made a stage road across the Ceriso, yet the parallel lines that are the wheel traces show from the height dark and well defined. Afoot in the Ceriso one looks in vain for any sign of it. So all the paths that wild creatures use going down to the Lone Tree

Spring are mapped out whitely from this level, which is also the level of the hawks.

There is little water in the Ceriso at the best of times, and that little brackish and smelling vilely, but by a lone juniper where the rim of the Ceriso breaks away to the lower country, there is a perpetual rill of fresh sweet drink in the midst of lush grass and watercress. In the dry season there is no water else for a man's long journey of a day. East to the foot of the Black Mountain, and north and south without counting, are the burrows of small rodents, rat and squirrel kind. Under the sage are the shallow forms of the jackrabbits, and in the dry banks of washes, and among the strewn fragments of black rock, lairs of bobcat, fox, and coyote.

The coyote is your true water-witch, one who snuffs and paws, snuffs and paws again at the smallest spot of moisture-scented earth until he has freed the blind water from the soil. Many water-holes are no more than this detected by the lean hobo of the hills in localities where not even an Indian would look for it.

It is the opinion of many wise and busy people that the hill-folk pass the ten-month interval between the end and renewal of winter rains, with no drink; but your true idler, with days and nights to spend beside the water trails, will not subscribe to it. The trails begin, as I said, very far back in the Ceriso, faintly, and converge in one span broad, white, hard-trodden way in the gully of the spring. And why trails if there are no travelers in that direction?

I have yet to find the land not scarred by the thin, far roadways of rabbits and what not of furry folks that run in them. Venture to look for some seldom-touched water-hole, and so long as the trails run with your general direction make sure you are right, but if they begin to cross yours at never so slight an angle, to converge toward a point left or right of your objective, no matter what the maps say, or your memory, trust them; they *know*.

It is very still in the Ceriso by day, so that were it not for the evidence of those white beaten ways, it might be the desert it looks. The sun is hot in the dry season, and the days are filled with the glare of it. Now and again some unseen coyote signals his pack in a long-drawn, dolorous whine that comes from no determinate point, but nothing stirs much before mid-afternoon. It is a sign when there begin to be hawks skimming above the sage that the little people are going about their business.

We have fallen on a very careless usage, speaking of wild creatures as if they were bound by some such limitation as hampers clockwork. When we say of one and another, they are night prowlers, it is perhaps true only as the things they feed upon are more easily come by in the dark, and they know well how to adjust themselves to conditions wherein food is more plentiful by day. And their accustomed performance is very much a matter of keen eye, keener scent, quick ear, and a better memory of sights and sounds than man dares boast. Watch a coyote come out of his lair and cast about in his mind where he will go for his daily killing. You cannot very well tell what decides him, but very easily that he has decided. He trots or breaks into short gallops, with very perceptible pauses to look up and about at landmarks, alters his tack a little, looking forward and back to steer his proper course. I am persuaded that the coyotes in my valley, which is narrow and beset with steep, sharp hills, in long passages steer by the pinnacles of the sky-line, going with head cocked to one side to keep to the left or right of such and such a promontory.

I have trailed a coyote often, going across country, perhaps to where some slant-winged scavenger hanging in the air signaled prospect of a dinner, and found his track such as a man, a very intelligent man accustomed to a hill country, and a little cautious, would make to the same point. Here a detour to avoid a stretch of too little cover, there a pause on the rim of gully to pick the better way,— and it is usually the best way,—and making his point with the greatest economy of effort. Since the time of Seyavi the deer have shifted their feeding ground across the valley at the beginning of deep snows, by way of the Black Rock, fording the river at Charley's Butte, and making straight for the mouth of the cañon that is the easiest going to the winter pastures on Waban. So they still cross, though whatever trail they had has been long broken by ploughed ground; but from the mouth of Tinpah Creek, where the deer come out of the Sierras, it is easily seen that the creek, the point of Black Rock, and Charley's Butte are in line with the wide bulk of shade that is the foot of Waban Pass. And along with this the deer have learned that Charley's Butte is almost the only possible ford, and all the shortest crossing of the valley. It seems that the wild creatures have learned all that is important to their way of life except the changes of the moon. I have seen some prowling fox or coyote, surprised by its sudden rising from behind the mountain wall, slink in its increasing glow, watch it furtively from the cover of near-by brush, unprepared and half uncertain of its identity until it rode clear of the peaks, and finally make off with all the air of one caught napping by an ancient joke. The moon in its wanderings must be a sort of exasperation to cunning beasts, likely to spoil by untimely risings some fore-planned mischief.

But to take the trail again; the coyotes that are astir in the Ceriso of late afternoons, harrying the rabbits from their shallow forms, and the hawks that sweep and swing above them, are not there from any mechanical promptings of instinct, but because they know of old experience that the small fry are about to take to seed gathering and the water trails. The rabbits begin it, taking the trail with long, light leaps, one eye and ear cocked to the hills from whence a coyote might descend upon them at any moment. Rabbits are a foolish people. They do not fight except with their own kind, nor use their paws except for feet, and appear to have no reason for existence but to furnish meals for meat-eaters. In flight they seem to rebound from the earth of their own elasticity, but keep a sober pace going to the spring. It is the young watercress that tempts them and the pleasures of society, for they seldom drink. Even in localities where there are flowing streams they seem to prefer the moisture that collects on herbage, and after rains may be seen rising on their haunches to drink delicately the clear drops caught in the tops of the young sage. But drink they must, as I have often seen them mornings and evenings at the rill that goes by my door. Wait long enough at the Lone Tree Spring and sooner or later they will all come in. But here their matings are accomplished, and though they are fearful of so little as a cloud shadow or blown leaf, they contrive to have some playful hours. At the spring the bobcat drops down upon them from the black rock, and the red fox picks them up returning in the dark. By day the hawk and eagle overshadow them, and the coyote has all times and seasons for his own.

Cattle, when there are any in the Ceriso, drink morning and evening, spending the night on the warm last lighted slopes of neighboring hills, stirring with the peep o' day. In these half wild spotted steers the habits of an earlier lineage persist. It must be long since they have made beds for themselves, but before lying down they turn themselves round and round as dogs do. They choose bare and stony ground, exposed fronts of westward facing hills, and lie down in companies. Usually by the end of the summer the cattle have been driven or gone of their own choosing to the mountain meadows. One year a maverick yearling, strayed or overlooked by the vaqueros, kept on until the season's end, and so betrayed another visitor to the spring that else I might have missed. On a certain morning the half-eaten carcass lay at the foot of the black rock, and in moist earth by the rill of the spring, the foot-pads of a cougar, puma, mountain lion, or whatever the beast is rightly called. The kill must have been made early in the evening, for it appeared that the cougar had been twice to the spring; and since the meat-eater drinks little until he has eaten, he must have fed and drunk, and after an interval of lying up in the black rock, had eaten and drunk again. There was no knowing how far he had come, but if he came again the second night he found that the coyotes had left him very little of his kill.

Nobody ventures to say how infrequently and at what hour the small fry visit the spring. There are such numbers of them that if each came once between the last of spring and the first of winter rains, there would still be water trails. I have seen badgers drinking about the hour when the light takes on the yellow tinge it has from coming slantwise through the hills. They find out shallow places, and are loath to wet their feet. Rats and chipmunks have been observed visiting the spring as late as nine o'clock mornings. The larger spermophiles that live near the spring and keep awake to work all day, come and go at no particular hour, drinking sparingly. At long intervals on half-lighted days, meadow and field mice steal delicately along the trail. These visitors are all too small to be watched carefully at night, but for evidence of their frequent coming there are the trails that may be traced miles out among the crisping grasses. On rare nights, in the places where no grass grows between the shrubs, and the sand silvers whitely to the moon, one sees them whisking to and fro on innumerable errands of seed gathering, but the chief witnesses of their presence near the spring are the elf owls. Those burrow-haunting, speckled fluffs of greediness begin a twilight flitting toward the spring, feeding as they go on grasshoppers, lizards, and small, swift creatures, diving into burrows to catch field mice asleep, battling with chipmunks at their own doors, and getting down in great numbers toward the lone juniper. Now owls do not love water greatly on its own account. Not to my knowledge have I caught one drinking or bathing, though on night wanderings across the mesa they flit up from under the horse's feet along stream borders. Their presence near the spring in great numbers would indicate the presence of the things they feed upon. All night the rustle and soft hooting keeps on in the neighborhood of the spring, with seldom small shrieks of mortal agony. It is clear day before they have all gotten back to their particular hummocks, and if one follows cautiously, not to frighten them into some near-by burrow, it is possible to trail them far up the slope.

The crested quail that troop in the Ceriso are the happiest frequenters of the water trails. There is no furtiveness about their morning drink. About the time the burrowers and all that feed upon them are addressing themselves to sleep, great flocks pour down the trails with that peculiar melting motion of moving quail, twittering, shoving, and shouldering. They splatter into the shallows, drink daintily, shake out small showers over their perfect coats, and melt away again into the scrub, preening and pranking, with soft contented noises.

After the quail, sparrows and ground-inhabiting birds bathe with the utmost frankness and a great deal of splutter; and here in the heart of noon hawks resort, sitting panting, with wings aslant, and a truce to all hostilities because of the heat. One summer there came a road-runner up from the lower valley, peeking and prying, and he had never any patience with the water baths of the sparrows. His own ablutions were performed in the clean, hopeful dust of the chaparral; and whenever he happened on their morning splatterings, he would depress his glossy crest, slant his shining tail to the level of his body, until he looked most like some bright venomous snake, daunting them with shrill abuse and feint of battle. The suddenly he would go tilting and balancing down the gully in fine disdain, only to return in a day or two to make sure the foolish bodies were still at it.

Out on the Ceriso about five miles, and wholly out of sight of it, near where the immemorial foot trail goes up from Saline Flat toward Black Mountain, is a water sign worth turning out of the trail to see. It is a laid circle of stones large enough not to be disturbed by any ordinary hap, with an opening flanked by two parallel rows of similar stones, between which were an arrow placed, touching the opposite rim of the circle, it would point as the crow flies to the spring. It is the old, indubitable water mark of the Shoshones. One still finds it in the desert ranges in Salt Wells and Mesquite valleys, and along the slopes of Waban. On the other side of Ceriso, where the black rock begins, about a mile from the

spring, is the work of an older, forgotten people. The rock here-
about is all volcanic, fracturing with a crystalline whitish surface,
but weathered outside to furnace blackness. Around the spring,
where must have been a gathering place of the tribes, it is scored
over with strange pictures and symbols that have no meaning to the
Indians of the present day; but out where the rock begins, there is
carved into the white heart of it a pointing arrow over the symbol
for distance and a circle full of wavy lines reading thus: "In this
direction three [units of measurement unknown] is a spring of
sweet water; look for it."

# BARRY LOPEZ

# *Encounter on the Tundra*

Barry Lopez (b. 1945) has become one of the nation's most respected natural
history writers. After a childhood spent in New York City and southern
California, he returned to the West Coast in 1967 to live in the Cascade
Mountains in Oregon with his wife, and has been there ever since. Somewhat
paradoxically, both a sense of place and a thirst for travel motivate Lopez. He
and his wife have spent more than twenty-five years mapping out their property in Oregon, getting to know intimately the land that they live on. But Lopez
has also described himself as "a writer who travels," a fact which is evident in
his work. "Encounter on the Tundra," an excerpt from *Arctic Dreams,* draws
from his experience in Alaska, where he went first to study wolves, and later
to study all the things other than wolves that he had missed before. He has
also written about experiences in Kenya, the Northern Territory of Australia,
and the Galápagos Islands.

IN CERTAIN PARTS OF THE ARCTIC—LANCASTER SOUND, THE SHORES
of Queen Maud Gulf, the Mackenzie River Delta, northern Bering
Sea, the Yukon-Kuskokwin Delta—great concentrations of wildlife
seem to belie violent fluctuations in this ecosystem. The Arctic
seems resplendent with life. But these are summer concentrations,

at well-known oases, widely separated over the land; and they consist largely of migratory creatures—geese, alcids, and marine mammals. When the rivers and seas freeze over in September they will all be gone. The winter visitor will find only caribou and muskoxen, and occasionally arctic hares, concentrated in any number, and again only in a few places.

All life, of course, cannot fly or swim or walk away to a warmer climate. When winter arrives, these animals must disperse to areas where they will have a good chance to find food and where there is some protection from the weather. A few hibernate for seven or eight months. Voles and lemmings go to ground too, but remain active all winter. Wolves shift their home ranges to places where caribou and moose are concentrated. Arctic foxes follow polar bears out onto the sea ice, where they scavenge the bear's winter kills. Arctic hares seek out windblown slopes where vegetation is exposed. All these resident animals have a measure of endurance about them. They expect to see you, as unlikely as it may seem, in the spring.

In my seasonal travels the collared lemming became prominent in my mind as a creature representative of winter endurance and resiliency. When you encounter it on the summer tundra, harvesting lichen or the roots of cotton grass, it rises on its back feet and strikes a posture of hostile alertness that urges you not to trifle. Its small size is not compromising; it displays a quality of heart, all the more striking in the spare terrain.

Lemmings are ordinarily sedentary, year-round residents of local tundra communities. They came into the central Arctic at the end of the Pleistocene some 8,000 years ago, crossing great stretches of open water and extensive rubble fields of barren sea ice to reach the places they live in today. In winter lemmings live under an insulating blanket of snow in a subnivean landscape, a dark, cool, humid world of quiet tunnels and windless corridors. They emerge in spring to a much brighter, warmer, and infinitely more open landscape—where they are spotted by hungry snowy owls and parasitic jaegers and are hunted adroitly by foxes and short-tailed weasels. In most years, in most places, there is not much perplexing about this single link in several arctic food chains. In some places, every three or four years, however, the lemming population explodes. Lemmings emerge from their subnivean haunts in extraordinary numbers and strike out—blindly is the guess—across the tundra.

The periodic boom in lemming populations—there are comparable, though more vaguely defined, cycles affecting the periodic rise and fall of snowshoe hare and lynx populations, and caribou and wolf populations—is apparently connected with the failure of the lemmings' food base. The supply of available forage reaches a peak and then collapses, and the lemmings move off smartly in all directions as soon as traveling conditions permit in the spring. Occasionally many thousands of them reach sea cliffs or a swift-moving river; those pushing in the rear force the vanguard into the water to perish.

Arctic scientist Laurence Irving, camped once on a gravel bar off the Alaska coast, wrote: "In the spring of a year of climaxing abundance, a lively and pugnacious lemming came into my camp . . . [more] tracks and a dead lemming were seen on the ice several kilometers from shore. The seaward direction of this mad movement was pointless, but it illustrates stamina that could lead to a far dispersal." Irving's regard, of course, is a regard for the animal itself, not for the abstract mechanisms of population biology of which it seems to merely be a part. Its apparently simple life on the tundra suggests it can be grasped, while its frantic migrations make it seem foolish. In the end, it is complex in its behavior, intricately fitted into its world, and mysterious.

Whenever I met a collared lemming on a summer day and took its stare I would think: Here is a tough animal. Here is a valuable life. In a heedless moment, years from now, will I remember more machinery here than mind? If it could tell me of its will to survive, would I think of biochemistry, or would I think of the analogous human desire? If it could speak of the time since the retreat of the ice, would I have the patience to listen?

One time I fell asleep on the tundra, a few miles from our camp. I was drowsy with sun and the weight of languid air. I nestled in the tussock heath, in the warm envelope of my down parka; and was asleep in a few moments. When I awoke I did not rise, but slowly craned my head around to see what was going on. At a distance I saw a ground squirrel crouched behind a limestone slab that rose six or eight inches out of the ground like a wall. From its attitude I thought it was listening, confirming the presence of some threat on the other side of the rock, in a shallow draw. After a while it put its paws delicately to the stone and slowly rose up to peer over, breaking the outline of the rock with the crown of its head. Then, with its paws still flat at the rim, it lowered itself and rested its forehead on the rock between its forelegs. The feeling that it was waiting for something deadly to go away was even stronger. I thought: Well, there is a fox over there, or a wolverine. Maybe a bear. He'd better be careful.

I continued to stare at him from the warm crevice in the earth that concealed me. If it is a bear, I thought, I should be careful too, not move from here until the ground squirrel loses that tension in its body. Until it relaxes, and walks away.

I lay there knowing something eerie ties us to the world of animals. Sometimes the animals pull you backward into it. You share hunger and fear with them like salt in blood.

The ground squirrel left. I went over to the draw beyond the rock but could find no tracks. No sign. I went back to camp mulling the arrangements animals manage in space and in time—their migrations, their patience, their lairs. Did they have intentions as well as courage and caution?

Few things provoke like the presence of wild animals. They pull at us like tidal currents with questions of volition, of ethical involvement, of ancestry.

For some reason I brooded often about animal behavior and the threads of evolution in the Arctic. I do not know whether it was the reserves of space, the simplicity of the region's biology, its short biological history, striking encounters with lone animals, or the realization of my own capacity to annihilate life here. I wondered where the animals had come from; and where we had come from; and where each of us was going. The ecosystem itself is only 10,000 years old, the time since the retreat of the Wisconsin ice. The fact that it is the youngest ecosystem on earth gives it a certain freshness and urgency. (Curiously, historians refer to these same ten millennia as the time of civilized man, from his humble beginnings in northern Mesopotamia to the present. Arctic ecosystems and civilized man belong, therefore, to the same, short epoch, the Holocene. Mankind is, in fact, even older than the Arctic, if you consider his history to have begun with the emergence of Cro-Magnon people in Europe 40,000 years ago.)

Human beings dwell in the same biological systems that contain the other creatures but, to put the thought bluntly, they are not governed by the same laws of evolution. With the development of various technologies—hunting weapons, protective clothing, fire-making tools; and then agriculture and herding—mankind has not only been able to take over the specific niches of other animals but has been able to move into regions that were formerly unavailable to him. The animals he found already occupying niches in these other areas he, again, either displaced or eliminated. The other creatures have had no choice. They are confined to certain niches—places of food (stored solar energy), water, and shelter—which they cannot leave without either speciating or developing tools. To finish the thought, the same technological advances and the enormous increase in his food base have largely exempted man from the effect of natural controls on the size of his population. Outside of some virulent disease, another ice age, or his own weapons technology, the only thing that promises to stem the continued increase in his population and the expansion of his food base (which now includes oil, exotic minerals, fossil ground water, huge tracts of forest, and so on, and entails the continuing, concomitant loss of species) is human wisdom.

Walking across the tundra, meeting the stare of a lemming, or coming on the tracks of a wolverine, it would be the frailty of our wisdom that would confound me. The pattern of our exploitation of the Arctic, our increasing utilization of its natural resources, our very desire to "put it to use," is clear. What is it that is missing, or tentative, in us, I would wonder, to make me so uncomfortable walking out here in a region of chirping birds, distant caribou, and redoubtable lemmings? It is restraint.

Because mankind can circumvent evolutionary law, it is incumbent upon him, say evolutionary biologists, to develop another law to abide by if he wishes to survive, to not outstrip his food base. He must learn restraint. He must derive some other, wiser way of behaving toward the land. He must be more attentive to the biological imperatives of the system of sun-driven protoplasm upon which he, too, is still dependent. Not because he must, because he lacks inventiveness, but because herein is the accomplishment of the wisdom that for centuries he has aspired to. Having taken on his own destiny, he must now think with critical intelligence about where to defer.

A Yup'ik hunter on Saint Lawrence Island once told me that what traditional Eskimos fear most about us is the extent of our power to alter the land, the scale of that power, and the fact that we can easily effect some of these changes electronically, from a distant city. Eskimos, who sometimes see themselves as still not quite separate from the animal world, regard us as a kind of people whose separation may have become too complete. They call us, with a mixture of incredulity and apprehension, "the people who change nature."

## £DWARD ABBEY

# Polemic: *Industrial Tourism and the National Parks*

Edward Abbey (1927–1989) fell in love with the American West after hitchhiking from his family's home in Pennsylvania to the West Coast at the age of 21. Abbey earned an MA in English Literature at the University of New Mexico, but his need to be close to the land and experience it in all of its hardships and beauty led him to work as a park ranger in Moab, Utah. Edward Abbey and his writing in such books as *The Monkey Wrench Gang* and *Abbey's Road* has been charged with creating the modern eco-terrorism movement. Although he wrote in favor of spiking trees and removing surveyors' marks, Abbey denied association with the eco-terrorist groups, and stressed that individuals should act on their own beliefs rather than blindly following a group. Although some readers may not agree with Abbey's radical environmentalism, the passion and enthusiasm in his writing is undeniable. "*Polemic:* Industrial Tourism and the National Parks" comes from *Desert Solitaire,* Abbey's fictional/autobiographical account of his experiences in Moab. This passage is an example of how Abbey used his sense of humor to point out the harms of "industrial tourism" and blatant misuse of the land.

I LIKE MY JOB. THE PAY IS GENEROUS; I MIGHT EVEN SAY MUNIFICENT: $1.95 per hour, earned or not, backed solidly by the world's most powerful Air Force, biggest national debt, and grossest national product. The fringe benefits are priceless: clean air to breathe (after the spring sandstorms); stillness, solitude and space; an unobstructed view every day and every night of sun, sky, stars, clouds, mountains, moon, cliffrock and canyons; a sense of time enough to let thought and feeling range from here to the end of the world and back; the discovery of something intimate—though impossible to name—in the remote.

The work is simple and requires almost no mental effort, a good thing in more ways than one. What little thinking I do is my own and I do it on government time. Insofar as I follow a schedule it goes about like this:

For me the work week begins on Thursday, which I usually spend in patrolling the roads and walking out the trails. On Friday I inspect the campgrounds, haul firewood, and distribute the toilet paper. Saturday and Sunday are my busy days as I deal with the influx of weekend visitors and campers, answering questions, pulling cars out of the sand, lowering children down off the rocks, tracking lost grandfathers and investigating picnics. My Saturday night campfire talks are brief and to the point. "Everything all right?" I say, badge and all, ambling up to what looks like a cheerful group. "Fine," they'll say; "how about a drink?" "Why not?" I say.

By Sunday evening most everyone has gone home and the heavy duty is over. Thank God it's Monday, I say to myself the next morning. Mondays are very nice. I empty the garbage cans, read the discarded newspapers, sweep out the outhouses and disengage the Kleenex from the clutches of cliffrose and cactus. In the afternoon I watch the clouds drift past the bald peak of Mount Tukuhnikivats. (*Someone* has to do it.)

Tuesday and Wednesday I rest. Those are my days off and I usually set aside Wednesday evening for a trip to Moab, replenishing my supplies and establishing a little human contact more vital than that possible with the tourists I meet on the job. After a week in the desert, Moab (pop. 5500, during the great uranium boom), seems like a dazzling metropolis, a throbbing dynamo of commerce and pleasure. I walk the single main street as dazed by the noise and neon as a country boy on his first visit to Times Square. (Wow, I'm thinking, this is great.)

After a visit to Miller's Supermarket, where I stock up on pinto beans and other necessities, I am free to visit the beer joints. All of them are busy, crowded with prospectors, miners, geologists, cowboys, truckdrivers and sheepherders, and the talk is loud, vigorous, blue with blasphemy. Although differences of opinion have been known to occur, open violence is rare, for these men treat one another with courtesy and respect. The general atmosphere is free and friendly, quite unlike the sad, sour gloom of most bars I have known, where nervous men in tight collars brood over their drinks between out-of-tune TV screens and a remorseless clock. Why the difference?

I have considered the question and come up with the following solution:

1. These prospectors, miners, etc. have most of them been physically active all day out-of-doors at a mile or more above sea level; they are comfortably tired and relaxed.
2. Most of them have been working alone; the presence of a jostling crowd is therefore not a familiar irritation to be borne with resignation but rather an unaccustomed pleasure to be enjoyed.
3. Most of them are making good wages and/or doing work they like to do; they are, you might say, happy. (The boom will not last, of course, but this is forgotten. And the ethical and political implications of uranium exploitation are simply unknown in these parts.)
4. The nature of their work requires a combination of skills and knowledge, good health and self-reliance, which tends to inspire self-confidence; they need not doubt their manhood. (Again, everything is subject to change.)
5. Finally, Moab is a Mormon town with funny ways. Hard booze is not sold across the bar except in the semiprivate "clubs." Nor even standard beer. These hard-drinking fellows whom I wish to praise are trying to get drunk on three-point-two! They rise somewhat heavily from their chairs and barstools and tramp, with frequency and a squelchy, sodden noise, toward the pissoirs at the back of the room, more waterlogged than intoxicated.

In the end the beer halls of Moab, like all others, become to me depressing places. After a few games of rotation pool with my friend Viviano Jacquez, a reformed sheepherder turned dude wrangler (a dubious reform), I am glad to leave the last of those smoky dens around midnight and to climb into my pickup and take the long drive north and east back to the silent rock, the unbounded space and the sweet clean air of my outpost in the Arches.

Yes, it's a good job. On the rare occasions when I peer into the future for more than a few days I can foresee myself returning here for season after season, year after year, indefinitely. And why not?

What better sinecure could a man with small needs, infinite desires, and philosophic pretensions ask for? The better part of each year in the wilderness and the winters in some complementary, equally agreeable environment—Hoboken perhaps, or Tiajuana, Nogales, Juarez . . . one of the border towns. Maybe Tonopah, a good tough Nevada mining town with legal prostitution, or possibly Oakland or even New Orleans—some place grimy, cheap (since I'd be living on unemployment insurance), decayed, hopelessly corrupt. I idle away hours dreaming of the wonderful winter to come, of the chocolate-colored mistress I'll have to rub my back, the journal spread open between two tall candles in massive silver candlesticks, the scrambled eggs with green chile, the crock of homebrew fermenting quietly in the corner, etc., the nights of desperate laughter with brave young comrades, burning billboards, and defacing public institutions. . . . Romantic dreams, romantic dreams.

For there is a cloud on my horizon. A small dark cloud no bigger than my hand. Its name is Progress.

The ease and relative freedom of this lovely job at Arches follow from the comparative absence of the motorized tourists, who stay away by the millions. And they stay away because of the unpaved entrance road, the unflushable toilets in the campgrounds, and the fact that most of them have never even heard of Arches National Monument. (Could there be a more genuine testimonial to its beauty and integrity?) All this must change.

I'd been warned. On the very first day Merle and Floyd had mentioned something about developments, improvements, a sinister Master Plan. Thinking that *they* were the dreamers, I paid little heed and had soon forgotten the whole ridiculous business. But only a few days ago something happened which shook me out of my pleasant apathy.

I was sitting out back on my 33,000-acre terrace, shoeless and shirtless, scratching my toes in the sand and sipping on a tall iced drink, watching the flow of evening over the desert. Prime time: the sun very low in the west, the birds coming back to life, the shadows rolling for miles over rock and sand to the very base of the brilliant mountains. I had a small fire going near the table—not for heat or light but for the fragrance of the juniper and the ritual appeal of the clear flames. For symbolic reasons. For ceremony. When I heard a faint sound over my shoulder I looked and saw a file of deer watching from fifty yards away, three does and a velvet-horned buck, all dark against the sundown sky. They began to move. I whistled and they stopped again, staring at me. "Come on over," I said, "have a drink." They declined, moving off with casual, unhurried grace, quiet as phantoms, and disappeared beyond the rise. Smiling, thoroughly at peace, I turned back to my drink, the little fire, the subtle transformations of the immense landscape before me. On the program: rise of the full moon.

It was then I heard the discordant note, the snarling whine of a jeep in low range and four-wheel-drive, coming from an unexpected direction, from the vicinity of the old foot and horse trail that leads from Balanced Rock down toward Courthouse Wash and on to park headquarters near Moab. The jeep came in sight from beyond some bluffs, turned onto the dirt road, and came up the hill toward the entrance station. Now operating a motor vehicle of any kind on the trails of a national park is strictly forbidden, a nasty bureaucratic regulation which I heartily support. My bosom swelled with the righteous indignation of a cop: by God, I thought, I'm going to write these sons of bitches a ticket. I put down the drink and strode to the housetrailer to get my badge.

Long before I could find the shirt with the badge on it, however, or the ticket book, or my shoes or my park ranger hat, the jeep turned in at my driveway and came right up to the door of the trailer. It was a gray jeep with a U.S. Government decal on the side—Bureau of Public Roads—and covered with dust. Two empty water bags flapped at the bumper. Inside were three sunburned men in twill britches and engineering boots, and a pile of equipment: transit case, tripod, survey rod, bundles of wooden stakes. (*Oh no!*) The men got out, dripping with dust, and the driver grinned at me, pointing to his parched open mouth and making horrible gasping noises deep in his throat.

"Okay," I said, "come on in."

It was even hotter inside the trailer than outside but I opened the refrigerator and left it open and took out a pitcher filled with ice cubes and water. As they passed the pitcher back and forth I got the full and terrible story, confirming the worst of my fears. They were a survey crew, laying out a new road into the Arches.

And when would the road be built? Nobody knew for sure; perhaps in a couple of years, depending on when the Park Service would be able to get the money. The new road—to be paved, of course—would cost somewhere between half a million and one million dollars, depending on the bids, or more than fifty thousand dollars per linear mile. At least enough to pay the salaries of ten park rangers for ten years. Too much money, I suggested—they'll never go for it back in Washington.

The three men thought that was pretty funny. Don't worry, they said, this road will be built. I'm worried, I said. Look, the party chief explained, you *need* this road. He was a pleasant-mannered, soft-spoken civil engineer with an unquestioning dedication to his work. A very dangerous man. Who *needs* it? I said; we get very few tourists in this park. That's why you need it, the engineer explained patiently; look, he said, when this road is built you'll get ten, twenty, thirty times as many tourists in here as you get now. His men nodded in solemn agreement, and he stared at me intently, waiting to see what possible answer I could have to that.

"Have some more water," I said. I had an answer all right but I was saving it for later. I knew that I was dealing with a madman.

As I type these words, several years after the little episode of the gray jeep and the thirsty engineers, all that was foretold has come to pass. Arches National Monument has been developed. The Master Plan has been fulfilled. Where once a few adventurous people came on weekends to camp for a night or two and enjoy a taste of the primitive and remote, you will now find serpentine streams of baroque automobiles pouring in and out, all through the spring and summer, in numbers that would have seemed fantastic when I worked there: from 3,000 to 30,000 to 300,000 per year, the "visitation," as they call it, mounts ever upward. The little campgrounds where I used to putter around reading three-day-old newspapers full of lies and watermelon seeds have now been consolidated into one master campground that looks, during the busy season, like a suburban village: elaborate housetrailers of quilted aluminum crowd upon gigantic camper-trucks of Fiberglas and molded plastic; through their windows you will see the blue glow of television and hear the studio laughter of Los Angeles; knobby-kneed oldsters in plaid Bermudas buzz up and down the quaintly curving asphalt road on motorbikes; quarrels break out between campsite neighbors while others gather around their burning charcoal briquettes (ground campfires no longer permitted—not enough wood) to compare electric toothbrushes. The Comfort Stations are there, too, all lit up with electricity, fully equipped inside, though the generator breaks down now and then and the lights go out, or the sewage backs up in the plumbing system (drain fields were laid out in sand over a solid bed of sandstone), and the water supply sometimes fails, since the 3000-foot well can only produce about 5gpm—not always enough to meet the demand. Down at the beginning of the new road, at park headquarters, is the new entrance station and visitor center, where admission fees are collected and where the rangers are going quietly nuts answering the same three basic questions five hundred times a day: (1) Where's the john? (2) How long's it take to see this place? (3) Where's the Coke machine?

Progress has come at last to the Arches, after a million years of neglect. Industrial Tourism has arrived.

What happened to Arches Natural Money-mint is, of course, an old story in the Park Service. All the famous national parks have the same problems on a far grander scale, as everyone knows, and many other problems as yet unknown to a little subordinate unit of the system in a backward part of southeastern Utah. And the same kind of development that has so transformed Arches is under way, planned or completed in many more national parks and national monuments. I will mention only a few examples with which I am personally familiar:

The newly established Canyonlands National Park. Most of the major points of interest in this park are presently accessible, over passable dirt roads, by car—Grandview Point, Upheaval Dome, part of the White Rim, Cave Spring, Squaw Spring campground and Elephant Hill. The more difficult places, such as Angel Arch or Druid Arch, can be reached by jeep, on horseback or in a one- or two-day hike. Nevertheless the Park Service had drawn up the usual Master Plan calling for modern paved highways to most of the places named and some not named.

Grand Canyon National Park. Most of the south rim of this park is now closely followed by a conventional high-speed highway and interrupted at numerous places by large asphalt parking lots. It is no longer easy, on the South Rim, to get away from the roar of motor traffic, except by descending into the canyon.

Navajo National Monument. A small, fragile, hidden place containing two of the most beautiful cliff dwellings in the Southwest—Keet Seel and Betatakin. This park will be difficult to protect under heavy visitation, and for years it was understood that it would be preserved in a primitive way so as to screen out those tourists unwilling to drive their cars over some twenty miles of dirt road. No longer so: the road has been paved, the campground enlarged and "modernized," and the old magic destroyed.

Natural Bridges National Monument. Another small gem in the park system, a group of three adjacent natural bridges tucked away in the canyon country of southern Utah. Formerly you could drive your car (over dirt roads, of course) to within sight of and easy walking distance—a hundred yards?—of the most spectacular of the three bridges. From there it was only a few hours walking time to the other two. All three could easily be seen in a single day. But this was not good enough for the developers. They have now constructed a paved road into the heart of the area, *between* the two biggest bridges.

Zion National Park. The northwestern part of this park, known as the Kolob area, has until recently been saved as almost virgin wilderness. But a broad highway, with banked curves, deep cuts and heavy fills, that will invade this splendid region, is already under construction.

Capitol Reef National Monument. Grand and colorful scenery in a rugged land—south-central Utah. The most beautiful portion of the park was the canyon of the Fremont River, a great place for hiking, camping, exploring. And what did the authorities do? They built a state highway through it.

Lee's Ferry. Until a few years ago a simple, quiet, primitive place on the shores of the Colorado, Lee's Ferry has now fallen under the protection of the Park Service. And who can protect it against the Park Service? Powerlines now bisect the scene; a 100-foot pink water tower looms against the red cliffs; tract-style houses are built to house the "protectors"; natural campsites along the river are closed off while all campers are now herded into an artificial steel-and-asphalt "campground" in the hottest, windiest spot in the area; historic buildings are razed by bulldozers to save the expense of maintaining them while at the same time hundreds of thousands of dollars are spent on an unneeded paved entrance road. And the administrators complain of *vandalism.*

I could easily cite ten more examples of unnecessary or destructive development for every one I've named so far. What has happened in these particular areas, which I chance to know a little and love too much, has happened, is happening, or will soon happen to the majority of our national parks and national forests, despite the illusory protection of the Wilderness Preservation Act, unless a great many citizens rear up on their hind legs and make vigorous political gestures demanding implementation of the Act.

. . .

This being the case, why is the Park Service generally so anxious to accommodate that other crowd, the indolent millions born on wheels and suckled on gasoline, who expect and demand paved highways to lead them in comfort, ease and safety into every nook and corner of the national parks? For the answer to that we must consider the character of what I call Industrial Tourism and the quality of the mechanized tourists—the Wheelchair Explorers—who are at once the consumers, the raw material and the victims of Industrial Tourism.

Industrial Tourism is a big business. It means money. It includes the motel and restaurant owners, the gasoline retailers, the oil corporations, the road-building contractors, the heavy equipment manufacturers, the state and federal engineering agencies and the sovereign, all-powerful automotive industry. These various interests are well organized, command more wealth than most modern nations, and are represented in Congress with a strength far greater than is justified in any constitutional or democratic sense. (Modern politics is expensive—power follows money.) Through Congress the tourism industry can bring enormous pressure to bear upon such a slender reed in the executive branch as the poor old Park Service, a pressure which is also exerted on every other possible level—local, state, regional—and through advertising and the well-established habits of a wasteful nation.

. . .

Industrial Tourism is a threat to the national parks. But the chief victims of the system are the motorized tourists. They are being robbed and robbing themselves. So long as they are unwilling to crawl out of their cars they will not discover the treasures of the national parks and will never escape the stress and turmoil of those urban-suburban complexes which they had hoped, presumably, to leave behind for a while.

How to pry the tourists out of their automobiles, out of their back-breaking upholstered mechanized wheelchairs and onto their feet, onto the strange warmth and solidity of Mother Earth again? This is the problem which the Park Service should confront directly, not evasively, and which it cannot resolve by simply submitting and conforming to the automobile habit. The automobile, which began as a transportation convenience, has become a bloody tyrant (50,000 lives a year), and it is the responsibility of the Park Service, as well as that of everyone else concerned with preserving both wilderness and civilization, to begin a campaign of resistance. The automotive combine has almost succeeded in strangling our cities; we need not let it also destroy our national parks. . . .

Having indulged myself in a number of harsh judgments upon the Park Service, the tourist industry, and the motoring public, I now feel entitled to make some constructive, practical, sensible proposals for the salvation of both parks and people.

(1) No more cars in national parks. Let the people walk. Or ride horses, bicycles, mules, wild pigs—anything—but keep the automobiles and the motorcycles and all their motorized relatives out. We have agreed not to drive our automobiles into cathedrals, concert halls, art museums, legislative assemblies, private bedrooms and the other sanctums of our culture; we should treat our national parks with the same deference, for they, too, are holy places. An increasingly pagan and hedonistic people (thank God!), we are learning finally that the forests and mountains and desert canyons are holier than our churches. Therefore let us behave accordingly. . . .

What about children? What about the aged and infirm? Frankly, we need waste little sympathy on these two pressure groups. Children too small to ride bicycles and too heavy to be borne on their parents' backs need only wait a few years—if they are not run over by automobiles they will grow into a lifetime of joyous adventure, if we save the parks and *leave them unimpaired for the enjoyment of future generations.* The aged merit even less sympathy: after all they had the opportunity to see the country when it was still relatively unspoiled. However, we'll stretch a point for those too old or too sickly to mount a bicycle and let them ride the shuttle buses. . . .

(2) No more new roads in national parks. After banning private automobiles the second step should be easy. Where paved roads are already in existence they will be reserved for the bicycles and essential in-park services, such as shuttle buses, the trucking of camping gear and concessioners' supplies. Where dirt roads already exist they too will be reserved for nonmotorized traffic. Plans for new roads can be discarded and in their place a program of trail-building begun, badly needed in some of the parks and in many of the national monuments. In mountainous areas it may be desirable to

build emergency shelters along the trails and bike roads; in desert regions a water supply might have to be provided at certain points—wells drilled and handpumps installed if feasible. . . .

(3) Put the park rangers to work. Lazy scheming loafers, they've wasted too many years selling tickets at toll booths and sitting behind desks filling out charts and tables in the vain effort to appease the mania for statistics which torments the Washington office. Put them to work. They're supposed to be rangers—make the bums range; kick them out of those overheated air-conditioned offices, yank them out of those overstuffed patrol cars, and drive them out on the trails where they should be, leading the dudes over hill and dale, safely into and back out of the wilderness. It won't hurt them to work off a little office fat; it'll do them good, help take their minds off each other's wives, and give them a chance to get out of reach of the boss—a blessing for all concerned.

• • •

Let us therefore steal a slogan from the Development Fever Faction in the Park Service. The parks, they say, are for people. Very well. At the main entrance to each national park and national monument we shall erect a billboard one hundred feet high, two hundred feet wide, gorgeously filigreed in brilliant neon and outlined with blinker lights, exploding stars, flashing prayer wheels and great Byzantine phallic symbols that gush like geysers every thirty seconds. (You could set your watch by them). Behind the fireworks will loom the figure of Smokey the Bear, taller than a pine tree, with eyes in his head that swivel back and forth, watching YOU, and ears that actually twitch. Push a button and Smokey will recite, for the benefit of children and government officials who might otherwise have trouble with some of the big words, in a voice ursine, loud and clear, the message spelled out on the face of the billboard. To wit:

HOWDY FOLKS. WELCOME. THIS IS YOUR NATIONAL PARK, ESTABLISHED FOR THE PLEASURE OF YOU AND ALL PEOPLE EVERYWHERE. PARK YOUR CAR, JEEP, TRUCK, TANK, MOTORBIKE, MOTORBOAT, JETBOAT, AIRBOAT, SUBMARINE, AIRPLANE, JETPLANE, HELICOPTER, HOVERCRAFT, WINGED MOTORCYCLE, SNOWMOBILE, ROCKETSHIP, OR ANY OTHER CONCEIVABLE TYPE OF MOTORIZED VEHICLE IN THE WORLD'S BIGGEST PARKINGLOT BEHIND THE COMFORT STATION IMMEDIATELY TO YOUR REAR. GET OUT OF YOUR MOTORIZED VEHICLE, GET ON YOUR HORSE, MULE, BICYCLE OR FEET, AND COME ON IN.

ENJOY YOURSELVES. THIS HERE PARK IS FOR *people.*

The survey chief and his two assistants did not stay very long. Letting them go in peace, without debate, I fixed myself another drink, returned to the table in the backyard and sat down to await the rising of the moon.

My thoughts were on the road and the crowds that would pour upon it as inevitably as water under pressure follows every channel which is opened to it. Man is a gregarious creature, we are told, a social being. Does that mean he is also a herd animal? I don't believe it, despite the character of modern life. The herd is for ungulates, not for men and women and their children. Are men no better than sheep or cattle, that they must live always in view of one another in order to feel a sense of safety? I can't believe it.

We are preoccupied with time. If we could learn to love space as deeply as we are now obsessed with time, we might discover a new meaning in the phrase *to live like men.*

At what distance should good neighbors build their houses? Let it be determined by the community's mode of travel: if by foot, four miles; if by horseback, eight miles; if by motorcar, twenty-four miles; if by airplane, ninety-six miles.

Recall the Proverb: "Set not thy foot too often in thy neighbor's house, lest he grow weary of thee and hate thee."

The sun went down and the light mellowed over the sand and distance and hoodoo rocks "pinnacled dim in the intense inane." A few stars appeared, scattered liberally through space. The solitary owl called.

Finally the moon came up, a golden globe behind the rocky fretwork of the horizon, a full and delicate moon that floated lightly as a leaf upon the dark slow current of the night. A face that watched me from the other side.

The air grew cool. I put on boots and shirt, stuffed some cheese and raisins in my pocket, and went for a walk. The moon was high enough to cast a good light when I reached the place where the gray jeep had first come into view. I could see the tracks of its wheels quite plainly in the sand and the route was well marked, not only by the tracks but by the survey stakes planted in the ground at regular fifty-foot intervals and by streamers of plastic ribbon tied to the brush and trees.

Teamwork, that's what made America what it is today. Teamwork and initiative. The survey crew had done their job; I would do mine. For about five miles I followed the course of their survey back toward headquarters, and as I went I pulled up each little wooden stake and threw it away, and cut all the bright ribbons from the bushes and hid them under a rock. A futile effort, in the long run, but it made me feel good. Then I went home to the trailer, taking a shortcut over the bluffs.

# ΑL GORE

# *Remarks to Climate Change Conference, April 21, 1994*

Al Gore (b. 1948) was born into politics. His father, Al Gore, Sr., had been a U.S. Congressional representative for ten years when Al, Jr. was born in Washington, D.C. in 1948. Though his experience growing up as a Congressman's son had made him vow that politics would be the last profession he entered, in 1976, when the congressional seat in his district opened up, he couldn't resist. He's been in politics ever since. After Gore was elected vice president in 1992, President Clinton assigned him the job of improving the environment. He's attacked the problem with characteristic zeal. What follows are remarks he made on the subject on Earth Day, 1994.

THIS IS THE WEEK THAT, 219 YEARS AGO, PAUL REVERE WENT ON HIS midnight ride celebrated by Henry Wadsworth Longfellow. "And so through the night went his cry of alarm/To every Middlesex village and farm," wrote Longfellow.

Well, Paul Revere actually did ride "on the 18th of April in '75."

But he wasn't alone. Some new research makes it clear that Revere was one of 60 riders. Not only that, these riders were helped out by boatmen ferrying them across the Mystic, sympathizers hanging lanterns in the church, farmers finding good horses—and at least one informer, probably the wife of a British general.

You get my point.

There are certainly individual acts of heroism. But many of them turn out on closer examination to be the result of a team effort. A partnership. All of us here this morning are Paul Reveres of the environmental movement. We too are working as a team. The enemy is more subtle than a British fleet. Climate change has caused enormous damage before in human history. The historical evidence for this is overwhelming. Even short-term changes—the volcanic eruptions near Crete 3600 years ago, or the devastating effects of the Tambora volcano eruptions in Indonesia, in 1815—can have disastrous effect.

And I'm talking about changes of one or two degrees. Today, we're setting forces in motion that can alter temperatures three or four times as much. I got a little taste of what the devastation could be like last spring during the floods that destroyed so many communities in the midwest.

It's one thing to read about these possibilities in scientific journals. It's another to fly over whole towns and see tops of houses and street signs poking above the water—or row a boat down what used to be streets. Or talk to people who have lost literally every family memento and every stick of furniture they own. No one is suggesting that the 1993 flood was caused by climate change from our air pollution. But we can expect more and more floods just like it if we don't cut greenhouse gases. This isn't just the scientific view.

Take this quote.

Even a modest 0.9 degree Fahrenheit increase in average global temperature by the year 2010 could produce a 20 day extension of the hurricane season, a 33% jump in hurricane landfalls in the U.S., an increase in the severity of the storms and a 30% annual rise in U.S. catastrophic losses from storms.

A treehugging enviro? Nope. A study by the insurance giant, the Travelers Corporation, based in Hartford.

As Franklin Nutter says—he's the President of the Reinsurance Association of America: "The insurance business is first in line to be affected by climate change. Global warming could bankrupt the industry." Insurance companies set their rates in anticipation of future calamities—and when they look ahead they see trouble.

So it's not just alarmists who say that the climate change will be devastating and we should try to prevent it. It's common sense. And it's good business sense, too. But the looming ecological and economic crisis of climate change is only the first of our problems.

The second is gridlock. For far too long shouting has taken the place of meaningful dialogue in the environmental arena. Litigation has taken the place of discussion. Lines have been drawn in the sand and progress has been stopped in its tracks.

And so, I am proud on this Earth Day, to be able to look back over the 16 months since Inauguration Day and see what a difference Presidential leadership—the leadership of Bill Clinton—has made on this issue. Two years ago in Rio, the United States was isolated from the world and fought *any* commitment for global warming. What a difference a year can make.

One year ago, President Clinton announced the Nation's commitment to address climate change. He directed his Administration to produce a plan to cut emissions to 1990 levels. At the time, he said it must be a "clarion call, not for more bureaucracy or regulation or unnecessary costs, but instead for American ingenuity and creativity, to produce the best and most energy-efficient technology."

That's what the plan does. It's a very aggressive attempt to address the world's most important environmental threat. It has 50 separate programs. It addresses every source of greenhouse gas emissions, in every sector of the economy. It will improve energy efficiency. It will save businesses, taxpayers, and consumers money. And it will create jobs. Like the commitment to fight global warming, the Climate Change Action Plan is a major break from the past. It's like no other major environmental initiative in history. It relies almost exclusively on *partnerships.* Partnerships with states. With business. With the environmental community. With Congress.

Now, when you make major breaks with the past—taking on huge environmental problems like global warming, or implementing a new style of environmental program—people get skeptical. Either they'll tell you the problem isn't worth fighting. Or they'll tell you you're not doing enough. And lots of folks will tell you it can't be done without wrecking the economy.

Sounds a lot like 1987. That's when the countries of the world took that first step to stopping ozone depletion from CFCs—the Montreal Protocol. The naysayers said it couldn't be done. Said it would wreck the world's economy to try. And the business community rose to the challenge. They developed substitutes. And that allowed us to accelerate the phase-out dates. Not once. Twice. Here again, I think businesses around the country will rise to the challenge.

Already we've seen evidence to show that's true. It's gathered here today, in the form of facility managers, farmers, and executives who are committed to the climate change programs. Whether or not the plan succeeds depends on the continuing commitment of all of you. And it depends on the same level of commitment from your peers across America. I challenge all of you here today to sign up in a partnership to take this problem on. States, businesses, and their associations, laborers, environmentalists, and Congress all must work together in a committed partnership to make it work. What's that mean?

FOR STATES AND LOCAL GOVERNMENTS: There are two challenges.
- First, lead by example. Set up programs in your own facilities. We have a couple of examples of this here today—the City of Philadelphia is one. They're partners with EPA in the Green Lights program for energy efficient lighting. And they're partners with EPA in its Jobs Through Recycling initiative.
- The second challenge for state and local governments: they should provide a flexible and innovative network for implementing programs. So, if EPA asks you to join Green Lights, do it. If your public utility commissions can help the Department of Energy with Climate Challenge, then they should do it.

FOR BUSINESS: Prove the skeptics wrong and be committed partners in the climate programs. We've got a number of new commitments here today, including some who've signed up recently. You're the ones this effort depends on most. You'll be the ones to make it happen.

The fact is, since last October, there has been a tremendous response from industry and others to the challenge to become partners with climate change programs. Dozens of new partners have signed up for the Agstar, Climate Wise, Energy Star Buildings, and Natural Gas Star programs. Motor Challenge has 86 new partners. Waste Wise: 145. Energy Star Computers: 189. Green Lights: 201. And Climate Change: 766. The totals keep changing. But there's still plenty of room—it's not like the Smith Center at a Colonials basketball game. We have sign up sheets available. To all the potential partners at this conference who have not signed up, I use the words of the Nike ad: Just Do It.

ENVIRONMENTAL GROUPS AND NGOS: Public interest groups and environmental groups are essential to the success in at least two ways:

- First, by keeping us honest. Hold our feet to the fire—but let us know when we've done well—not just when we're well done. Many of you have been working at this subject for longer than many of us. So review our programs. Scrutinize every detail. Tell us what works and what doesn't. And tell Congress to support what works. We'll change what doesn't.
- The second way environmental groups are essential to fighting climate change is to mobilize the American people. Knock on doors. Educate them about the seriousness of the problem. Like the environmental community, *Congress* needs to contribute its views as we implement the Climate Plan. Much of it is based on the Energy Policy Act, which Congress passed in 1992.

The next one's tougher: We've got to fund the Climate Programs. The programs will not succeed if they're poorly designed. We'll work on that. But if we can't get them off the ground for lack of funding—they don't have a chance. The Federal government is committed to this plan.

Will we have to monitor our work? Yes. Constantly. Are we willing to modify it? If necessary. But we still believe that if all the partners do their share, a cooperative approach can succeed.

And this Administration plans to lead by example. We've signed executive order after executive order to put our money where our mouth is. Just last month, I announced an executive order for federal energy efficiency. Under the order, our own building managers will do what we're asking you to do. We'll improve energy efficiency, prevent pollution, and save money—up to $1 billion worth every year.

And when I say that we're starting at home, you can believe it. The White House itself is in the midst of an energy and environmental overhaul. The "greening" White House will be a showcase for practical measures that all Americans can take to save money, protect the environment and improve the comfort of their surroundings. Many of the technologies you're signing up to use in the

Climate Plan will be installed at 1600 Pennsylvania Avenue. We're starting at home. We're going to cut greenhouse gas emissions to 1990 levels. We're breaking gridlock with a new way of doing business—partnerships. It's up to you to prove the new way will work. So be careful out there.

There's a story about a chicken who asked the pig to invest with him on a ham n'egg place. "No thanks," the pig said. "For you ham n'eggs is an investment. For me it's a total commitment."

Earth Day is about commitment. It's about commitment to the most important task of our generation: preserving life on this planet. Commitment to something larger than oneself is the glue that holds society together. And society wins when each of us, one by one, makes that commitment.

In 1988, a group of 8-year-old girls planted a tree as penance for using paper plates on a camping trip. Today those girls form a group called the Tree Musketeers. The President, 15-year old Sabrina Alimahomed, has taken Tree Musketeers from a vacant lot at the edge of El Segundo, California to national recognition. They've planted hundreds of trees. Adopted thousands of others, developed the city's waste management plan and helped open El Segundo's first drop-off recycling plan. Last year they ran the first National Youth Environmental Summit. Sabrina Alimahomed is at this Conference, along with three other Tree Musketeers.

To them, I say: we applaud your commitment. If we succeed in blocking climate change . . . if we succeed in keeping our air and water clean . . . it will be because of the dedication you have demonstrated. Sabrina, you're not alone. On Earth Day, we should all resolve to be as dedicated as you. It's the people who work as a team that accomplish the real revolutions. After all . . . just look at Paul Revere.

*Student APA Essay*

# (AREY M(ALISTER

# Spatial Memory in Pigeons and Rats

Here is an example of scientific writing about nature. In a sense, this paper addresses some of the same issues as many of the other selections in this chapter: how organisms interact with the world around them. In the case of the other readings, however, the organism doing the interacting is a human, who can write down his or her thoughts. When we scientifically study animal behavior, we can't read their minds—we can only observe their behavior. In this paper, Carey McAlister discusses scientific experiments on the behavior of pigeons and rats, coming to an interesting conclusion about how these organisms interact with their environment.

FORAGING BEHAVIOR IN ANIMALS AND THE MEMORY STRATEGIES THEY use have become of great interest to psychologists over the years. Researchers have discovered a great deal about learning processes, including spatial memory, by observing animals both in their natural environments and in the laboratory. In order to evaluate learning and to compare the importance of stimulus characteristics such as spatial distinction and visual distinction to memory, researchers often use maze tasks or analog maze tasks which require certain learned behavior in order to obtain a reinforcer (i.e. food pellets).

Research into the use of spatial memory in pigeons and rats indicates that spatial distinctiveness of stimuli does affect these animals' ability to perform accurately in maze tasks (Bond, et al., 1981; Olton & Samuelson, 1976). However, researchers disagree about the spatial memory capacity and the importance of this memory strategy among animals with different foraging patterns. Overall, findings from research display a strong dependence among rats on spatial memory in making accurate choices in maze tasks.

Rats' reliance on spatial memory in discrimination learning is a well known and well researched phenomenon. Olton and Samuelson (1976), using a radial-arm maze with eight arms (unequal in width), tested the spatial memory of rats in order "to assess the capacity of rats to discriminate, remember, and process information . . . in searching for food" (97). The researchers aided place learning by allowing both intramaze cues, such as varying arm widths and odor trails, and extramaze cues, such as a sink, columns, and a table to be present during testing. The rats in this study rarely visited the same arm twice, displaying strong support for the use of spatial memory. Even when intramaze cues such as arm widths and odor trails were controlled, the rats continued to choose arms in spatial locations which had not been previously chosen. This dependence on extramaze cues lends further support to the importance of spatial memory in discrimation learning, and perhaps in foraging.

Pigeons have displayed similar responding to spatial locations on radial-arm-maze analog tasks. However, findings are mixed as to whether pigeons benefit from spatial distinctions when other visual distinctions, such as colors, are present. Zentall, Steirn, and Jackson-Smith (1990) used one chamber with a horizontal line of three pecking keys spaced .8 cm apart, and another chamber with a matrix configuration of five keys (four as corners of a square and one in the center) spaced 3.1 cm apart to simulate the maze task. If spatial distinction is key to correct responding, the pigeons should have responded more accurately to the matrix condition with larger separations between the pecking keys. Zentall, et al. (1990) defined correct choice responses as pecking a key not previously chosen. The results of this study revealed that when the pecking keys were illuminated white, pigeons responded more accurately to the matrix formation. However, when the pecking keys were illuminated with different colors, there was no significant difference between the performance in the linear condition and the matrix condition.

In view of these results, Steirn, Zentall, and Sherburne (1992) conducted further research into this area using four experimental conditions: (a) a large two-dimensional matrix with four corner keys and a center key, (b) a smaller two-dimensional matrix with keys spaced apart half as much as in the larger matrix, (c) a one-dimensional horizontal configuration of five pecking keys, and (d) a one-dimensional vertical configuration of pecking keys. They defined a response as five consecutive pecks to a single key, and a correct choice involved responding to a key not previously chosen. Pigeons displayed no significant differences in responding accuracy for the horizontal condition versus the vertical condition. Both of the two-dimensional matrix conditions produced better response accuracy than did the one-dimensional configurations. Although there was some indication that spatial distinctiveness affected learning, the improvement due solely to key spacing was not significant.

Strong evidence exists in support of learning through spatial memory in rats. Both Zentall, et al. (1990) and Steirn, et al. (1992) suggest that spatial memory also plays a role in the learning process for pigeons. However, some researchers disagree, arguing that pigeons have little need for, and therefore little, if any, ability to use spatial memory. For example, in one study which compared the performance of rats and pigeons in a radial-arm maze task, pigeons exhibited only minimal use of spatial memory (Bond, Cook, and Lamb, 1981).

A reasonable explanation of the differences that appear to be present in the spatial memory capacity of pigeons and rats is that species differences may exist. The resource-distribution hypothesis states, "the ability of an animal to remember the spatial location of past events is related to the typical distribution of food resources for the species" (Bond, et al., 1981, 575). Based on the theory of natural selection and the resource-distribution hypothesis, Bond, et al. (1981) hypothesized that rats who must generally seek food from many locations would be more naturally predisposed to use short-term spatial memory than pigeons who generally have a more concentrated area of food resources. In an eight-arm radial maze task similar to the one in Olton and Samuelson (1976), rats exhibited a significantly higher capacity for spatial memory than did pigeons. According to the results, the pigeons utilized only half the spatial memory capacity of the rats (Bond, et al., 1981).

The reasons behind the mixed findings on the effects of using spatially distinct stimuli with pigeons are unclear. Poor performance by pigeons, as in the Bond, et al. (1981) study, may have been the result of the experimental design, the memory capacity of the pigeons, or a combination of such factors. For example, pigeons may not perform as well as rats or other land animals when a good deal of physical motion or exploration is involved in a task. Some researchers speculate that species differences, as well as foraging patterns within species, could be crucial factors in spatial memory capacity.

In fact, a more telling difference concerning spatial memory, as related to the resource-distribution theory, may be the comparison of performances in discrimination learning of two or more avian species who possess different foraging patterns. Olson (1991) addressed this issue by comparing the performance of Clark's nutcrackers, scrub jays, and pigeons on a nonmatching to sample task. According to the resource-distribution theory, species differences in spatial memory should exist between the nutcrackers who depend heavily on cached food for survival, scrub jays who depend partially on cached food, and pigeons who do not cache food. Nutcrackers performed more accurately both in cache recovery and in the operant nonmatching to sample task (Olson, 1991). The scrub jays, in turn, performed more accurately in the operant condition than the pigeons. The results of this study lend further support to species differences in spatial memory ability.

Due to the mixed findings concerning spatial memory, more research into this area needs to be conducted. Researchers need to carefully analyze experiment designs to find if differences exist in pigeon and rat performance in maze tasks versus analog maze tasks. Analog maze tasks may prove to be better alternatives in testing pigeon performance than actual maze tasks. More research is also needed in determining the significance of species differences, and under what conditions these differences may appear. Overall, the research suggests that both rats and pigeons utilize spatial memory in maze performance, albeit to different extents.

## References

Bond, A. B., Cook, R. G., & Lamb, M. R. (1981). Spatial memory and the performance of rats and pigeons in the radial-arm maze. *Animal Learning & Behavior, 9,* 575-580.

Olson, D. J. (1991). Species differences in spatial memory among Clark's nutcrackers, scrub jays, and pigeons. *Journal of Experimental Psychology: Animal Behavior Processes, 17,* 363-376.

Olton, D. S., & Samuelson, R. J. (1976). Remembrance of places passed: spatial memory in rats *Journal of Experimental Psychology: Animal Behavior Processes, 2,* 97-116.

Steirn, J. N., Zentall, T. R., & Sherburne, L. M. (1992). Pigeons' performances of a radial-arm-maze analog task: effect of spatial distinctiveness. *The Psychological Record, 42,* 255-272.

Zentall, T. R., Steirn, J. N., & Jackson-Smith, P. (1990). Memory strategies in pigeons; performance of a radial-arm-maze analog task. *Journal of Experimental Psychology: Animal Behavior Processes, 16,* 358-371.

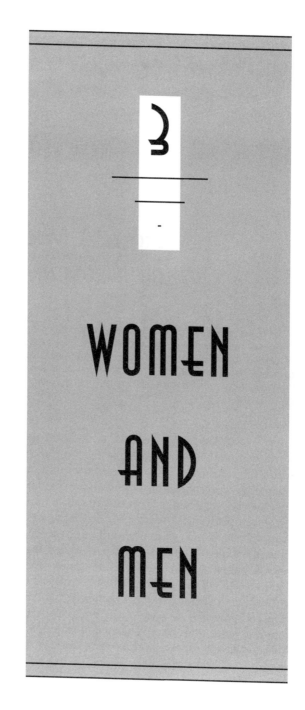

3

WOMEN

AND

MEN

# MARY WOLLSTONECRAFT

# from *A Vindication of the Rights of Woman*

Mary Wollstonecraft (1759–1797), a novelist and translator, helped found the feminist movement with the publication in 1792 of *A Vindication of the Rights of Woman.* Unfortunately, after her death, when her husband published the details of their passionate pre-marital affair, her work was largely discredited. Wollstonecraft was not given the recognition she deserved until over a century later.

AFTER CONSIDERING THE HISTORIC PAGE, AND VIEWING THE LIVING world with anxious solicitude, the most melancholy emotions of sorrowful indignation have depressed my spirits, and I have sighed when obliged to confess, that either nature has made a great difference between man and man, or that the civilization which has hitherto taken place in the world has been very partial. I have turned over various books written on the subject of education, and patiently observed the conduct of parents and the management of schools; but what has been the result?—a profound conviction that the neglected education of my fellow-creatures is the grand source of the misery I deplore; and that women, in particular, are rendered weak and wretched by a variety of concurring causes, originating from one hasty conclusion. The conduct and manners of women, in fact, evidently prove that their minds are not in a healthy state; for, like the flowers which are planted in too rich a soil, strength and usefulness are sacrificed to beauty; and the flaunting leaves, after having pleased a fastidious eye, fade, disregarded on the stalk, long before the season when they ought to have arrived at maturity. —One cause of this barren blooming I attribute to a false system of education, gathered from the books written on this subject by men who, considering females rather as women than human creatures, have been more anxious to make them alluring mistresses than affectionate wives and rational mothers; and the understanding of the sex has been so bubbled by this specious homage, that the civilized women of the present century, with a few exceptions, are only anxious to inspire love, when they ought to cherish a nobler ambition, and by their abilities and virtues exact respect.

In a treatise, therefore, on female rights and manners, the works which have been particularly written for their improvement must not be overlooked; especially when it is asserted, in direct terms, that the minds of women are enfeebled by false refinement; that the books of instruction, written by men of genius, have had the same tendency as more frivolous productions; and that, in the true style of Mahometanism, they are treated as a kind of subordinate beings, and not as a part of the human species, when improvable reason is allowed to be the dignified distinction which raises men above the brute creation, and puts a natural sceptre in a feeble hand.

Yet, because I am a woman, I would not lead my readers to suppose that I mean violently to agitate the contested question respecting the equality or inferiority of the sex; but as the subject lies in my way, and I cannot pass it over without subjecting the main tendency of my reasoning to misconstruction, I shall stop a moment to deliver, in a few words, my opinion.—In the government of the physical world it is observable that the female in point of strength is, in general, inferior to the male. This is the law of nature; and it does not appear to be suspended or abrogated in favour of woman. A degree of physical superiority cannot, therefore, be denied—and it is a noble prerogative! But not content with this natural pre-eminence, men endeavour to sink us still lower, merely to render us alluring objects for a moment; and women, intoxicated by the adoration which men, under the influence of their senses, pay them, do not seek to obtain a durable interest in their hearts, or to become the friends of the fellow creatures who find amusement in their society.

I am aware of an obvious inference:—from every quarter have I heard exclamations against masculine women; but where are they to be found? If by this appellation men mean to inveigh against their ardour in hunting, shooting, and gaming, I shall most cordially join in the cry; but if it be against the imitation of many virtues, or, more properly speaking, the attainment of those talents and virtues, the exercise of which ennobles the human character, and which raise females in the scale of animal being, when they are comprehensively termed mankind;—all those who view them with a philosophic eye must, I should think, wish with me, that they may every day grow more and more masculine.

This discussion naturally divides the subject. I shall first consider women in the grand light of human creatures, who, in common with men, are placed on this earth to unfold their faculties; and afterwards I shall more particularly point out their peculiar designation.

I wish also to steer clear of an error which many respectable writers have fallen into; for the instruction which has hitherto been addressed to women, has rather been applicable to *ladies*, if the little indirect advice, that is scattered through Sandford and Merton, be excepted; but, addressing my sex in a firmer tone, I pay particular attention to those in the middle class, because they appear to be in the most natural state. Perhaps the seeds of false refinement, immorality, and vanity, have ever been shed by the great. Weak, artificial beings, raised above the common wants and affections of their race, in a premature unnatural manner, undermine the very foundation of virtue, and spread corruption through the whole mass of society! As a class of mankind they have the strongest claim to pity; the education of the rich tends to render them vain and helpless, and the unfolding mind is not strengthened by the practice of those duties which dignify the human character.—They only live to amuse themselves, and by the same law which in nature invariably produces certain effects, they soon only afford barren amusement.

But as I purpose taking a separate view of the different ranks of society, and of the moral character of women, in each, this hint is, for the present, sufficient, and I have only alluded to the subject, because it appears to me to be the very essence of an introduction to give a cursory account of the contents of the work it introduces.

My own sex, I hope, will excuse me, if I treat them like rational creatures, instead of flattering their *fascinating* graces, and viewing them as if they were in a state of perpetual childhood, unable to stand alone. I earnestly wish to point out in what true dignity and human happiness consists—I wish to persuade women to endeavour to acquire strength, both of mind and body, and to convince them that the soft phrases, susceptibility of heart, delicacy of sentiment, and refinement of taste, are almost synonymous with epithets of weakness, and that those beings who are only the objects of pity and that kind of love, which has been termed its sister, will soon become objects of contempt.

Dismissing then those pretty feminine phrases, which the men condescendingly use to soften our slavish dependence, and despising that weak elegancy of mind, exquisite sensibility, and sweet docility of manners, supposed to be the sexual characteristics of the weaker vessel, I wish to shew that elegance is inferior to virtue, that the first object of laudable ambition is to obtain a character as a human being, regardless of the distinction of sex; and that secondary views should be brought to this simple touchstone.

This is a rough sketch of my plan; and should I express my conviction with the energetic emotions that I feel whenever I think of the subject, the dictates of experience and reflection will be felt by some of my readers. Animated by this important object, I shall disdain to cull my phrases or polish my style;—I aim at being useful, and sincerity will render me unaffected; for, wishing rather to persuade by the force of my arguments, than dazzle by the elegance of my language, I shall not waste my time in rounding periods, or in fabricating the turgid bombast of artificial feelings, which, coming from the head, never reach the heart. I shall be employed about things, not words!—and, anxious to render my sex more respectable members of society, I shall try to avoid that flowery diction which has slided from essays into novels, and from novels into familiar letters and conversation

These pretty superlatives, dropping glibly from the tongue, vitiate the taste, and create a kind of sickly delicacy that turns away from simple unadorned truth; and a deluge of false sentiments and over-stretched feelings, stifling the natural emotions of the heart, render the domestic pleasures insipid, that ought to sweeten the exercise of those severe duties which educate a rational and immortal being for a nobler field of action.

The education of women has, of late, been more attended to than formerly; yet they are still reckoned a frivolous sex, and ridiculed or pitied by the writers who endeavour by satire or instruction to improve them. It is acknowledged that they spend many of the first years of their lives in acquiring a smattering of accomplishments; meanwhile strength of body and mind are sacrificed to libertine notions of beauty, to the desire of establishing themselves,–the only way women can rise in the world,–by marriage. And this desire making mere animals of them, when they marry they act as such children may be expected to act:–they dress; they paint, and nickname God's creatures.–Surely these weak beings are only fit for a seraglio!–Can they be expected to govern a family with judgment, or take care of the poor babes whom they bring into the world?

If then it can be fairly deduced from the present conduct of the sex, from the prevalent fondness for pleasure which takes place of ambition and those nobler passions that open and enlarge the soul; that the instruction which women have hitherto received has only tended, with the constitution of civil society, to render them insignificant objects of desire—mere propagators of fools!—if it can be proved that in aiming to accomplish them, without cultivating their understandings, they are taken out of their sphere of duties, and made ridiculous and useless when the short-lived bloom of beauty is over, I presume that *rational* men will excuse me for endeavouring to persuade them to become more masculine and respectable.

Indeed the word masculine is only a bugbear: there is little reason to fear that women will acquire too much courage or fortitude; for their apparent inferiority with respect to bodily strength, must render them, in some degree, dependent on men in the various relations of life; but why should it be increased by prejudices that give a sex to virtue, and confound simple truths with sensual reveries?

Women are, in fact, so much degraded by mistaken notions of female excellence, that I do not mean to add a paradox when I assert, that this artificial weakness produces a propensity to tyrannize, and gives birth to cunning, the natural opponent of strength, which leads them to play off those contemptible infantine airs that undermine esteem even whilst they excite desire. Let men become more chaste and modest, and if women do not grow wiser in the same ratio it will be clear that they have weaker understandings. It seems scarcely necessary to say, that I now speak of the sex in general. Many individuals have more sense than their male relatives; and, as nothing preponderates where there is a constant struggle for an equilibrium, without it has naturally more gravity, some women govern their husbands without degrading themselves, because intellect will always govern.

# JOHN STUART MILL

# from *The Subjection of Women*

John Stuart Mill (1806–1873), philosopher and political economist, was given an accelerated education by his father James Mill, an important utilitarian thinker. By the age of fourteen, he had read many of the great Greek and Roman works—in the original Greek and Latin. Later in life, he departed from his father's philosophy and generated many important works of his own. In this selection, Mill describes his theory of the cause of the subjection of women. He must make a lengthy argument to dismiss the idea that the subordination of women to men reflects the natural order of things. His explanation of why women continue to be suppressed continues to have value today. As you read this piece, pay special attention to the rights Mill seeks for women, and how they differ from those Wollstonecraft sought for women half a century earlier.

THE OBJECT OF THIS ESSAY IS TO EXPLAIN AS CLEARLY AS I AM ABLE, the grounds of an opinion which I have held from the very earliest period when I had formed any opinions at all on social or political matters, and which, instead of being weakened or modified, has been constantly growing stronger by the progress of reflection and the experience of life: That the principle which regulates the existing social relations between the two sexes—the legal subordination of one sex to the other—is wrong in itself, and now one of the chief hindrances to human improvement; and that it ought to be replaced by a principle of perfect equality, admitting no power or privilege on the one side, nor disability on the other.

Some will object, that a comparison cannot fairly be made between the government of the male sex and the forms of unjust power which I have adduced in illustration of it, since these are arbitrary, and the effect of mere usurpation, while it on the contrary is natural. But was there ever any domination which did not appear natural to those who possessed it? There was a time when the division of mankind into two classes, a small one of masters and a numerous one of slaves, appeared, even to the most cultivated minds, to be a natural, and the only natural, condition of the human race. No less an intellect, and one which contributed no less to the progress of human thought, than Aristotle, held this opinion without doubt or misgiving; and rested it on the same premises on which the same assertion in regard to the dominion of men over women is usually based, namely that there are different natures among mankind, free natures, and slave natures; that the Greeks were of a free nature, the barbarian races of Thracians and Asiatics of a slave nature. But why need I go back to Aristotle? Did not the slaveowners of the Southern United States maintain the same doctrine, with all the fanaticism with which men cling to the theories that justify their passions and legitimate their personal interests? Did they not call heaven and earth to witness that the dominion of the white man over the black is natural, that the black race is by nature incapable of freedom, and marked out for slavery? some even going so far as to say that the freedom of manual laborers is an unnatural order of things anywhere. Again, the theorists of absolute monarchy have always affirmed it to be the only natural form of government; issuing from the patriarchal, which was the primitive and spontaneous form of society, framed on the model of the paternal, which is anterior to society itself, and, as they contend, the most natural authority of all. Nay, for that matter, the law of force itself, to those who could not plead any other, has always seemed the most natural of all grounds for the exercise of authority. Conquering races hold it to be Nature's own dictate that the conquered should obey the conquerors, or, as they euphoniously paraphrase it, that the feebler and more unwarlike races should submit to the braver and manlier. The smallest acquaintance with human life in the middle ages, shows how supremely natural the dominion of the feudal nobility over men of low condition appeared to the nobility themselves, and how unnatural the conception seemed, of a person of the inferior class claiming equality with them, or exercising authority over them. It hardly seemed less so to the class held in subjection. The emancipated serfs and burgesses, even in their most vigorous struggles, never made any pretension to a share of authority; they only demanded more or less of limitation to the power of tyrannizing over them. So true is it that unnatural generally means only uncustomary, and that everything which is usual appears natural. The subjection of women to men being a universal custom, any departure from it quite naturally appears unnatural. But how entirely, even in this case, the feeling is dependent on custom, appears by ample experience. Nothing so much astonishes the people of distant parts of the world, when they first learn anything about England, as to be told that it is under a queen: the thing seems to them so unnatural as to be almost incredible. To Englishmen this does not seem in the least degree unnatural, because they are used to it; but they do feel it unnatural that women should be soldiers or members of Parliament. In the feudal ages, on the contrary, war and politics were not thought unnatural to women, because not unusual; it seemed natural that women of the privileged classes should be of manly character, inferior in nothing but bodily strength to their husbands and fathers. The independence of women seemed rather less unnatural to the Greeks than to other ancients, on account of the fabulous Amazons (whom they believed to be historical), and the partial example afforded by the Spartan women; who, though no less subordinate by law than in other Greek states, were more free in fact, and being trained to bodily exercises in the same manner with men, gave ample proof that they were not naturally disqualified for them. There can be little doubt that Spartan experience suggested to Plato, among many other of his doctrines, that of the social and political equality of the two sexes.

But, it will be said, the rule of men over women differs from all these others in not being a rule of force: it is accepted voluntarily; women make no complaint, and are consenting parties to it. In the first place, a great number of women do not accept it. Ever since there have been women able to make their sentiments known by their writings (the only mode of publicity which society permits to them), an increasing number of them have recorded protests against their present social condition: and recently many thousands of them, headed by the most eminent women known to the public, have petitioned Parliament for their admission to the Parliamentary Suffrage. The claim of women to be educated as solidly, and in the same branches of knowledge, as men, is urged with growing intensity, and with a great prospect of success; while the demand for their admission into professions and occupations hitherto closed against them, becomes every year more urgent. Though there are not in this country, as there are in the United States, periodical Conventions and an organized party to agitate for the Rights of Women, there is a numerous and active Society organized and managed by women, for the more limited object of obtaining the political franchise. Nor is it only in our own country and in America that women are beginning to protest, more or less collectively, against the disabilities under which they labor. France, and Italy, and Switzerland, and Russia now afford examples of the same thing. How many more women there are who silently cherish similar aspirations, no one can possibly know; but there are abundant tokens how many *would* cherish them, were they not so strenuously taught to repress them as contrary to the proprieties of their sex. It must be remembered, also, that no enslaved class ever asked for complete liberty at once. When Simon de Montfort called the deputies of the commons to sit for the first time in Parliament, did any of them dream of demanding that an assembly, elected by their constituents, should make and destroy ministries, and dictate to the king in affairs of state? No such thought entered into the imagination of the most ambitious of them. The nobility had already these pretensions; the commons pretended to nothing but to be exempt from arbitrary taxation, and from the gross individual oppression of the king's officers. It is a political law of nature that those who are under any power of ancient origin, never begin by complaining of the power itself, but only of its oppressive exercise. There is never any want of women who complain of ill usage by their husbands. There would be infinitely more, if complaint were not the greatest of all provocatives to a repetition and increase of the ill usage. It is this which frustrates all attempts to maintain the power but protect the woman against its abuses. In no other case (except that of a child) is the person who has been proved judicially to have suffered an injury, replaced under the physical power of the culprit who inflicted it. Accordingly wives, even in the most extreme and protracted cases of bodily ill usage, hardly ever dare avail themselves of the laws made for their protection: and if, in a moment of irrepressible indignation, or by the interference of neighbors, they are induced to do so, their whole effort afterward is to disclose as little as they can, and to beg off their tyrant from his merited chastisement.

All causes, social and natural, combine to make it unlikely that women should be collectively rebellious to the power of men. They are so far in a position different from all other subject classes, that their masters require something more from them than actual service. Men do not want solely the obedience of women, they want their sentiments. All men, except the most brutish, desire to have, in the woman most nearly connected with them, not a forced slave but a willing one, not a slave merely, but a favorite. They have therefore put everything in practice to enslave their minds. The masters of all other slaves rely, for maintaining obedience, on fear; either fear of themselves, or religious fears. The masters of women wanted more than simple obedience, and they turned the whole force of education to effect their purpose. All women are brought up from the very earliest years in the belief that their ideal of character is the very opposite to that of men; not self-will, and government by self-control, but submission, and yielding to the control of others. All the moralities tell them that it is the duty of women, and all the current sentimentalities that it is their nature, to live for others; to make complete abnegation of themselves, and to have no life but in their affections. And by their affections are meant the only ones they are allowed to have—those to the men with whom they are connected, or to the children who constitute an additional and indefeasible tie between them and a man. When we put together three things—first, the natural attraction between opposite sexes; secondly, the wife's entire dependence on the husband, every privilege or pleasure she has being either his gift, or depending entirely on his will; and lastly, that the principal object of human pursuit, consideration, and all objects of social ambition, can in general be sought or obtained by her only through him, it would be a miracle if the object of being attractive to men had not become the polar star of feminine education and formation of character. And, this great means of influence over the minds of women having been acquired, an instinct of selfishness made men avail themselves of it to the utmost as a means of holding women in subjection, by representing to them meekness, submissiveness, and resignation of all individual will into the hands of a man, as an essential part of sexual attractiveness. Can it be doubted that any of the other yokes which mankind have succeeded in breaking, would have subsisted till now if the same means had existed, and had been as sedulously used, to bow down their minds to it? If it had been made the object of the life of every young plebeian to find personal favor in the eyes

of some patrician, of every young serf with some seigneur; if do-
mestication with him, and a share of his personal affections, had
been held out as the prize which they all should look out for, the
most gifted and aspiring being able to reckon on the most desirable
prizes; and if, when this prize had been obtained, they had been
shut out by a wall of brass from all interests not centering in him,
all feelings and desires but those which he shared or inculcated;
would not serfs and seigneurs, plebeians and patricians, have been
as broadly distinguished at this day as men and women are? and
would not all but a thinker here and there, have believed the distinction to be a fundamental and unalterable fact in human nature?

The preceding considerations are amply sufficient to show that
custom, however universal it may be, affords in this case no presumption, and ought not to create any prejudice, in favor of the
arrangements which place women in social and political subjection
to men. But I may go farther, and maintain that the course of history, and the tendencies of progressive human society, afford not
only no presumption in favor of this system of inequality of rights,
but a strong one against it; and that, so far as the whole course of
human improvement up to this time, the whole stream of modern
tendencies, warrants any inference on the subject, it is, that this
relic of the past is discordant with the future, and must necessarily
disappear.

For, what is the peculiar character of the modern world—the difference which chiefly distinguishes modern institutions, modern
social ideas, modern life itself, from those of times long past? It is,
that human beings are no longer born to their place in life, and
chained down by an inexorable bond to the place they are born to,
but are free to employ their faculties, and such favourable chances
as offer, to achieve the lot which may appear to them most
desirable.

# ELIZABETH CADY STANTON

# *Declaration of Sentiments and Resolutions*

Elizabeth Cady Stanton (1815–1902) led the women's movement in the United States in the 19th century. She was an organizer of the Seneca Falls Convention in 1848, where this declaration and resolutions were adopted. The convention has come to be recognized as the start of the women's movement in America, and many similar conventions were held until women finally gained suffrage in 1920. The Declaration imitates the Declaration of Independence because at the time, opponents of the women's movement liked to quote the line, "all *men* are created equal."

WHEN, IN THE COURSE OF HUMAN EVENTS, IT BECOMES NECESSARY for one portion of the family of man to assume among the people of the earth a position different from that which they have hitherto occupied, but one to which the laws of nature and of nature's God entitle them, a decent respect to the opinions of mankind requires that they should declare the causes that impel them to such a course.

We hold these truths to be self-evident: that all men and women are created equal; that they are endowed by their Creator with certain inalienable rights; that among these are life, liberty, and the pursuit of happiness; that to secure these rights governments are instituted, deriving their just powers from the consent of the governed. Whenever any form of government becomes destructive of these ends, it is the right of those who suffer from it to refuse allegiance to it, and to insist upon the institution of a new government, laying its foundation on such principles, and organizing its powers in such form, as to them shall seem most likely to effect their safety and happiness. Prudence, indeed, will dictate that governments long established should not be changed for light and transient causes; and accordingly all experience hath shown that mankind are more disposed to suffer, while evils are sufferable, than to right themselves by abolishing the forms to which they were accustomed.

But when a long train of abuses and usurpations, pursuing invariably the same object, evinces a design to reduce them under absolute despotism, it is their duty to throw off such government, and to provide new guards for their future security. Such has been the patient sufferance of the women under this government, and such is now the necessity which constrains them to demand the equal station to which they are entitled.

The history of mankind is a history of repeated injuries and usurpations on the part of man toward woman, having in direct object the establishment of an absolute tyranny over her. To prove this, let facts be submitted to a candid world.

He has never permitted her to exercise her inalienable right to the elective franchise.

He has compelled her to submit to laws, in the formation of which she had no voice.

He has withheld from her rights which are given to the most ignorant and degraded men—both natives and foreigners.

Having deprived her of this first right of a citizen, the elective franchise, thereby leaving her without representation in the halls of legislation, he has oppressed her on all sides.

He has made her, if married, in the eye of the law, civilly dead.

He has taken from her all right in property, even to the wages she earns.

He has made her, morally, an irresponsible being, as she can commit many crimes with impunity, provided they be done in the presence of her husband. In the covenant of marriage, she is compelled to promise obedience to her husband, he becoming to all intents and purposes, her master—the law giving him power to deprive her of her liberty, and to administer chastisement.

He has so framed the laws of divorce, as to what shall be the proper causes, and in case of separation, to whom the guardianship of the children shall be given, as to be wholly regardless of the happiness of women—the law, in all cases, going upon a false supposition of the supremacy of man, and giving all power into his hands.

After depriving her of all rights as a married woman, if single, and the owner of property, he has taxed her to support a government which recognizes her only when her property can be made profitable to it.

He has monopolized nearly all the profitable employments, and from those she is permitted to follow, she receives but a scanty remuneration. He closes against her all the avenues to wealth and distinction which he considers most honorable to himself. As a teacher of theology, medicine, or law, she is not known.

He has denied her the facilities for obtaining a thorough education, all colleges being closed against her.

He allows her in Church, as well as State, but a subordinate position, claiming Apostolic authority for her exclusion from the ministry, and, with some exceptions, from any public participation in the affairs of the Church.

He has created a false public sentiment by giving to the world a different code of morals for men and women, by which moral delinquencies which exclude women from society, are not only tolerated, but deemed of little account in man.

He has usurped the prerogative of Jehovah himself, claiming it as his right to assign for her a sphere of action, when that belongs to her conscience and to her God.

He has endeavored, in every way that he could, to destroy her confidence in her own powers, to lessen her self-respect, and to make her willing to lead a dependent and abject life.

Now, in view of this entire disfranchisement of one-half the people of this country, their social and religious degradation—in view of the unjust laws above mentioned, and because women do feel themselves aggrieved, oppressed, and fraudulently deprived of their most sacred rights, we insist that they have immediate admission to all the rights and privileges which belong to them as citizens of the United States.

In entering upon the great work before us, we anticipate no small amount of misconception, misrepresentation, and ridicule; but we shall use every instrumentality within our power to effect our object. We shall employ agents, circulate tracts, petition the State and National legislatures, and endeavor to enlist the pulpit and the press in our behalf. We hope this Convention will be followed by a series of Conventions embracing every part of this country.

[The following resolutions were discussed by Lucretia Mott, Thomas and Mary Ann McClintock, Amy Post, Catharine A. F. Stebbins, and others, and were adopted:]

Whereas, The great precept of nature is conceded to be, that "man shall pursue his own true and substantial happiness." Blackstone in his Commentaries remarks, that this law of Nature being coeval with mankind, and dictated by God himself, is of course superior in obligation to any other. It is binding over all the globe, in all countries, and at all times; no human laws are of any validity if contrary to this, and such of them as are valid, derive all their force, and all their validity, and all their authority, mediately and immediately, from this original; therefore,

*Resolved*, That such laws as conflict, in any way, with the true and substantial happiness of woman, are contrary to the great precept of nature and of no validity, for this is "superior in obligation to any other."

*Resolved*, That all laws which prevent woman from occupying such a station in society as her conscience shall dictate, or which place her in a position inferior to that of man, are contrary to the great precept of nature, and therefore of no force or authority.

*Resolved*, That woman is man's equal—was intended to be so by the Creator, and the highest good of the race demands that she should be recognized as such.

*Resolved*, That the women of this country ought to be enlightened in regard to the laws under which they live, that they may no longer publish their degradation by declaring themselves satisfied with their present position, nor their ignorance, by asserting that they have all the rights they want.

*Resolved*, That inasmuch as man, while claiming for himself intellectual superiority, does accord to woman moral superiority, it is preeminently his duty to encourage her to speak and teach, as she has an opportunity, in all religious assemblies.

*Resolved*, That the same amount of virtue, delicacy, and refinement of behavior that is required of woman in the social state, should also be required of man, and the same transgressions should be visited with equal severity on both man and woman.

*Resolved*, That the objection of indelicacy and impropriety, which is so often brought against woman when she addresses a public audience, comes with a very ill-grace from those who encourage, by their attendance, her appearance on the stage, in the concert, or in feats of the circus.

*Resolved*, That woman has too long rested satisfied in the circumscribed limits which corrupt customs and a perverted application of the Scriptures have marked out for her, and that it is time she should move in the enlarged sphere which her great Creator has assigned her.

*Resolved,* That it is the duty of the women of this country to secure to themselves their sacred right to the elective franchise.

*Resolved,* That the equality of human rights results necessarily from the fact of the identity of the race in capabilities and responsibilities.

*Resolved, therefore,* That, being invested by the Creator with the same capabilities, and the same consciousness of responsibility for their exercise, it is demonstrably the right and duty of woman, equally with man, to promote every righteous cause by every righteous means; and especially in regard to the great subjects of morals and religion, it is self-evidently her right to participate with her brother in teaching them, both in private and in public, by writing and by speaking, by any instrumentalities proper to be used, and in any assemblies proper to be held; and this being a self-evident truth growing out of the divinely implanted principles of human nature, any custom or authority adverse to it, whether modern or wearing the hoary sanction of antiquity, is to be regarded as a self-evident falsehood, and at war with mankind.

[At the last session Lucretia Mott offered and spoke to the following resolution:]

*Resolved,* That the speedy success of our cause depends upon the zealous and untiring efforts of both men and women, for the overthrow of the monopoly of the pulpit, and for the securing to woman an equal participation with men in the various trades, professions, and commerce.

# OLIVE SCHREINER

# Sex-Parasitism

South African novelist Olive Schreiner was the daughter of a missionary father and a stern and rigid Victorian mother who believed in the superiority of the British over native black Africans and the Boers. Schreiner's parents met any show of sympathy for those two groups with severe punishment. Rather than adopt the same views, Schreiner resolved to spend her life defending the weak against the strong. In 1889 she met and married a cattle rancher, Samuel Cronwright, another anti-imperialist who, at her request, took her name when they married. The first novel Schreiner published, *The Story of an African Farm,* was an immediate best-seller. Her 1911 work *Women and Labour* is the volume from which this selection is taken. In this work Schreiner outlines the history and fate of any nation in which prosperity, because of the subjugation of a slavery class, leads to its women becoming useless except as vessels in which to breed the next generation.

THERE NEVER HAS BEEN, AND AS FAR AS CAN BE SEEN, THERE NEVER will be, a time when the majority of the males in any society will be supported by the rest of the males in a condition of perfect mental and physical inactivity. "*Find labour or die,*" is the choice ultimately put before the human male today, as in the past; and *this* constitutes his labour problem.

The labour of the man may not always be useful in the highest sense to his society, or it may even be distinctly harmful and anti-social, as in the case of the robber-barons of the Middle Ages, who lived by capturing and despoiling all who passed by their castles; or as in the case of the share speculators, stockjobbers, ring-and-corner capitalists, and monopolists of the present day, who feed upon the productive labours of society without contributing anything to its welfare. But even males so occupied are compelled to expend a vast amount of energy and even a low intelligence in their callings; and, however injurious to their societies, they run no personal risk of handing down effete and enervated constitutions to their race. Whether beneficially or unbeneficially, the human male must, generally speaking, employ his intellect, or his muscle, or die.

The position of the unemployed modern female is one wholly different. The choice before her, as her ancient fields of domestic labour slip from her, is not generally or often at the present day the choice between finding new fields of labour, or death; but one far more serious in its ultimate reaction on humanity as a whole—it is the choice between finding new forms of labour or sinking into a condition of more or less complete and passive *sex-parasitism!*

Again and again in the history of the past, when among human creatures a certain stage of material civilization has been reached, a curious tendency has manifested itself for the human female to become more or less parasitic; social conditions tend to rob her of all forms of active conscious social labour, and to reduce her, like the field-bug, to the passive exercise of her sex functions alone. And the result of this parasitism has invariably been the decay in vitality and intelligence of the female, followed after a longer or shorter period by that of her male descendants and her entire society.

Nevertheless, in the history of the past the dangers of the sex-parasitism have never threatened more than a small section of the females of the human race, those exclusively of some dominant race or class; the mass of women beneath them being still compelled to assume many forms of strenuous activity. It is at the present day, and under the peculiar conditions of our modern civilization, that for the first time sex-parasitism has become a danger, more or less remote, to the mass of civilized women, perhaps ultimately to all.

In the very early stages of human growth, the sexual parasitism and degeneration of the female formed no possible source of social danger. Where the conditions of life rendered it inevitable that all the labour of a community should be performed by the members of that community for themselves, without the assistance of slaves or machinery, the tendency has always been rather to throw an excessive amount of social labour on the female. Under no conditions, at no time, in no place, in the history of the world have the males of any period, of any nation, or of any class, shown the slightest inclination to allow their own females to become inactive or parasitic, so long as the actual muscular labour of feeding and clothing them would in that case have devolved upon *themselves!*

The parasitism of the human female becomes a possibility only when a point in civilization is reached (such as that which was attained in the ancient civilizations of Greece, Rome, Persia, Assyria, India, and such as today exists in many of the civilizations of the East, such as those of China and Turkey), when, owing to the extensive employment of the labour of slaves, or of subject races or classes, the dominant race or class has become so liberally supplied with the material goods of life that mere physical toil on the part of its own female members has become unnecessary.

It is when this point has been reached, and never before, that the symptoms of female parasitism have in the past almost invariably tended to manifest themselves, and have become a social danger. The males of the dominant class have almost always contrived to absorb to themselves the new intellectual occupations, which the absence of necessity for the old forms of physical toil made possible in their societies and the females of the dominant class or race, for whose muscular labours there was now also no longer any need, not succeeding grasping or attaining to these new forms of labour, have sunk into a state in which, performing no species of active social duty, they have existed through the passive performance of sexual functions alone, with how much or how little of discontent will now never be known, since no literary record has been made by the woman of the past, of her desires or sorrows. Then, in place of the active labouring woman, upholding society—by her toil, has come the effete wife, concubine or prostitute, clad in fine raiment, the work of others' fingers; fed on luxurious viands, the result of others' toil, waited on and tended by the labour of others. The need for her physical labour having gone, and mental industry not having taken its place, she bedecked and scented her person, or had it bedecked and scented for her, she lay upon her sofa, or drove or was carried out in her vehicle, and, loaded with jewels, she sought by dissipations and amusements to fill up the inordinate blank left by the lack of productive activity. And the hand whitened and frame softened, till, at last, the very duties of motherhood, which were all the constitution of her life left her, became distasteful, and, from the instant when her infant came damp from her womb, it passed into the hands of others, to be tended and reared by them; and from youth to age her offspring often owed nothing to her personal toil. In many cases so complete was her enervation, that at last the very joy of giving life, the glory and beatitude of a virile womanhood, became distasteful; and she sought to evade it, not because of its interference with more imperious duties to those already born of her, or to her society, but because her existence of inactivity had robbed her of all joy in strenuous exertion and endurance in any form. Finely clad, tenderly housed, life became for her merely the gratification of her own physical and sexual appetites, and the appetites of the male, through the stimulation of which she could maintain herself. And, whether as kept wife, kept mistress, or prostitute, she contributed nothing to the active and sustaining labours of her society. She had attained to the full development of that type which, whether in modern Paris or New York or London, or in ancient Greece, Assyria, or Rome, is essentially one in its features, its nature, and its results. She was the "fine lady," the human female parasite—the most deadly microbe which can make its appearance on the surface of any social organism.

Wherever in the history of the past this type has reached its full development and has comprised the bulk of the females belonging to any dominant class or race, it has heralded its decay. In Assyria, Greece, Rome, Persia, as in Turkey today, the same material conditions have produced the same social disease among wealthy and dominant races and again and again when the nation so affected has come into contact with nations more healthily constituted, the diseased condition has contributed to its destruction.

# D. H. LAWRENCE

# Pornography

D. H. Lawrence (1885–1930) was a controversial figure in English literature because of the vivid descriptions of sex in his novels. His most famous work, *Lady Chatterley's Lover*, was banned in both England and the United States when it was published in 1928. In fact, the version published in 1928 was actually *toned down* by Lawrence in an attempt to elude censorship. After a widely publicized trial in 1960, the work was finally allowed to be published in unexpurgated form. Though the passages in question are actually quite tame by today's standards, some have even credited the re-release of *Lady Chatterley's Lover* in 1961 with causing the "free-love" movement of the 1960s. Here Lawrence defends his work by constructing a definition of pornography which carefully excludes his novels.

WHAT IS PORNOGRAPHY TO ONE MAN IS THE LAUGHTER OF GENIUS TO
another. The word itself, we are told, means "pertaining to harlots"—the graph of the harlot. But nowadays, what is a harlot? If she
was a woman who took money from a man in return for going to
bed with him—really, most wives sold themselves, in the past, and
plenty of harlots gave themselves, when they felt like it, for nothing.
If a woman hasn't got a tiny streak of harlot in her, she's a dry stick
as a rule. And probably most harlots had somewhere a streak of
womanly generosity. Why be so cut and dried? The law is a dreary
thing, and its judgments have nothing to do with life. . . .

One essay on pornography, I remember, comes to the conclusion that pornography in art is that which is calculated to arouse
sexual desire, or sexual excitement. And stress is laid on the fact,
whether the author or artist *intended* to arouse sexual feelings. It is
the old vexed question of intention, become so dull today, when we
know how strong and influential our unconscious intentions are.
And why a man should be held guilty of his conscious intentions,
and innocent of his unconscious intentions, I don't know, since
every man is more made up of unconscious intentions than of conscious ones. I am what I am, not merely what I think I am.

However! We take it, I assume, that *pornography* is something
base, something unpleasant. In short, we don't like it. And why
don't we like it? Because it arouses sexual feelings?

I think not. No matter how hard we may pretend otherwise,
most of us rather like a moderate rousing of our sex. It warms us,
stimulates us like sunshine on a grey day. After a century or two of
Puritanism, this is still true of most people. Only the mob-habit of
condemning any form of sex is too strong to let us admit it naturally. And there are, of course, many people who are genuinely
repelled by the simplest and most natural stirrings of sexual feeling.
But these people are perverts who have fallen into hatred of their
fellow men; thwarted, disappointed, unfulfilled people, of whom,
alas, our civilisation contains so many. And they nearly always enjoy
some unsimple and unnatural form of sex excitement, secretly.

Even quite advanced art critics would try to make us believe that
any picture or book which had "sex appeal" was *ipso facto* a bad
book or picture. This is just canting hypocrisy. Half the great
poems, pictures, music, stories, of the whole world are great by
virtue of the beauty of their sex appeal. Titian or Renoir, the Song
of Solomon or *Jane Eyre*, Mozart or "Annie Laurie," the loveliness is

all interwoven with sex appeal, sex stimulus, call it what you will. Even Michelangelo, who rather hated sex, can't help filling the Cornucopia with phallic acorns. Sex is a very powerful, beneficial and necessary stimulus in human life, and we are all grateful when we feel its warm, natural flow through us, like a form of sunshine. . . .

Then what is pornography, after all this? It isn't sex appeal or sex stimulus in art. It isn't even a deliberate intention on the part of the artist to arouse or excite sexual feelings. There's nothing wrong with sexual feelings in themselves, so long as they are straightforward and not sneaking or sly. The right sort of sex stimulus is invaluable to human daily life. Without it the world grows grey. I would give everybody the gay Renaissance stories to read; they would help to shake off a lot of grey self-importance, which is our modern civilised disease.

But even I would censor genuine pornography, rigorously. It would not be very difficult. In the first place, genuine pornography is almost always underworld, it doesn't come into the open. In the second, you can recognise it by the insult it offers, invariably, to sex and to the human spirit.

Pornography is the attempt to insult sex, to do dirt on it. This is unpardonable. Take the very lowest instance, the picture postcard sold underhand, by the underworld, in most cities. What I have seen of them have been of an ugliness to make you cry. The insult to the human body, the insult to a vital human relationship! Ugly and cheap they make the human nudity, ugly and degraded they make the sexual act, trivial and cheap and nasty.

It is the same with the books they sell in the underworld. They are either so ugly they make you ill, or so fatuous you can't imagine anybody but a cretin or a moron reading them, or writing them.

It is the same with the dirty limericks that people tell after dinner, or the dirty stories one hears commercial travellers telling each other in a smoke-room. Occasionally there is a really funny one, that redeems a great deal. But usually they are just ugly and repellent, and the so-called "humour" is just a trick of doing dirt on sex.

Now the human nudity of a great many modern people is just ugly and degraded, and the sexual act between modern people is just the same, merely ugly and degrading. But this is nothing to be proud of. It is the catastrophe of our civilisation. I am sure no other civilisation, not even the Roman, has showed such a vast proportion of ignominious and degraded nudity, and ugly, squalid dirty sex. Because no other civilisation has given sex into the underworld, and nudity to the W.C.

The intelligent young, thank heaven, seem determined to alter in these two respects. They are rescuing their young nudity from the stuffy, pornographical hole-and-corner underworld of their elders, and they refuse to sneak about the sexual relation. This is a change the elderly grey ones of course deplore, but it is in fact a very great change for the better, and a real revolution.

But it is amazing how strong is the will in ordinary, vulgar people, to do dirt on sex. It was one of my fond illusions, when I was young, that the ordinary healthy-seeming sort of men in railway carriages, or the smoke-room of an hotel or a pullman, were healthy in their feelings and had a wholesome, rough devil-may-care attitude towards sex. All wrong! All wrong! Experience teaches that common individuals of this sort have a disgusting attitude towards sex, a disgusting contempt of it, a disgusting desire to insult it. If such fellows have intercourse with a woman, they triumphantly feel that they have done her dirt, and now she is lower, cheaper, more contemptible than she was before.

It is individuals of this sort that tell dirty stories, carry indecent picture postcards, and know the indecent books. This is the great pornographical class—the really common men-in-the-street and women-in-the-street. They have as great a hate and contempt of sex as the greyest Puritan, and when an appeal is made to them, they are always on the side of the angels. They insist that a film heroine shall be a neuter, a sexless thing of washed-out purity. They insist that real sex-feeling shall only be shown by the villain or villainess, low lust. They find a Titian or a Renoir really indecent, and they don't want their wives and daughters to see it.

Why? Because they have the grey disease of sex-hatred, coupled with the yellow disease of dirt-lust. The sex functions and the excrementory functions in the human body work so close together, yet they are, so to speak, utterly different in direction. Sex is a creative flow, the excrementory flow is towards dissolution, decreation, if we may use such a word. In the really healthy human being the distinction between the two is instant, our profoundest instincts are perhaps our instincts of opposition between the two flows. But in the degraded human being the deep instincts have gone dead, and then the two flows become identical. *This* is the secret of really vulgar and of pornographical people: the sex flow and the excrement flow is the same to them. It happens when the psyche deteriorates, and the profound controlling instincts collapse. Then sex is dirt and dirt is sex, and sexual excitement becomes a playing with dirt, and any sign of sex in a woman becomes a show of her dirt. This is the condition of the common, vulgar human being whose name is legion, and who lifts his voice, and it is the *Vox populi, vox Dei*. And this is the source of all pornography.

# MARGARET ATWOOD

# *Pornography*

Margaret Atwood (b. 1939), a novelist, poet, and essayist, is best known as the author of novels such as *The Handmaid's Tale* (1986) and *Cat's Eye* (1989). In this essay, Atwood clearly has a much narrower definition of pornography than D. H. Lawrence. Instead of merely defining pornography, however, she is more interested in determining how to regulate it. The issues she brings up are not without consequence: how can we balance the need for freedom of expression against the rights of potential victims of rape or incest? If pornography incites people to violence, shouldn't it be banned? Should we define a movie depicting the horrible consequences of rape as "pornography" or "education"?

WHEN I WAS IN FINLAND A FEW YEARS AGO FOR AN INTERNATIONAL writers' conference, I had occasion to say a few paragraphs in public on the subject of pornography. The context was a discussion of political repression, and I was suggesting the possibility of a link between the two. The immediate result was that a male journalist took several large bites out of me. Prudery and pornography are two halves of the same coin, said he, and I was clearly a prude. What could you expect from an Anglo-Canadian? Afterward, a couple of pleasant Scandinavian men asked me what I had been so worked up about. All "pornography" means, they said, is graphic depictions of whores, and what was the harm in that?

Not until then did it strike me that the male journalist and I had two entirely different things in mind. By "pornography," he meant naked bodies and sex. I, on the other hand, had recently been doing the research for my novel *Bodily Harm*, and was still in a state of shock from some of the material I had seen, including the Ontario Board of Film Censors' "outtakes." By "pornography," I meant women getting their nipples snipped off with garden shears, having meat hooks stuck into their vaginas, being disemboweled; little girls being raped; men (yes, there are some men) being smashed to a pulp and forcibly sodomized. The cutting edge of pornography, as far as I could see, was no longer simple old copulation, hanging from the chandelier or otherwise: it was death, messy, explicit and highly sadistic. I explained this to the nice Scandinavian men. "Oh, but that's just the United States," they said. "Everyone knows they're sick." In their country, they said, violent "pornography" of that kind was not permitted on television or in movies; indeed, excessive violence of any kind was not permitted. They had drawn a clear line between erotica, which earlier studies had shown did not incite men to more aggressive and brutal behavior toward women, and violence, which later studies indicated did.

Some time after that I was in Saskatchewan, where, because of the scenes in *Bodily Harm*, I found myself on an open-line radio show answering questions about "pornography." Almost no one who phoned in was in favor of it, but again they weren't talking about the same stuff I was, because they hadn't seen it. Some of them were all set to stamp out bathing suits and negligees, and, if possible, any depictions of the female body whatsoever. God, it was implied, did not approve of female bodies, and sex of any kind, including that practised by bumblebees, should be shoved back into the dark, where it belonged. I had more than a suspicion that *Lady Chatterley's Lover*, Margaret Laurence's *The Diviners*, and indeed most books by most serious modern authors would have ended up as confetti if left in the hands of these callers.

For me, these two experiences illustrate the two poles of the emotionally heated debate that is now thundering around this issue. They also underline the desirability and even the necessity of defining the terms. "Pornography" is now one of those catchalls, like "Marxism" and "feminism," that have become so broad they can mean almost anything, ranging from certain verses in the Bible, ads for skin lotion and sex tests for children to the contents of Penthouse, Naughty '90s postcards and films with titles containing the word *Nazi* that show vicious scenes of torture and killing. It's easy to say that sensible people can tell the difference. Unfortunately, opinions on what constitutes a sensible person vary.

But even sensible people tend to lose their cool when they start talking about this subject. They soon stop talking and start yelling, and the name calling begins. Those in favor of censorship (which may include groups not noticeably in agreement on other issues, such as some feminists and religious fundamentalists) accuse the others of exploiting women through the use of degrading images, contributing to the corruption of children, and adding to the general climate of violence and threat in which both women and children live in this society; or, though they may not give much of a hoot about actual women and children, they invoke moral standards and God's supposed aversion to "filth," "smut" and deviated *preversion*, which may mean ankles.

The camp in favor of total "freedom of expression" often comes out howling as loud as the Romans would have if told they could no longer have innocent fun watching the lions eat up Christians. It too may include segments of the population who are not natural bedfellows: those who proclaim their God-given right to freedom, including the freedom to tote guns, drive when drunk, drool over chicken porn and get off on videotapes of women being raped and beaten, may be waving the same anticensorship banner as responsible liberals who fear the return of Mrs. Grundy, or gay groups for whom sexual emancipation involves the concept of "sexual theatre." *Whatever turns you on* is a handy motto, as is *A man's home is his castle* (and if it includes a dungeon with beautiful maidens strung up in chains and bleeding from every pore, that's his business).

Meanwhile, theoreticians theorize and speculators speculate. Is today's pornography yet another indication of the hatred of the body, the deep mind-body split, which is supposed to pervade Western Christian society? Is it a backlash against the women's movement by men who are threatened by uppity female behavior in real life, so like to fantasize about women done up like outsize parcels, being turned into hamburger, kneeling at their feet in slave-like adoration or sucking off guns? Is it a sign of collective impotence, of a generation of men who can't relate to real women at all but have to make do with bits of celluloid and paper? Is the current flood just a result of smart marketing and aggressive promotion by the money men in what has now become a multi-billion dollar industry? If they were selling movies about men getting their testicles stuck full of knitting needles by women with swastikas on their sleeves, would they do as well, or is this penchant somehow peculiarly male? If so, why? Is pornography a power trip rather than a sex one? Some say that those ropes, chains, muzzles and other restraining devices are an argument for the immense power female sexuality still wields in the male imagination: you don't put these things on dogs unless you're afraid of them. Others, more literary, wonder about the shift from the 19th-century Magic Woman or Femme Fatale image to the lollipop-licker, airhead or turkey-carcass treatment of women in porn today. The proporners don't care much about theory; they merely demand product. The antiporners don't care about it in the final analysis either; there's dirt on the street, and they want it cleaned up, now.

It seems to me that this conversation, with its *You're-a-prude/You're-a-pervert* dialectic, will never get anywhere as long as we continue to think of this material as just "entertainment." Possibly we're deluded by the packaging, the format: magazine, book, movie, theatrical presentation. We're used to thinking of these things as part of the "entertainment industry," and we're used to thinking of ourselves as free adult people who ought to be able to see any kind of "entertainment" we want to. That was what the First Choice pay-TV debate was all about. After all, it's only entertainment, right? Entertainment means fun, and only a killjoy would be antifun. What's the harm?

This is obviously the central question: *What's the harm?* If there isn't any real harm to any real people, then the antiporners can tsk-tsk and/or throw up as much as they like, but they can't rightfully expect more legal controls or sanctions. However, the no harm position is far from being proven.

(For instance, there's a clear-cut case for banning—as the federal government has proposed—movies, photos and videos that depict children engaging in sex with adults: real children are used to make the movies, and hardly anybody thinks this is ethical. The possibilities for coercion are too great.)

To shift the viewpoint, I'd like to suggest three other models for looking at "pornography"—and here I mean the violent kind.

Those who find the idea of regulating pornographic materials repugnant because they think it's Fascist or Communist or otherwise not in accordance with the principles of an open democratic society should consider that Canada has made it illegal to disseminate material that may lead to hatred toward any group because of race or religion. I suggest that if pornography of the violent kind depicted these acts being done predominantly to Chinese, to blacks, to Catholics, it would be off the market immediately, under the present laws. Why is hate literature illegal? Because whoever made the law thought that such material might incite real people to do real awful things to other real people. The human brain is to a certain extent a computer: garbage in, garbage out. We only hear about the extreme cases (like that of American multimurderer Ted Bundy) in which pornography has contributed to the death and/or mutilation of women and/or men. Although pornography is not the only factor involved in the creation of such deviance, it certainly has upped the ante by suggesting both a variety of techniques and the social acceptability of such actions. Nobody knows yet what effect this stuff is having on the less psychotic.

Studies have shown that a large part of the market for all kinds of porn, soft and hard, is drawn from the 16-to-21-year-old population of young men. Boys used to learn about sex on the street, or (in Italy, according to Fellini movies) from friendly whores, or, in more genteel surroundings, from girls, their parents, or, once upon a time, in school, more or less. Now porn has been added, and sex education in the schools is rapidly being phased out. The buck has been passed, and boys are being taught that all women secretly like to be raped and that real men get high on scooping out women's digestive tracts.

Boys learn their concept of masculinity from other men: is this what most men want them to be learning? If word gets around that rapists are "normal" and even admirable men, will boys feel that in order to be normal, admirable and masculine they will have to be rapists? Human beings are enormously flexible, and how they turn out depends a lot on how they're educated, by the society in which they're immersed as well as by their teachers. In a society that advertises and glorifies rape or even implicitly condones it, more women get raped. It becomes socially acceptable. And at a time when men and the traditional male role have taken a lot of flak and men are confused and casting around for an acceptable way of being male (and, in some cases, not getting much comfort from women on that score), this must be at times a pleasing thought.

It would be naïve to think of violent pornography as just harmless entertainment. It's also an educational tool and a powerful propaganda device. What happens when boy educated on porn meets girl brought up on Harlequin romances? The clash of expectations can be heard around the block. She wants him to get down on his knees with a ring, he wants her to get down on all fours with a ring in her nose. Can this marriage be saved?

Pornography has certain things in common with such addictive substances as alcohol and drugs: for some, though by no means for all, it induces chemical changes in the body, which the user finds exciting and pleasurable. It also appears to attract a "hard core" of habitual users and a penumbra of those who use it occasionally but aren't dependent on it in any way. There are also significant numbers of men who aren't much interested in it, not because they're undersexed but because real life is satisfying their needs, which may not require as many appliances as those of users.

For the "hard core," pornography may function as alcohol does for the alcoholic: tolerance develops, and a little is no longer enough. This may account for the short viewing time and fast turnover in porn theatres. Mary Brown, chairwoman of the Ontario Board of Film Censors, estimates that for every one mainstream movie requesting entrance to Ontario, there is one porno flick. Not only the quantity consumed but the quality of explicitness must escalate, which may account for the growing violence: once the big deal was breasts, then it was genitals, then copulation, then that was no longer enough and the hard users had to have more. The ultimate kick is death, and after that, as the Marquis de Sade so boringly demonstrated, multiple death.

The existence of alcoholism has not led us to ban social drinking. On the other hand, we do have laws about drinking and driving, excessive drunkenness and other abuses of alcohol that may result in injury or death to others.

This leads us back to the key question: what's the harm? Nobody knows, but this society should find out fast, before the saturation point is reached. The Scandinavian studies that showed a connection between depictions of sexual violence and increased impulse toward it on the part of male viewers would be a starting point, but many more questions remain to be raised as well as answered.

What, for instance, is the crucial difference between men who are users and men who are not? Does using affect a man's relationship with actual women, and, if so, adversely? Is there a clear line between erotica and violent pornography, or are they on an escalating continuum? Is this a "men versus women" issue, with all men secretly siding with the proporners and all women secretly siding against? (I think not; there *are* lots of men who don't think that running their true love through the Cuisinart is the best way they can think of to spend a Saturday night, and they're just as nauseated by films of someone else doing it as women are.) Is pornography merely an expression of the sexual confusion of this age or an active contributor to it?

Nobody wants to go back to the age of official repression, when even piano legs were referred to as "limbs" and had to wear pantaloons to be decent. Neither do we want to end up in George Orwell's 1984, in which pornography is turned out by the State to keep the proles in a state of torpor, sex itself is considered dirty and the approved practise it only for reproduction. But Rome under the emperors isn't such a good model either.

If all men and women respected each other, if sex were considered joyful and life-enhancing instead of a wallow in germ-filled glop, if everyone were in love all the time, if, in other words, many people's lives were more satisfactory for them than they appear to be now, pornography might just go away on its own. But since this is obviously not happening, we as a society are going to have to make some informed and responsible decisions about how to deal with it.

*Student Essay*

# LISA SHIN

# Response to Lawrence and Atwood on Pornography

Between Atwood and Lawrence's definitions of pornography, there is a lot of gray area. Lisa's essay explores that gray area and attempts a reconciliation— and a questioning—of both essays.

MARGARET ATWOOD AND D. H. LAWRENCE, TWO OF THE TWENTIETH century's most respected and sensuous writers, both have a lot to say on the subject of pornography. For each of them, the question of definition is central, and they both make a distinction between pornography and depictions of sex and bodies.

For Atwood, real pornography is found in violence and sadism used as entertainment, in depictions of "women getting their nipples sheared off . . . little girls being raped . . . men . . . being smashed to a pulp and forcibly sodomized." To her, this is hate literature, and as such, should be banished (as racially based hate literature is currently banned in Canada). Too often, she says, people either think of pornography as graphic depictions of whores or "naked bodies and sex" or "bathing suits and negligees."

Atwood would probably take exception with Lawrence when he says "If a woman hasn't got a tiny streak of harlot in her, she's a dry stick as a rule," but she might agree with him that literature that arouses sexual feelings is a good thing, and quite different from literature which "does dirt to sex." Pornography, he says, occurs when people want to hide sex, to keep in underground, when people confuse sex functions with excretory functions. He want to suppress this kind of thinking and celebrate the body.

The question of suppression is one of the key questions surrounding the issue of pornography today. For Atwood, the question boils down to "What is the harm?" which comes off as a question that is both sardonically rhetorical and straightforwardly serious. A variety of studies involving showing pornographic movies and magazines to men to determine the answer to this question has produced an inconclusive bunch of conclusions, and we end up forced to make a decision based on our original position. If pornography does affect men's ability to see women as human, then there is great harm, and that window of possibility is enough for Atwood to suggest that certain pornographic works be classed as hate literature and censored, if not banned.

According to Lawrence, the harm is done in pornography's "attempt to insult sex." Sex is big and beautiful and people want to make it small and dirty. Sex should be celebrated; it is and should be found in great literature and great paintings. Lawrence is something of a snob; first by giving too much credit to the common men and women in the street, believing them to be more in touch with the earth and therefore aware of and happy with the earthy, then by seeing those common people as the ones responsible for cheapening and dirtying sex.

Though both writers bring up the question of what to do about pornography, neither one has an ultimate or fully satisfactory answer. I would say that pornography isn't found in those kittenishly cute photos of prom queens in Playboy—except possibly insofar as those are by nature embarrassing, to both the women who pose and the men who buy. But at this point there seems to be nothing to do about such degradation. Atwood would get rid of the violent and sadistic, Lawrence would get rid of the degrading and dirtying. My own fear is that by getting rid of potentially pornographic material you allow for suppression of all material that mentions sex—including Atwood's and Lawrence's works. Including, in fact, this essay—and I would hate to see that happen.

## MARK GERZON

# *Manhood: The Elusive Goal*

Mark Gerzon, journalist, activist, consultant, lecturer, and writer, has spent much of his life trying to reconcile differences between groups with different beliefs. His journey started with the publication in 1969 of *The Whole World is Watching: A Young Man Looks at Youth's Dissent*, which explored the conflict between the baby-boom generation and their parents' generation. He spent the seventies cofounding and editing *WorldPaper*, a "global newspaper" with contributing editors from the cultures of four continents. In *A Choice of Heroes: The Changing Faces of American Manhood*, published in 1982, Gerzon tried to connect the feminist movement with the emerging men's movement. In this excerpt from *A Choice of Heroes*, Gerzon recounts an episode from his own youth and contrasts it with modern expectations for men.

> There is no steady unretracing progress in this life. . . . Once gone through, we trace the round again; and are infants, boys, and men, and Ifs eternally.
>
> HERMAN MELVILLE, *MOBY DICK*

IT WAS NOT COINCIDENCE THAT WHEN LOVE ENTERED MY LIFE SO DID violence. I fell in love for the first time with a high school classmate, Diana. She was a cheerleader, the most feminine of all roles. Even now, almost twenty years later, I think of her when I see cheerleaders practicing. In one cheer, they would shout each letter of each member of the starting line-up's name as they ran onto the basketball court heralding them as if they were heroes. They had mastered the art of feminine support: they remained on the sidelines while acclaiming the men who played the game.

In this, Diana was wholehearted. In winter, her face would glow when the ball swished through the hoop; she would look crestfallen when it fell short. In autumn, chanting "Hit 'em again, hit 'em again, harder, harder," her body pulsed to the rhythm of her words. Even if she was not the most beautiful cheerleader, she was certainly the most magnetic. She made us feel like men.

Before she and I started dating, she went with a fellow two years my senior, a leading figure in one of the male clubs known for its toughness. Since he and Diana had broken up (or so she said), I felt no qualms when our study dates became romantic. Soon she and I were together almost constantly. When she invited me to a party sponsored by her club, I accepted. After all, she was "mine."

Midway through the evening, however, her former beau arrived with several of his hefty club brothers behind him. "They want you," a friend warned me, then quickly disappeared. My strategy, which was to pretend that I had not noticed their arrival, became impractical when three of them had me cornered. And I had no club brothers to back me up.

"Let's go outside," said Diana's old beau.

"What for?" I was still playing dumb.

The purpose of our outing was to settle with our fists who Diana belonged to. He obviously felt that he had staked his claim first and that I was trespassing on his territory. I believed that she had the right to choose for herself to whom she wanted to belong. Neither of us, perhaps not even Diana herself, considered it odd that at the age of sixteen she should belong to anyone.

As it turned out, the other boyfriend and I didn't fight, at least not that night. "Why'd you let him talk you out of it?" one of his buddies asked him. He was outraged at being deprived of what was to be the high point of his evening.

A few weeks later, after a basketball game, my adversary and I passed each other under the bleachers. Without warning, he punched me hard in my right eye. My fist was raised to return the blow when several arms pressed me back against the wall.

"Whatsa matter?" he shouted at me contemptuously. "Are you gonna cry?"

The impatient crowd pushed us in opposite directions. Stunned, I felt my eye to check if it was bleeding. Only then did I feel the tell-tale moistness. Although no tears trickled down my cheeks, they were still evidence against my manliness. First, I had weaseled out of a fight. Next, I let him hit me without ever returning the blow. But the most damaging evidence of all were my barely averted tears. To be hit and to cry was the ultimate violation of the code of masculine conduct.

That happened half a lifetime ago. I no longer see my unwillingness to fight as an indictment of my character. Had I been as old and as tough as my adversary, perhaps I would have handled our conflict differently. Perhaps I would have fought. Perhaps I even might have won. Instead, aware of my relative weakness and inexperience, I chose not to. I wanted to protect my eyes, my mouth, my groin. I thought I might need them in the future. But the deeper reason had nothing to do with self-protection but with love. I could not understand what the winner of a fight would gain. Would Diana accept the verdict of our brawl? Like a Kewpie doll at the fairgrounds, would she let herself be claimed by whichever contestant came out on top? If her love could be won by violence, I was not sure I wanted it. I wanted her to love me for who I was, not for how I fought.

My problem, my friends told me then, was that I was too sensitive.

Strange how things change. The image of manhood against which I am measured has changed so much that now, almost twenty years later, I am told I am not sensitive *enough*. When tensions build in our relationship, Shelley will admonish me for being out of touch with my feelings. "You are always so defensive, always trying to protect yourself," she will say. "Why can't you be more open to your feelings?"

How can I explain it to her? How can any man explain it to any woman? Women are not raised to abort all tears. They are not measured by their toughness. They are not expected to bang against each other on hockey rinks and football fields and basketball courts. They do not go out into the woods to play soldiers. They do not settle disagreements by punching each other. For them, tears are a badge of femininity. For us, they are a masculine demerit.

Nothing has made me see this more clearly than talking with Richard Ryan, a former alcoholic. Sitting in the sun one afternoon by a lake near his home, Richard reminded me of a masculine rite of passage I had almost forgotten.

"After I gave this rap about alcoholism at the high school, this kid came up to me and said, 'Can I talk with you privately, Mr. Ryan?' Usually that means that either the kid's parents are alcoholic or he is. But not this kid. He said to me, 'Mr. Ryan, I've never been drunk, never smoked a joint. What's wrong with me?'

"So I said to him, 'Nothing's wrong with you, man. You're doin' fine.'

"'But why do I feel I have to lie to my friends about it?' he asked. 'If they knew I didn't drink or smoke they'd make fun of me.'"

Richard Ryan rolled over onto his stomach as he finished the story. Either the sun or his emotions made him hide his face.

"I always felt like I had to lie as a kid," Ryan told me. "I liked to bake cookies. I liked to watch my kid brothers and sisters. I liked to write poetry. But my dad made me feel that was wrong somehow. So I started to pretend I *didn't* want to do it."

I had heard the lament so often now that I pushed him for specifics. "But what did your dad do? Did he walk in and say, 'Get out of the kitchen' or 'That's women's work'?"

"No, no. Nothing like that. It was more subtle." He thought for a moment. "For example, when my mother's mother died, I wanted to be her pallbearer. Grandma had been very special to me. I felt like she'd carried me all my life. When she died, I wanted to carry her once. So I asked my dad if I could be a pallbearer. He said, 'Only if you promise not to cry. Pallbearers can't cry!' I knew if I lied and said I wouldn't, he'd let me. But I felt like that'd be betraying her. How could I go to her funeral and not cry? Since I wouldn't promise, my dad refused to let me do it."

Now in his mid-thirties, Ryan runs a project called Creative Drug Education. He visits high schools and talks about alcohol and drug abuse. But he doesn't preach. He tells his own story:

"When I used to go out and get bombed, guys would say, 'He drinks like a man' or 'He holds it like a man.' Being drunk, I really felt like I was something great. The other guys and I, we were like a pack, and drinking was our bond. We'd get together and, because we drank, we'd say stuff and hug each other and do all sorts of things we'd never let ourselves do if we were sober."

Only after reaching the age of thirty did Richard realize he was an alcoholic. "I've only recently felt I can be who I am," he continues. "All those years I felt I had to blot out a whole side of myself. I used alcohol to make myself feel good about myself. After I quit drinking, I thought I was free. But then I realized I was addicted to smoking. And I mean *addicted*. My withdrawal from nicotine was almost as bad as from booze—the shakes, sweating, couldn't sleep. I found it hard to be around people without a cigarette in my hand. It was the whole Marlboro man thing—it made me look cool, made me feel like a man. When a friend told me I should stop, I told him, 'Anybody can quit smoking. It takes a real man to face cancer.' I said it as a joke, but I meant it. That's how sick I was."

Richard no longer looks sick. He is big and muscular. We swam out to the middle of the lake and back and, when we dried off, he wasn't even out of breath. He is respected by the people with whom he works. Teachers tell me he is more effective with young people who use drugs than anyone they've ever met.

As we walked back to the car, I saw a sadness in him, a wound that had not yet healed.

"What you thinking about?" I asked, not knowing a better way to probe.

He laughed. "Oh, I was just thinking about Grandma's funeral. You know what? Every one of those pallbearers cried."

In Western societies, there are clearly no longer any rites of passage. The very existence of terms such as teenager (the German word is *Halbwüchsiger*, half-grown) shows that the absence of this social institution results in an in-between stage. All too often adult society avoids this whole question by regarding those in their teens in terms of the high school health book definition. Adolescence, it says, is the period when the person is no longer a child, but not yet an adult. This is defining the concept of adolescence by avoiding it altogether. This is why we have a youth culture. It is where adolescents go (and sometimes stay) before they become grownups.

Despite the absence of any established initiation rite, young men need one. By default, other institutions take the place of these missing rites. Some commentators on growing up in America point to sports or fraternities for example, to demonstrate that our culture does have various kinds of initiation rites. But they are wrong.

Sports, for instance, can hardly serve as the means for gaining manhood. Sports are games. Except for the professionals who make their living from them, these games have little connection with real life. Moreover, only a small minority of males in American high schools and colleges can participate in athletics. As dozens of articles document, sports play a key role in enabling boys and young men to test their physical prowess, but they do not alone make a boy a man.

Fraternities, too, are a painfully inadequate means for gaining manhood. Except for token community service projects once a year, most fraternities are disconnected from society. How can they provide a socially recognized initiation rite when they involve only members of the younger generation? Frat members do not go off into seclusion with the adults of the "tribe." They go off into seclusion with themselves. They are initiated into youth culture, perhaps, but not into the world of adults.

The young man facing adulthood cannot reach across this great divide. He has only rites of impasse. There is no ritual—not sexual, economic, military, or generational—that can confirm his masculinity. Maturity eludes him. Our culture is famous for its male adolescent pain. From James Dean in *Rebel Without a Cause* and Dustin Hoffman in *The Graduate* to the more recent box office hits *Breaking Away*, *My Bodyguard*, and *Ordinary People*, young men try to prove they are grown men. But to no avail. None of the surrogate initiation rites—car duels, college diplomas, after-work drinking rituals, first paychecks, sports trophies—answers their deepest needs. None has proven to be what William James called the "moral equivalent of war."

The only rituals that confirm manhood now are imitations of war. The military academies, for example, like boot camp itself, involve many of the ingredients of primitive rites of passage. Young men are secluded with older men. They must endure tests of psychological or physical endurance.

Pat Conroy's novel *The Lords of Discipline*, which depicts life in a southern military academy, and Lucian K. Truscott IV's *Dress Gray*, which portrays West Point, showed how boys are turned into men—the kind of men the military needs. But, as we have recognized, the Soldier is no longer the hero. The Vietnam war was "billed on the marquee as a John Wayne shoot-'em-up test of manhood," wrote Mark Baker in *Nam*, but it ended up "a warped version of *Peter Pan* . . . a brutal Never Never Land where little boys didn't have to grow up. They just grew old before their time." Similarly, the heroes of Conroy's and Truscott's tales are not the brave soldier but the dissenter. Nevertheless, because military service is the only rite of passage available, men are drawn to it like moths to light. We need to prove our manhood and will take whatever paths our culture offers.

With the option of going to war foreclosed, young men seek to prove themselves by performing other manly deeds. The most obvious surrogates for war often involve violence too. It is not directed at the enemy, but at each other, and ourselves.

Each week, the news media overflow with accounts of young men between the ages of fifteen and twenty-five who have committed acts of violence. Too old to be boys, too young to have proven themselves men, they are finding their own rites of passage. Here are three, culled from the newspapers:

A Boy Scout leader smashes his new car on a country road at 100 miles per hour: he is "showing off" to the four scouts who were riding with him. Now they are all dead.

A sixteen-year-old who lives in a comfortable suburb throws a large rock from a freeway overpass through the windshield of a car. The victim, a thirty-one-year-old housewife, suffers a concussion but survives. "You do it for the thrill," the boy says. "It's a boring town," says one of his classmates.

A teenage boy is so upset that his girlfriend has jilted him that he threatens to kill himself. Talking to her on the phone, he says he will drive over to her house and smash his car into the tree in her front yard if she will not go out with him. She refuses. So he does it, killing himself.

Many movies are made as surrogate rites of passage for young men. They are designed for the guy who, in actor Clint Eastwood's words, "sits alone in the theater. He's young and he's scared. He doesn't know what he's going to do with his life. He wishes he could be self-sufficient, like the man he sees up there on the screen, somebody who can look out for himself, solve his own problems." The heroes of these films are men who are tough and hard, quick to use violence, wary of women. Whether cowboys, cops, or superheroes, they dominate everything—women, nature, and other men. Young men cannot outmaneuver the Nazis as Indiana Jones did in *Raiders of the Lost Ark*, or battle Darth Vader, or outsmart Dr. No with James Bond's derring-do. To feel like heroes they turn to the other sex. They ask young women for more than companionship, or sex, or marriage. They ask women to give them what their culture could not—their manhood.

Half the nation's teenagers have had sex before they graduate from high school. The easiest way to prove oneself a man today is to make it with a girl. First we make out or put the make on her. Then we make it. We are not, like our "primitive" forebearers, joining together with a woman as adults. We are coming together in order to become adults, if not in society's eyes, then in our own.

"You in her pants yet?" one of the high school jocks asks his classmate in *Ordinary People*, the Academy Award-winning movie directed by Robert Redford. We prove our manhood on the football field or the basketball court by scoring points against other men. We prove our manhood in sex by scoring with women.

The young man, armed with lines like "Don't you love me?" is always ready for action. He wants to forge ahead, explore new territory. After all, he has nothing to lose. He has no hymen, no uterus. He is free to play the role of bold adventurer, coaxing the reluctant girl to let him sow his wild oats in her still virgin land. "I love you, but I don't feel ready," she may say. She may be afraid that her refusal may jeopardize her relationship with her young explorer, but she is even more afraid to get pregnant. She may feel less mature than her sex-hungry companion. But the emotional reality may be precisely the opposite. Certain of her femininity and of her pregnability, she dares to wait until the time is right. Insecure about his masculinity and obsessed with proving it—to himself and his buddies, if not to her—he needs to score in order to feel that he has made the team.

Sonny Burns, the sexually insecure hero of Dan Wakefield's *Going All the Way*, finds himself engaged in an amorous overture on a double date. But he admits to himself, and to a generation of readers, that he is doing so not because he finds his date exciting. On the contrary, she bores him. He does so because he wants to impress his buddy in the front seat. He must prove he is a man, and a man takes whatever "pussy" he can get. Pretending to be passionate, he thinks about the high school rating system, according to which boys reported their sexual scores: "The next day, when the guys asked you what you got the night before, you could say you got finger action inside the pants. That wasn't as good as really fucking but it rated right along with dry-humping and was much better than just the necking stuff like frenching and getting covered-tit or bare-tit. It was really pretty much of a failure if you parked with a girl and got only covered-tit."

Even if he wins, the victory is private. There are no fans in the bleachers as he crosses home plate and scores. He has not proved himself a man to adult males, as did young men in traditional rites of passage. His sexual conquest is a rite of passage only in his own mind. If adult society were to pass judgment on these back-seat gymnastics, it would probably be negative. The responsible adult would ask him if he was ready for marriage. Could he support her if he had to? And of course the answers are no. He has become an adult sexually, not socially. He has proved his virility in the dark of night. By the light of day, the proof has vanished.

As Margaret Mead pointed out in *Male and Female*, our culture

leaves adolescents in a quandary. We give them extraordinary freedom but tell them not to use it. "We permit and encourage situations in which young people can indulge in any sort of sex behavior
that they elect," wrote Mead a generation ago. "We actually place
our young people in a virtually intolerable situation, giving them
the entire setting for behaviour for which we then punish them
when it occurs." It is a cultural arrangement for which some young
women pay an awful price.

Whether veiled in fiction or revealed in autobiography, women
recall the ritual of modern courtship with caustic humor at best,
more often with bitterness. So objectified do they feel that they
develop a detached attitude toward their bodies. Reports the cheerleader heroine in Lisa Alther's *Kinflicks*: "Joe Bob would dutifully
knead my breasts through my uniform jacket and padded bra, as
though he were a housewife poking plums to determine their
ripeness." Later, she would observe him sucking "at my nipples
while I tried to decide what to do with my hands to indicate my continuing involvement in the project."

But Alther's good-natured response is not typical. Other sagas of
car-seat courtships and apartment affairs leave their heroines har-
boring a deep distaste for men. Some declare themselves feminists
or lesbians. Some become depressed. Others, as in Judith Rossner's
*Looking for Mr. Goodbar*, are killed by their lovers. And a few, after
great turmoil, find a man who will treat them gently, with genuine
care.

The movie theater, that public living room for a nation of young
lovers, reflects this yearning too. For those who have grown weary
of the macho hero whose physical prowess is enough, Hollywood
has provided a countertype. For those who are not infatuated with
the Soldier, there are now movies about the anti-soldier. "In what
may be an emerging genre in the movies," wrote Paul Starr in his
review of *Coming Home*, *An Unmarried Woman*, and *Alice Doesn't Live
Here Anymore*, "there appears a character who expresses in his personality and in his relations with the heroine a new idea of masculinity. He might be described as the emotionally competent hero.
. . . He is the man to whom women turn as they try to change their
own lives: someone who is strong and affectionate, capable of inti-
macy . . . masculine without being dominating." The new hero,
though perhaps not rugged and tough in the familiar mold, can be
intimate. He can feel. "The new softer image of masculinity seems

to represent what is distinctive and significant in recent films, and I expect we will see more of the post-feminist hero because the old, strong, silent type no longer seems adequate as lover—or as person."

Who, then, is to be the young man's hero? The gentle, post-feminist figure extolled by the new genre of films and by the roughly five thousand men's consciousness-raising groups across America? Or the self-sufficient, hard-hitting tough that Eastwood tries to embody and that the military breeds? Faced with such polarized and politicized choices, how does a boy become a man? By being hard or by being soft?

From the sensible to the absurd, we have answers. We have so many shifting, contradictory criteria for manhood that they confuse rather than inspire.

American boys coming of age encounter sexual chaos. A chorus of liberation advocates, now with bass as well as soprano voices, encourages them to free themselves from the oppressive male role, to become softer, and to consider themselves women's equals. But another vociferous group beckons them in another direction. For every pro-feminist man, there is his counterpart, who denounces those "fuzzy-headed housemales, purporting to represent 'men's liberation,' but sponsored by NOW." One Minnesota men's rights leader argued, for example, that men who support women's liberation are "eunuchs," motivated by an "urge to slip into a pair of panties." According to him and his followers: "Men's liberation means establishing the right of males to be men, not to liberate them from being men."

The hard-liners and soft-liners both have their respective magazines, organizations, and conferences. Repulsed by the cacophony, most young men try to ignore it. But the questions gnaw at them anyway. Although the pro- and anti-feminist activists irritate them, young men cannot deny their own uncertainty. They are caught between the competing ideals of chauvinism and liberation. The old archetypes do not work; the new ones remain vague and incomplete. If we are not to be John Wayne, then who?

Into the vacuum created by the demise of the old archetypes rush myriad images. Each hopes to inspire a following. Masculinity becomes the target for everyone from toothpaste advertisers to Hollywood superstars. These salesmen of self-help all have their diagnoses for the young man struggling to find his own identity. Some take the pose of proud aging lions, defending the traditional masculine role as Western civilization enters a precipitous, psycho-sexual decline. In *Sexual Suicide*, George Gilder warned of the imminent feminization of man and masculinization of woman and called on men to reassert their superiority.

Others do not oppose liberation but rather seem to exploit it. Cynically catering to masculine insecurity, they describe the world of white-collar commuters as a stark and brutal asphalt jungle in which men must constantly flex their aggressive personalities in order to survive. According to Michael Korda, author of *Power!* and *Success!*, life is nothing more than a series of encounters in which one dominates or is dominated, intimidates or is intimidated, achieves power over or is oneself overpowered. "Your gain is inevitably someone else's loss," philosophizes this latter-day Nietzsche, "your failure someone else's victory."

There are also the advocates of liberation who seek to free us from the manacles of machismo. Although they are constructive in intent, they too increase the confusion. In their attempt to free us from one-sidedness, they double our load. They now want us to be "assertive *and* yielding, independent *and* dependent, job *and* people oriented, strong *and* gentle, in short, both masculine *and* feminine." The prescriptions are not wrong, just overwhelming. Their lists of do's and don'ts, like Gail Sheehy's *Passages*, seem too neat, too tidy. They write of "masculinity in crisis" with such certainty. They encourage us to cry with such stoicism. They advise us to "be personal, be intimate with men" with such authority. It is all too much.

Whichever model young men choose, they know the traditional expectation of their culture. At least until the seventies, Americans of all ages and of all educational and income levels were in wide agreement about what traits are masculine. According to one study, based on more than a thousand interviews, men are expected to be very aggressive, not at all emotional, very dominant, not excitable, very competitive, rough, and unaware of others' feelings. And women are expected to be more or less the opposite.

If this is what maleness is, then a young man must find ways to demonstrate those traits. Without a rite of passage he can only prove what he is not. Not a faggot, a pussy, a queer. Not a pushover, a loser, or a lightweight. Not a dimwit or a dunce or a jerk or a nobody. Not a prick or a pansy. Not, above all, anything that is feminine. Indeed, without clear rites of passage, the only way to be a man is essentially negative: to not be a woman.

If we are to be masculine, then they must be feminine. We convince ourselves that women are yielding, that they are more interested in our careers than in their own, that they are interested in sex whenever we are, that they are fulfilled by raising children. That, we assume, is who they are. Should one of them act differently, then something is wrong, not with our assumptions, but with her.

Having entered physical manhood, we are nevertheless emotionally unsure of ourselves. The more unsure we are, the more we stress that we are not "feminine" and the more we are threatened when women act "masculine." We try to rid ourselves of any soft, effeminate qualities. We gravitate toward all-male cliques in the form of sports teams, social clubs, or professional groups. When we are with a woman, it is virtually always in a sexually charged atmosphere. To be merely friends is nearly impossible because it suggests that we have something in common. We are trying, after all, to prove precisely the opposite, which is why so many marriages fail.

# PAUL THEROUX

# *Being a Man*

Novelist, teacher, and master of the travel narrative, Paul Theroux (b. 1941) received an early education in writing from the novelist V. S. Naipaul, who was a faculty colleague of Theroux when he was teaching English at Makerere University in Uganda. Theroux has traveled all over the world, usually taking copious notes of both the people and places he visits. Both Theroux's novels and his travel narratives make extensive use of those notes. In "Being a Man," Theroux applies the skills honed from years of travel and observation to a subject much closer to home: the American male.

THERE IS A PATHETIC SENTENCE IN THE CHAPTER "FETISHISM" IN DR. Norman Cameron's book *Personality Development and Psychopathology*. It goes, "Fetishists are nearly always men; and their commonest fetish is a woman's shoe." I cannot read that sentence without thinking that it is just one more awful thing about being a man—and perhaps it is an important thing to know about us.

I have always disliked being a man. The whole idea of manhood in America is pitiful, in my opinion. This version of masculinity is a little like having to wear an ill-fitting coat for one's entire life (by contrast, I imagine femininity to be an oppressive sense of nakedness). Even the expression "Be a man!" strikes me as insulting and abusive. It means: Be stupid, be unfeeling, obedient, soldierly and stop thinking. Man means "manly"—how can one think about men without considering the terrible ambition of manliness? And yet it is part of every man's life. It is a hideous and crippling lie; it not only insists on difference and connives at superiority, it is also by its very nature destructive, emotionally damaging, and socially harmful. The youth who is subverted, as most are, into believing in the masculine ideal is effectively separated from women and he spends the rest of his life finding women a riddle and a nuisance. Of course, there is a female version of this male affliction. It begins with mothers encouraging little girls to say (to other adults) "Do you like my new dress?" In a sense, little girls are traditionally urged to please adults with a kind of coquettishness while boys are enjoined to behave like monkeys towards each other. The nine-year-old coquette proceeds to become womanish in a subtle power game in which she learns to be sexually indispensable, socially decorative and always alert to a man's sense of inadequacy.

Femininity—being lady-like—implies needing a man as witness and seducer; but masculinity celebrates the exclusive company of men. That is why it is so grotesque; and that is also why there is no manliness without inadequacy—because it denies men the natural friendship of women.

It is very hard to imagine any concept of manliness that does not belittle women, and it begins very early. At an age when I wanted to meet girls—let's say the treacherous years of thirteen to sixteen—I was told to take up a sport, get more fresh air, join the Boy Scouts, and I was urged not to read so much. It was the 1950s and if you asked too many questions about sex you were sent to camp—boy's camp, of course: the nightmare. Nothing is more unnatural or prison-like than a boy's camp, but if it were not for them we would have no Elks' Lodges, no pool rooms, no boxing matches, no Marines.

And perhaps no sports as we know them. Everyone is aware of how few in number are the athletes who behave like gentlemen. Just as high school basketball teaches you how to be a poor loser, the manly attitude towards sports seems to be little more than a recipe for creating bad marriages, social misfits, moral degenerates, sadists, latent rapists and just plain louts. I regard high school sports as a drug far worse than marijuana, and it is the reason that the average tennis champion, say, is a pathetic oaf.

Any objective study would find the quest for manliness essentially right-wing, puritanical, cowardly, neurotic and fueled largely by a fear of women. It is also certainly philistine. There is no book-hater like a Little League coach. But indeed all the creative arts are obnoxious to the manly ideal, because at their best the arts are pursued by uncompetitive and essentially solitary people. It makes it very hard for a creative youngster, for any boy who expresses the desire to be alone seems to be saying that there is something wrong with him.

It ought to be clear by now that I have something of an objection to the way we turn boys into men. It does not surprise me that when the President of the United States has his customary weekend off he dresses like a cowboy—it is both a measure of his insecurity and his willingness to please. In many ways, American culture does little more for a man than prepare him for modeling clothes in the L. L. Bean catalogue. I take this as a personal insult because for many years I found it impossible to admit to myself that I wanted to be a writer. It was my guilty secret, because being a writer was incompatible with being a man. There are people who might deny this, but that is because the American writer, typically, has been so at pains to prove his manliness that we have come to see literariness and manliness as mingled qualities. But first there was a fear that writing was not a manly profession—indeed, not a profession at all. (The paradox in American letters is that it has always been easier for a woman to write and for a man to be published.) Growing up, I had thought of sports as wasteful and humiliating, and the idea of manliness was a bore. My wanting to become a writer was not a flight from that oppressive role-playing, but I quickly saw that it was at odds with it. Everything in stereotyped manliness goes against the life of the mind. The Hemingway personality is too tedious to go into here, and in any case his exertions are well-known, but certainly it was not until this aberrant behavior was examined by feminists in the 1960s that any male writer dared question the pugnacity in Hemingway's fiction. All the bullfighting and arm wrestling and elephant shooting diminished Hemingway as a writer, but it is consistent with a prevailing attitude in American writing: one cannot be a male writer without first proving that one is a man.

It is normal in America for a man to be dismissive or even somewhat apologetic about being a writer. Various factors make it easier. There is a heartiness about journalism that makes it acceptable—journalism is the manliest form of American writing and, therefore, the profession the most independent-minded women seek (yes, it is an illusion, but that is my point). Fiction-writing is equated with a kind of dispirited failure and is only manly when it produces wealth—money is masculinity. So is drinking. Being a drunkard is another assertion, if misplaced, of manliness. The American male writer is traditionally proud of his heavy drinking. But we are also a very literal-minded people. A man proves his manhood in America in old-fashioned ways. He kills lions, like Hemingway; or he hunts ducks, like Nathanael West; or he makes pronouncements like, "A man should carry enough knife to defend himself with," as James Jones once said to a *Life* interviewer. Or he says he can drink you under the table. But even tiny drunken William Faulkner loved to mount a horse and go fox hunting, and Jack Kerouac roistered up and down Manhattan in a lumberjack shirt (and spent every night of *The Subterraneans* with his mother in Queens). And we are familiar with the lengths to which Norman Mailer is prepared, in his endearing way, to prove that he is just as much a monster as the next man.

When the novelist John Irving was revealed as a wrestler, people took him to be a very serious writer, and even a bubble reputation like Eric (*Love Story*) Segal's was enhanced by the news that he ran the marathon in a respectable time. How surprised we would be if Joyce Carol Oates were revealed as a sumo wrestler or Joan Didion active in pumping iron. "Lives in New York City with her three children" is the typical woman writer's biographical note, for just as the male writer must prove he has achieved a sort of muscular manhood, the woman writer—or rather her publicists—must prove her motherhood.

There would be no point in saying any of this if it were not generally accepted that to be a man is somehow—even now in feminist-influenced America—a privilege. It is on the contrary an unmerciful and punishing burden. Being a man is bad enough; being manly is appalling (in this sense, women's lib has done much more for men than for women). It is the sinister silliness of men's fashions, and a clubby attitude in the arts. It is the subversion of good students. It is the so-called "Dress Code" of the Ritz-Carlton Hotel in Boston, and it is the institutionalized cheating in college sports. It is the most primitive insecurity.

And this is also why men often object to feminism but are afraid to explain why: of course women have a justified grievance, but most men believe—and with reason—that their lives are just as bad.

# ANITA K. BLAIR

# *Shattering the Myth of the Glass Ceiling*

Anita K. Blair is the executive vice president of the Independent Women's Forum, a conservative women's lobbying group based in Arlington, Virginia. She has been outspoken as a defender of the status quo in the women's rights movement. As a trustee of the all-male Virginia Military Institute, she defended the college's decision not to admit women into its ranks. Here, she suggests that women have moved to a position of near-equality with men, and so no special efforts are necessary to "raise" the status of women any further.

WE OFTEN HEAR THAT WOMEN HAVE BEEN THE BIGGEST BENEFICIARIES of affirmative action. In fact, whether the credit belongs to affirmative action policies, the birth control pill, economic growth or a combination of factors, women have made remarkable progress in the last 30 years. Why have women succeeded so well while other minorities have not?

First, of course, women aren't a minority; they constitute more than 51% of the U.S. population. But like racial and ethnic minorities, until the 1960s, women generally lacked access to educational and employment opportunities. What did they do when previously closed doors began to open for them? Government-gathered statistics tell the story.

Women went to college. In 1960, only 19% of bachelor's degrees were awarded to women. By 1992, women received 55% of bachelor's degrees and 54% of master's degrees. Note that these figures exceed the percentage of women in the population.

In 1960, women received only 5.5% of medical doctor degrees and 2.5% of juris doctor degrees. By 1992, women represented more than 35% of new physicians and 42% of new lawyers. Today, women constitute more than 22% of doctors and almost 25% of lawyers and judges.

Women also left home and went to work. Today, women constitute 46% of the civilian work force overall. Among women 25 to 54, 74% work outside the home. This includes 60% of married women, up from 32% in 1960.

We often hear about a "wage gap" between women and men. In 1992, the ratio of female to male, year-round, fulltime earnings was 71 cents to the dollar. This includes workers of all ages and all types of jobs. Among workers 25 to 34, the 1992 ratio was 82 cents on the dollar. And in a real "apples to apples" comparison, the gap narrows more. June E. O'Neill, director of the Congressional Budget Office, did a study based on the National Longitudinal Survey of Youth by Ohio State University's Center for Human Resources Research. O'Neill found that among people 27 to 33 who have never had a child, women's earnings were about 98% of men's. Similar results occur if you compare the earnings of women and men of the same education and experience in the same professions.

Women outnumber men in several significant job areas. For example, women far outnumber men in health and medicine management (79% female) and personnel and labor relations management (61% female). Women constitute 64% of workers in technical, sales and administrative support and about 60% of workers in service jobs. These are among the fastest growing occupations in America.

Consider, on the other hand, the jobs where men predominate. Women constitute only 24% of machine operators and laborers, 19% of farming, forestry and fishing workers and 9% of production, craft, and repair workers. The Bureau of Labor Statistics says these are among America's fastest declining occupations. Thus women are concentrated in occupations with good prospects for growth.

Women also have created jobs, for themselves and others. In 1980, there were about 2 million women-owned businesses with about $25 billion in sales. Today, according to the National Foundation for Women Business Owners, nearly 8 million companies with more than $2.25 trillion in sales are owned by women. One in four American workers is employed by a woman-owned business.

Should affirmative action policies receive the credit for women's success? Assume it's true. What lessons can we learn about the future of affirmative action? First, merely opening doors—the classic meaning of "affirmative action"—can accomplish a lot if the people who walk through the doors have done their homework by staying in school and getting the training necessary to qualify for jobs they want.

Second, dictating results—as "affirmative action" has come to do through quotas, goals, preferences and set-asides—not only doesn't help but probably hurts. Suppose women had dedicated all their efforts to penetrating the male-dominated trades mentioned above? They'd have a bleak future, as technology would have marched on anyway, and women would have missed the new opportunities made possible by the technological revolution. Instead, women today are well positioned to participate in the information age.

Finally, the era of affirmative action should teach us that any program purportedly designed to achieve goals must achieve or die. If affirmative action has served its purpose, it should be ended. If, after 30 years, it has not served its purpose, it definitely should be ended.

# LESTER C. THUROW

# Why Women Are Paid Less Than Men

Lester Thurow (b. 1938), an economist at the Massachusetts Institute of Technology, has been called "the most influential economist of his generation." While that title can be debated, he has had an undeniable influence on the left side of the political spectrum. Most of his writings address the social inequalities inherent in capitalism. He has proposed, among other things, a 77 percent tax bracket, a 10 percent national sales tax, and a three dollar a gallon gasoline tax. In "Why Women are Paid Less than Men," Thurow applies his very clear and logical reasoning to yet another controversial issue: women's status in the business world.

IN THE 40 YEARS FROM 1939 TO 1979 WHITE WOMEN WHO WORK full time have with monotonous regularity made slightly less than 60 percent as much as white men. Why?

Over the same time period, minorities have made substantial progress in catching up with whites, with minority women making even more progress than minority men. Black men now earn 72 percent as much as white men (up 16 percentage points since the mid-1950s) but black women earn 92 percent as much as white women. Hispanic men make 71 percent of what their white counterparts do, but Hispanic women make 82 percent as much as white women. As a result of their faster progress, fully employed black women make 75 percent as much as fully employed black men while Hispanic women earn 68 percent as much as Hispanic men.

This faster progress may, however, end when minority women finally catch up with white women. In the bible of the New Right, George Gilder's *Wealth and Poverty*, the 60 percent is just one of Mother Nature's constants like the speed of light or the force of gravity. Men are programmed to provide for their families economically while women are programmed to take care of their families emotionally and physically. As a result men put more effort into their jobs than women. The net result is a difference in work intensity that leads to that 40 percent gap in earnings. But there is no discrimination against women—only the biological facts of life.

The problem with this assertion is just that. It is an assertion with no evidence for it other than the fact that white women have made 60 percent as much as men for a long period of time.

"Discrimination against women" is an easy answer but it also has its problems as an adequate explanation. Why is discrimination against women not declining under the same social forces that are leading to a lessening of discrimination against minorities? In recent years women have made more use of the enforcement provisions of the Equal Employment Opportunities Commission and the courts than minorities. Why do the laws that prohibit discrimination against women and minorities work for minorities but not for women?

When men discriminate against women, they run into a problem. To discriminate against women is to discriminate against your own wife and to lower your own family income. To prevent women from working is to force men to work more.

When whites discriminate against blacks, they can at least think that they are raising their own incomes. When men discriminate against women they have to know that they are lowering their own family income and increasing their own work effort.

While discrimination undoubtedly explains part of the male-female earnings differential, one has to believe that men are monumentally stupid or irrational to explain all of the earnings gap in terms of discrimination. There must be something else going on.

Back in 1939 it was possible to attribute the earnings gap to large differences in educational attainments. But the educational gap between men and women has been eliminated since World War II. It is no longer possible to use education as an explanation for the lower earnings of women. Some observers have argued that women earn less money since they are less reliable workers who are more apt to leave the labor force. But it is difficult to maintain this position since women are less apt to quit one job to take another and as a result they tend to work as long, or longer, for any one employer. From any employer's perspective they are more reliable, not less reliable, than men.

Part of the answer is visible if you look at the lifetime earnings profile of men. Suppose that you were asked to predict which men in a group of 25-year-olds would become economically successful. At age 25 it is difficult to tell who will be economically successful and your predictions are apt to be highly inaccurate. But suppose that you were asked to predict which men in a group of 35-year-olds would become economically successful. If you are successful at age 35, you are very likely to remain successful for the rest of your life. If you have not become economically successful by age 35, you are very unlikely to do so later.

The decade between 25 and 35 is when men either succeed or fail. It is the decade when lawyers become partners in the good firms, when business managers make it onto the "fast track," when academics get tenure at good universities, and when blue collar workers find the job opportunities that will lead to training opportunities and the skills that will generate high earnings. If there is any one decade when it pays to work hard and to be consistently in the labor force, it is the decade between 25 and 35. For those who succeed, earnings will rise rapidly. For those who fail, earnings will remain flat for the rest of their lives.

But the decade between 25 and 35 is precisely the decade when women are most apt to leave the labor force or become part-time workers to have children. When they do, the current system of promotion and skill acquisition will extract an enormous lifetime price.

This leaves essentially two avenues for equalizing male and female earnings. Families where women who wish to have successful careers, compete with men, and achieve the same earnings should alter their family plans and have their children either before 25 or after 35. Or society can attempt to alter the existing promotion and skill acquisition system so that there is a longer time period in which both men and women can attempt to successfully enter the labor force. Without some combination of these two factors, a substantial fraction of the male-female earnings differentials are apt to persist for the next 40 years, even if discrimination against women is eliminated.

# KAY EBELING

# The Failure of Feminism

Perhaps, as Kay Ebeling argues in her provocative essay, "The Failure of Feminism," all of the tremendous "progress" made by the women's movement over the last two centuries isn't really progress at all. Might it just be that single motherhood, perhaps the most significant inheritance of the feminist tradition, is more of a curse than a blessing? In this essay, Ebeling pursues the paradoxical argument that men may have benefited from the feminist movement more than women have.

THE OTHER DAY I HAD THE WORLD'S FASTEST BLIND DATE. A YUPPIE from Eureka penciled me in for 50 minutes on a Friday and met me at a watering hole in the rural northern California town of Arcata. He breezed in, threw his jammed daily planner on the table and shot questions at me, watching my reactions as if it were a job interview. He eyed how much I drank. Then he breezed out to his next appointment. He had given us 50 minutes to size each other up and see if there was any chance for romance. His exit was so fast that as we left he let the door slam back in my face. It was an interesting slam.

Most of our 50-minute conversation had covered the changing state of male-female relationships. My blind date was 40 years old, from the Experimental Generation. He is "actively pursuing new ways for men and women to interact now that old traditions no longer exist." That's a real quote. He really did say that, when I asked him what he liked to do. This was a man who'd read Ms. Magazine and believed every word of it. He'd been single for 16 years but had lived with a few women during that time. He was off that evening for a ski weekend, meeting someone who was paying her own way for the trip.

I too am from the Experimental Generation, but I couldn't even pay for my own drink. To me, feminism has backfired against women. In 1973 I left what could have been a perfectly good marriage, taking with me a child in diapers, a 10-year-old Plymouth and

Volume 1, Number One of *Ms.* Magazine. I was convinced I could make it on my own. In the last 15 years my ex has married or lived with a succession of women. As he gets older, his women stay in their 20s. Meanwhile, I've stayed unattached. He drives a BMW. I ride buses.

Today I see feminism as the Great Experiment That Failed, and women in my generation, its perpetrators, are the casualties. Many of us, myself included, are saddled with raising children alone. The resulting poverty makes us experts at cornmeal recipes and ways to find free recreation on weekends. At the same time, single men from our generation amass fortunes in CDs and real-estate ventures so they can breeze off on ski weekends. Feminism freed men, not women. Now men are spared the nuisance of a wife and family to support. After childbirth, if his wife's waist doesn't return to 20 inches, the husband can go out and get a more petite woman. It's far more difficult for the wife, now tied down with a baby, to find a new man. My blind date that Friday waved goodbye as he drove off in his RV. I walked home and paid the sitter with laundry quarters.

The main message of feminism was: woman, you don't need a man; remember, those of you around 40, the phrase: "A woman without a man is like a fish without a bicycle?" That joke circulated through "consciousness raising" groups across the country in the '70s. It was a philosophy that made divorce and cohabitation casual and routine. Feminism made women disposable. So today a lot of females are around 40 and single with a couple of kids to raise on their own. Child-support payments might pay for a few pairs of shoes, but in general, feminism gave men all the financial and personal advantages over women.

What's worse, we asked for it. Many women decided: you don't need a family structure to raise your children. We packed them off to day-care centers where they could get their nurturing from professionals. Then we put on our suits and ties, packed our briefcases and took off on this Great Experiment, convinced that there was no difference between ourselves and the guys in the other offices.

### "Biological Thing"

How wrong we were. Because like it or not, women have babies. It's this biological thing that's just there, these organs we're born with. The truth is, a woman can't live the true feminist life unless she denies her childbearing biology. She has to live on the pill, or have her tubes tied at an early age. Then she can keep up with the guys with an uninterrupted career and then, when she's 30, she'll be paying her own way on ski weekends too.

The reality of feminism is a lot of frenzied and overworked women dropping kids off at day-care centers. If the child is sick, they just send along some children's Tylenol and then rush off to underpaid jobs that they don't even like. Two of my working-mother friends told me they were mopping floors and folding laundry after midnight last week. They live on five hours of sleep, and it shows in their faces. And they've got husbands! I'm not advocating that women retrogress to the brainless housewives of the '50s who spent afternoons baking macaroni sculptures and keeping Betty Crocker files. Post-World War II women were the first to be left with a lot of free time, and they weren't too creative in filling it. Perhaps feminism was a reaction to that Brainless Betty, and in that respect, feminism has served a purpose.

Women should get educations so they can be brainy in the way they raise their children. Women can start small businesses, do consulting, write freelance out of the home. But women don't belong in 12-hour-a-day executive office positions, and I can't figure out today what ever made us think we would want to be there in the first place. As long as that biology is there, women can't compete equally with men. A ratio cannot be made using disproportionate parts. Women and men are not equal, we're different. The economy might even improve if women came home, opening up jobs for unemployed men, who could then support a wife and children, the way it was, pre-feminism.

Sometimes on Saturday nights I'll get dressed up and go out club-hopping or to the theater, but the sight of all those other women my age, dressed a little too young, made up to hide encroaching wrinkles, looking hopefully into the crowds, usually depresses me. I end up coming home, to spend my Saturday night with my daughter asleep in her room nearby. At least the NBC Saturday-night lineup is geared demographically to women at home alone.

*Student Essay*

# FELICIA ANDERSEN

# *Why I Am Not a Feminist*

Growing up in the '70s and '80s means growing up *after* the '60s, when many of American society's attitudes were turned upside-down. Suddenly, it was OK for a man to stay home and raise children. Suddenly, it was OK for a woman to have a career. Felicia grew up in the '70s, and the result has been perhaps somewhat different than expected. As you read, consider how the times you grew up in have affected your politics.

I AM NOT A FEMINIST. WHERE I COME FROM, I COULD GET IN BIG trouble saying that. My mother, while never exactly an agitator, was a divorced mother from about 1970 on, and she found herself in a position of "liberating" the men around her. She gender-integrated a men's exercise class, she learned (and taught) that women could pick up the check in a restaurant without castrating men, and she was a charter subscriber to Ms. magazine. Yet I am not a feminist— so where did she fail?

I guess she made the world too easy, too much better for her daughters. Nobody could get away with telling me or my sister that we couldn't take shop or try out for the football team or join the Boy Scouts of America—but we never wanted those things. Nobody ever told my brother that he should be "manly" and avoid cooking or housework for more masculine activities like lawn-mowing and watching televised sports—he just ended up inept at all those skills. Without an atmosphere of denial, suppression, obviously unfair rules or social structures inhibiting us, my brother and sister and I grew up expecting the world to treat us fairly, or each as fairly as the others, and it always has.

Well, fair-to-middling. I have noticed that my sister and I, having followed my mother's wishes for *all* her children, became proficient typists and have been able to get secretarial jobs in a flash. My brother, on the other hand, graduated from college with a B.A. in English and no such manual skills, only intellectual ones, and was able to begin work immediately as a paralegal, earning $23,000 a year to start. He never had to type after that; all his typing was done by a secretary, also with a B.A., who earned $17,000 a year, probably because she had listened to her mother and excelled at typing.

Granted, both of those positions are dead-end. The difference between them is primarily status, and kind of work required. I don't point this out because I'm a feminist, because I'm not, merely because it's true.

On the other hand, my mother managed, over the course of 20 years, to parlay her typing skills and a B.A. in English into a career in city government, in which she earned $48,000 a year. My father, on the other hand, never much of a typist but armed with an M.S. in mathematics, plateaued at around $36,000 a year in software engineering. It's hard to see any systematic forces at work here. I see instead two personalities, two different lives lived differently. My mother likes work and my father doesn't. My mother raised three children (not without my father's help, but as primary caregiver), while my father began ten years ago to raise his fourth. My father is intensely involved in his leisure activities; my mother prefers work activity. Perhaps the discrepancy in my brother's office between his earnings and the earnings of a similarly qualified woman is due to an ambition discrepancy as well. I point this out because I'm not a feminist, because a feminist would never bother to point this out.

I'll bet you my brother will never be asked to take a typing test. And neither will my father. But though I try to, I can't begin to feel outraged at this. I have the same opportunity to go to college as my mother and her mother, the same as my father and brother and sister. I can take exercise classes with men (even at formerly all-male clubs), I can buy a man dinner, and I can get a job using my mind. I thank my mother for these opportunities, but I have always been secure that they will be there. No one has ever suggested otherwise to me. If anyone did, I'd black his eye—with my typing hand.

# 4

## CUSTOMS AND HABITS

# JANE AUSTEN

# from *Pride and Prejudice*

A novelist and social critic, Jane Austen (1775–1817) wrote most often about society and marriage. Ironically, she never married, and kept herself quite removed from society. This excerpt from her novel, *Pride and Prejudice*, offers a penetrating description of the relationship between the Bennets, and the urgency which accompanied the custom of marriage.

IT IS A TRUTH UNIVERSALLY ACKNOWLEDGED THAT A SINGLE MAN IN possession of a good fortune must be in want of a wife.

However little known the feelings or views of such a man may be on his first entering a neighbourhood, this truth is so well fixed in the minds of the surrounding families that he is considered as the rightful property of some one or other of their daughters.

"My dear Mr. Bennet," said his lady to him one day, "have you heard that Netherfield Park is let at last?"

Mr. Bennet replied that he had not.

"But it is," returned she; "for Mrs. Long has just been here, and she told me all about it."

Mr. Bennet made no answer.

"Do not you want to know who has taken it?" cried his wife impatiently.

"*You* want to tell me, and I have no objection to hearing it."

This was invitation enough.

"Why, my dear, you must know, Mrs. Long says that Netherfield is taken by a young man of large fortune from the north of England; that he came down on Monday in a chaise and four to see the place, and was so much delighted with it that he agreed with Mr. Morris immediately; that he is to take possession before Michaelmas,* and some of his servants are to be in the house by the end of next week."

"What is his name?"

"Bingley."

"Is he married or single?"

"Oh! single, my dear, to be sure! A single man of large fortune; four or five thousand a year. What a fine thing for our girls!"

"How so? How can it affect them?"

"My dear Mr. Bennet," replied his wife, "how can you be so tiresome! You must know that I am thinking of his marrying one of them."

"Is that his design in settling here?"

"Design! nonsense, how can you talk so! But it is very likely that he *may* fall in love with one of them, and therefore you must visit him as soon as he comes."

"I see no occasion for that. You and the girls may go, or you may send them by themselves, which perhaps will be still better, for as you are as handsome as any of them, Mr. Bingley might like you the best of the party."

"My dear, you flatter me. I certainly *have* had my share of beauty, but I do not pretend to be anything extraordinary now. When a woman has five grown up daughters, she ought to give over thinking of her own beauty."

"In such cases, a woman has not often much beauty to think of."

"But, my dear, you must indeed go and see Mr. Bingley when he comes into the neighbourhood."

"It is more than I engage for, I assure you."

"But consider your daughters. Only think what an establishment it would be for one of them. Sir William and Lady Lucas are determined to go, merely on that account, for in general you know they visit no newcomers. Indeed you must go, for it will be impossible for us to visit him if you do not."

"You are over scrupulous surely. I dare say Mr. Bingley will be

---

*A religious holiday celebrated on September 29, the end of summer.

very glad to see you; and I will send a few lines by you to assure him of my hearty consent to his marrying whichever he chooses of the girls; though I must throw in a good word for my little Lizzy."

"I desire you will do no such thing. Lizzy is not a bit better than the others; and I am sure she is not half so handsome as Jane, nor half so good-humoured as Lydia. But you are always giving *her* the preference."

"They have none of them much to recommend them," replied he; "they are all silly and ignorant like other girls; but Lizzy has something more of quickness than her sisters."

"Mr. Bennet, how can you abuse your own children in such a way? You take delight in vexing me. You have no compassion on my poor nerves."

"You mistake me, my dear. I have a high respect for your nerves. They are my old friends. I have heard you mention them with consideration these twenty years at least."

"Ah! you do not know what I suffer."

"But I hope you will get over it, and live to see many young men of four thousand a year come into the neighbourhood."

"It will be no use to us if twenty such should come since you will not visit them."

"Depend upon it, my dear, that when there are twenty, I will visit them all."

Mr. Bennet was so odd a mixture of quick parts, sarcastic humour, reserve, and caprice, that the experience of three and twenty years had been insufficient to make his wife understand his character. *Her* mind was less difficult to develop. She was a woman of mean understanding, little information, and uncertain temper. When she was discontented she fancied herself nervous. The business of her life was to get her daughters married; its solace was visiting and news.

# LEAH NEUMAN

# Calling a "Boy" for a "Date"

We've all experienced it (men, still, probably more than women)—the anxiety about asking a potential love-interest on a date. Here, Leah Neuman (yes, the names have been changed to protect the innocent) tells all about one such experience. As you read, notice how much easier—and more fun—it is to read about these awkward moments than it would be to actually go through them yourself.

THE FIRST TIME I CALLED UP A "BOY" ("A MALE HUMAN OF ALMOST any age whom I would consider going out with") to ask for a "date" ("an unspecified romantic activity that two people who don't know each other very well participate in"), I wrote down everything I wanted to say on a scrap of paper, so I wouldn't flub it. My cues went through several revisions before I settled on: "You are Daniel Clark. I am Leah Neuman. We know each other. I was wondering if you'd like to have dinner with me on Saturday." I wasn't planning to actually say the first three sentences; probably something like "Hello, Daniel? This is Leah Neuman. Yeah, that's right . . ." would come out. The last sentence, though, seemed to me to strike a perfect balance among all the necessary elements:

a) It didn't end in a question mark;
b) It referred to a specific activity;
c) It referred to a specific day;
d) It referred to a potentially romantic activity.

All these elements were necessary in order to make it easy for him to answer either yes or no graciously, without making me feel personally rejected. A question like "Do you want to go out with me?" for example, would leave not enough room for doubt. (Several desperate but charming young men I know have actually used this ploy with moderate, or at least temporary, success; it makes them look desperate but charming, neurotic in the way that certain neurotic hearers respond to very well indeed.)

Now that I had rehearsed and paced for a few hours, all that was left was to place the call. I figured that there were three possible desirable outcomes to dialing: Busy, no answer, or CONTACT! I received, on this call, the second-best option: CONTACT!, but with a brother—Argh! Daniel wasn't home; I left a message. Daniel would call back tonight; time for a new plan of attack. All that rehearsal time out the window. Now I had to reshape my evening, around the central theme of Waiting for the Return Call—Without Sounding Like You're Waiting.

Let me step aside for a moment to tell you how I felt about Daniel. I knew him barely, briefly, but I had talked to him twice, at two different parties, once before Christmas vacation and once after. At the party before Christmas I had sprained my ankle and was sitting on a couch, trying to look as if I had chosen my fate, as if I liked to sit alone, as if all I was there for was people-watching, anyway. All of a sudden, a gorgeous stranger walked across the room, said hello, introduced himself, and sat beside me on the couch for fifteen minutes! I kept my cool, and we had a conversation about writing (mine) and painting (his). At the exact appropriate time, he excused himself, and a friend of mined eagerly filled his place to pump me for information. The next time I saw him, I walked by him several times (proving just how much more mobile I'd become since last we spoke), before I saw him alone and moved in for the kill—which turned out to be a conversation about painting (his) and writing (mine). Even so, I continued to find him charming, handsome, and friendly. In other words, good enough for a stranger.

So I got his number from my brother who knows his brother, who of course told him that somebody's brother had asked him for the phone number for her—so he had advance warning. However, I did not let advance warning take the place of proper rehearsal. Nosiree. He was a little older, he knew the score, and rehearsing my lines was the only way I could think of to equalize us at all. And now, waiting for his call, I had to devise a new plan that would serve the same equalizing function.

Simplicity was the answer. I would wait to pick up the phone until the middle of the third ring (time enough to clear my throat, not enough time to frustrate him), say hello, act unsurprised that he'd returned my call, and go directly from "Howareyougreat-iamfine" to "I was wondering if you'd like to have dinner with me on Saturday night."

He called, I answered, it actually worked. I chose the restaurant; turns out he loves Thai! Great! Everything worked perfectly, charmingly, and we had a perfectly charming date. Over shrimp dumplings and sweet ice coffee, we discoursed at length on the topics of writing (mine) and painting (his). Our first, best, and only date.

## STEPHANIE A. CROCKETT

# "Haven't We Met . . . ?":
## The Pickup Line Just Goes On and On

"Picking up" a member of the opposite sex has never been easy. It's even harder in these times of political correctness, where a wrong move can be interpreted as a moral affront. In "Haven't We Met . . . ?" Stephanie Crockett, a reporter for the *Washington Post,* covers the basics of meeting people in today's extra-sensitive dating environment.

IT'S A PHENOMENON AS OLD AS THE BATTLE BETWEEN THE SEXES. THE pickup line.

"What's up, sexy."

"I know my name, what's yours?"

Or the oldest line in the book—"Can I talk to you for a minute?"

Walter Cloud, "30-ish," divorced owner of a graphic design company in Arlington, has it down to a science. He enters the club, rakes his eyes over the crowd until he spots a subject, then moves in.

He chooses his words carefully, tailoring them to the way the woman is dressed, the event and the atmosphere. A woman in pearls or a business suit gets the gentle approach—polite conversation about the weather, the president, the O. J. trial.

"I would like to make them feel like the effort that they made to put that all together is well-deserved," explains Cloud.

But for sisters in sexier garb, no telling. "The base is the dress, that's how you decide what you're going to say to a woman," he says. "Believe it or not, people wear clothes that are appropriate for the event. If she's wearing something that is raunchy just to show off, you don't have as much respect for them."

Judson Tallandier, 22, a senior at Howard University majoring in telecommunications, says the key to his pickup lines is getting a woman to smile. "I say, 'Would you be offended if I ask you a personal question?' Then they have to tell me yes or no. Most girls say no, they wouldn't be offended," Tallandier says. Then he continues. "'Would you be offended if I asked you what your name was?' Then they smile. If they break a smile, a smile says so much."

Next thing, he says, he's buying her a drink or a hamburger and they're getting acquainted. Hopefully, he gets a telephone number.

Pickup lines are as varied as the people who deliver them. Some men and women looking to meet someone they have spotted across a room, in a grocery store aisle or along a trail in the park simply walk up, say hello and introduce themselves.

That's how Tony Mack, a 25-year-old administrative assistant at the National Institutes of Health, does it. He says pickup lines don't work. "Basically, I just say, 'How are you, what's your name, where are you from?' . . . stuff like that," says Mack. "Then I tell them a little about myself."

But for others, the pickup line is alive and well in an intricate series of verbal volleys and return shots that will either be entertaining enough to elicit a positive response or stupid enough to ensure rejection.

"Don't I know you from somewhere?" almost always results in an answer of "I don't think so," "I hope not," or "No, and you won't."

A typical response to "What's your sign?" is almost always "A stop sign."

"Can I go with you?" is sure to receive a curt "No."

Several pickup artists say the delivery is the key element to success in the introduction: "Everybody uses the same lines. It's like sex. Sex is sex, but lovers make it what it is," says Cloud, using a comparison to a familiar subject.

The general consensus, among several unscientifically polled people, is that men are more prone to use pickup lines than women, even in comparable social situations. "I have tried every trick in the book," says Cloud. "Guys have a whole head full of pickup lines."

Kimberly Turrentine, 24, an administrative assistant at Bolling Air Force Base, doesn't use lines on men in an effort to gain their affection. "Pickup lines are a last resort or desperate plea for attention for women," says Turrentine, turning up her nose at the thought of using one.

"Women should never put themselves in positions where they can be rejected," she goes on. "If a man approaches me or I see a man that I am attracted to, I will give him eye contact in the hope that he will notice that I am interested in him."

Men always are the ones who have to set themselves up for rejection, complains Dale Rudolph, a 28-year-old delivery driver.

"Girls want to look nice so guys can talk to them, then when we talk to them, they shove us away," he says. "You [women] shoot us down, but you can't do our job," he says. "Then you wonder why we get so mad."

Flattery, they say, will get you nowhere. But unabashed flattery is what Bernard Sumlin, a 30-year-old copyright technician, recommends.

"I say, 'Do you know that you are the most beautiful woman in the world?'" Sumlin says, lowering his voice seductively and moving closer, for a second assuming the pickup role.

Then he straightens up and his voice returns to its normal tone: "And it works, I guarantee you, that works," he says.

# KATHLEEN DOHENY

# *Desperately Seeking . . . Anyone*

What lengths would you go to meet the "perfect match"? When singles bars and blind dates fail, what's the busy, single, successful businessperson to do? In this selection, Kathleen Doheny, a freelance writer, takes a look at the extreme measures some have taken to meet their life-long companion. Does any of it work? Hard to say, but it doesn't keep some people from spending a lot of time and money trying. . . .

PAUL WALTON'S SEARCH FOR A WIFE CONSUMES MUCH OF HIS TIME and $3,000 a month.

Ever since the 38-year-told San Diego millionaire told Oprah's viewers last year that he is looking for a mate who wants to "give it up to live it up," he has been jetting around the country to meet the candidates.

Jerilyn Walter has taken to the skies to meet Mr. Right, too. Actually *lots* of Mr. Rights.

Tired of hearing her single female friends complain about their lack of dates, the 36-year-old Newport Beach businesswoman took action.

First, she advertised in the Anchorage Daily News, tipped off by television reports about great numbers of Alaskan men in search of mates. She invited all available men to meet women from Southern California and elsewhere who would fly in for a dinner-dance and other events.

"I got 70 calls in three days," says Walter. Meanwhile, word was spreading here, too, and in September, Walter and 127 other women flew to Alaska.

"We had 20 couples by the end of the trip," says Walter, who has formed Females for New Frontiers, a Costa Mesa-based group whose members go to great lengths—and rack up frequent-flier miles—to find relationships.

Singles on more modest budgets often invest just as much interest and time in the hunt. While some make a habit of checking every ring finger they encounter, others develop more ingenious strategies. A Los Angeles woman plans to find office buildings where many men work—and then hang out.

A San Fernando Valley single slipped on a bogus wedding ring, convinced that men would feel more comfortable talking with her if they thought she was married. (If something clicked, she figured, she could explain later.)

While singles engaged in such activities call themselves *dedicated, determined* or *dogged* in their pursuit of a partner, other folks (especially married ones) label them with another "D" word: *desperate.*

Like bad breath and body odor, desperation usually belongs to someone else. While some singles know other desperate singles and married folks know lots of desperate singles, desperate singles rarely describe themselves that way.

After all, *desperate* is defined in "The American Heritage Dictionary" as "nearly hopeless, critical, grave." The listing follows *despair.*

"Everyone has their own definition of *desperate*," notes Walton, the megabuck bachelor. When he appeared on another television talk show recently, two female guests described how they staged a car accident just to meet firemen. That meets Walton's definition of desperate.

Ditto, personal ads.

"To me, *desperate* is placing an ad in the paper because I'm really lonely. Or, I write Oprah, 'Please help me.' But I didn't call Oprah. They called me. I'm not desperate, I'm *opportunistic.*"

Not that anyone—regardless of marital status—is blaming singles for feeling desperate, by the way.

First, there's the car culture, which makes it difficult to meet people out and about. (Although one woman tried to solve that problem by writing her cell-phone number on a large pad of paper and holding it up to her window so the handsome driver in the next lane could see. He was married, but probably was admiring her chutzpah as he waved his left hand.)

Then there are changing expectations that lead naturally to desperation. This is the "blame-it-on-society" excuse, but in this case it's valid, sort of.

In generations past, no one expected the sun, moon and stars in a relationship, says Kathleen Mojas, a Beverly Hills psychologist. Now, she says, people expect more, and some people expect too much—*way* too much from their partner-to-be.

"Some people want to make someone else responsible for their happiness," she says. "There's a desperation that they won't find the right one. Some people are continually looking—and mistakenly thinking that the right person is the one who holds the key to their fulfillment."

Excuses out of the way, there are ways *not* to look desperate, even if you are, say mental-health experts who specialize in singles' issues.

Singles appear desperate when they're full of self-doubt, says Sharyn Wolf, a New York psychotherapist. Eliminate the self-doubt, and poof! go those desperate vibes.

It's easy for some singles to cluck, cluck over stories of extreme efforts to find mates, reassuring themselves they're not that desperate. But Wolf says they might take a page from that book.

As she sees it, many self-doubting singles—even those seemingly obsessed with finding a partner—often don't go far enough in their efforts.

"We think if we say, 'Hi,' something should happen," says Wolf, who wrote "Guerrilla Dating Tactics" (Plume, 1994) and teaches seminars by the same title. "But frequently it takes more than a hello."

It takes creativity, she contends. Even boldness, perhaps.

Suppose a guy is approaching a woman to ask her to dance. There's the traditional way to ask—and then there's Wolf's way: "Would you like to dance—if only to prove to my friends that I have excellent taste?"

Or, suppose you're at that most ancient of hunting grounds, the bar.

"This is a risky one," warns Wolf. "Ask, 'Can I buy you a drink or would you rather just have the money?'"

Says Wolf: "Nothing breaks the ice like humor. If you can get them to laugh, you know a lot about them. If you can't get them to laugh, you also know a lot about them."

And of course it's difficult to laugh and look desperate simultaneously.

In her counseling sessions and her seminars, Wolf has collected a plethora of other sure-fire ways to look less desperate. In each case the emphasis is on creativity—and the other person:

- One woman donating blood noticed a fellow donor who was a bit green around the gills. She offered him a plate of cookies and said, "I guess natural childbirth is out of the question?" (The couple dated—and married. )
- A news photographer covering a fire was surprised when a neighborhood woman brought him a glass of lemonade—and even more pleased when he discovered she had taped her name and telephone number on it. (Status of couple unknown.)

While the title "Guerrilla Dating Tactics" has a martial tone, Wolf emphasizes that the enemy isn't the potential partner. "The enemy is actually self-doubt. And extreme self-doubt often has people behaving in ways that seem desperate."

Think guts, not desperation.

"You make a bold first move and then you give 100% of the power to the other person," Wolf advises. "You make it clear there's interest on your part and then let them take it from there."

Whatever technique is used, creativity is vital to camouflage desperation, agrees Mojas, the Beverly Hills psychologist. She knows firsthand that some singles can get so desperate that they rely on a standard, one-size-fits-all opening line.

Big mistake, no matter how smooth it sounds.

On the way into her gym, Mojas noticed a man a few cars away looking at her and waving.

"Then he came over and said what a beautiful smile I had." He asked for her phone number. Hesitant, she said her business listing was in the yellow pages—but never heard from him.

"About six weeks later, standing in the line at the movies, I noticed a guy looking at me," Mojas says. He came over and told her what a beautiful smile she had. Mojas didn't recognize him at first because he was wearing a baseball cap. But then came the line—and déjà vu.

Reason enough, Mojas figured, to let him have it.

"Wait a minute," she said. "You've done this before. You didn't call the first time. You're probably here with a date. [He was.] I think your picture is in the lobby—you're the popcorn pickup artist!"

The movie episode brought home a point to Mojas, who now shares it with clients she counsels about relationships. ( No, it's not, "Don't pick up a date on a date.")

"The more gimmicky you are, the more insecure [you'll be seen as being]," Mojas says. "These gimmicky one-liners are much more likely to be turned down," she says.

"Unless, of course, the person who hears them is equally desperate."

*Student Essay*

# ADAM BURRELL

# *Time Torture*

In this essay, Adam describes what truly must be every student's object of hatred—the clock radio. Notice how he uses the device of personification to make his loathing of his clock seem more . . . well, personal. Adam uses hyperbole—like the "millions" of dials—to excellent comic effect. You must be brave to use comedy well: there are many situations where it may be seen as inappropriate.

DON'T GET ME WRONG—I'M REALLY NOT PARANOID. I MEAN, MY alarm clock looks like a typical generic style clock radio. Nothing appears outwardly abnormal at all. In fact, it doesn't have any truly distinguishing features at all, and I'm tempted to say that it's an average, run-of-the-mill, nondescript clock radio. But, since it's a cop-out to describe something as "nondescript" (if not outright contradictory), I'll give a quick rundown of it. I've owned this clock radio, a Realistic Chronomatic 213, for a month now, and it's still difficult to remember exactly what it looks like. There it is, a rectangular box sitting on my desk in the corner, six feet from my bed, with a bright red digital readout saying 9:39. The colon between the 9 and the 39—no, now 40—flashes on and off once per second, 24 hours a day. To the right of the time display is the radio tuning dial, set near 97 FM, probably KBCO Boulder. Also on the rectangular front face, just below the clock display and the radio tuning dial, is a row of four small round switches, used to set the time and the alarm. The top and the sides of the radio are an artificial wood-grain finish, trimmed with black and separated from the front panel by a chrome strip. Centered on its top is a small square speaker grill.

Yeah, this alarm clock would seem like a normal, well-adjusted appliance to most people, but that's because they don't have to live with it. Just by looking at it, a person wouldn't sense that this clock radio carried a grudge and had general anti-social tendencies. Even I didn't notice anything strange until recently. First, small irritating things became apparent. For instance, the way it stares at night, annoyingly blinking its stupid red colon. After a half-hour of watching the clock gaze back, it's obvious that the stare isn't a benign one; it has the qualities of an unpleasant sneer, that certain executioner's look of someone in ultimate control. Then, I noticed how time always seemed to speed up at night while I slept. I could almost hear that damn blood-red colon flashing faster and faster, but as soon as I would open my eyes it would skid back down to once per second, once per second. The unnerving part, though, is that the clock speeds up in direct proportion to the amount of sleep that I need— so even if I go to bed early the night before a big exam, I still wake up with severe jetlag.

This clock's attitude problem doesn't become blatantly apparent until early morning, however. The hours of darkness slowly convert it into a remorseless predatory creature, primed to terrorize. Yes, terrorize. Remaining utterly silent and motionless so as not to stir its unsuspecting comatose victim, the clock waits. Mercilessly it savors its position of power as the final seconds slip by. And then it strikes. Noise and chaos, resembling the detonation of a medium-sized nuclear device in the corner of my room, slam out of its tiny speaker. At five in the morning. Actually, at five in the morning, the sound has more of a physical quality, roughly equivalent to a chain-saw being started in the left ear while a rake crashes into the jaw. Instinctively, my body, instantly brought from suspended animation to adrenalin overload, lunges in the general direction of the demonic box on the desk. My hand swats at every small knob—there are now millions of them—until it slaps the right switch in the right direction, snuffing out the noise and the pain.

Every morning, as I lie limply on the floor, I can see the clock display staring straight ahead, blinking its damned red colon in the morning sun, once per second, once per second, and I know it's trying not to snicker. I'm not paranoid—the clock really does hate me.

# W. E. B. DUBOIS

# The Souls of White Folk

William Edgar Burghardt DuBois was a descendant of a French Huguenot and an African slave. He received B.A. degrees from both Fisk and Harvard Universities and a Ph.D. from the University of Berlin. He taught, at various times, at Wilberforce, the University of Pennsylvania, and Atlanta University, holding professorships in Greek, Latin, Sociology, Economics, and History. In addition, he edited many publications, including *Crisis*, the journal of the National Association for the Advancement of Colored People, from 1910 to 1934. One of his most famous works was *The Souls of Black Folk*—both a fine piece of English prose and a plea for greater understanding of blacks by whites. Seven years later, in 1910, he wrote this essay as a plea to whites to understand themselves.

HIGH IN THE TOWER WHERE I SIT BESIDE THE LOUD COMPLAINING OF the human sea I know many souls that toss and whirl and pass, but none there are that puzzle me more than the Souls of White Folk. Not, mind you, the souls of them that are white, but souls of them that have become painfully conscious of their whiteness; those in whose minds the paleness of their bodily skins is fraught with tremendous and eternal significance.

Forgetting (as I can at times forget) the meaning of this singular obsession to me and my folk, I become the more acutely sensitive to the marvelous part this thought is playing today, and to the way it is developing the Souls of White Folk, and I wonder what the end will be.

The discovery of personal whiteness among the world's people is a very modern thing—a nineteenth- and twentieth-century matter, indeed. The ancient world would have laughed at such a distinction. The Middle Ages regarded it with mild curiosity, and even up into the eighteenth century we were hammering our national manikins into one great Universal Man with fine frenzy, which ignored color and race as well as birth. Today we have changed all that, and the world, in sudden emotional conversation, has discovered that it is white, and, by that token, wonderful.

When I seek to explain this, to me, inexplicable phenomenon, there always creeps first to my mind the analogy of the child and his candy. To every child there comes a time when the toothsomeness of his sweets is strangely enhanced by the thought that his playmate has none. Further than this, however, the analogy fails, for with one accord the mother world seeks to teach this child the third new joy of sharing. Any thought, however, of sharing their color is to white folk not simply unthinkable, but its mention is liable to lead to violent explosions of anger and vituperation. Not only is there this unrebuked and vociferously applauded greediness, but something that sounds like: "I shall keep my candy and you shall not have yours." Or, in other words, it is not the obvious proposition: "I am white and you are black," but the astonishing declaration, "I am white and you are nothing."

This assumption that of all the hues of God, whiteness alone is candy to the world child—is inherently and obviously better than brownness or tan—leads to curious acts; even the sweeter souls of the dominant world, as they discourse with me on weather, weal and woe, are continually playing above their actual words an obligato of turn and tone, saying:

"My poor unwhite thing! Weep not nor rage. I know, too well, that the curse of God lies heavy on you. Why? That is not for me to say; but be brave! Do your work in your lowly sphere, praying the good Lord that into heaven above, where all is love, you may one day, be born—white!"

At such times I have an unholy desire to laugh, and to ask with seemingly irrelevance and certain irreverence: "But what on earth is whiteness, that one should so desire it?"

Then always somehow, some way, silently but clearly, I am given to understand that whiteness is the ownership of the earth, forever and ever, Amen!

Now, what is the effect on a man or a nation when it comes passionately to believe such an extraordinary dictum as this? That nations are coming to believe it is manifest daily. Wave on wave, each with increasing virulence, is dashing this new religion of whiteness on the shores of our time. Its first effects are funny; the strut of the Southerner, the arrogance of the Englishman amuck, the whoop of the hoodlum who vicariously leads your mob. Next it appears dampening generous enthusiasm in what we once counted glorious: To free the slave is discovered to be tolerable only insofar as it freed his master. Do we sense somnolent writhings in black Africa, or angry groans in India, or triumphant "banzais" in Japan? "To your tents, O Israel!" These nations are not white. Build warships and heft the Big Stick.

After the more comic manifestations and chilling of generous enthusiasm, come subtler, darker deeds. Everything considered, the title to the universe claimed by white folk is faulty. It ought at least to look plausible. How easy, then, by emphasis and omission, to make every child believe that every great soul the world ever saw was a white man's soul; that every great thought the world ever knew was a white man's thought; that every great deed the world ever did was a white man's deed; that every great dream the world ever sang was a white man's dream. In fine, that if from the world were dropped everything that could not fairly be attributed to white folk the world would, if anything, be even greater, truer, better than now. And if all this be a lie, is it not a lie in a great cause?

Here it is that the comedy verges to tragedy. The first minor note is struck all unconsciously by those worthy souls in whom consciousness of high descent brings burning desire to spread the gift abroad—the obligation of nobility to the ignoble. Such sense of duty assumes two things: A real possession of the heritage and its frank appreciation by the humbly born. So long, then, as humble black folk, voluble with thanks, receive barrels of old clothes from lordly and generous whites, there is much mental peace and moral satisfaction. But when the black man begins to dispute the white man's title to certain alleged bequests of the Father's in wage and position, authority and training; and when his attitude toward charity is sullen anger rather than humble jollity; when he insists on his human rights to swagger and swear and waste—then the spell is suddenly broken and the philanthropist is apt to be ready to believe that Negroes are impudent, that the South is right, and that Japan wants to fight us.

Mentally the blight has fallen on American science. The race problem is not insoluble if the correct answer is sought. It is insoluble if the wrong answer is insisted upon as it has been insisted upon for thrice a hundred years. A very moderate brain can show that two and two is four. But no human ingenuity can make that sum three or five. This American science has long attempted to do. It has made itself the handmaid of a miserable prejudice. In its attempt to justify the treatment of black folk it has repeatedly suppressed evidence, misquoted authority, distorted fact and deliberately lied. It is wonderful that in the very lines of social study, where America should shine, it has done nothing.

Worse than this is our moral and religious plight. We profess a religion of high ethical advancement, a spiritual faith, of respect for truth, despising of personal riches, a reverence for humility, and not simply justice to our fellows, but personal sacrifice of our good for theirs. It is a high aim, so high that we ought not utterly to be condemned for not reaching it, so long as we strive bravely toward it. Do we, as a people? On the contrary, we have injected into our creed a gospel of human hatred and prejudice, a despising of our less fortunate fellows, not to speak of our reverence for wealth, which flatly contradicts the Christian ideal. Granting all that American Christianity has done to educate and uplift black men, it must be frankly admitted that there is absolutely no logical method by which the treatment of black folk by white folk in this land can be squared with any reasonable statement or practice of the Christian ideal.

What is the result? It is either the abandonment of the Christian ideal or hypocrisy. Some frankly abandon Christianity when it comes to the race problem and say: Religion does not enter here. They then retire to some more primitive paganism and live there, enlightened by such prejudices as they adopt or inherit. This is retrogression toward barbarism, but it is at least honest. It is infinitely better than its widely accepted alternative, which attempts to reconcile color caste and Christianity, and sees or affects to see no incongruity. What ails the religion of a land when its strongholds of orthodoxy are to be found in those regions where race prejudice is most uncompromising, vindictive, and cruel; where human brotherhood is a lie?

The one great moral issue of America upon which the Church of Christ comes nearest being dumb is the question as to the application of the golden rule between white and black folk.

All this I see and hear up in my tower above the thunder of the seven seas. From my narrowed windows I stare into the night that looms beneath the cloud-swept stars. Eastward and westward storms are brewing great, ugly whirlwinds of hatred and blood and cruelty. I will not believe them inevitable. I will not believe that all that was must be—that all the shameful drama of the past must be done again today before the sunlight sweeps the silver seas.

If I cry amid this roar of elemental forces, must my cry be vain because it is but a cry—a small and human cry amid Promethean gloom?

Back beyond the world and swept by these wild white faces of the awful dead, why will this Soul of the White Folk, this modern Prometheus, hang bound by his own binding, tethered by a labor of the past? I hear his mighty cry reverberating through the world, "I am white!" Well and good, O Prometheus, divine thief! The world is wide enough for two colors, two little shinings of the sun; why then devour your own vitals when I answer, "I am black"?

# WILLIAM RASPBERRY

# *The Handicap of Definition*

William Raspberry (b. 1935) is a Pulitzer Prize-winning writer and a professor of journalism and communications at Duke University. His *Washington Post* column on minority affairs now appears in over 180 newspapers. While his columns often cover the difficult issues of race relations and social development, he remains cautiously optimistic. "I am a hopeful person," commented Raspberry in a 1995 interview, "and I think that there is a reasonable chance that people here and there, not all at once, will wake up to what we need to do and not sit around waiting for the politicians to come riding in to save us. It's the only way we're going to get anywhere." In this essay, he comments on the problems created by society's narrow definition of "black."

I KNOW ALL ABOUT BAD SCHOOLS, MEAN POLITICIANS, ECONOMIC deprivation and racism. Still, it occurs to me that one of the heaviest burdens black Americans—and black children in particular— have to bear is the handicap of definition: the question of what it means to be black.

Let me explain quickly what I mean. If a basketball fan says that the Boston Celtics' Larry Bird plays "black," the fan intends it—and Bird probably accepts it—as a compliment. Tell pop singer Tom Jones he moves "black" and he might grin in appreciation. Say to Teena Marie or The Average White Band that they sound "black" and they'll thank you.

But name one pursuit, aside from athletics, entertainment or sexual performance in which a white practitioner will feel complimented to be told he does it "black." Tell a white broadcaster he talks "black" and he'll sign up for diction lessons. Tell a white reporter he writes "black" and he'll take a writing course. Tell a white lawyer he reasons "black" and he might sue you for slander.

What we have here is a tragically limited definition of blackness, and it isn't only white people who buy it.

Think of all the ways black children can put one another down with charges of "whiteness." For many of these children, hard study and hard work are "white." Trying to please a teacher might be criticized as acting "white." Speaking correct English is "white." Scrimping today in the interest of tomorrow's goals is "white." Educational toys and games are "white."

An incredible array of habits and attitudes that are conducive to success in business, in academia, in the non-entertainment professions are likely to be thought of as somehow "white." Even economic success, unless it involves such "black" undertakings as numbers banking, is defined as "white."

And the results are devastating. I wouldn't deny that blacks often are better entertainers and athletes. My point is the harm that comes from too narrow a definition of what is black.

One reason black youngsters tend to do better at basketball, for instance, is that they assume they can learn to do it well, and so they practice constantly to prove themselves right.

Wouldn't it be wonderful if we could infect black children with the notion that excellence in math is "black" rather than white, or possibly Chinese? Wouldn't it be of enormous value if we could create the myth that morality, strong families, determination, courage and love of learning are traits brought by slaves from Mother Africa and therefore quintessentially black?

There is no doubt in my mind that most black youngsters could develop their mathematical reasoning, their elocution and their attitudes the way they develop their jump shots and their dance steps: by the combination of sustained, enthusiastic practice and the unquestioned belief that they can do it.

In one sense, what I am talking about is the importance of developing positive ethnic traditions. Maybe Jews have an innate talent for communication; maybe the Chinese are born with a gift for mathematical reasoning; maybe blacks are naturally blessed with athletic grace. I doubt it. What is at work, I suspect, is assumption, inculcated early in their lives, that this is a thing our people do well.

Unfortunately, many of the things about which blacks make this assumption are things that do not contribute to their career success—except for that handful of the truly gifted who can make it as entertainers and athletes. And many of the things we concede to whites are the things that are essential to economic security. So it is with a number of assumptions black youngsters make about what it is to be a "man": physical aggressiveness, sexual prowess, the refusal to submit to authority. The prisons are full of people who, by this perverted definition, are unmistakably men.

But the real problem is not so much that the things defined as "black" are negative. The problem is that the definition is much too narrow.

Somehow, we have to make our children understand that they are intelligent, competent people, capable of doing whatever they put their minds to and making it in the American mainstream, not just in a black subculture.

What we seem to be doing, instead, is raising up yet another generation of young blacks who will be failures—by definition.

# MELVIN KONNER

# Kick Off Your Heels

Melvin Konner, an M.D. and professor of anthropology at Emory University, is an expert on health-care reform who has testified before the U.S. Congress on the issue. He has written several books for the popular press including *The Tangled Wing: Biological Constraints On the Human Spirit*, *Becoming a Doctor*, and *The Paleolithic Prescription*. In this essay, he examines the allure and the dangers of high-heeled shoes.

A FRIEND OF MINE, A SEDATE HISTORIAN, ALLOWS HOW HE USED TO sit in the library as a graduate student at Princeton trying to bury his thoughts in some thick tome. In those bad old days, when Princeton was all-male, the appearance of a female visitor would sometimes be signaled by a sound outside the window in the summer evening: the unmistakable click, click of high heels on the garden walk. Like the bell that made Pavlov's dog salivate, the mere sound of the walk triggered a physiological cascade. Such is the drift of the male brain that it can be drawn off course, for at least minutes, by the sound of a symbol of sexuality.

Yet consider what those heels do with the female form. The legs are slimmed and lengthened; this makes them what students of animal behavior call a supernormal stimulus—recalling, yet exaggerating the lengthening that occurs at puberty. (Pin-up drawings always exaggerate length.) At the same time, the feet are shortened—daintier? For some reason, both men and women seem to prefer smaller feet. Heels tighten the calves and make them prominent. The buttocks are thrown up and out (a distant echo, perhaps, of the sexual "presenting" of female mammals) and the bosom thrust forward, producing the S-curve for which women bustled and corseted brutally in time past. That certain something—not a ponytail—that sways when she walks (because women's hips are wider and not poised over the knees) sways more than usual. And she is hobbled. She is charmingly (to him) off-balance on her pedestal, and unable to flee. (A convicted mugger has said, "We would wait under a stairwell in the subway station and, when we heard the click of the wobbly spiked heel, we knew we had one.")

The message is not unambiguous helplessness. The heels just about abolish the average male advantage in height. The points of the heels and the toes are suitable weapons. But regardless of ambiguity, they convey a message: Look at me; get close if you can—or, if you haven't the courage, try to go back to your book.

Courting creatures signal sex in myriad ways. Often the males do the strutting. The peacock spreads his magnificent eyed feathers, and antelope like the Uganda kob prance and clang great antlers against each other. Other species leave some posing to the female. In the 10-spined stickleback, a little fresh-water fish of the British Isles, the female flashes a bit of swollen silver belly and triggers the male's courtship dance. The female zebra finch, an Australian perching bird, sits on a branch and stretches in a horizontal posture. While the male watches nearby, she bends her legs, sleeks her gray feathers and flutters her black-and-white tail. The female great crested grebe, ordinarily a graceful diving waterbird, assumes an even more awkward posture, sitting on the water with her wings spread and shoulders pointing down.

Humans are no slouches when it comes to sexual signaling. On the contrary, we take the signals nature has given us—an arched brow, a descending eyelid, a smile—and embellish them with every conceivable cultural brush stroke. Draping or painting or piercing or molding the body has gone on for millenniums. New Guinea men paint themselves dramatically for dancing, and marriageable Papuan maidens bear elegant tattoos. Extensive, patterned scars variously signified femininity and manliness in many African cultures. Lip plugs, head molding, circumcision, ear stretching, tooth filing—the list goes on.

Fewer than a hundred years ago, Western women tied themselves in corsets that damaged abdominal organs and made them respiratory wrecks. At the same time, the Chinese were still practicing the extraordinary 1,000-year-old tradition of foot-binding. The resulting foot was shortened, with all toes but the first curled under and the arch drastically raised—essentially, high heels made of bone. This distortion was a matter of pride, a sign of nobility and allure.

How close do our own artificial high heels come to that old Chinese ideal? Not very, but there are similarities. Both signify sex and class, and achieve femininity. And both, to different degrees, result in impairment.

Orthopedists and chiropractors see the consequences in back-ache and knee problems. One orthopedics textbook describes the gait in such shoes as "ungainly" and "mincing," and notes that the normal cushioning is lost. Authorities agree that the toes and balls of the feet in high heels must bear too much weight in striking the ground, and that they transmit the shock upward. After prolonged wearing of high heels, the calf muscles and the Achilles' tendon may permanently contract. Robert Donatelli, a physical therapist, says shortened calf muscles may cause the knees to be slightly flexed; this in turn may cause chronic flection of hips. The ultimate result may produce a shape of buttocks suggestive to the male, but at the cost of increased lumbar lordosis, harmful pressure on the lumbar discs that can cause low-back pain.

Richard Benjamin, a podiatrist at the Greater Southeastern Hospital in Washington, says, too, that throwing the weight on the ball of the foot diminishes the normal roles of both heel and big toe. Incorrect turning of the foot throws the knee out, affecting the hip and back. Like the S-shaped stance, the exaggerated pelvic sway provides allure at a cost in physical damage.

Podiatrists do see several times more women than men, pri-marily because of high-heeled shoes with pointed toes. Pain in foot bones is almost inevitable, but this is only the beginning. Abrasions, calluses, bunions (*hallux valgus*), tendinitis, ingrown toe-nails and serious bone deformities such as hammer toes and "pump bump"—a bony enlargement of the heel where the shoe rim bites into it—are frequent. Bunions can be serious; they can force the joint between the big toe and the adjacent metatarsal bone to be-come so bent for so long that calcium buildup renders it perma-nently and painfully deviated. The ratio of women to men who have this disorder is estimated to be 40-to-1. High heels also cause abnor-mal thickening of skin and bone at the ball of the foot, and this can force the small toes under the foot, crushing them, in some rare cases. Sheldon Flaxman, a foot surgeon, concludes: "These shoes should be worn for special occasions only." Even then, he says, they should not be pointed and the heels should be as low as possible.

High heels are, after all, relatively new in Western tradition. In the 16th century, the elegant—men and women alike—began to like upward-tilting footwear. Before the Elizabethan period in England, flatness in shoes was consistent with both elegance and sex. One will search in vain in earlier paintings and sculpture for evidence of shoes that lever people off the ground. By the mid-18th century, men's shoes had returned to normalcy, but women were stuck on their awkward platforms, and there they have remained. The most extreme form—the stiletto of the 1950s—was often banned, to prevent damage to floors. No laws, written or unwritten, prevent damage to feet—or to women's sense of freedom.

Why do we have such an attachment to this hurtful fashion? The Freudians have had a field day with it, likening it to a mild version of the condition in which a fetishist (always a man) can be aroused only by a shoe. They even invoke sadomasochism as well, and in this explanation the pain and harm are no longer incidental. As I get older, the pain is what I most often see. But I have to admit that a woman will sometimes take me by surprise—dressed to the nines, high-heeled shoes and all.

I'm fighting it though, the part of it that comes from bad shoes. I expect to win. I think of adjectives that apply to women in flat shoes: lithe, graceful, earthy, athletic, sensible, fleet, dancing, practical, fresh, nimble, strong—and sexy, definitely sexy. (Don't look for logic here, we're talking about hormones.) I think of the women depicted by Greek and Roman art—they didn't need to be hobbled to interest men. I think of the polka and the hora instead of the waltz and the tango—and as for whatever it is we do to rock music, that works just as well in flats.

Still, it's hard to visualize a great formal party without stylish women kicking up their high heels. Like some of the other indulgences of that and like occasions, they're probably O.K. in moderation. But for everyday wear they make as little sense as a three-martini lunch. They're a relatively recent innovation. They've wormed their way into our sexual imagery. But it's hard to see why they have to stay there.

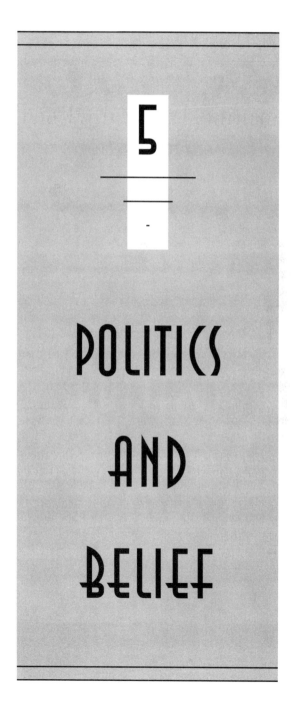

# 5

## POLITICS AND BELIEF

# Translations of the Bible

The Bible has always been a political document, from the decision of which texts to include in the book, to how (or whether) to translate it. In response to numerous complaints about the accuracy of the various available English translations of the Bible, the authoritative 1611 "King James" Bible gained acceptance for hundreds of years. Yet today, we once again have dozens of translations of the Bible, from the Revised Standard version to the Good News Bible. But many people have complained that all of these translations suffer from the same flaw: they include many instances of sexist language—for example, characterizing "God" as a "he." In 1990 a group of scholars undertook the revision of the Bible to not only eliminate this sexist language, but also other pejorative or prejudiced language. The result, in 1995, was the Inclusive Version of the New Testament and Psalms. Here, on the left, are two familiar passages from the King James version; on the right, the Inclusive version of the same texts.

## Psalm 23 (King James)

THE LORD IS MY SHEPHEARD, I shall not want.

He maketh me to lie downe in green pastures: he leadeth me beside the still waters.

He restoreth my soule: he leadeth me in the pathes of righteousness, for his names sake.

Yea though I walk through the valley of the shadow of death, I will fear no evil: for thou art with me, thy rod and thy staff, they comfort me.

Thou preparest a table before me, in the presence of

## Psalm 23 (Inclusive)

GOD IS MY SHEPHERD, I SHALL not want.

God makes me lie down in green pastures, and leads me beside still waters;

God restores my soul.

God leads me in paths of righteousness for the sake of God's name.

Even though I walk through the valley of the shadow of death, I fear no evil; for you are with me; your rod and your staff—they comfort me.

You prepare a table before me in the presence of my ene-

mine enemies: thou anointest my head with oil, my cup runneth over.

Surely goodness and mercy shall follow me all the days of my life: and I will dwell in the house of the Lord for ever.

mies; you anoint my head with oil; my cup overflows.

Surely goodness and mercy shall follow me all the days of my life, and I shall dwell in the house of GOD my whole life long.

### Matthew 6.5-14

BUT WHEN THOU PRAYEST, EN-ter into thy closet, and when thou hast shut thy door, pray to thy father which is in secret, and thy father which seeth in secret, shall reward thee openly.

But when you pray, use not vain repetitions, as the heathen do. For they think that they shall be heard for their much speaking. Be not ye therefore like unto them; For your father knoweth what things you have need of, before you ask him.

After this manner therefore pray you: Our Father which art in heaven, hallowed be thy name. Thy kingdom come, Thy will be done, in earth, as it is in heaven.

Give us this day our daily bread.

And forgive us our debts, as we forgive our debtors. And lead us not into temptation, but deliver us from evil: For thine is the kingdom, and the power, and the glory, for ever, Amen.

For if you forgive men their trespasses, your heavenly father will also forgive you.

### Matthew 6.5-14

"BUT WHENEVER YOU PRAY, GO into your room and shut the door and pray to your Father-Mother who is in secret; and your Father-Mother who sees in secret will reward you.

"When you are praying, do not heap up empty phrases as the Gentiles do; for they think that they will be heard because of their many words. Do not be like them, for your Father-Mother knows what you need before you ask.

"Pray then in this way:

Our Father-Mother in hea-ven, hallowed be your name. Your dominion come. Your will be done, on earth as it is in heaven.

Give us this day our daily bread.

And forgive us our debts, as we also have forgiven our debtors. And do not bring us to the time of trial, but rescue us from the evil one.

"For if you forgive others their trespasses, your heavenly Father-Mother will also forgive you . . ."

# D. T. SUZUKI

# *What is Zen?*

Daisetz Teitaro Suzuki (1870-1966) was not only one of the great interpreters of Eastern religion for the West; he also published translations of great Western religious works into his native Japanese. Suzuki traveled extensively in the West in his life, and lived for an extensive period in New York City, where he was a visiting professor at Columbia University. Though he did not claim to adhere to strict Zen principles, he did write several landmark books on Zen in English, including *An Introduction to Zen Buddhism*, *Essays in Zen Buddhism*, *Zen and Japanese Culture*, and *A Manual of Zen*. This selection, from *Zen and Japanese Culture*, begins to explain the fundamental Zen concept of *Satori*, or "enlightenment."

THE OBJECT OF ZEN TRAINING CONSISTS IN MAKING US REALIZE THAT Zen is our daily experience and that it is not something put in from the outside. Tennō Dōgo (T'ien-huang Tao-wu, 748-807) illustrates the point most eloquently in his treatment of a novice monk, while an unknown Japanese swordmaster demonstrates it in the more threatening manner characteristic of his profession. Tennō Dōgo's story runs as follows:

Dōgo had a disciple called Sōshin (Ch'ung-hsin). When Sōshin was taken in as a novice, it was perhaps natural of him to expect lessons in Zen from his teacher the way a schoolboy is taught at school. But Dōgo gave him no special lessons on the subject, and this bewildered and disappointed Sōshin. One day he said to the master, "It is some time since I came here, but not a word has been given me regarding the essence of the Zen teaching." Dōgo replied, "Since your arrival I have ever been giving you lessons on the matter of Zen discipline."

"What kind of lesson could it have been?"

"When you bring me a cup of tea in the morning, I take it; when you serve me a meal, I accept it; when you bow to me I return it with a nod. How else do you expect to be taught in the mental discipline of Zen?"

Sōshin hung his head for a while, pondering the puzzling words of the master. The master said, "If you want to see, see right at once. When you begin to think, you miss the point."

The swordsman's story is this:

> When a disciple came to a master to be disciplined in the art of sword-play, the master, who was in retirement in his mountain hut, agreed to undertake the task. The pupil was made to help him gather kindling, draw water from the nearby spring, split wood, make fires, cook rice, sweep the rooms and the garden, and generally look after his house-hold. There was no regular or technical teaching in the art. After some time the young man became dissatisfied, for he had not come to work as servant to the old gentleman, but to learn the art of swordsmanship. So one day he approached the master and asked him to teach him. The master agreed.
>
> The result was that the young man could not do any piece of work with any feeling of safety. For when he began to cook rice early in the morning, the master would appear and strike him from behind with a stick. When he was in the midst of his sweeping, he would be feeling the same sort of blow from somewhere, some unknown direction. He had no peace of mind, he had to be always on the *qui vive*. Some years passed before he could successfully dodge the blow from wherever it might come. But the master was not quite satisfied with him yet.
>
> One day the master was found cooking his own vegetables over an open fire. The pupil took it into his head to avail himself of this oppor-tunity. Taking up his big stick, he let it fall over the head of the master, who was then stooping over the cooking pan to stir its contents. But the pupil's stick was caught by the master with the cover of the pan. This opened the pupil's mind to the secrets of the art, which had hith-erto been kept from him and to which he had so far been a stranger. He then, for the first time, appreciated the unparalleled kindness of the master.

The secrets of perfect swordsmanship consist in creating a certain frame or structure of mentality which is made always ready to respond instantly, that is, im-mediately, to what comes from the outside. While technical training is of great importance, it is after all something artificially, consciously, calculatingly added and acquired. Unless the mind that avails itself of the technical skill somewhat attunes itself to a state of the utmost fluidity or mobil-ity, anything acquired or superimposed lacks spontaneity of nat-ural growth. This state prevails when the mind is awakened to a *satori*. What the swordsman aimed at was to make the disciple attain to this realization. It cannot be taught by any system specifically designed for the purpose, it must simply grow from within. The master's system was really no system in the proper sense. But there was a "natural" method in his apparent craziness, and he succeeded in awakening in his young disciple's mind something that touched off the mechanism needed for the mastery of swordsmanship.

Dōgo the Zen master did not have to be attacking his disciple all the time with a stick. The swordsman's object was more definite and limited to the area of the sword, whereas Dōgo wanted to teach by getting to the source of being from which everything making up our daily experience ensues. Therefore, when Sōshin began to reflect on the remark Dōgo made to him, Dōgo told him: "No reflecting whatever. When you want to see, see immediately. As soon as you tarry [that is, as soon as an intellectual interpretation or mediation takes place], the whole thing goes awry." This means that, in the study of Zen, conceptualization must go, for as long as we tarry at this level we can never reach the area where Zen has its life. The door of enlightenment-experience opens by itself as one finally faces the deadlock of intellectualization.

We now can state a few things about Zen in a more or less summary way:

1. Zen discipline consists in attaining enlightenment (or *satori*, in Japanese).
2. *Satori* finds a meaning hitherto hidden in our daily concrete particular experiences, such as eating, drinking, or business of all kinds.
3. The meaning thus revealed is not something added from the outside. It is in being itself, in becoming itself, in living itself. This is called, in Japanese, a life of *kono-mama* or *sono-mama*.* Kono- or sonomama means the "isness" of a thing. Reality in its isness.
4. Some may say, "There cannot be any meaning in mere isness." But this is not the view held by Zen, for according to

---

*Kono* is "this," *sono* "that" and *mama* means "as-it-is-ness." Kono-mama or song-mama thus corresponds to the Sanskrit *tathatā*, "suchness," and to the Chinese *chih-mo* or *shih-mo*.

it, isness is the meaning. When I see into it I see it as clearly as I see myself reflected in a mirror.

5. This is what made Hō Koji (P'ang Chü-shih), a lay disciple of the eighth century, declare:

> How wondrous this, how mysterious!
> I carry fuel, I draw water.

The fuel-carrying or the water-drawing itself, apart from its utilitarianism, is full of meaning; hence its "wonder," its "mystery."

6. Zen does not, therefore, indulge in abstraction or in conceptualization. In its verbalism it may sometimes appear that Zen does this a great deal. But this is an error most commonly entertained by those who do not at all know Zen.

7. *Satori* is emancipation, moral, spiritual, as well as intellectual. When I am in my isness, thoroughly purged of all intellectual sediments, I have my freedom in its primary sense.

8. When the mind, now abiding in its isness—which, to use Zen verbalism, is not isness—and thus free from intellectual complexities and moralistic attachments of every description, surveys the world of the senses in all its multiplicities, it discovers in it all sorts of values hitherto hidden from sight. Here opens to the artist a world full of wonders and miracles.

9. The artist's world is one of free creation, and this can come only from intuitions directly and im-mediately rising from the isness of things, unhampered by senses and intellect. He creates forms and sounds out of formlessness and soundlessness. To this extent, the artist's world coincides with that of Zen.

10. What differentiates Zen from the arts is this: While the artists have to resort to the canvas and brush or mechanical instruments or some other mediums to express themselves, Zen has no need of things external, except "the body" in which the Zen-man is so to speak embodied. From the absolute point of view this is not quite correct; I say it only in concession to the worldly way of saying things. What Zen does is to delineate itself on the infinite canvas of time and space the way the flying wild geese cast their shadow on the water below without any idea of doing so, while the water reflects the geese just as naturally and unintentionally.

11.  The Zen-man is an artist to the extent that, as the sculptor chisels out a great figure deeply buried in a mass of inert matter, the Zen-man transforms his own life into a work of creation, which exists, as Christians might say, in the mind of God.

# JOHN F. KENNEDY

# *Inaugural Address*

John F. Kennedy (1917-1963) set forth a tall agenda as he began his short presidency in 1961. He had been a war hero, a best-selling historian, and a popular senator. Nonetheless, his margin of victory in the election had been one of the smallest in history, and he needed to begin his term of office by bringing popular sentiment to his side. He needed to allay fears from the right that he would not be tough enough in the middle of the cold war, and fears from the left that he would not be aggressive enough in gaining civil rights for all. The result was a highly patriotic, highly allusive speech, which includes some lines which are still quoted today.

WE OBSERVE TODAY NOT A VICTORY OF PARTY BUT A CELEBRATION OF freedom—symbolizing an end as well as a beginning—signifying renewal as well as change. For I have sworn before you and Almighty God the same solemn oath our forebears prescribed nearly a century and three quarters ago.

The world is very different now. For man holds in his mortal hands the power to abolish all forms of human poverty and all forms of human life. And yet the same revolutionary beliefs for which our forebears fought are still at issue around the globe—the belief that the rights of man come not from the generosity of the state but from the hand of God.

We dare not forget today that we are the heirs of that first revolution. Let the word go forth from this time and place, to friend and foe alike, that the torch has been passed to a new generation of Americans—born in this century, tempered by war, disciplined by a hard and bitter peace, proud of our ancient heritage—and unwilling to witness or permit the slow undoing of those human rights to which this nation has always been committed, and to which we are committed today at home and around the world.

Let every nation know, whether it wishes us well or ill, that we shall pay any price, bear any burden, meet any hardship, support any friend, oppose any foe, to assure the survival and the success of liberty.

This much we pledge—and more.

To those old allies whose cultural and spiritual origins we share, we pledge the loyalty of faithful friends. United, there is little we cannot do in a host of cooperative ventures. Divided, there is little we can do—for we dare not meet a powerful challenge at odds and split asunder.

To those new states whom we welcome to the ranks of the free, we pledge our word that one form of colonial control shall not have passed away merely to be replaced by a far more iron tyranny. We shall not always expect to find them supporting our view. But we shall always hope to find them strongly supporting their own freedom—and to remember that in the past, those who foolishly sought power by riding the back of the tiger ended up inside.

To those peoples in the huts and villages of half the globe struggling to break the bonds of mass misery, we pledge our best efforts to help them help themselves, for whatever period is required—not because the Communists may be doing it, not because we seek their votes, but because it is right. If a free society cannot help the many who are poor, it cannot save the few who are rich.

To our sister republics south of our border, we offer a special pledge—to convert our good words into good deeds—in a new alliance for progress—to assist free men and free governments in casting off the chains of poverty. But this peaceful revolution of hope cannot become the prey of hostile powers. Let all our neighbors know that we shall join with them to oppose aggression or subversion anywhere in the Americas. And let every other power know that this hemisphere intends to remain the master of its own house.

To that world assembly of sovereign states, the United Nations, our last best hope in an age where the instruments of war have far outpaced the instruments of peace, we renew our pledge of support—to prevent it from becoming merely a forum for invective—to strengthen its shield of the new and the weak—and to enlarge the area in which its writ may run.

Finally, to those nations who would make themselves our adversary, we offer not a pledge but a request: that both sides begin anew the quest for peace, before the dark powers of destruction unleashed by science engulf all humanity in planned or accidental self-destruction.

We dare not tempt them with weakness. For only when our arms are sufficient beyond doubt can we be certain beyond doubt that they will never be employed.

But neither can two great and powerful groups of nations take comfort from our present course—both sides overburdened by the cost of modern weapons, both rightly alarmed by the steady spread of the deadly atom, yet both racing to alter that uncertain balance of terror that stays the hand of mankind's final war.

So let us begin anew—remembering on both sides that civility is not a sign of weakness, and sincerity is always subject to proof. Let us never negotiate out of fear. But let us never fear to negotiate.

Let both sides explore what problems unite us instead of belaboring those problems which divide us.

Let both sides, for the first time, formulate serious and precise proposals for the inspection and control of arms—and bring the absolute power to destroy other nations under the absolute control of all nations.

Let both sides seek to invoke the wonders of science instead of its terrors. Together let us explore the stars, conquer the deserts, eradicate disease, tap the ocean depths, and encourage the arts and commerce.

Let both sides unite to heed in all corners of the earth the command of Isaiah—to "undo the heavy burdens [and] let the oppressed go free."

And if a beachhead of cooperation may push back the jungle of suspicion, let both sides join in creating a new endeavor, not a new balance of power, but a new world of law, where the strong are just and the weak secure and the peace preserved.

All this will not be finished in the first one hundred days. Nor will it be finished in the first one thousand days, nor in the life of this administration, nor even perhaps in our lifetime on this planet. But let us begin.

In your hands, my fellow citizens, more than mine, will rest the final success or failure of our course. Since this country was founded, each generation of Americans has been summoned to give testimony to its national loyalty. The graves of young Americans who answered the call to service surround the globe.

Now the trumpet summons us again—not as a call to bear arms, though arms we need—not as a call to battle, though embattled we are—but as a call to bear the burden of a long twilight struggle, year in and year out, "rejoicing in hope, patient in tribulation"—a struggle against the common enemies of man: tyranny, poverty, disease, and war itself.

Can we forge against these enemies a grand and global alliance, North and South, East and West, that can assure a more fruitful life for all mankind? Will you join in that historic effort?

In the long history of the world, only a few generations have been granted the role of defending freedom in its hour of maximum danger. I do not shrink from this responsibility—I welcome it. I do not believe that any of us would exchange places with any other people or any other generation. The energy, the faith, the devotion which we bring to this endeavor will light our country and all who serve it—and the glow from that fire can truly light the world.

And so, my fellow Americans: ask not what your country can do for you—ask what you can do for your country.

My fellow citizens of the world: ask not what America will do for you, but what together we can do for the freedom of man.

Finally, whether you are citizens of America or citizens of the world, ask of us here the same high standards of strength and sacrifice which we ask of you. With a good conscience our only sure reward, with history the final judge of our deeds, let us go forth to lead the land we love, asking His blessing and His help, but knowing that here on earth God's work must truly be our own.

# ADLAI E. STEVENSON

# *Veto of the "Cat Bill"*

Adlai Stevenson was elected governor of Illinois in 1948, was the Democratic candidate for president in 1952 and in 1956, and in 1961 was named ambassador to the United Nations by President John F. Kennedy. In spite of his great wit, Stevenson was called an "egg-head" by his political opponents—particularly when he tried "to talk sense to the American people." His candidacy had little appeal for a nation which, so soon after four years of World War II, wanted to think little, if at all.

For many years some of the more fun-loving members of the Illinois legislative branch had submitted to new governors a bill, the purpose of which was (on its face) to restrict the free movement of cats in the State of Illinois. In truth, its purpose was to force a gubernatorial veto. In 1949, Adlai E. Stevenson obliged them with this message. The "Cat Bill" has not reappeared in the Illinois General Assembly since then.

To the honorable, the members of the Senate of the 66th general assembly:

I herewith return, without my approval, Senate bill 93 entitled, "an act to provide protection to insectivorous birds by restraining cats." This is the so-called "cat bill." I veto and withhold my approval from this bill for the following reasons:

It would impose fines on owners or keepers who permitted their cats to run at large off their premises. It would permit any person to capture, or call upon the police to pick up and imprison, cats at large. It would permit the use of traps. The bill would have statewide application—on farms, in villages, and in metropolitan centers.

This legislation has been introduced in the past several sessions of the legislature, and it has, over the years, been the source of much comment—not all of which has been in a serious vein. It may be that the general assembly has now seen fit to refer it to one who can view it with a fresh outlook. Whatever the reasons for passage at this session, I cannot believe there is a widespread public demand for this law or that it could, as a practical matter, be enforced.

Furthermore, I cannot agree that it should be the declared public policy of Illinois that a cat visiting a neighbor's yard or crossing the highway is a public nuisance. It is in the nature of cats to do a certain amount of unescorted roaming. Many live with their owners in apartments or other restricted premises, and I doubt if we want to make their every brief foray an opportunity for a small game hunt by zealous citizens—with traps or otherwise.

I am afraid this bill could only create discord, recrimination and enmity. Also consider the owner's dilemma: To escort a cat abroad on a leash is against the nature of the cat, and to permit it to venture forth for exercise unattended into a night of new dangers is against the nature of the owner. Moreover, cats perform useful service, particularly in rural areas, in combating rodents—work they necessarily perform alone and without regard for party lines.

We are all interested in protecting certain varieties of birds. That cats destroy some birds, I well know, but I believe this legislation would further but little the worthy cause to which its proponents give such unselfish effort.

The problem of cat versus bird is as old as time. If we attempt to resolve it by legislation, who knows but what we may be called upon to take sides as well in the age old problems of dog versus cat, bird versus bird, or even bird versus worm. In my opinion, the state of Illinois and its local governing bodies already have enough to do without trying to control feline delinquency.

For these reasons, and not because I love birds the less or cats the more, I veto and withhold my approval from Senate bill No. 93.

*Student MLA Essay*

# EILEEN WILLIAMS

# Mandatory AIDS Testing for Job Applicants

There is no need to shy away from controversial topics in research papers. Here, Eileen puts forth a very convincing case for banning AIDS testing of job applicants. Note that her case is consistently supported by research—she doesn't just make undocumented assertions.

AIDS IS A RAPIDLY SPREADING DISEASE THAT IS REACHING EPIDEMIC proportions. According to a brochure entitled *Facts About AIDS* put out by the Public Health Service, AIDS was first reported in the United States in 1981 (*Facts*). By early 1987, an estimated 1.5 million Americans had been infected with the AIDS virus, more than 30,000 had developed AIDS, and 17,000 had died from it. Researchers are predicting that by 1991, these latter two figures will be ten times as high ("AIDS: What We Know Now" 143). An issue evolving from the AIDS problem is that of whether or not employers can require job applicants to take a blood test for AIDS before the employers will consider hiring them. Although many workers feel they have the right to refuse to work with an AIDS victim because they do not want to risk contracting the illness, and although an employer might not want to invest in a person whose condition ends in death, these tests should not be made mandatory. They will only lead to discrimination in both the workplace and with insurance, and they are an invasion of privacy.

Once an AIDS test for a job applicant has come back positive, discrimination is likely to start. Many employees feel they do not have to work with a person infected with AIDS because they risk contracting the disease. This shows ignorance because over and over the U.S. Public Health Service has assured the public that

AIDS cannot be transmitted through casual contact ("AIDS: No Need" 51). The only ways known to transmit the virus are through sexual contact, the sharing of needles for intravenous drugs, blood transfusions, and rarely, a mother's breast milk (*Facts*). One cannot contract the AIDS virus from a toilet seat or from sharing some-one's eating utensils. These concerned employees have no logical or medical evidence to support them, only emotional input.

An employer might also want to require AIDS testing so he'll know if he wants to invest in a person whom he expects always to be sick and to have a short life expectancy. But in the *Facts About AIDS* brochure, it is stated that it might be up to five years after a person is infected with the virus before he starts experiencing symptoms. So even though he may have several good years to live and work, the employer will probably label him an AIDS victim and not hire him. This is discrimination because a person's life should not end the moment he or she is diagnosed as having AIDS. As long as he can, he should be allowed to lead a normal life, including working for as long as he is able. Fortunately, according to the article, "Workplace AIDS," most authorities feel that people with AIDS are included in the laws that protect the handicapped from discrimination. So if they don't have any symptoms that interfere with their work ability, they cannot be fired ("Workplace AIDS" 30). In all fairness, this should apply to hiring as well.

Discrimination doesn't remain only in the workplace, though. If job applicants' test results are passed on to insurance companies, they sometimes discriminate also. Fortunately, as stated in a *U.S. News and World Report* article, "contract law forbids insurers from barring newly diagnosed AIDS patients from group health plans" ("AIDS: A Time of Testing" 58). Yet, according to another *U.S. News* article, a man in Colorado sent a copy of his negative AIDS test to his insurance company, and they still refused him "on the basis that the fact he got tested at all made him too great a risk" ("Mandatory Tests" 62). These companies are presently fighting bills that would keep them from refusing AIDS victims ("AIDS: A Time of Testing" 58).

Along with causing discrimination, the AIDS tests are invading persons' privacy. Employers, by testing job applicants for AIDS, are prying into their personal lives. Employers don't test prospective employees for other diseases that aren't contagious through casual contact such as cancer, syphillis, and cerebral palsy, and for that matter, for diseases that are more easily contagious, such as hepatitis and pneumonia, so why should AIDS be an exception? Besides, once employers explore all aspects of applicants' health and discover positive AIDS tests, what's to stop employers from looking into causes and discriminating against the applicants, not necessarily because of AIDS, but perhaps because they are homosexual? That is quite a generalization, and perhaps most employers are more unbiased than this, but it is certainly possible that discrimination could become this out-of-hand.

Yes, the population of AIDS victims is rapidly growing, and it is frightening because everyone is afraid of contracting this dreadful illness. But if we refrain from the activities known to transmit AIDS, we have no need to worry, even in the workplace. AIDS victims—like everyone else—have the right to live normal lives, and as long as they are able to perform their job duties, they should not be discriminated against. So, until the medical community finds any evidence that AIDS can be transmitted through casual contact, I don't see any risk with an AIDS victim in the workplace. Therefore, mandatory blood tests to check for AIDS in job applicants are unnecessary.

## Works Cited
"AIDS: No Need for Worry in the Workplace." *Newsweek* 25 Nov. 1985: 51.

"AIDS: What We Know Now." *McCall's* Apr. 1987: 143-44.

*Facts About AIDS*. U.S. Dept. of Health and Human Services, Spring 1986.

"Mandatory Tests for AIDS?" *U.S. News & World Report* 9 March 1987: 62.

"Workplace AIDS." *Nation's Business* Nov. 1986: 30.

# JONATHAN SWIFT

# A Modest Proposal

Jonathan Swift (1667-1745), Irish writer, poet, and clergyman, used his works as an opportunity to comment on the society he lived in. He is best known for his novel, *Gulliver's Travels*, but "A Modest Proposal" is perhaps his most effective social commentary. At the time "A Modest Proposal" appeared, Ireland was afflicted by a great famine, made worse by the oppressive rule of England. Harsh taxation by the invading English made it difficult for all but a few to sustain themselves at a reasonable level. Master of satire, Swift offered his "Modest Proposal" as a means of solving the tremendous problems Ireland faced. If "A Modest Proposal" didn't accomplish that, it has, for over two centuries, enlightened us all on the art of satire.

IT IS A MELANCHOLY OBJECT TO THOSE WHO WALK THROUGH THIS great town or travel in the country, when they see the streets, the roads, and cabin doors crowded with beggars of the female sex, followed by three, four, or six children, all in rags and importuning every passenger for an alms. These mothers, instead of being able to work for their honest livelihood, are forced to employ all their time in strolling to beg sustenance for their helpless infants, who, as they grow up, either turn thieves for want of work, or leave their dear native country to fight for the Pretender in Spain, or sell themselves to the Barbadoes.

I think it is agreed by all parties that this prodigious number of children in the arms, or on the backs, or at the heels of their mothers, and frequently of their fathers, is in the present deplorable state of the kingdom a very great additional grievance; and, therefore, whoever could find out a fair, cheap, and easy method of making these children sound, useful members of the commonwealth, would deserve so well of the public as to have his statue set up for a preserver of the nation.

But my intention is very far from being confined to provide only for the children of professed beggars; it is of a much greater extent, and shall take in the whole number of infants at a certain age who are born of parents in effect as little able to support them as those who demand our charity in the streets.

As to my own part, having turned my thoughts for many years upon this important subject, and maturely weighed the several schemes of other projectors, I have always found them grossly mistaken in their computation. It is true, a child just dropped from its dam may be supported by her milk for a solar year, with little other nourishment; at most not above the value of two shillings, which the mother may certainly get, or the value in scraps, by her lawful occupation of begging; and it is exactly at one year old that I propose to provide for them in such a manner as instead of being a charge upon their parents or the parish, or wanting food and raiment for the rest of their lives, they shall on the contrary contribute to the feeding, and partly to the clothing, of many thousands.

There is likewise another great advantage in my scheme, that it will prevent those voluntary abortions, and that horrid practice of women murdering their bastard children, alas! too frequent among us! sacrificing the poor innocent babes I doubt more to avoid the expense than the shame, which would move tears and pity in the most savage and inhuman breast.

The number of souls in Ireland being usually reckoned one million and a half, of these I calculate there may be about two hundred thousand couples whose wives are breeders; from which number I subtract thirty thousand couples who are able to maintain their own children, although I apprehend there cannot be so many, under the present distresses of the kingdom; but this being granted, there will remain an hundred and seventy thousand breeders. I again subtract fifty thousand for those women who miscarry, or whose children die by accident or disease within the year. There only remain a hundred and twenty thousand children of poor parents annually born. The question therefore is, how this number shall be reared and provided for? which, as I have already said, under the present situation of affairs, is utterly impossible by all the methods hitherto proposed. For we can neither employ them in handicraft or agriculture; we neither build houses (I mean in the country) nor cultivate land. They can very seldom pick up a livelihood by stealing, till they arrive at six years old, except where they are of towardly parts; although I confess they learn the rudiments much earlier, during which time they can, however, be properly looked upon only as probationers; as I have been informed by a principal gentleman in the county of Cavan, who protested to me that he never knew above one or two instances under the age of six, even in a part of the kingdom so renowned for the quickest proficiency in that art.

I am assured by our merchants, that a boy or a girl before twelve years old is no saleable commodity; and even when they come to this age they will not yield above three pounds or three pounds and half a crown at most on the Exchange; which cannot turn to account either to the parents or the kingdom, the charge of nutriment and rags having been at least four times that value.

I shall now therefore humbly propose my own thoughts, which I hope will not be liable to the least objection.

I have been assured by a very knowing American of my acquaintance in London, that a young healthy child well nursed is, at year old, a most delicious, nourishing, and wholesome food, whether stewed, roasted, baked, or boiled; and I make no doubt that it will equally serve in a fricassee or a ragout.

I do therefore humbly offer it to public consideration that of the hundred and twenty thousand children already computed, twenty thousand may be reserved for breed, whereof only one-fourth part to be males; which is more than we allow to sheep, black cattle, or swine; and my reason is, that these children are seldom the fruits of marriage, a circumstance not much regarded by our savages; therefore one male will be sufficient to serve four females. That the remaining hundred thousand may, at a year old, be offered in sale to the persons of quality and fortune through the kingdom, always advising the mother to let them suck plentifully in the last month, so as to render them plump and fat for a good table. A child will make two dishes at an entertainment for friends; and when the family dines alone, the fore or hind quarter will make a reasonable dish, and seasoned with a little pepper or salt will be very good boiled on the fourth day, especially in winter.

I have reckoned upon a medium that a child just born will weigh twelve pounds, and in a solar year, if tolerably nursed, will increase to twenty-eight pounds.

I grant this food will be somewhat dear, and therefore very proper for landlords, who, as they have already devoured most of the parents, seem to have the best title to the children.

Infant's flesh will be in season throughout the year, but more plentiful in March, and a little before and after: for we are told by a grave author, an eminent French physician, that fish being a prolific diet, there are more children born in Roman Catholic countries about nine months after Lent than at any other season; therefore, reckoning a year after Lent, the markets will be more glutted than usual, because the number of popish infants is at least three to one in this kingdom; and therefore it will have one other collateral advantage, by lessening the number of papists among us.

I have already computed the charge of nursing a beggar's child (in which list I reckon all cottagers, laborers, and four-fifths of the farmers) to be about two shillings per annum, rags included; and I believe no gentleman would repine to give ten shillings for the carcass of a good fat child, which, as I have said, will make four dishes of excellent nutritive meat, when he has only some particular friend or his own family to dine with him. Thus the squire will learn to be a good landlord, and grow popular among his tenants; the mother will have eight shillings net profit, and be fit for work till she produces another child.

Those who are more thrifty (as I must confess the times require) may flay the carcass; the skin of which artificially dressed will make admirable gloves for ladies, and summer boots for fine gentlemen.

As to our city of Dublin, shambles may be appointed for this purpose in the most convenient parts of it, and butchers we may be assured will not be wanting: although I rather recommend buying the children alive, and dressing them hot from the knife as we do roasting pigs.

A very worthy person, a true lover of his country, and whose virtues I highly esteem, was lately pleased in discoursing on this matter to offer a refinement upon my scheme. He said that many gentlemen of this kingdom, having of late destroyed their deer, he conceived that the want of venison might be well supplied by the bodies of young lads and maidens, not exceeding fourteen years of age nor under twelve; so great a number of both sexes in every county being now ready to starve for want of work and service; and these to be disposed of by their parents, if alive, or otherwise by their nearest relations. But with due deference to so excellent a friend and so deserving a patriot, I cannot be altogether in his sentiments. For as to the males, my American acquaintance assured me from frequent experience that their flesh was generally tough and lean, like that of our schoolboys by continual exercise, and their taste disagreeable; and to fatten them would not answer the charge.

Then as to the females, it would, I think, with humble submission be a loss to the public, because they soon would become breeders themselves; and besides, it is not improbable that some scrupulous people might be apt to censure such a practice (although indeed very unjustly) as a little bordering upon cruelty; which, I confess, has always been with me the strongest objection against any project, how well soever intended.

But in order to justify my friend, he confessed that this expedient was put into his head by the famous Psalmanazar, a native of the island Formosa, who came from thence to London above twenty years ago, and in conversation told my friend that in his country when any young person happened to be put to death, the executioner sold the carcass to persons of quality as a prime dainty; and that in his time the body of a plump girl of fifteen, who was crucified for an attempt to poison the emperor, was sold to his imperial majesty's prime minister of state, and other great mandarins of the court, in joints from the gibbet, at four hundred crowns. Neither indeed can I deny that if the same use were made of several plump young girls in this town, who without one single groat to their fortunes cannot stir abroad without a chair, and appear at the playhouse and assemblies in foreign fineries which they never will pay for, the kingdom would not be the worse.

Some persons of a desponding spirit are in great concern about that vast number of poor people who are aged, diseased, or maimed, and I have been desired to employ my thoughts what course may be taken to ease the nation of so grievous an encumbrance. But I am not in the least pain upon that matter, because it is very well known that they are every day dying and rotting by cold and famine, and filth and vermin, as fast as can be reasonably expected. And as to the younger labourers, they are now in almost as hopeful a condition. They cannot get work, and consequently pine away for want of nourishment, to a degree that if at any time they are accidentally hired to common labour, they have not strength to perform it; and thus the country and themselves are in a fair way of being soon delivered from the evils to come.

I have too long digressed, and therefore shall return to my subject. I think the advantages by the proposal which I have made are obvious and many, as well as of the highest importance.

For first, as I have already observed, it would greatly lessen the number of papists, with whom we are yearly overrun, being the principal breeders of the nation as well as our most dangerous enemies; and who stay at home on purpose with a design to deliver the kingdom to the Pretender, hoping to take their advantage by the absence of so many good Protestants, who have chosen rather to leave their country than stay at home and pay tithes against their conscience to an idolatrous Episcopal curate.

Secondly, the poor tenants will have something valuable of their own, which by law may be made liable to distress, and help to pay their landlord's rent, their corn and cattle being already seized and money a thing unknown.

Thirdly, whereas the maintenance of an hundred thousand children from two years old and upward, cannot be computed at less than ten shillings apiece per annum, the nation's stock will be thereby increased fifty thousand pounds per annum, besides the profit of a new dish introduced to the tables of all gentlemen of fortune in the kingdom who have any refinement in taste. And the money will circulate among ourselves, the goods being entirely of our own growth and manufacture.

Fourthly, the constant breeders, besides the gain of eight shillings sterling per annum by the sale of their children, will be rid of the charge of maintaining them after the first year.

Fifthly, this food would likewise bring great custom to taverns, where the vintners will certainly be so prudent as to procure the best receipts for dressing it to perfection, and consequently have their houses frequented by all the fine gentlemen, who justly value themselves upon their knowledge in good eating; and a skillful cook, who understands how to oblige his guests, will contrive to make it as expensive as they please.

Sixthly, this would be a great inducement to marriage, which all wise nations have either encouraged by rewards or enforced by laws and penalties. It would increase the care and tenderness of mothers towards their children, when they were sure of a settlement for life to the poor babes, provided in some sort by the public, to their annual profit instead of expense. We should see an honest emulation among the married women, which of them could bring the fattest child to the market. Men would become as fond of their wives during the time of their pregnancy as they are now of their mares in foal, their cows in calf, their sows when they are ready to farrow; nor offer to beat or kick them (as is too frequent a practice) for fear of a miscarriage.

Many other advantages might be enumerated. For instance, the addition of some thousand carcasses in our exportation of barreled beef, the propagation of swine's flesh, and improvement in the art of making good bacon, so much wanted among us by the great destruction of pigs, too frequent at our tables, and which are no way comparable in taste or magnificence to a well-grown, fat, yearling child, which roasted whole will make a considerable figure at a lord mayor's feast or any other public entertainment. But this and many others I omit, being studious of brevity.

Supposing that one thousand families in this city would be constant customers for infants' flesh, besides others who might have it at merry meetings, particularly weddings and christenings, I compute that Dublin would take off annually about twenty thousand carcasses, and the rest of the kingdom (where probably they will be sold somewhat cheaper) the remaining eighty thousand.

I can think of no one objection that will possibly be raised against this proposal, unless it should be urged that the number of people will be thereby much lessened in the kingdom. This I freely own, and it was indeed one principal design in offering it to the world. I desire the reader will observe, that I calculate my remedy for this one individual kingdom of Ireland and for no other that ever was, is, or I think ever can be upon earth. Therefore let no man talk to me of other expedients: of taxing our absentees at five shillings a pound: of using neither clothes nor household furniture except what is of our own growth and manufacture: of utterly rejecting the materials and instruments that promote foreign luxury: of curing the expensiveness of pride, vanity, idleness, and gaming in our women: of introducing a vein of parsimony, prudence, and temperance: of learning to love our country, wherein we differ even from Laplanders and the inhabitants of Topinamboo: of quitting our animosities and factions, nor act any longer like the Jews, who were murdering one another at the very moment their city was taken: of being a little cautious not to sell our country and conscience for nothing: of teaching landlords to have at least one degree of mercy toward their tenants: lastly, of putting a spirit of honesty, industry, and skill into our shopkeepers; who, if a resolution could now be taken to buy only our native goods, would immediately unite to cheat and exact upon us in the price, the measure, and the goodness, nor could ever yet be brought to make one fair proposal of just dealing, though often and earnestly invited to it.

Therefore, I repeat, let no man talk to me of these and the like expedients, till he has at least a glimpse of hope that there will ever be some hearty and sincere attempt to put them in practice.

But as to myself, having been wearied out for many years with offering vain, idle, visionary thoughts, and at length utterly despairing of success, I fortunately fell upon this proposal, which, as it is wholly new, so it has something solid and real, of no expense and little trouble, full in our own power, and whereby we can incur no danger in disobliging England. For this kind of commodity will not bear exportation, the flesh being of too tender a consistence to admit a long continuance in salt, although perhaps I could name a country which would be glad to eat up our whole nation without it.

After all, I am not so violently bent upon my own opinion as to reject any offer proposed by wise men, which shall be found equally innocent, cheap, easy, and effectual. But before something of that kind shall be advanced in contradiction to my scheme, and offering a better, I desire the author or authors will be pleased maturely to consider two points. First, as things now stand, how they will be able to find food and raiment for a hundred thousand useless mouths and backs. And secondly, there being a round million of creatures in human figure throughout this kingdom, whose whole subsistence put into a common stock would leave them in debt two millions of pounds sterling, adding those who are beggars by profession to the bulk of farmers, cottagers, and labourers, with their wives and children who are beggars in effect; I desire those politicians who dislike my overture, and may perhaps be so bold to attempt an answer, that they will first ask the parents of these mortals, whether they would not at this day think it a great happiness to have been sold for food at a year old in the manner I prescribe, and thereby have avoided such a perpetual scene of misfortunes as they have since gone through by the oppression of landlords, the impossibility of paying rent without money or trade, the want of common sustenance, with neither house nor clothes to cover them from the inclemencies of weather, and the most inevitable prospect of entailing the like or greater miseries upon their breed for ever.

I profess, in the sincerity of my heart, that I have not the least personal interest in endeavouring to promote this necessary work, having no other motive than the public good of my country, by advancing our trade, providing for infants, relieving the poor, and giving some pleasure to the rich. I have no children by which I can propose to get a single penny; the youngest being nine years old, and my wife past child-bearing.

ΜΛRΚ TWΛIΝ

# *Running for President*

This essay contains enough of Twain's typical wry wit and dry humor to make up for *Two Views of the Mississippi* (see the introduction to that selection in Chapter 2). It was that irrepressible humor that made Twain both a favorite of American readers in his nationally syndicated newspaper stories and an exceptionally gifted public speaker. Indeed, Twain made as much money from speaking engagements as he did with his writing. Neither his speaking nor his writing would have flourished as much as it did had Twain not squandered most of his earnings on bad investments. Those failings forced Twain to be a prolific writer—and our nation's literary coffers are so much the wealthier for it. In "Running for President," Twain makes light of many of his failings. While some of his "admissions" in this selection are obviously fallacious, many are based on the truth—including the story of his desertion in the Civil War.

I HAVE PRETTY MUCH MADE UP MY MIND TO RUN FOR PRESIDENT. What the country wants is a candidate who cannot be injured by investigation of his past history, so that the enemies of the party will be unable to rake up anything against him that nobody ever heard of before. If you know the worst about a candidate, to begin with, every attempt to spring things on him will be checkmated. Now I am going to enter the field with an open record. I am going to own up in advance to all the wickedness I have done, and if any Congressional committee is disposed to prowl around my biography in the hope of discovering any dark and deadly deed that I have secreted, why–let it prowl.

In the first place, I admit that I treed a rheumatic grandfather of mine in the winter of 1850. He was old and inexpert in climbing trees, but with the heartless brutality that is characteristic of me I ran him out of the front door in his nightshirt at the point of a shotgun, and caused him to bowl up a maple tree, where he remained all night, while I emptied shot into his legs. I will do it again if I ever have another grandfather. I am as inhuman now as I was in 1850. I candidly acknowledge that I ran away at the battle of Gettysburg. My friends have tried to smooth over this fact by asserting that I did so for the purpose of imitating Washington, who went into the woods at Valley Forge for the purpose of saying his prayers. It was a miserable subterfuge. I struck out in a straight line for the Tropic of Cancer because I was scared. I wanted my country saved, but I preferred to have somebody else save it. I entertain that preference yet. If the bubble reputation can be obtained only at the cannon's mouth, I am willing to go there for it provided the cannon is empty. If it is loaded my immortal and inflexible purpose is to get over the fence and go home. My invariable practice in war has been to bring out of every fight two-thirds more men than when I went in. This seems to me Napoleonic in its grandeur.

My financial views are of the most decided character, but they are not likely, perhaps, to increase my popularity with the advocates of inflation. I do not insist upon the special supremacy of rag money or hard money. The great fundamental principle of my life is to take any kind I can get.

The rumor that I buried a dead aunt under my grapevine was correct. The vine needed fertilizing, my aunt had to be buried, and I dedicated her to this high purpose. Does that unfit me for the Presidency? The Constitution of this country does not say so. No other citizen was ever considered unworthy of this office because he enriched his grapevines with his dead relatives. Why should I be selected as the first victim of an absurd prejudice?

I admit also that I am not a friend of the poor man. I regard the poor man, in his present condition, as so much wasted raw material. Cut up and properly canned, he might be made useful to fatten the natives of the cannibal islands and to improve our export trade in that region. I shall recommend legislation upon the subject in my first message. My campaign cry will be: "Desiccate the poor workingman; stuff him into sausages."

These are about the worst parts of my record. On them I come before the country. If my country doesn't want me, I will go back again. But I recommend myself as a safe man—a man who starts from the basis of total depravity and proposes to be fiendish to the last.

# ΛMƐRICΛNS UNITƐD FOR THƐ
# SƐPΛRΛTION OF CHURCH ΛND STΛTƐ

# *School Prayer (con position)*

Discussing politics or religion has always been a sure way to get into a fight. It's no surprise that the issue of school prayer has caused its own share of conflicts. As this selection points out, Americans have been fighting about prayer in public schools for almost as long as public schools have existed. Why all the strident debate over perhaps one minute of our children's time in schools? Isn't the Constitution clear on this point? Perhaps the problem *is* the Constitution, for nowhere does the Constitution say "separation of church and state" or "freedom of religion." The actual text of the First Amendment reads as follows: "Congress shall make no law respecting an establishment of religion, or prohibiting the free exercise thereof. . . ." If you place the emphasis on the first part of the passage, you could argue that school prayer respects "an establishment of religion," and so should not be allowed. On the other hand, if you focus on the second part, which says that Congress can't "prohibit the free exercise" of religion, you can come to the opposite conclusion. Here's a reading that takes the first position. It's a statement by Americans United for the Separation of Church and State, whose belief is that the best way to preserve religion is to keep the government out of it.

IN 1843, AN UGLY RIOT ROCKED THE PHILADELPHIA SUBURB OF Kensington. For three days, mobs roamed the streets of the City of Brotherly Love as the police struggled to regain control. When it was all over, several buildings had been reduced to rubble, and 13 people were dead.

The Philadelphia riot was notable for its particularly violent character, but what's even more unusual is what sparked it. The country was restless with pre-Civil War tensions at the time, but it wasn't race relations, slavery, or "preserving the union" that tore the community asunder. The people of Philadelphia rioted over prayer in public schools.

Tensions between Roman Catholics and Protestants were near the breaking point in mid-19th century America, and public schools had become the flash point. When local education officials in southeastern Pennsylvania assented to Catholic demands and ruled that Catholic children could be excused from mandatory daily—and generally Protestant—Bible reading and prayer, the Protestant majority generated a violent backlash.

The incident is worth remembering as the nationwide debate over religion in public schools resumes again, thanks to soon-to-be Speaker of the House Newt Gingrich's promise to hold a congressional vote on a school prayer amendment by July 4.

Prayer in schools is one of the most misunderstood social concerns Americans face today. Many people wonder why the issue is so emotional. What is the harm, they ask, in a little prayer.

What these people fail to understand is that religious passions run deep. Many Americans are offended by the idea that their children may be forced to participate in religious exercises in public school that clash with what the children are taught at home or at the family's house of worship. These parents rightly see school prayer as a usurpation of parental authority.

Other parents have no desire to have their children participate in the type of bland, watered-down prayers that are commonly offered for public consumption. They cite the words of Jesus from the sixth book of Matthew who, in cautioning against gaudy public displays of religion, said, "When you pray, enter your closet and shut the door. Pray to your Father, who is in secret, and your Father, who sees in secret, will reward you openly."

As the religious pluralism of the United States continues to expand, it is impossible that a "To-Whom-It-May-Concern" prayer could be fashioned that would please fundamentalist Protestants and Roman Catholics as well as Jews, Buddhists, Muslims, and the thousands of other religious groups. Even if this type of prayer could be written, who would care to recite such theological pablum?

Some school prayer advocates suggest letting each community decide what prayer is recited. If Southern Baptists predominate, for example, the Lord's Prayer would be recited. If Catholics hold sway, it will be the Our Father.

Such a "majority rules" set-up would violate the right of conscience of millions of American schoolchildren. Their choice would be to either participate in religious ceremonies alien to them or risk ostracism by getting up and leaving the room.

In a country that was founded on religious freedom, this is an unfair situation to put any child in, especially very young children, who may not even understand what is going on.

The great tragedy of the school prayer debate is that it is unnecessary. Nothing in the Constitution now prohibits children from engaging in truly voluntary prayer. They may pray at the beginning of the day, over lunch, before tests, at any time they have a free moment.

Under the Federal Equal Access Act, high school students may even form prayer clubs and meet outside class hours for Bible study and worship. No court in the land has ever struck down personal religious devotions.

Despite the rhetoric, what Gingrich and some of his colleagues are offering is not voluntary prayer. The wording of the proposed amendment says that "group prayer" will be permitted in public schools.

In other words, the entire class, at the direction of a teacher or school official, can be ordered to recite a prayer. The only option for those who choose not to take part is to grin and bear it or get up and leave. There is nothing "voluntary" about this type of coercion.

Religion is best left as a private matter, as the Nation's founders intended. It should never be forced onto anyone, especially a child. Public schools are for educating children about the basics—reading, 'riting, and 'rithmetic. Let's leave the "fourth R," religion, where it rightly belongs—in the homes and houses of worship of our country.

## THE AMERICAN CENTER FOR LAW AND JUSTICE

# School Prayer (pro position)

Freedom of religion is one of the fundamental rights on which our nation is based. Many of the first settlers of America came here to escape a government that made it difficult to practice their chosen religion. Isn't it ironic, then, that children are restricted from practicing religion in schools supported by that same government? The Supreme Court has ruled that the Constitution allows student prayer on school grounds during noninstructional time if a school allows other student activities the same privilege (in the *Mergens* case mentioned below). The American Center for Law and Justice, an organization devoted to preserving the freedom of religious speech, argues that that right is not enough. If students can't pray at graduation ceremonies, or are told they can't do book reports on religious figures, all in the name of separation of church and state, then the Constitution itself must be changed.

FOR THE PAST SIX YEARS, WE HAVE DEDICATED A SUBSTANTIAL amount of our resources to defend students who desire to pray and have Bible and prayer clubs at the public schools. In 1990, when we argued the Bible club case, *Westside Community Schools v. Mergens* before the U.S. Supreme Court, we committed substantial resources in order for our organization to stand up for students whenever their rights are being denied because of their faith.

The amount of requests for assistance for cases involving the public schools are increasing at an unprecedented rate. Despite the passage of the Equal Access Act in 1984 and the Supreme Court's decision in *Mergens,* students across our land are being denied fundamental rights of freedom of speech, including the right to pray.

This fact hit home most recently when the U.S. Court of Appeals for the Ninth Circuit, on November 18, 1994, ruled that student prayer at a graduation ceremony was unconstitutional. The Ninth Circuit held that there was "no meaningful distinction between school authorities actually organizing the religious activities and officials merely permitting students to direct the exercises" *(Harris v. Joint School District No. 241).*

This decision of the Ninth Circuit runs contrary to the language written by the Supreme Court in the *Mergens* case, which noted that "there is a crucial difference between government speech endorsing religion which the Establishment Clause forbids, and private speech endorsing religion which the Free Speech and Free Exercise Clauses protect."

We have consistently taken the position that students have the right to share their faith at graduation ceremonies through testimony, or through prayer. This apparently is not the view of the U.S. Court of Appeals for the Ninth Circuit. This decision, left unchecked, could create a further zone of hostility for religious students on public school campuses. This is why we need some affirmative protection for religious liberty for students.

When the debate began on the constitutional amendment for prayer these past few weeks, we initially were hesitant to take a public position. After reviewing the proposed amendment to the Constitution, however, and then recommending to Congressman Istook and others significant changes to the language, we are convinced that if we work through the amendment process we can obtain justice for students in our Nation's public schools.

The language we have proposed is this:

Nothing in this Constitution shall be construed to prohibit individual or group prayer by students in the public schools, or individual or group prayer in other public institutions. No person shall be required by the United States or by any State to participate in prayer. Neither the United States nor any State shall compose the words of any prayer to be said in public schools.

Our proposed language focuses on students not being denied the right to have prayer at their pubic schools. We have seen the abuses that students have been confronted with when they have been threatened with arrest, have been arrested for praying around their school flagpole, suspected for possession of Christian material on campus, or told that establishing a Bible club would violate the separation of church and state. By using the word "students," and possibly including the word student-initiated or student-led, we will be in a position to affirmatively protect students who desire to pray on public school campuses.

We need to see affirmative protection for students on the public school campus who want to exercise their faith. We have reached a point in our country where we have more of a freedom from religion than a freedom of religion.

When students are told that they cannot pray at graduation ceremonies, when the president of a Christian Bible club is told to remove the word "God" or "Jesus" from a sign advertising the club meetings, and when students are told that they cannot do book reports on historical figures if those figures are referenced in the Bible, we have a serious misunderstanding of freedom and liberty.

Based on the surveys we have seen, and the phone calls and letters that pour into our offices, it's time for affirmative protection for students who want to engage in prayer in our Nation's public schools. Do we want to have a constitutional amendment? No. We certainly would have been more satisfied if the courts simply upheld the true understanding of freedom and liberty, but in many circumstances they have not.

For those students involved in the Ninth Circuit decision, their freedom was lost on November 18, 1994, when the Court held that students could not pray at graduation. Through this constitutional amendment process not only is the issue of school prayer placed before the Nation, but we have an opportunity to see a change in the right direction for freedom.

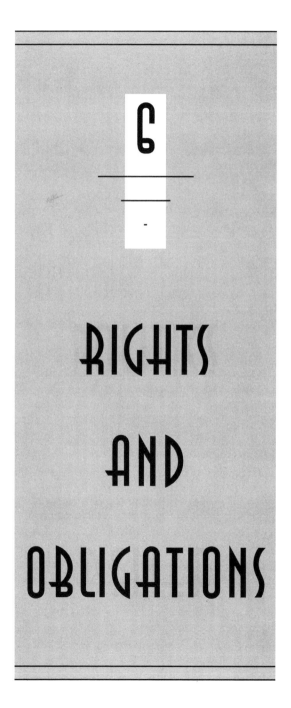

# 6

# RIGHTS AND OBLIGATIONS

# THOMAS JEFFERSON

# The Declaration of Independence

Though he was criticized for owning slaves at a time when his writings supported liberty, Thomas Jefferson's influence, perhaps more than any other's, helped shape the foundation of rights that we enjoy today. A relatively young, shy Jefferson drafted the eloquent Declaration that would be adopted on July 4, 1776—fifty years, to the day, before his death. During those years, he became the nation's first secretary of state, its third president, and a founder of the University of Virginia—many of whose buildings were also designed by Jefferson. It was partly at his insistence that the Bill of Rights was added to the Constitution. The Declaration itself is truly an American masterpiece, for not only does it set forth the reasons for secession, but it also provides the intellectual groundwork for a new nation.

### In Congress, July 4, 1776
### The Unanimous Declaration of the
### Thirteen United States of America

WHEN IN THE COURSE OF HUMAN EVENTS IT BECOMES NECESSARY for one people to dissolve the political bands which have connected them with another, and to assume among the powers of the earth, the separate and equal station to which the Laws of Nature and of Nature's God entitle them, a decent respect to the opinions of mankind requires that they should declare the causes which impel them to the separation.

We hold these truths to be self-evident, that all men are created equal, that they are endowed by their Creator with certain unalienable Rights, that among these are Life, Liberty and the pursuit of Happiness.

That to secure these rights, Governments are instituted among Men, deriving their just powers from the consent of the governed.

That whenever any Form of Government becomes destructive of these ends, it is the Right of the People to alter or to abolish it, and to institute new Government, laying its foundation on such principles and organizing its powers in such form, as to them shall seem most likely to affect their Safety and Happiness. Prudence, indeed, will dictate that Governments long established should not be changed for light and transient causes; and accordingly all experience hath shewn, that mankind are more disposed to suffer, while evils are sufferable, than to right themselves by abolishing the forms to which they are accustomed. But when a long train of abuses and usurpations, pursuing invariably the same Object evinces a design to reduce them under absolute Despotism, it is their right, it is their duty, to throw off such Government, and to provide new Guards for their future security.

Such has been the patient sufferance of these Colonies; and such is now the necessity which constrains them to alter their former Systems of Government. The history of the present King of Great Britain is a history of repeated injuries and usurpations, all having in direct object the establishment of an absolute Tyranny over these States. To prove this, let Facts be submitted to a candid world.

He has refused his Assent to Laws, the most wholesome and necessary for the public good.

He has forbidden his Governors to pass Laws of immediate and pressing importance, unless suspended in their operation till his Assent should be obtained; and when so suspended, he has utterly neglected to attend to them.

He has refused to pass other Laws for the accommodation of large districts of people, unless those people would relinquish the right of Representation in the Legislature, a right inestimable to them and formidable to tyrants only.

He has called together legislative bodies at places unusual, uncomfortable, and distant from the depository of their public Records, for the sole purpose of fatiguing them into compliance with his measures.

He has dissolved Representative Houses repeatedly, for opposing with manly firmness his invasions on the rights of the people.

He has refused for a long time, after such dissolutions, to cause others to be elected; whereby the Legislative powers, incapable of Annihilation, have returned to the People at large for their exercise; the State remaining in the mean time exposed to all the dangers of invasion from without, and convulsions within.

He has endeavored to prevent the population of these States; for that purpose obstructing the Laws for Naturalization of Foreigners; refusing to pass others to encourage their migrations hither, and raising the conditions of new Appropriations of Lands.

He has obstructed the Administration of Justice, by refusing his Assent to Laws for establishing Judiciary powers.

He has made Judges dependent on his Will alone, for the tenure of their offices, and the amount and payment of their salaries.

He has erected a multitude of New Offices, and sent hither swarms of Officers to harass our people, and eat out their substance.

He has kept among us, in times of peace, Standing Armies without the Consent of our legislatures.

He has affected to render the Military independent of and superior to the Civil power.

He has combined with others to subject us to a jurisdiction foreign to our constitution, and unacknowledged by our laws; giving his Assent to their Acts of pretended Legislation:

For Quartering large bodies of armed troops among us:

For Protecting them, by a mock Trial, from punishment for any Murders which they should commit on the Inhabitants of these States:

For cutting off our Trade with all parts of the world:

For imposing Taxes on us without our Consent:

For depriving us in many cases, of the benefits of Trial by Jury:

For transporting us beyond Seas to be tried for pretended offences:

For abolishing the free System of English Laws in a neighbouring Province, establishing therein an Arbitrary government, and enlarging its Boundaries so as to render it at once an example and fit instrument for introducing the same absolute rule into these Colonies:

For taking away our Charters, abolishing our most valuable

Laws, and altering fundamentally the Forms of our Governments:

For suspending our own Legislatures, and declaring themselves invested with power to legislate for us in all cases whatsoever.

He has abdicated Government here, by declaring us out of his Protection and waging War against us:

He has plundered our seas, ravaged our Coasts, burnt our towns, and destroyed the lives of our people.

He is at this time transporting large Armies of foreign Mercenaries to complete the works of death, desolation and tyranny, already begun with circumstances of Cruelty & perfidy scarcely paralleled in the most barbarous ages, and totally unworthy of the Head of a civilized nation.

He has constrained our fellow Citizens taken Captive on the high Seas to bear Arms against their Country, to become the executioners of their friends and Brethren, or to fall themselves by their Hands.

He has excited domestic insurrections amongst us, and has endeavoured to bring on the inhabitants of our frontiers, the merciless Indian Savages, whose known rule of warfare, is an undistinguished destruction of all ages, sexes, and conditions. In every stage of these Oppressions We have Petitioned for Redress in the most humble terms: Our repeated Petitions have been answered only by repeated injury. A Prince, whose character is thus marked by every act which may define a Tyrant, is unfit to be the ruler of a free people. Nor have We been wanting in attentions to our British brethren. We have warned them from time to time of attempts by their legislature to extend an unwarrantable jurisdiction over us. We have reminded them of the circumstances of our emigration and settlement here. We have appealed to their native justice and magnanimity, and we have conjured them by the ties of our common kindred to disavow these usurpations, which, would inevitably interrupt our connections and correspondence. They too have been deaf to the voice of justice and of consanguinity. We must, therefore, acquiesce in the necessity, which denounces our Separation, and hold them, as we hold the rest of mankind, Enemies in War, in Peace Friends.

We, THEREFORE the Representatives of the UNITED STATES OF AMERICA, in General Congress, Assembled, appealing to the Supreme Judge of the world for the rectitude of our intentions, do, in the Name and by Authority of the good People of these Colonies, solemnly publish and declare, That these United

Colonies are, and of Right ought to be FREE AND INDEPENDENT STATES; that they are Absolved from all Allegiance to the British Crown, and that all political connection between them and the State of Great Britain, is and ought to be totally dissolved; and that as Free and Independent States, they have full Power to levy War, conclude Peace, contract Alliances, establish Commerce, and to do all other Acts and Things which Independent States may of right do.

And for the support of this Declaration, with a firm reliance on the protection of divine Providence, we mutually pledge to each other our Lives, our Fortunes and our sacred Honor.

## ABRAHAM LINCOLN

# Gettysburg Address

President Abraham Lincoln (1809–1965) gave this speech in 1863 after the most crucial Union victory of the Civil War. If the Confederate army had won at Gettysburg, it would have had the potential to deal severe damage to the North, if not win the war outright. Perhaps the reason that this speech is so memorable is in its allusion to the great works of our nation's history—the Declaration of Independence, the Constitution—and also those of the world—the Bible, Pericles' Funeral Oration. Yet all these ideas are integrated into a work of just a few paragraphs, constituting a speech less than two minutes long.

FOUR SCORE AND SEVEN YEARS AGO OUR FATHERS BROUGHT FORTH on this continent, a new nation, conceived in Liberty, and dedicated to the proposition that all men are created equal.

Now we are engaged in a great civil war, testing whether that nation, or any nation so conceived and so dedicated, can long endure. We are met on a great battle-field of that war. We have come to dedicate a portion of that field, as a final resting place for those who here gave their lives that that nation might live. It is altogether fitting and proper that we should do this.

But, in a larger sense, we can not dedicate—we can not conse-crate—we can not hallow—this ground. The brave men, living and dead, who struggled here, have consecrated it, far above our poor power to add or detract. The world will little note, nor long remember what we say here, but it can never forget what they did here. It is for us the living, rather, to be dedicated here to the unfinished work which they who fought here have thus far so nobly advanced. It is rather for us to be here dedicated to the great task remaining before us—that from these honored dead we take increased devotion to that cause for which they gave the last full measure of devotion—that we here highly resolve that these dead shall not have died in vain—that this nation, under God, shall have a new birth of freedom—and that government of the people, by the people, for the people, shall not perish from the earth.

# FREDERICK DOUGLASS

# The Meaning of the 4th of July for the Negro

Frederick Douglass (1817–1895) escaped from slavery at age twenty-one and dedicated his life to abolishing it. In 1845, after he had begun to gain acclaim as a powerful speaker at abolitionist meetings, he published his autobiography, *The Narrative Life of Frederick Douglass, an American Slave*. The book was an immediate bestseller, but because it identified Douglass's master, it actually placed Douglass in danger of being returned to slavery by bounty hunters, forcing Douglass to flee to England. After his freedom was "purchased" by British supporters, Douglass returned to America, where he became the central figure of the abolitionist movement. This speech, given at an abolitionist meeting in Rochester, New York, on July 5, 1852, reveals much of the empassioned power of Douglass' speaking style.

New York, July 5, 1852

WHAT, TO THE AMERICAN SLAVE, IS YOUR 4TH OF JULY? I ANSWER; A day that reveals to him, more than all other days in the year, the gross injustice and cruelty to which he is the constant victim. To him, your celebration is a sham; your boasted liberty, an unholy license; your national greatness, swelling vanity; your sounds of rejoicing are empty and heartless; your denunciation of tyrants, brass-fronted impudence; your shouts of liberty and equality, hollow mockery; your prayers and hymns, your sermons and thanksgivings, with all your religious parade and solemnity, are, to Him, mere bombast, fraud, deception, impiety, and hypocrisy—a thin veil to cover up crimes which would disgrace a nation of savages. There is not a nation on the earth guilty of practices more shocking and bloody than are the people of the United States, at this very hour.

Go where you may, search where you will, roam through all the monarchies and despotisms of the Old World, travel through South America, search out every abuse, and when you have found the last, lay your facts by the side of the everyday practices of this nation, and you will say with me, that, for revolting barbarity and shameless hypocrisy, America reigns without a rival. . . .

To me the American slave-trade is a terrible reality. When a child, my soul was often pierced with a sense of its horrors. I lived on Philpot Street, Fell's Point, Baltimore, and have watched from the wharves the slave ships in the Basin, anchored from the shore, with their cargoes of human flesh, waiting for favorable winds to waft them down the Chesapeake. There was, at that time, a grand slave mart kept at the head of Pratt Street, by Austin Woldfolk. His agents were sent into every town and county in Maryland, announcing their arrival, through the papers, and on flaming *"hand-bills,"* headed cash for Negroes. These men were generally well dressed men, and very captivating in their manners; ever ready to drink, to treat, and to gamble. The fate of many a slave has depended upon the turn of a single card; and many a child has been snatched from the arms of its mother by bargains arranged in a state of brutal drunkenness.

The flesh-mongers gather up their victims by dozens, and drive them, chained, to the general depot at Baltimore. When a sufficient number has been collected here, a ship is chartered for the purpose of conveying the forlorn crew to Mobile, or to New Orleans. From the slave prison to the ship, they are usually driven in the darkness of night; for since the anti-slavery agitation, a certain caution is observed.

In the deep, still darkness of midnight, I have been often aroused by the dead, heavy footsteps, and the piteous cries of the chained gangs that passed our door. The anguish of my boyish heart was intense; and I was often consoled, when speaking to my mistress in the morning, to hear her say that the custom was very wicked; that she hated to hear the rattle of the chains and the heart-rending cries. I was glad to find one who sympathized with me in my horror.

Fellow-citizens, this murderous traffic is, to-day, in active operation in this boasted republic. In the solitude of my spirit I see clouds of dust raised on the highways of the South; I see the bleeding footsteps; I hear the doleful wail of fettered humanity on the way to the slave-markets, where the victims are to be sold like *horses, sheep,* and *swine,* knocked off to the highest bidder. There I see the tenderest ties ruthlessly broken, to gratify the lust, caprice, and rapacity of the buyers and sellers of men. My soul sickens at the sight.

> *Is this the land your Fathers loved,*
> *The freedom which they toiled to win?*
> *Is this the earth whereon they moved?*
> *Are these the graves they slumber in?*

. . . Americans! your republican politics, not less than your republican religion, are flagrantly inconsistent. You boast of your love of liberty, your superior civilization, and your pure Christianity, while the whole political power of the nation (as embodied in the two great political parties) is solemnly pledged to support and perpetuate the enslavement of three millions of your countrymen. You hurl your anathemas at the crowned headed tyrants of Russia and Austria and pride yourselves on your Democratic institutions, while you yourselves consent to be the mere *tools* and *body-guards* of the tyrants of Virginia and Carolina. You invite to your shores fugitives of oppression from abroad, honor them with banquets, greet them with ovations, cheer them, toast them, salute them, protect them, and pour out your money to them like water; but the fugitives from your own land you advertise, hunt, arrest, shoot, and kill. You glory in your refinement and your universal education; yet you maintain a system as barbarous and dreadful as ever stained the character of a nation—a system begun in avarice, supported in pride, and perpetuated in cruelty. You shed tears over fallen Hungary, and make the sad story of her wrongs the theme of your poets, statesmen, and orators, till your gallant sons are ready to fly to arms to vindicate her cause against the oppressor; but, in regard to the ten thousand wrongs of the American slave, you would enforce the strictest silence, and would hail him as an enemy of the nation who dares to make those wrongs the subject of public discourse! You are all on fire at the mention of liberty for France or for Ireland; but are as cold as an iceberg at the thought of liberty for the enslaved of America. You discourse eloquently on the dignity of labor; yet you sustain a system which, in its very essence, casts a stigma upon labor. You can bare your bosom to the storm of British artillery to throw off a three-penny tax on tea; and yet wring the last hard earned farthing from the grasp of the black laborers of your country. You profess to believe "that, of one blood, God made all nations of men to dwell on the face of all the earth," and hath commanded all men, everywhere, to love one another; yet you notoriously hate (and glory in your hatred) all men whose skins are not colored like your own. You declare before the world, and are understood by the world to declare that you *"hold these truths to be self-evident, that all men are created equal; and are endowed by their Creator with certain inalienable rights; and that among these are, life, liberty, and the pursuit of happiness"*; and yet, you hold securely, in a bondage which, according to your own Thomas Jefferson, *"is worse than ages of that which your fathers rose in rebellion to oppose,"* a seventh part of the inhabitants of your country.

Fellow-citizens, I will not enlarge further on your national inconsistencies. The existence of slavery in this country brands your republicanism as a sham, your humanity as a base pretense, and your Christianity as a lie. It destroys your moral power abroad: it corrupts your politicians at home. It saps the foundation of religion; it makes your name a hissing and a byword to a mocking earth. It is the antagonistic force in your government, the only thing that seriously disturbs and endangers your *Union*. It fetters your progress; it is the enemy of improvement; the deadly foe of education; it fosters pride; it breeds insolence; it promotes vice; it shelters crime; it is a curse to the earth that supports it; and yet you cling to it as if it were the sheet anchor of all your hopes. Oh! be warned! be warned! a horrible reptile is coiled up in your nation's bosom; the venomous creature is nursing at the tender breast of your youthful republic; *for the love of God, tear away*, and fling from you the hideous monster, and *let the weight of twenty millions crush and destroy it forever!*

## HENRY DAVID THOREAU

# *An Immoral Law*

Henry David Thoreau (1817–1862) was known in his time as an odd sort of educated vagrant, rarely employed, who mostly kept to himself. He wrote voraciously in his journals at the suggestion of his most notable friend, Ralph Waldo Emerson. Occasionally, to earn extra money, he lectured about life in the backwoods, peppering his rather dry talks with folksy anecdotes. The one exception was when he spoke or wrote about slavery, when his laconic wit became an intense fire of emotion. In his most significant book, *Walden*, he expresses his seemingly contradictory individualist philosophy of civil responsibility. The following selection, from his journal entry of June 16, 1854, is an application of the principles expressed in *Walden* to an event which deeply affected Thoreau's community—the enforcement of the Fugitive Slave Act by the forcible returning of a black man (possibly not even an escaped slave) to the South. The Fugitive Slave Act was never again enforced in Massachusetts.

THE EFFECT OF A GOOD GOVERNMENT IS TO MAKE LIFE MORE VALUable,—of a bad government, to make it less valuable. We can afford that railroad and all merely material stock should depreciate, for that only compels us to live more simply and economically; but suppose the value of life itself should be depreciated. Every man in New England capable of the sentiment of patriotism must have lived the last three weeks with the sense of having suffered a vast, indefinite loss. I had never respected this government, but I had foolishly thought that I might manage to live here, attending to my private affairs, and forget it. For my part, my old and worthiest pursuits have lost I cannot say how much of their attraction, and I feel that my investment in life here is worth many per cent, less since Massachusetts last deliberately and forcibly restored an innocent man, Anthony Burns, to slavery. I dwelt before in the illusion that my life passed somewhere only between heaven and hell, but now I cannot persuade myself that I do not dwell wholly within hell. The sight of that political organization called Massachusetts is to me morally covered with scoriae and volcanic cinders, such as Milton imagined. If there is any hell more unprincipled than our rulers and our people, I feel curious to visit it. Life itself being worthless, all things with it, that feed it, are worthless. Suppose you have a small library, with pictures to adorn the walls,—a garden laid out around—and contemplate scientific and literary pursuits, etc., etc., and discover suddenly that your villa, with all its contents, is located in hell, and that the justice of the peace is one of the devil's angels, has a cloven foot and forked tail,—do not these things suddenly lose their value in your eyes? Are you not disposed to sell at a great sacrifice?

I feel that, to some extent, the State has fatally interfered with my just and proper business. It has not merely interrupted me in my passage through Court Street on errands of trade, but it has, to some extent, interrupted me and every man on his onward and upward path, on which he had trusted soon to leave Court Street far behind. I have found that hollow which I had relied on for solid.

I am surprised to see men going about their business as if nothing had happened, and say to myself, "Unfortunates! they have not heard the news"; that the man whom I just met on horseback should be so earnest to overtake his newly bought cows running away,—since all property is insecure, and if they do not run away again, they may be taken away from him when he gets them. Fool! does he not know that his seed-corn is worth less this year,—that all beneficent harvests fail as he approaches the empire of hell? No prudent man will build a stone house under these circumstances, or engage in any peaceful enterprise which it requires a long time to accomplish. Art is as long as ever, but life is more interrupted and less available for a man's proper pursuits. It is time we had done referring to our ancestors. We have used up all our inherited freedom, like the young bird the albumen in the egg. It is not an era of repose. If we would save our lives, we must fight for them.

The discovery is what matter of men your countrymen are. They steadily worship mammon—and on the seventh day curse God with a tintamarre from one end of the *Union* to the other. I heard the other day of a meek and sleek devil of a Bishop Somebody, who commended the law and order with which Burns was given up. I would like before I sit down to a table to inquire if there is one in the company who styles himself or is styled Bishop, and he or I should go out of it. I would have such a man wear his bishop's hat and his clerical bib and tucker, that we may know him.

Why will men be such fools as [to] trust to lawyers for a *moral* reform? I do not believe that there is a judge in this country pre-pared to decide by the principle that a law is immoral and therefore of no force. They put themselves, or rather are by character, exactly on a level with the marine who discharges his musket in any direc-tion in which he is ordered. They are just as much tools, and as lit-tle men.

# MARTIN LUTHER KING, JR.

# *Letter from Birmingham Jail**

In 1955, after a resolute Rosa Parks was arrested for refusing to give up her seat to a white man on a Montgomery bus, a young, articulate black minister was thrust into the national spotlight—as the unlikely leader of the ensuing bus

---

*This response to a published statement by eight fellow clergymen from Alabama (Bishop C. C. J. Carpenter, Bishop Joseph A. Durick, Rabbi Milton L. Grafman, Bishop Paul Hardin, Bishop Holan B. Harmon, the Reverend George M. Murray, the Reverend Edward V. Ramage, and the Reverend Earl Stallings) was composed under somewhat constricting circumstances. Begun on the margins of the newspaper in which the statement appeared while I was in jail, the letter was continued on scraps of writing paper supplied by a friendly Negro trusty, and concluded on a pad my attorneys were eventually permitted to leave me. Although the text remains in substance unaltered, I have indulged in the author's prerogative of polishing it for publication.

boycott which ignited the modern civil rights movement. Over the next twelve years, Martin Luther King, Jr. became one of the most influential figures in American history. A powerful presence on both the podium and the pulpit, his command of written English made him a figure of admiration around the globe. In 1964 he was awarded the Nobel Peace Prize. In 1986, eighteen years after his tragic assassination, he became one of only three Americans honored with a national holiday.

Perhaps the most eloquent statement of King's philosophy of passive resistance, the "Letter from Birmingham Jail" was written in 1963 after King was arrested for demonstrating in defiance of a court order. Soon thereafter, it was widely circulated. It has become a classic of the civil rights movement.

APRIL 16, 1963

MY DEAR FELLOW CLERGYMEN:

While confined here in the Birmingham city jail, I came across your recent statement calling my present activities "unwise and untimely." Seldom do I pause to answer criticism of my work and ideas. If I sought to answer all the criticisms that cross my desk, my secretaries would have little time for anything other than such correspondence in the course of the day, and I would have no time for constructive work. But since I feel that you are men of genuine good will and that your criticisms are sincerely set forth, I want to try to answer your statement in what I hope will be patient and reasonable terms.

I think I should indicate why I am here in Birmingham, since you have been influenced by the view which argues against "outsiders coming in." I have the honor of serving as president of the Southern Christian Leadership Conference, an organization operating in every southern state, with headquarters in Atlanta, Georgia. We have some eighty-five affiliated organizations across the South, and one of them is the Alabama Christian Movement for Human Rights. Frequently we share staff, educational and financial resources with our affiliates. Several months ago the affiliate here in Birmingham asked us to be on call to engage in a nonviolent direct-action program if such were deemed necessary. We readily consented, and when the hour came we lived up to our promise. So I, along with several members of my staff, am here because I was invited here. I am here because I have organizational ties here.

But more basically, I am in Birmingham because injustice is here. Just as the prophets of the eighth century B.C. left their villages and carried their "thus saith the Lord" far beyond the boundaries of their home towns, and just as the Apostle Paul left his village of Tarsus and carried the gospel of Jesus Christ to the far corners of the Greco-Roman world, so am I compelled to carry the gospel of freedom beyond my own home town. Like Paul, I must constantly respond to the Macedonian call for aid.

Moreover, I am cognizant of the interrelatedness of all communities and states. I cannot sit idly by in Atlanta and not be concerned about what happens in Birmingham. Injustice anywhere is a threat to justice everywhere. We are caught in an inescapable network of mutuality, tied in a single garment of destiny. Whatever affects one directly, affects all indirectly. Never again can we afford to live with the narrow, provincial "outside agitator" idea. Anyone who lives inside the United States can never be considered an outsider anywhere within its bounds.

You deplore the demonstrations taking place in Birmingham. But your statement, I am sorry to say, fails to express a similar concern for the conditions that brought about the demonstrations. I am sure that none of you would want to rest content with the superficial kind of social analysis that deals merely with effects and does not grapple with underlying causes. It is unfortunate that demonstrations are taking place in Birmingham, but it is even more unfortunate that the city's white power structure left the Negro community with no alternative.

In any nonviolent campaign there are four basic steps: collection of the facts to determine whether injustices exist; negotiation; self-purification; and direct action. We have gone through all these steps in Birmingham. There can be no gainsaying the fact that racial injustice engulfs this community. Birmingham is probably the most thoroughly segregated city in the United States. Its ugly record of brutality is widely known. Negroes have experienced grossly unjust treatment in the courts. There have been more unsolved bombings of Negro homes and churches in Birmingham than in any other city in the nation. These are the hard, brutal facts of the case. On the basis of these conditions, Negro leaders sought to negotiate with the city fathers. But the latter consistently refused to engage in good-faith negotiation.

Then, last September, came the opportunity to talk with leaders of Birmingham's economic community. In the course of the negotiations, certain promises were made by the merchants—for example, to remove the stores' humiliating racial signs. On the basis of

these promises, the Reverend Fred Shuttlesworth and the leaders of
the Alabama Christian Movement for Human Rights agreed to a
moratorium on all demonstrations. As the weeks and months went
by, we realized that we were the victims of a broken promise. A few
signs, briefly removed, returned; the others remained.

As in so many past experiences, our hopes had been blasted,
and the shadow of deep disappointment settled upon us. We had
no alternative except to prepare for direct action, whereby we would
present our very bodies as a means of laying our case before the conscience of the local and the national community. Mindful of the
difficulties involved, we decided to undertake a process of self-
purification. We began a series of workshops on nonviolence, and
we repeatedly asked ourselves: "Are you able to accept blows without retaliating?" "Are you able to endure the ordeal of jail?" We
decided to schedule our direct-action program for the Easter season, realizing that except for Christmas, this is the main shopping
period of the year. Knowing that a strong economic-withdrawal program would be the by-product of direct action, we felt that this
would be the best time to bring pressure to bear on the merchants
for the needed change.

Then it occurred to us that Birmingham's mayoral election was
coming up in March, and we speedily decided to postpone action
until after election day. When we discovered that the Com-
missioner of Public Safety, Eugene "Bull" Connor, had piled up
enough votes to be in the runoff, we decided again to postpone
action until the day after the runoff so that the demonstrations
could not be used to cloud the issues. Like many others, we wanted
to see Mr. Connor defeated, and to this end we endured postponement after postponement. Having aided in this community
need, we felt that our direct-action program could be delayed no
longer.

You may well ask, "Why direct action? Why sit-ins, marches and
so forth? Isn't negotiation a better path?" You are quite right in calling for negotiation. Indeed, this is the very purpose of direct action.
Nonviolent direct action seeks to create such a crisis and foster such
a tension that a community which has constantly refused to negotiate is forced to confront the issue. It seeks so to dramatize the
issue that it can no longer be ignored. My citing the creation of tension as part of the work of the nonviolent-resister may sound rather
shocking. But I must confess that I am not afraid of the word "ten-

sion." I have earnestly opposed violent tension, but there is a type of constructive, nonviolent tension which is necessary for growth. Just as Socrates felt that it was necessary to create a tension in the mind so that individuals could rise from the bondage of myths and half-truths to the unfettered realm of creative analysis and objective appraisal, so must we see the need for nonviolent gadflies to create the kind of tension in society that will help men rise from the dark depths of prejudice and racism to the majestic heights of understanding and brotherhood.

The purpose of our direct-action program is to create a situation so crisis-packed that it will inevitably open the door to negotiation. I therefore concur with you in your call for negotiation. Too long has our beloved Southland been bogged down in a tragic effort to live in monologue rather than dialogue.

One of the basic points in your statement is that the action that I and my associates have taken in Birmingham is untimely. Some have asked: "Why didn't you give the new city administration time to act?" The only answer that I can give to this query is that the new Birmingham administration must be prodded about as much as the outgoing one, before it will act. We are sadly mistaken if we feel that the election of Albert Boutwell as mayor will bring the millennium to Birmingham. While Mr. Boutwell is a much more gentle person than Mr. Connor, they are both segregationists, dedicated to maintenance of the status quo. I have hoped that Mr. Boutwell will be reasonable enough to see the futility of massive resistance to desegregation. But he will not see this without pressure from devotees of civil rights. My friends, I must say to you that we have not made a single gain in civil rights without determined legal and nonviolent pressure. Lamentably, it is an historical fact that privileged groups seldom give up their privileges voluntarily. Individuals may see the moral light and voluntarily give up their unjust posture; but, as Reinhold Niebuhr has reminded us, groups tend to be more immoral than individuals.

We know through painful experience that freedom is never voluntarily given by the oppressor; it must be demanded by the oppressed. Frankly, I have yet to engage in a direct-action campaign that was "well timed" in the view of those who have not suffered unduly from the disease of segregation. For years now I have heard the word "Wait!" It rings in the ear of every Negro with piercing familiarity. This "Wait" has almost always meant "Never." We must come to see, with one of our distinguished jurists, that "justice too long delayed is justice denied."

We have waited for more than 340 years for our constitutional and God-given rights. The nations of Asia and Africa are moving with jetlike speed toward gaining political independence, but we still creep at horse-and-buggy pace toward gaining a cup of coffee at a lunch counter. Perhaps it is easy for those who have never felt the stinging darts of segregation to say "Wait." But when you have seen vicious mobs lynch your mothers and fathers at will and drown your sisters and brothers at whim; when you have seen hate-filled policemen curse, kick and even kill your black brothers and sisters; when you see the vast majority of your twenty million Negro brothers smothering in an airtight cage of poverty in the midst of an affluent society; when you suddenly find your tongue twisted and your speech stammering as you seek to explain to your six-year-old daughter why she can't go to the public amusement park that has just been advertised on television, and see tears welling up in her eyes when she is told that Funtown is closed to colored children, and see ominous clouds of inferiority beginning to form in her little mental sky, and see her beginning to destroy her personality by developing an unconscious bitterness toward white people; when you have to concoct an answer for a five-year-old son who is asking: "Daddy, why do white people treat colored people so mean?"; when you take a cross-country drive and find it necessary to sleep night after night in the uncomfortable corners of your automobile because no motel will accept you; when you are humiliated day in and day out by nagging signs "white" and "colored"; when your first name becomes "nigger," your middle name becomes "boy" (however old you are) and your last name becomes "John," and your wife and mother are never given the respected title "Mrs."; when you are harried by day and haunted by night by the fact that you are a Negro, living constantly at tiptoe stance, never quite knowing what to expect next, and are plagued with inner fears and outer resentments; when you are forever fighting a degenerating sense of "nobodiness"—then you will understand why we find it difficult to wait. There comes a time when the cup of endurance runs over, and men are no longer willing to be plunged into the abyss of despair. I hope, sirs, you can understand our legitimate and unavoidable impatience.

You express a great deal of anxiety over our willingness to break laws. This is certainly a legitimate concern. Since we so diligently urge people to obey the Supreme Court's decision of 1954 outlawing segregation in the public schools, at first glance it may seem rather paradoxical for us consciously to break laws. One may well ask: "How can you advocate breaking some laws and obeying others?" The answer lies in the fact that there are two types of laws: just and unjust. I would be the first to advocate obeying just laws. One has not only a legal but a moral responsibility to obey just laws. Conversely, one has a moral responsibility to disobey unjust laws. I would agree with St. Augustine that "an unjust law is no law at all."

Now, what is the difference between the two? How does one determine whether a law is just or unjust? A just law is a man-made code that squares with the moral law or the law of God. An unjust law is a code that is out of harmony with the moral law. To put it in the terms of St. Thomas Aquinas: An unjust law is a human law that is not rooted in eternal law and natural law. Any law that uplifts human personality is just. Any law that degrades human personality is unjust. All segregation statutes are unjust because segregation distorts the soul and damages the personality. It gives the segregator a false sense of superiority and the segregated a false sense of inferiority. Segregation, to use the terminology of the Jewish philosopher Martin Buber, substitutes an "I-it" relationship for an "I-thou" relationship and ends up relegating persons to the status of things. Hence segregation is not only politically, economically and sociologically unsound, it is morally wrong and sinful. Paul Tillich has said that sin is separation. Is not segregation an existential expression of man's tragic separation, his awful estrangement, his terrible sinfulness? Thus it is that I can urge men to obey the 1954 decision of the Supreme Court, for it is morally right; and I can urge them to disobey segregation ordinances, for they are morally wrong.

Let us consider a more concrete example of just and unjust laws. An unjust law is a code that a numerical or power majority group compels a minority group to obey but does not make binding on itself. This is *difference* made legal. By the same token, a just law is a code that a majority compels a minority to follow and that it is willing to follow itself. This is *sameness* made legal.

Let me give another explanation. A law is unjust if it is inflicted on a minority that, as a result of being denied the right to vote, had no part in enacting or devising the law. Who can say that the legislature of Alabama which set up that state's segregation laws was democratically elected? Throughout Alabama all sorts of devious methods are used to prevent Negroes from becoming registered voters, and there are some counties in which, even though Negroes constitute a majority of the population, not a single Negro is registered. Can any law enacted under such circumstances be considered democratically structured?

Sometimes a law is just on its face and unjust in its application. For instance, I have been arrested on a charge of parading without a permit. Now, there is nothing wrong in having an ordinance which requires a permit for a parade. But such an ordinance becomes unjust when it is used to maintain segregation and to deny citizens the First-Amendment privilege of peaceful assembly and protest.

I hope you are able to see the distinction I am trying to point out. In no sense do I advocate evading or defying the law, as would the rabid segregationist. That would lead to anarchy. One who breaks an unjust law must do so openly, lovingly, and with a willingness to accept the penalty. I submit that an individual who breaks a law that conscience tells him is unjust, and who willingly accepts the penalty of imprisonment in order to arouse the conscience of the community over its injustice, is in reality expressing the highest respect for law.

Of course, there is nothing new about this kind of civil disobedience. It was evidenced sublimely in the refusal of Shadrach, Meshach, and Abednego to obey the laws of Nebuchadnezzar, on the ground that a higher moral law was at stake. It was practiced superbly by the early Christians, who were willing to face hungry lions and the excruciating pain of chopping blocks rather than submit to certain unjust laws of the Roman Empire. To a degree, academic freedom is a reality today because Socrates practiced civil disobedience. In our own nation, the Boston Tea Party represented a massive act of civil disobedience.

We should never forget that everything Adolf Hitler did in Germany was "legal" and everything the Hungarian freedom fighters did in Hungary was "illegal." It was "illegal" to aid and comfort a Jew in Hitler's Germany. Even so, I am sure that, had I lived in Germany at the time, I would have aided and comforted my Jewish brothers. If today I lived in a Communist country where certain principles dear to the Christian faith are suppressed, I would openly advocate disobeying that country's antireligious laws.

I must make two honest confessions to you, my Christian and Jewish brothers. First, I must confess that over the past few years I have been gravely disappointed with the white moderate. I have almost reached the regrettable conclusion that the Negro's great stumbling block in his stride toward freedom is not the White Citizen's Counciler or the Ku Klux Klanner, but the white moderate, who is more devoted to "order" than to justice; who prefers a negative peace which is the absence of tension to a positive peace which is the presence of justice; who constantly says: "I agree with you in the goal you seek, but I cannot agree with your methods of direct action"; who paternalistically believes he can set the time table for another man's freedom; who lives by a mythical concept of time and who constantly advises the Negro to wait for a "more convenient season." Shallow understanding from people of good will is more frustrating than absolute misunderstanding from people of ill will. Lukewarm acceptance is much more bewildering than outright rejection.

I had hoped that the white moderate would understand that law and order exist for the purpose of establishing justice and that when they fail in this purpose they become the dangerously structured dams that block the flow of social progress. I had hoped that the white moderate would understand that the present tension in the South is a necessary phase of the transition from an obnoxious negative peace, in which the Negro passively accepted his unjust plight, to a substantive and positive peace, in which all men will respect the dignity and worth of human personality. Actually, we who engage in nonviolent direct action are not the creators of tension. We merely bring to the surface the hidden tension that is already alive. We bring it out in the open, where it can be seen and dealt with. Like a boil that can never be cured so long as it is covered up but must be opened with all its ugliness to the natural medicines of air and light, injustice must be exposed, with all the tension its exposure creates, to the light of human conscience and the air of national opinion before it can be cured.

In your statement you assert that our actions, even though peaceful, must be condemned because they precipitate violence. But is this a logical assertion? Isn't this like condemning a robbed man because his possession of money precipitated the evil act of robbery? Isn't this like condemning Socrates because his unswerving commitment to truth and his philosophical inquiries precipitated the act by the misguided populace in which they made him drink hemlock? Isn't this like condemning Jesus because his unique God-consciousness and never-ceasing devotion to God's will pre-cipitated the evil act of crucifixion? We must come to see that, as the federal courts have consistently affirmed, it is wrong to urge an individual to cease his efforts to gain his constitutional rights because the quest may precipitate violence. Society must protect the robbed and punish the robber.

I had also hoped that the white moderate would reject the myth concerning time in relation to the struggle for freedom. I have just received a letter from a white brother in Texas. He writes: "All Christians know that the colored people will receive equal rights eventually, but it is possible that you are in too great a religious hurry. It has taken Christianity almost two thousand years to ac-complish what it has. The teachings of Christ take time to come to earth." Such an attitude stems from a tragic misconception of time, from the strangely irrational notion that there is something in the very flow of time that will inevitably cure all ills. Actually, time itself is neutral; it can be used either destructively or constructively. More and more I feel that the people of ill will have used time much more effectively than have the people of good will. We will have to repent in this generation not merely for the hateful words and actions of the bad people but for the appalling silence of the good people. Human progress never rolls in on wheels of inevitability; it comes through the tireless efforts of men willing to be co-workers with God, and without this hard work, time itself becomes an ally of the forces of social stagnation. We must use time creatively, in the knowledge that the time is always ripe to do right. Now is the time to make real the promise of democracy and transform our pending national elegy into a creative psalm of brotherhood. Now is the time to lift our national policy from the quicksand of racial injustice to the solid rock of human dignity.

You speak of our activity in Birmingham as extreme. At first I was rather disappointed that fellow clergymen would see my non-violent efforts as those of an extremist. I began thinking about the fact that I stand in the middle of two opposing forces in the Negro community. One is a force of complacency, made up in part of Negroes who, as a result of long years of oppression, are so drained of self-respect and a sense of "somebodiness" that they have adjusted to segregation; and in part of a few middle-class Negroes who, because of a degree of academic and economic security and because in some ways they profit by segregation, have become insensitive to the problems of the masses. The other force is one of bitterness and hatred, and it comes perilously close to advocating violence. It is expressed in the various black nationalist groups that are springing up across the nation, the largest and best-known being Elijah Muhammad's Muslim movement. Nourished by the Negro's frustration over the continued existence of racial discrimination, this movement is made up of people who have lost faith in America, who have absolutely repudiated Christianity, and who have concluded that the white man is an incorrigible "devil."

I have tried to stand between these two forces, saying that we need emulate neither the "do-nothingism" of the complacent nor the hatred and despair of the black nationalist. For there is the more excellent way of love and nonviolent protest. I am grateful to God that, through the influence of the Negro church, the way of nonviolence became an integral part of our struggle.

If this philosophy had not emerged, by now many streets of the South would, I am convinced, be flowing with blood. And I am further convinced that if our white brothers dismiss as "rabble-rousers" and "outside agitators" those of use who employ nonviolent direct action, and if they refuse to support our nonviolent efforts, millions of Negroes will, out of frustration and despair, seek solace and security in black-nationalist ideologies—a development that would inevitably lead to a frightening racial nightmare.

Oppressed people cannot remain oppressed forever. The yearning for freedom eventually manifests itself, and that is what has happened to the American Negro. Something within has reminded him of his birthright of freedom, and something without has reminded him that it can be gained. Consciously or unconsciously, he has been caught up by the *Zeitgeist*, and with his black brothers of Africa and his brown and yellow brothers of Asia, South America, and the Caribbean, the United States Negro is moving with a sense of great urgency toward the promised land of racial justice. If one recognizes this vital urge that has engulfed the Negro community, one should readily understand why public demonstrations are taking place. The Negro has many pent-up resentments and latent frustrations, and he must release them. So let him march; let him make prayer pilgrimages to the city hall; let him go on freedom rides—and try to understand why he must do so. If his repressed emotions are not released in nonviolent ways, they will seek expression through violence; this is not a threat but a fact of history. So I have not said to my people, "Get rid of your discontent." Rather, I have tried to say that this normal and healthy discontent can be channeled into the creative outlet of nonviolent direct action. And now this approach is being termed extremist.

But though I was initially disappointed at being categorized as an extremist, as I continued to think about the matter I gradually gained a measure of satisfaction from the label. Was not Jesus an extremist for love: "Love your enemies, bless them that curse you, do good to them that hate you, and pray for them which despitefully use you, and persecute you." Was not Amos an extremist for justice: "Let justice roll down like waters and righteousness like an everflowing stream." Was not Paul an extremist for the Christian gospel: "I bear in my body the marks of the Lord Jesus." Was not Martin Luther an extremist: "Here I stand; I cannot do otherwise, so help me God." And John Bunyan: "I will stay in jail to the end of my days before I make a butchery of my conscience." And Abraham Lincoln: "This nation cannot survive half slave and half free." And Thomas Jefferson: "We hold these truths to be self-evident, that all men are created equal. . . ." So the question is not whether we will be extremists, but what kind of extremists we will be. Will we be extremists for hate or for love? Will we be extremists for the preservation of injustice or for the extension of justice? In that dramatic scene on Calvary's hill three men were crucified. We must never forget that all three were crucified for the same crime—the crime of extremism. Two were extremists for immorality, and thus fell below their environment. The other, Jesus Christ, was an extremist for love, truth, and goodness, and thereby rose above his environment. Perhaps the South, the nation and the world are in dire need of creative extremists.

I had hoped that the white moderate would see this need. Perhaps I was too optimistic; perhaps I expected too much. I suppose I should have realized that few members of the oppressor race can understand the deep groans and passionate yearnings of the oppressed race, and still fewer have the vision to see that injustice must be rooted out by strong, persistent, and determined action. I am thankful, however, that some of our white brothers in the South have grasped the meaning of this social revolution and committed themselves to it. They are still all too few in quantity, but they are big in quality. Some—such as Ralph McGill, Lillian Smith, Harry Golden, James McBride Dabbs, Ann Braden and Sarah Patton Boyle—have written about our struggle in eloquent and prophetic terms. Others have marched with us down nameless streets of the South. They have languished in filthy, roach-infested jails, suffering the abuse and brutality of policemen who view them as "dirty nigger-lovers." Unlike so many of their moderate brothers and sisters, they have recognized the urgency of the moment and sensed the need for powerful "action" antidotes to combat the disease of segregation.

Let me take note of my other major disappointment. I have been so greatly disappointed with the white church and its leadership. Of course, there are some notable exceptions. I am not unmindful of the fact that each of you has taken some significant stands on this issue. I commend you, Reverend Stallings, for your Christian stand on this past Sunday, in welcoming Negroes to your worship service on a nonsegregated basis. I commend the Catholic leaders of this state for integrating Spring Hill College several years ago.

But despite these notable exceptions, I must honestly reiterate that I have been disappointed with the church. I do not say this as one of those negative critics who can always find something wrong with the church. I say this as a minister of the gospel, who loves the church; who was nurtured in its bosom; who has been sustained by its spiritual blessings and who will remain true to it as long as the cord of life shall lengthen.

When I was suddenly catapulted into the leadership of the bus protest in Montgomery, Alabama, a few years ago, I felt we would be supported by the white church. I felt that the white ministers, priests and rabbis of the South would be among our strongest allies. Instead, some have been outright opponents, refusing to understand the freedom movement and misrepresenting its leaders; all too many others have been more cautious than courageous and have remained silent behind the anesthetizing security of stained-glass windows.

In spite of my shattered dreams, I came to Birmingham with the hope that the white religious leadership of this community would see the justice of our cause and, with deep moral concern, would serve as the channel through which our just grievances could reach the power structure. I had hoped that each of you would understand. But again I have been disappointed.

I have heard numerous southern religious leaders admonish their worshippers to comply with a desegregation decision because it is the law, but I have longed to hear white ministers declare: "Follow this decree because integration is morally right and because the Negro is your brother." In the midst of blatant injustices inflicted upon the Negro, I have watched white churchmen stand on the sideline and mouth pious irrelevancies and sanctimonious trivialities. In the midst of a mighty struggle to rid our nation of racial and economic injustice, I have heard many ministers say: "Those are social issues, with which the gospel has no real concern." And I have watched many churches commit themselves to a completely otherworldly religion which makes a strange, un-Biblical distinction between body and soul, between the sacred and the secular.

I have traveled the length and breadth of Alabama, Mississippi and all the other southern states. On sweltering summer days and crisp autumn mornings I have looked at the South's most beautiful churches with their lofty spires pointing heavenward. I have beheld the impressive outlines of her massive religious-education buildings. Over and over I have found myself asking: "What kind of people worship here? Who is their God? Where were their voices when the lips of Governor Barnett dripped with words of interposition and nullification? Where were they when Governor Wallace gave a clarion call for defiance and hatred? Where were their voices of support when bruised and weary Negro men and women decided to rise from the dark dungeons of complacency to the bright hills of creative protest?"

Yes, these questions are still in my mind. In deep disappointment I have wept over the laxity of the church. But be assured that my tears have been tears of love. There can be no deep disappointment where there is not deep love. Yes, I love the church. How could I do otherwise? I am in the rather unique position of being the son, the grandson and the great-grandson of preachers. Yes, I see the church as the body of Christ. But, oh! How we have blemished and scarred that body through social neglect and through fear of being nonconformists.

There was a time when the church was very powerful—in the time when the early Christians rejoiced at being deemed worthy to suffer for what they believed. In those days the church was not merely a thermometer that recorded the ideas and principles of popular opinion; it was a thermostat that transformed the mores of society. Whenever the early Christians entered a town, the people in power became disturbed and immediately sought to convict the Christians for being "disturbers of the peace" and "outside agitators." But the Christians pressed on, in the conviction that they were "a colony of heaven," called to obey God rather than man. Small in number, they were big in commitment. They were too God-intoxicated to be "astronomically intimidated." By their effort and example they brought an end to such ancient evils as infanticide and gladiatorial contests.

Things are different now. So often the contemporary church is a weak, ineffectual voice with an uncertain sound. So often it is an archdefender of the status quo. Far from being disturbed by the presence of the church, the power structure of the average community is consoled by the church's silent—and often even vocal— sanction of things as they are.

But the judgment of God is upon the church as never before. If today's church does not recapture the sacrificial spirit of the early church, it will lose its authenticity, forfeit the loyalty of millions, and be dismissed as an irrelevant social club with no meaning for the twentieth century. Every day I meet young people whose disappointment with the church has turned into outright disgust.

Perhaps I have once again been too optimistic. Is organized religion too inextricably bound to the status quo to save our nation and the world? Perhaps I must turn my faith to the inner spiritual church, the church within the church, as the true *ekklesia* and the hope of the world. But again I am thankful to God that some noble souls from the ranks of organized religion have broken loose from the paralyzing chains of conformity and joined us as active partners in the struggle for freedom. They have left their secure congregations and walked the streets of Albany, Georgia, with us. They have gone down the highways of the South on tortuous rides for freedom. Yes, they have gone to jail with us. Some have been dismissed from their churches, have lost the support of their bishops and fellow ministers. But they have acted in the faith that right defeated is stronger than evil triumphant. Their witness has been the spiritual salt that has preserved the true meaning of the gospel in these troubled times. They have carved a tunnel of hope through the dark mountain of disappointment.

I hope the church as a whole will meet the challenge of this de-

cisive hour. But even if the church does not come to the aid of justice, I have no despair about the future. I have no fear about the
outcome of our struggle in Birmingham, even if our motives are at
present misunderstood. We will reach the goal of freedom in
Birmingham and all over the nation, because the goal of America
is freedom. Abused and scorned though we may be, our destiny is
tied up with America's destiny. Before the pilgrims landed at
Plymouth, we were here. Before the pen of Jefferson etched the
majestic words of the Declaration of Independence across the pages
of history, we were here. For more than two centuries our forebears
labored in this country without wages; they made cotton king; they
built the homes of their masters while suffering gross injustice and
shameful humiliation—and yet out of a bottomless vitality they continued to thrive and develop. If the inexpressible cruelties of slavery
could not stop us, the opposition we now face will surely fail. We
will win our freedom because the sacred heritage of our nation and
the eternal will of God are embodied in our echoing demands.

Before closing I feel impelled to mention one other point in your
statement that has troubled me profoundly. You warmly commended
the Birmingham police force for keeping "order" and "preventing
violence." I doubt that you would have so warmly commended the
police force if you had seen its dogs sinking their teeth into unarmed,
nonviolent Negroes. I doubt that you would so quickly commend the
policemen if you were to observe their ugly and inhumane treatment
of Negroes here in the city jail; if you were to watch them push and
curse old Negro women and young Negro girls; if you were to see
them slap and kick old Negro men and young boys; if you were to
observe them, as they did on two occasions, refuse to give us food
because we wanted to sing our grace together. I cannot join you in
your praise of the Birmingham police department.

It is true that the police have exercised a degree of discipline in
handling the demonstrators. In this sense they have conducted
themselves rather "nonviolently" in public. But for what purpose?
To preserve the evil system of segregation. Over the past few years I
have consistently preached that nonviolence demands that the
means we use must be as pure as the ends we seek. I have tried to
make clear that it is wrong to use immoral means to attain moral
ends. But now I must affirm that it is just as wrong, or perhaps even
more so, to use moral means to preserve immoral ends. Perhaps Mr.
Connor and his policemen have been rather nonviolent in public,

as was Chief Pritchett in Albany, Georgia, but they have used the moral means of nonviolence to maintain the immoral end of racial injustice. As T. S. Eliot has said: "The last temptation is the greatest treason: To do the right deed for the wrong reason."

I wish you had commended the Negro sit-inners and demonstrators of Birmingham for their sublime courage, their willingness to suffer and their amazing discipline in the midst of great provocation. One day the South will recognize its real heroes. They will be the James Merediths, with the noble sense of purpose that enables them to face jeering and hostile mobs, and with the agonizing loneliness that characterizes the life of the pioneer. They will be old, oppressed, battered Negro women, symbolized in a seventy-two-year-old woman in Montgomery, Alabama, who rose up with a sense of dignity and with her people decided not to ride segregated buses, and who responded with ungrammatical profundity to one who inquired about her weariness: "My feets is tired, but my soul is at rest." They will be the young high school and college students, the young ministers of the gospel and a host of their elders, courageously and nonviolently sitting in at lunch counters and willingly going to jail for conscience' sake. One day the South will know that when these disinherited children of God sat down at lunch counters, they were in reality standing up for what is best in the American dream and for the most sacred values in our Judaeo-Christian heritage, thereby bringing our nation back to those great wells of democracy which were dug deep by the founding fathers in their formulation of the Constitution and the Declaration of Independence.

Never before have I written so long a letter. I'm afraid it is much too long to take your precious time. I can assure you that it would have been much shorter if I had been writing from a comfortable desk, but what else can one do when he is alone in a narrow jail cell, other than write long letters, think long thoughts and pray long prayers?

If I have said anything in this letter that overstates the truth and indicates an unreasonable impatience, I beg you to forgive me. If I have said anything that understates the truth and indicates my having a patience that allows me to settle for anything less than brotherhood, I beg God to forgive me.

I hope this letter finds you strong in the faith. I also hope that circumstances will soon make it possible for me to meet each of you, not as an integrationist or a civil-rights leader but as a fellow clergyman and a Christian brother. Let us all hope that the dark clouds of racial prejudice will soon pass away and the deep fog of misunderstanding will be lifted from our fear-drenched communities, and in some not too distant tomorrow the radiant stars of love and brotherhood will shine over our great nation with all their scintillating beauty.

> Yours for the cause of Peace and Brotherhood,
> MARTIN LUTHER KING, JR.

*Student Essay*

# CATHERINE GARALDI

# King's Way with Words

Catherine wrote this essay as a sort of free-associative response King's "Letter from Birmingham Jail." She responds to what King writes, and addresses specific issues within King's "Letter," but the essay can't be said to have a thesis, or even a conclusion. The essay does make some sense of the complexities in the "Letter," and would be an excellent starting point for a more formal essay.

IN MARTIN LUTHER KING, JR.'S OWN NOTE ON THE WRITING OF THE "Letter from Birmingham Jail," he says that it was begun in secret, on smuggled scraps of paper at first, then on a notepad he was eventually permitted. "Although the text remains in substance unaltered," he wrote, "I have indulged the author's prerogative of polishing it for publication." Yet the letter reads like spoken words, with some of the natural diction of speech, combined with the power and righteous force of a sermon. King's skill as a preacher is highlighted in the "Letter," as is his talent as a letter-writer.

That particular talent is for some people hard to come by. A good letter-writer may have a large point to make, or a small tale to relate, but both kinds of things are expressed in a clear, relaxed manner. Although what King was writing is powerful, both in subject matter and tone, he easily visualizes his audience and is able to address them as though he were speaking to them in person. It is this semblance of real speech that distinguishes a good, readable letter from one that is too formal to struggle through.

King's rhetoric is so powerful at times that his stated subject matter—his controversial personal involvement in Birmingham racial politics and consequent jailing—sometimes disappears under waves of great truth that splash across and wash away his detractors' criticisms. He is accused of being an outside agitator, and therefore impolitic in his participation; he replies "Injustice anywhere is a threat to justice everywhere." He echoes the poetic "No man is an island" when he declares that "Whatever affects one directly, affects all indirectly." It is difficult to disagree, difficult not to nod and say "Amen." The force of his rhetoric, combined with the truth of his vision and the personal yet speechlike style of his address bring weight and persuasion to his argument.

King suggests that he and his stated audience of eight clergy may already be on the same side. He and they share the same goal: desegregation of Alabama's—and the nation's—institutions, specifically at this time, Birmingham's economic community. When he writes, he assumes that all people of good will share this goal. Starting with this assumption of agreement allows him to draw his audience in, believing that they are already with him, or, if they aren't, they should be. He assumes they are united, and uses his words to gently but powerfully instill that belief in them.

It is difficult to say anything new—or anything at all—about the subject matter of King's "Letter." As you read it, it is difficult to resist agreeing with the truth and beauty of what he had to say on the subject of growing up in Black America, hated by White America. You feel as if he is writing, speaking, directly to your heart. Next to his works, it is King's way with words we will remember him for. As the results in America today confirm, the two make a powerful combination.

# LINDA HASSELSTROM

## *The Cow versus the Animal Rights Activist*

People often ask Linda Hasselstrom (b. 1943) why she doesn't devote herself fulltime to either writing or ranching, although she's been quite successful doing both. Her response is characteristcally down-to-earth: "I'm often tired, but never bored. When I'm confronted with a job I detest, six other jobs I prefer can delay it another day." Her writings often focus on her own connection to the land and the lessons she has learned from that association. While the result, in less apt hands, would soon devolve into dogmatic drivel, Hasselstrom somehow strikes the right balance—she rarely sounds like she's preaching. In this excerpt from *Land Circle*, Hasselstrom again uses her own experience as a rancher to dispute animal rights activists' claims that raising and killing animals for food is immoral.

I'M A RANCHER; BEEF CATTLE PROVIDE MOST OF MY MONEY AND FOOD. I *like* cows; I've had a warm partnership with them for thirty-five years. I admire a cow's instincts, and suspect her of having a sense of humor, as well as of knowing more than we think. I envy her adaptation to the arid plains, and her apparent serenity in emergencies.

I also love to cut into a tender sirloin steak with a hint of pink in the center, and dip each bite into the luscious brown juice surrounding the potatoes on my plate. I relish each mouthful, thinking dreamily of the cow whose flesh I'm eating; I remember when she was born, how she became crippled so that her destiny became the dark freezer in my basement rather than the meat department of a brightly lighted supermarket. I have always considered that the relationship between me and my cattle was a little like a good marriage, with good days and bad days, but considerable satisfaction on both sides.

Suddenly my personal paradox has frightening possibilities, because animal rights activists are declaring in sizeable headlines that it is not possible to love animals and also kill them. Anyone who says so, they declare, is vicious, sadistic, and untrustworthy. Some extremists declare that doing anything at all with an animal but letting it follow its normal patterns is immoral, and others declare that we have no right to experiment with animals even to save human lives. Ranchers are targets because we confine cattle in pastures, brand them with hot irons, and cut sections out of their ears to show ownership. Those, say the activists, are the actions of exploiters, unfit to be environmentalists or associate with your daughter. Activists have destroyed research labs to free the animals, sometimes loosing dangerous bacteria. Some deer and bison lovers follow hunters into the woods, shouting to frighten the game. One screaming activist repeatedly whacked and poked a bison hunter with the point of a ski pole; the hunter, a model of nonviolence, neither screamed back nor made threatening gestures with his Rolling Block .45-70, capable of decimating an activist with one shot. In a middle-sized town near our ranch, activists scream obscenities and spit on women in fur coats. At a National Cattlemen's Association meeting, a speaker warned ranchers that new employees may work undercover for animal rights groups. An auction yard in Dixon, California, and a meatpacking plant in San Jose were torched by arsonists, and an unlit Molotov cocktail lobbed into the offices of the California Cattlemen's Association. A popular country singer, k.d. lang, was part of a "Meat Stinks" campaign supported by People for the Ethical Treatment of Animals, a group that opposes using animals "other than for companionship." Radio and television stations in beef-producing areas, including South Dakota, promptly stopped playing all of lang's records. I was disappointed; watching lang croon sweet nothings into the ear of a dairy cow—in no danger of being eaten because she is too valuable as a milk factory, and tough as guitar strings—was the highlight of my television watching.

Her problem, and the difficulty of the ski pole-wielding activist confronting the bison hunter, is lack of information. The beef cattle industry has three major phases. First, farmers and ranchers own basic herds and produce breeding cattle, or yearlings sold as feeders. They keep the breeding cattle, and sell the yearlings at a sale market where the price is determined by supply and demand, and by bidders. When the ranchers sell, they have no opportunity to add costs of materials to the product, passing expenses on to the consumer as most businesses do. Ranchers take the price offered on sale day, or take the cattle home—where they will require more care, more expense.

The second phase of the beef cattle industry consists of stocker operators whose pastures put additional weight on feeder cattle before they enter feedlots, the third phase. Confined in muddy, stinking feedlots, cattle consume huge quantities of pesticide-laced grain designed to make the meat fat enough for consumer preference, and produce immense amounts of polluted runoff. The dangers posed to humans by the chemicals in both the meat and runoff have drawn environmentalists' attention to the cattle industry—but they are attacking the wrong end of production. Feedlots are generally operated by corporations that control feeding, butchering, and in some cases supermarket sales of meat, grain, and associated products. In 1988, three companies—Iowa Beef Packing (IBP, owned by Occidental Petroleum), ConAgra, and Excel (Cargill)—accounted for 70 percent of all fed cattle slaughtered in the United States. These monopolies, which also control a considerable amount of the nation's grain, flour, pork, egg, and poultry production, do pass costs to the consumers, hiking prices far above what ranchers get for their labor. But enormous corporations are tough to find and difficult to move; it's easier to attack individual hunters and ranchers.

I'm afraid that one day I'll be sweating and swearing in the corral, struggling to brand calves twice my weight, and suddenly find I'm surrounded by people with no sense of humor who have come to "liberate" my cows.

I'd like to discourage that kind of behavior, partly because some ranchers are impatient and armed, and partly because it's based on lack of information. Unchecked ignorance and paranoia can escalate misunderstandings to bloodshed. And some of my cows, unaccustomed to noise and rudeness, might kick the strangers, who would sue me, not the cows.

I recognize the difficulty many people face in reconciling their love of animals with their love of meat, but I believe the problem is increasing because we are getting further from the realities of human existence. As we developed our large brain, we also built a complicated set of desires that seems to imply that enough wealth will allow us to sit still. We want our food to be easily obtainable; now that we no longer have to run it down and beat it to death, many of us buy it precooked. When someone markets predigested dinners, there will be buyers. But many of us will continue to wear leather shoes, lust after leather skirts and jackets and leather upholstery on our car seats, and relish a good steak or hamburger. As long as humans have such desires but remain unwilling or unable to slaughter and skin the animals that can satisfy them, ranchers will be needed.

In defense, beef industry representatives say a pregnant woman produces four hundred thousand times as much estrogen every day as she would get from the average serving of beef injected with growth-inducing hormones. I've spent my life doing hard physical labor while eating organically raised cattle, so I understand the healthy properties of red meat, and I despair at the perception among many Americans that this tasty stuff isn't good for them. I am part of an industry that requires me to donate one dollar from each animal sold to the Beef Check-Off plan, which promotes the facts about eating beef and health—a group defense instituted, reluctantly, by cattle ranchers in response to misinformation spread by antibeef activists. In part, this idea comes from paranoia about cholesterol and growth hormones; in part, it's a result of government-subsidized campaigns by producers of other foods. In many countries, the beef I eat in a year would make a family wealthy, but I am frustrated by being unable to sell directly to consumers beef raised on grass that is the natural product of my land.

Like most ranchers, I work more closely with cows than any animal rights activist I've ever met. I kneel in steaming cow manure and hot urine while talking kindly to a cow and urging a calf from her birth canal. I must brand calves so they won't stray or be stolen; castrate bulls to make them edible steers and protect bloodlines. I've cut cows' throats, helped gut and skin them, and canned every edible part of them for my family's use; in the process I've gained a deep appreciation for what killing our own meat can mean to humans. Because of this close involvement with the lives of cows, I feel I have worked hard for the right to eat their flesh. My relationship with cows is intimate, balanced—the cow is capable of killing or injuring me—and demands the most complete responsibility from the human half of the equation. The relationship is reviewed by both parties almost daily, and its implications carefully considered at least by the human half. Who knows what the cows are thinking?

Animal rights activists seem to me guilty of simplistic thinking and tunnel vision, although I envy people who forswear *all* killing and eating of flesh; I believe they have an easier road than those of us who try to strike a balance between exploitation and love. Similarly, I don't consider strolling along behind a fur-wearing woman screaming epithets, or shooting a cow, or burning a packing plant, to be meaningful activism; such actions are too simplistic, and too close to terrorism. During the easy environmentalism of the 1960s, one could lie on the lawn smoking grass on "Gentle Thursdays," sing "We Shall Overcome" and shout "No More War," and go back to class, one's pacifist duty done for the week. During that period, a few hard-working environmentalists passed strict laws which gave us a sense of power, but were sometimes as narrow and poorly thought out as the actions behind the corporate greed that made them necessary.

All of us—ranchers, environmentalists, and animal rights activists—if we expect to be taken seriously, should put as much work into defining and achieving realistic, fair goals as ranchers spend trying to keep cows alive. Few of us are born with that kind of dedication; we have to develop an interest in detail, a respect for our fellow animals—even Democrats, feminists, and snail darters—and an understanding of our responsibilities to the whole spectrum of life on the planet. What E. B. White wrote nearly sixty years ago is still true:

> Before you can be an internationalist you have first to be a naturalist and feel the ground under you making a whole circle. It is easier for a man to be loyal to his club than to his planet; the by-laws are shorter, and he is personally acquainted with the other members.
>
> The effect of any organization of a social and brotherly nature is to strengthen rather than to diminish the lines which divide people into classes; the effect of states and nations is the same, and eventually these lines will have to be softened, these powers will have to be generalized. It is written on the wall that this is so. I'm not inventing it, I'm just copying it off the wall.

Statistics from a few years ago declared that the average American ate fourteen cows in a lifetime, but consumption will drop to a twenty-five-year low in 1990 as hysterical and ill-informed folks screech about the dangers of beef. I've eaten more than my share in an effort to make up for vegetarian relatives and friends. When I calculated this my own family consisted of my parents, and my husband and me; we would butcher two animals, usually heifers, per year. Assuming each of us ate about one-fourth of each animal, I was eating an entire cow every four years, which means I've gobbled upwards of ten so far. If I live to be eighty, as I hope to do, I'll have eaten at least twenty of my own herd, not to mention the beef I eat in restaurants when I'm upholding the honor and economy of ranchers while surrounded by midwesterners lying about how good the frozen fish tastes. I am willing to take responsibility for the deaths of those twenty bovines, because I've saved the lives of many more than that.

Vegetarians may whittle the number of beefeaters down, but I'm confident beef will remain part of the American diet. Ranchers are learning to produce lean meat; I believe we will soon begin to move away from the dangerous chemicals and growth hormones we've been talked into using in order to raise productivity above sensible limits. At the same time, we are becoming aware of growing criticism of the damage cattle do to public lands by poorly controlled grazing. Little has been done, however, to control the meat and grain monopolies which will eventually control our food supplies and determine grocery prices.

It's a popular pastime now to debunk the myth of the independent cowboy and the cattle baron, and rightly so in many ways. Although there's truth to the legends, they were popularized and distorted by dime novels and bad movies; and some cow folk even bought their own advertising campaign or fantasy, and played their roles more eagerly than pulp heroes. They deserve to be reminded of reality.

But simply pronouncing the death of the age of the cattle baron and cowboy is too simple. Sure, those men—and their womenfolk—treated the West as if it was their kingdom. They battled its hardships, "civilized" it as they thought best—because they were given a challenge to do so by the wisest spirits of their age. Where I live was "the Great American Desert," shunned by all but the hardiest explorers. Later, the thinkers in their comfy New England offices decided that "rain follows the plow," and all that was needed to make the desert bloom were a few hardy souls to build claim shanties and plow to the horizon. The New England philosophers had no idea what difficult conditions westerners faced, but the westerners went right on working until they controlled everything but the weather.

We now see their errors, but we might have been guilty of the same actions, now seen as abuse, had we been cattle barons in those days. And some changes have been made not out of lack of concern, but through economic necessity. Cowboys, paid "forty a month and found," used to ride the range constantly, moving cattle around so that grazing was spread evenly over a wide area. Today workers who might once have become cowboys and cowgirls are instead making big wages in a city, and many ranchers operate alone, or assisted only by their smaller number of children or seasonal help. They have tried to adapt the advice given to farmers by agricultural experts within the government to invest more money, get big, and become efficient, but it didn't work as well on mobile cattle as on rows of corn; it didn't work on corn either, but that's another story, and Wes Jackson is telling it in his sustainable agriculture research at The Land Institute.

This generation's heroes are people who work to save our environment: the dead Saint Ed Abbey, Wendell Berry, Wes Jackson, Annie Dillard, Ann Zwinger, Gary Snyder, Barry Lopez, Gretel Ehrlich, Bil Gilbert, Kim Stafford, and other writers who contemplate humanity and nature. Some have attained almost mythical stature themselves, and we all try to learn from and imitate them. We believe, fervently, that they are right; those old ranchers believed in Manifest Destiny and the American Way just as passionately. What if we're wrong again?

Instead of blaming ranchers and farmers for doing what they were told to do, environmentalists need to show us what's wrong with the way we graze cattle, if they know. Most of the complainers have never been personally introduced to a cow, have no clear idea what's wrong with her grazing habits, and wouldn't know a good stand of native grass if they were lying in it reciting poetry or reading Abbey. They're willing to take someone else's word—just as the ranchers took the government's word for how to use the land. Too many environmentalists condemn without knowledge. None of the rhetoric changes the fact that the grasslands are in trouble, and only the people who own the land are likely to resolve the problems.

When I left the ranch, bound for a life of comfortable academic superiority in some ivory tower, I cared considerably less about cows than I do now, though I already knew more than the average American about the brutal facts of bovine life. Living beside a packing plant for a few months made a temporary vegetarian out of me.

I saw cows unloaded daily, heard the thud as the knacker's maul struck their foreheads, the bawl of pain as they were swung, only stunned, off their hooves by a hook thrust into an ankle. Sometimes, I could hear the bubbling, choking screech cut short as a worker finally opened a steer's throat. My cat grew sleek dragging home fleshy bones larger than he was, and I watched smugly when a steer escaped and ran through the streets, ineffectually pursued by a police force with little experience in cattle management. But as soon as I moved back to South Dakota, where I look out on my walking larder through every window, I went back to eating meat without hesitation. I earn every mouthful. The outmoded butchering practices used in packing plants have been changed; animals are killed with a gun, rather than stunned, before butchering begins. Other changes in the beef industry show increased awareness of public scrutiny.

When I returned to the ranch, I had shed some of the narrow attitudes with which I grew up, and I became involved in the complicated process of keeping a cow alive. I've learned, but I've remained a part of a wider world. Critics think ranch men read only *Farm Journal* and their wives do nothing but cook and raise children, but many are college graduates, and even those who aren't read more widely than their ancestors did. They also watch television; the rest of the world is no longer distant and inaccessible to them. They are informed about conditions in the "outer" world, and aware that most consumers know little about ranching or the food processing industry. For example, while farmers and ranchers know a good deal about what happens to their products—meat, grains, hay—when these leave the land, many folks who buy those products or by-products neatly wrapped in polyethylene haven't a clue about their production, and don't want to. Knowing the origins of our food and frivolities helps us make sensible choices about what we really want; in some cases, the sacrifice is not worth the benefit. When I shop for groceries, I carry a booklet that categorizes products by how socially responsible the producer is. I avoid products if the Council on Economic Priorities reports no reductions in animal testing by those companies, and no company contributions toward alternative research. On the other hand, I wouldn't hesitate to use any compatible animal heart to save the life of a child. But if the child was cocaine-addicted in the womb, and the operation was at taxpayers' expense, I could not support it.

Cattle have been domesticated for centuries, and belong in a separate category from animals bred for laboratory tests, and from wildlife; we are not likely to stop eating and managing cattle herds, nor should we. Wild cattle herds would be hardly more aesthetically satisfying than tame ones, as Indians have discovered while dodging sacred cows. A poorly managed herd of cattle can be as repugnant as Edward Abbey insisted, but that's the fault of the human manager, not the cows. With adequate feed and water and space to move while grazing selectively, a herd of cattle can be at least as acceptable in polite society as the average dog or child. Cattle do attract flies; before poisonous sprays and other costly forms of fly control existed, we built "oilers," slinging old feed sacks on a wire between two posts. We poured used crankcase oil on the cloth (recycling!) and cows rubbed oil on their bodies to discourage flies and lice. When the chemical companies noticed us using a product we didn't buy, they developed spray, injections, and fly-killing ear tags.

But most folks don't know this, because they spend more time with domesticated cats and dogs, and half-savage children, than with cows; and it is the activities that result from ignorance that bother me. Since I have become moderately well known as an articulate ranch woman, I've been questioned several times about animal rights.

What do I think of proposed laws to make branding illegal, for example? My reply: the folks who pass that law can find and return or replace the stolen cattle, catch and prosecute the thieves, and pay the costs of the confusion and crime. Branding does hurt, but it places a permanent mark on a cow, so even if she's illegally butchered, an owner has some chance of proving it. No other method is as useful, and I'll consider another method of marking my cattle when we stop licensing cars to identify them and prevent their theft. Every few years, someone suggests that acid brands are more merciful; I'd like that idea tested on the folks who suggest it: which hurts most, a burn with a hot iron, or an acid burn? Even if they are less painful, acid brands might not be enough; local old-timers talk about the days when government agencies used them. Enterprising cowboys sometimes roped the cows, smeared axle grease on the brands to neutralize the acid, turned the cows out until the hair grew back, and a few months later branded cows that appeared ownerless. Speaking of pain, what about breeds of dogs—Boxers, Doberman Pinschers, Schnauzers—not considered attractive unless their ears and tails are chopped off? Poodles, among the most widely popular dog breeds, just have their tails trimmed, though dogs with extremities intact are now allowed in some shows. What about the thousands of pets killed each year because owners couldn't be bothered with them any longer? Is it more merciful to keep a wild predator like a cat confined to an apartment for its entire life than to brand a cow once? So-called "pet" cats slaughter wild songbirds by the millions in most cities, but few animal rights activists picket pet owners. Why do suburbanites let their dogs run loose to chase and kill wildlife and calves?

Today's cattle live very well compared to their ancestors, perhaps too well for the health of the species; some old breeds are dying out. We may need their genetic diversity in coming years, if we continue to breed cattle for beef and milk production instead of their ability to survive, coddling them with medications until they can no longer resist disease. The average calf is observed and protected from predators at birth, and quickly vaccinated against many diseases. When necessary operations like branding, earmarking, castration, and dehorning occur, they are done with sterile equipment, supplemented with healing sprays to keep flies and maggots from the wounds. In the wild, only the fittest animals would survive a tough winter; modern cattle operators carefully control herd feed throughout the year for maximum gain, and maximum protection of pasture. Sick, weak, crippled, or otherwise unfit animals are culled from the herd, instead of being allowed to suffer and pass on their genes and illnesses. Ranchers who habitually abuse their cattle damage their own income and endanger themselves, both indirectly—by hurting their own profits—and directly; an abused or frightened cow can be a dangerous proposition.

As the rancher's awareness of chemical dangers increases, and as costs climb, some of us are realizing that we could raise organic, lean beef with less effort and expense, with the help of a real demand in the market from an informed public. Some ranchers already nervous about growth hormone implants would give them up if the steers didn't gain; heavier steers mean more income. As I write this, several tuna-packing companies have finally instituted policies that will make the killing of dolphins unprofitable. If the public demands chemical-free beef, it will be produced; ideally, South Dakota could encourage the sale of cattle straight from the organic grass of our pastures to the hungry customer—rather than selling the land for garbage dumps. I have heard of no state-sponsored efforts to keep native grass unplowed and grazed by cows for organic beef. If state officials put half the energy and cash spent on tourism into promoting the state's ranchers—whose product can keep the land relatively undamaged—we might discover a strong demand for grass-fed beef. And why not give tourists the chance to visit real, working ranches?

So if you like beef but don't like chemicals, cholesterol, or high food prices, get acquainted with a rancher who raises cattle on grass. Get a few friends together, buy a fat young "beef," and butcher it yourself—or ask a hunter to help. If one person does it, you'll just be a well-fed oddity. If two people do it, or five, it might become a movement. Think of it! Ranchers and beef eaters, joining together to beat chemical companies and monopolies; why, it's the stuff democracy is made of.

I'll say it again: I love cows, and consider my care and understanding of them superior to the treatment they'd get at the hands of the average animal rights activist.

# TOM REGAN

# *Animal Rights, Human Wrongs*

Philosophers were the first in academe to begin arguing the case for animal rights, and one of the pioneers of the academic movement for animal rights was Tom Regan. Regan (b. 1938) is a professor of philosophy at North Carolina State University. His work has focused on moral philosophy—an area that doesn't often attract popular interest—until the publication of his landmark book, *The Case for Animal Rights*, which not only established some of the major philosophical underpinnings of the animal rights movement, but also attracted a large popular audience. In this selection from *All That Dwell Therein*, Regan's forceful prose style supports his carefully crafted argument while helping to defuse some of the popular perception of animal rights activists as sentimental bunny-huggers.

AT THIS MOMENT WORKERS ON BOARD THE MOTHER SHIP OF A WHAL-
ing fleet are disassembling the carcass of a whale. Though the
species is officially protected by agreement of the member nations
of the International Whaling Commission, it is not too fanciful to
imagine the crew butchering a great blue whale, the largest creature
ever known to have lived on the earth—larger than thirty elephants,
larger even than three of the largest dinosaurs laid end to end. A
good catch, this leviathan of the deep. And, increasingly, a rare one.
For the great blue, like hundreds of other animal species, is endan-
gered, may, in fact, already be beyond the point of recovery.

But the crew has other things on their mind. It will take hours
of hard work to butcher the huge carcass, a process now carried out
at sea. Nor is butchering at sea the only thing in whaling that has
changed. The fabled days of a real hunt, of an individual Ahab pit-
ted against a treacherous whale, must remain the work of fiction
now. Whaling is applied technology, from the use of the most
sophisticated sonar to on-board refrigeration, from tracking heli-
copters to explosive harpoons, the latter a technological advance
that expedites a whale's death. Average time to die: sometimes as
long as twenty minutes; usually three to five. Here is one man's
account of a whale's demise:

> The gun roars. The harpoon hurls through the air and the whale-line
> follows. There is a momentary silence, and then the muffled explosion
> as the time fuse functions and fragments the grenade. . . . There is now
> a fight between the mammal and the crew of the catching vessel—a fight
> to the death. It is a struggle that can have only one result. . . . Deep in
> the whale's vast body is the mortal wound, and even if it could shake
> off the harpoon it would be doomed. . . . A second harpoon buries it-
> self just behind the dorsal fin . . . There is another dull explosion in
> the whale's vitals. Then comes a series of convulsions—a last despairing
> struggle. The whale spouts blood, keels slowly over and floats belly up-
> ward. It is dead.

For what? To what end? Why is this being done to the last remaining members of an irreplaceable species, certainly until recently,
possibly at this very moment, by supposedly civilized men? For can-
dle wax. For soap and oil. For pet food, margarine, fertilizer. For
perfume.

In Thailand, at this moment, another sort of hunt, less techno-
logically advanced, is in progress. The Thai hunter has hiked two

miles through thick vegetation and now, with his keen vision, spots a female gibbon and her infant, sleeping high in a tree. Jean-Yves Domalain describes what follows:

> Down below, the hunter rams the double charge of gun-powder down the barrel with a thin iron rod, then the lead shot. The spark flashes from two flints, and the gun goes off in a cloud of white smoke. . . . Overhead there is an uproar. The female gibbon, mortally wounded, clings to life. She still has enough strength to make two gigantic leaps, her baby still clinging to the long hair of her left thigh. At the third leap she misses the branch she was aiming for, and in a final desperate effort manages to grasp a lower one; but her strength is ebbing away and she is unable to pull herself up. Slowly her fingers begin to loosen her grip. Death is there, staining her pale fur. The youngster flattens himself in terror against her bloodstained flank. Then comes the giddy plunge of a hundred feet or more, broken by a terrible rebound off a tree trunk.

The object of this hunt is not to kill the female gibbon, but to capture the baby. Unfortunately, in this case the infant's neck is broken by the fall, so the shots were wasted. The hunter will have to move on, seeking other prospects.

We are not dealing in fantasies when we consider the day's work of the Thai hunter. Domalain makes it clear that both the method of capture (killing the mother to get the infant) and the results just seen (the death of both) are the rule rather than the exception in the case of gibbons. And chimpanzees. And tigers. And orangutans. And lions. Some estimate that for every one animal captured alive, ten have been killed. Domalain further states that for every ten captured only two will live on beyond a few months. The mortality rate stemming from hunts that aim to bring animals back alive thus is considerable.

Nor do we romanticize when we regard the female gibbon's weakening grip, the infant's alarmed clutching, the bonds of surprise and terror that unite them as they begin their final descent. And for what? To what end? Why is this scene played out again and again? So that pet stores might sell "exotic animals." So that roadside zoos might offer "new attractions." So that the world's scientists might have "subjects" for their experiments.

Not far from here, perhaps at this moment, a rabbit makes a futile effort to escape from a restraining device, called a stock, which holds the creature in place by clamping down around its neck. Immediately the reader thinks of trapping in the wild—that the stock must be a sort of trap, like the infamous leg-hold trap—but this is not so. The stock is a handmaiden of science, and the rabbit confined by it is not in the wild but in a research laboratory. If we look closely, we will see that one of the rabbit's eyes is ulcerated. It is badly inflamed, an open, running sore. After some hours the sore increases in size until barely half the eye is visible. In a few days the eye will become permanently blind. Sometimes the eye is literally burned out of its socket.

This rabbit is a research subject in what is known as the Draize test, named after its inventor. This rabbit, and hundreds like it, is being used because rabbits happen not to have tear ducts and so cannot flush irritants from their eyes. Nor can they dilute them. The Draize test proceeds routinely as follows: concentrated solutions of a substance are made to drip into one of the rabbit's eyes; the other eye, a sort of control, is left untroubled. Swelling, redness, destruction of iris or cornea, loss of vision are measured and the substance's eye-irritancy is thereby scientifically established.

What is this substance which in concentrated form invades the rabbit's eye? Probably a cosmetic, a new variety of toothpaste, shampoo, mouthwash, talcum, hand lotion, eye cosmetic, face cream, hair conditioner, perfume, cologne. Why? To what end? In the name of what purpose does this unanesthetized rabbit endure the slow burning destruction of its eye? So that a researcher might establish the eye-irritancy of mouthwash and talc, toothpaste and cologne.

A final individual bids for our attention at this moment. A bobbie calf is a male calf born in a dairy herd. Since the calf cannot give milk, something must be done with it. A common practice is to sell it as a source of veal, as in veal Parmigiana. To make this commercially profitable the calf must be raised in highly unnatural conditions. Otherwise the youngster would romp and play, as is its wont; equally bad, it would forage and consume roughage. From a businessman's point of view, this is detrimental to the product. The romping produces muscle, which makes for tough meat, and the roughage will contain natural sources of iron, which will turn the calf's flesh red. But studies show that consumers have a decided preference for pale veal. So the calf is kept permanently indoors, in a stall too narrow for it to turn around, frequently tethered to confine it further, its short life lived mostly in the dark on a floor of wood slats, its only contact with other living beings coming when it is fed and when, at the end, it is transported to the slaughterhouse.

Envision then the tethered calf, unable to turn around, unable to sit down without hunching up, devoid of companionship, its natural urges to romp and forage denied, fed a wholly liquid diet deliberately deficient in iron so as not to compromise its pale flesh but to keep it anemic. For what? To what end? In the name of what purpose does the calf live so? So that humans might have pale veal!

·    ·    ·

It would be grotesque to suggest that the whale, the rabbit, the gibbon, the bobbie calf, the millions of animals brought so much pain and death at the hands of humans are not harmed, for harm is not restricted to human beings. They are harmed, harmed in a literal, not a metaphorical sense. They are made to endure what is detrimental to their welfare, even death. Those who would harm them, therefore, must justify doing so. Thus, members of the whaling industry, the cosmetics industry, the farming industry, the network of hunters-exporters-importers must justify the harm they bring animals in a way that is consistent with recognizing the animals' right not to be harmed. To produce such a justification it is not enough to argue that people profit, satisfy their curiosity, or derive pleasure from allowing animals to be treated in these ways. These facts are not the morally relevant ones. Rather, what must be shown is that overriding the right of animals not to be harmed is justified because of further facts. For example, because we have very good reason to believe that overriding the individual's right prevents, and is the only realistic way to prevent, vastly greater harm to other innocent individuals.

Let us ask the whaling industry whether they have so justified their trade. Have they made their case in terms of the morally relevant facts? Our answer must be: No! And the cosmetic industry? No! The farmers who raise veal calves? No! The retailer of exotic animals? No! A thousand times we must say: No! I do not say that they cannot possibly justify what they do. The individual's right not to be harmed, we have argued, almost always trumps the interests of the group, but it is possible that such a right must sometimes give way. Possibly the rights of animals must sometimes give way to human interests. It would be a mistake to rule this possibility out. Nevertheless, the onus of justification must be borne by those who cause the harm to show that they do not violate the rights of the individuals involved.

We allow then that it is *possible* that harming animals might be justified; but we also maintain that those harming animals typically fail to show that the harm caused is *actually* justified. A further question we must ask ourselves is what, morally speaking, we ought to do in such a situation? Reflection on comparable situations involving human beings will help make the answer clear.

Consider racism and sexism. Imagine that slavery is an institution of the day and that it is built on racist or sexist lines. Blacks or women are assigned the rank of slave. Suppose we are told that in extreme circumstances even slavery might conceivably be justified, and that we ought not to object to it or try to bring it down, even though no one has shown that it is actually justified in the present case. Well, I do not believe for a moment that we would accept such an attempt to dissuade us from toppling the institution of slavery. Not for a moment would we accept the general principle involved here, that an institution actually is justified because it might conceivably be justified. We would accept the quite different principle that we are morally obligated to oppose any practice that appears to violate rights unless we are shown that it really does not do so. To be satisfied with anything less is to cheapen the value attributable to the victims of the practice.

Exactly the same line of reasoning applies in the case where animals are regarded as so many dispensable commodities, models, subjects, and the like. We ought not to back away from bringing these industries and related practices to a halt just because it is *possible* that the harm caused to the animals *might* be justified. If we do, we fail to mean it when we say that animals are not mere things, that they are the subjects of a life that is better or worse for them, that they have inherent value. As in the comparable case involving harm to human beings, our duty is to act, to do all that we can to put an end to the harm animals are made to endure. That the animals themselves cannot speak out on their own behalf, that they cannot organize, petition, march, exert political pressure, or raise our level of consciousness—all this does not weaken our obligation to act on their behalf. If anything, their impotence makes our obligation the greater.

We can hear, if we will but listen, the muffled detonation of the explosive harpoon, the sharp crack of the Thai hunter's rifle, the

drip of the liquid as it strikes the rabbit's eye, the bobbie calf's forlorn sigh. We can see, if we will but look, the last convulsive gasps
of the great blue whale, the dazed terror of the gibbons' eyes, the
frenzied activity of the rabbit's feet, the stark immobility of the bobbie calf. But not at this moment only. Tomorrow, other whales,
other rabbits will be made to suffer; tomorrow, other gibbons, other
calves will be killed, and others the day after. And others, stretching
into the future. All this we know with certainty. All this and more,
incalculably more, *will* go on, if we do not act today, as act we must.
Our respect for the value and rights of the animals cannot be satisfied with anything less.

# ſTЄPHЄП ᴚOſЄ

# *Proud to Be Speciesist*

The animal rights movement has had a powerful impact on scientific research
in the academic community. While philosophers like Tom Regan were carefully
crafting bulletproof arguments for animal rights, biologists, biochemists, neu-
roscientists, and psychologists were busily carrying on their research in the
same manner they had for decades, largely ignoring the efforts of what they
thought to be a few eccentric radicals. Then college administrators started listening to these "radicals," and animal research laboratories began closing.
Now scientists are beginning to respond to the animal rights movement, and
they are doing it with the same bulletproof logic so adeptly used against them
by the philosophers. Stephen Rose, a professor of biology at Open University
in England, is one of the scientists who is beginning to fight back. "Proud to
Be Speciesist" takes a term near to the heart of many animal rights activists—
"speciesism"—and turns it around, using it to make his own case for using animals in research.

I RESEARCH ON ANIMALS. I STUDY THE INTIMATE CHEMICAL AND ELEC-
trical processes that are the brain's mechanisms for storing information, for learning and memory. To discover those mechanisms, I

analyse the cellular changes that occur when young chicks learn and remember simple tasks. An antivivisectionist once asked me whether my research didn't make me feel rather like Dr. Mengele. No, it doesn't, though I can't resist pointing out that the only country ever to have moved to ban animal experimentation was Germany in the Nazi 1930s, showing a sensitivity that certainly didn't extend to those categories of humans regarded as "lives not worth living."

I won't cheapen the justification for my work by claiming that it will have *immediate* health benefits in helping children with learning problems or in treating the devastating consequences of Alzheimer's disease, though the fundamental biological mechanisms I am uncovering are certainly of relevance to both. I will insist that what I do is part of that great endeavor to understand human biological nature, and to interpret some of the deepest of philosophical questions about the nature of mind and brain. Of course, science is a social activity, and in a democratic society should be democratically controlled.

But the absolutists within the animal rights movement care little for that sort of democratic control. They want to have their argument both ways. On the one hand they claim the *discontinuites* between animals and humans are so great that animal experiments can tell us nothing relevant to the human condition. On the other, they say that because animals are sentient, the *continuities* between animals and humans mean that to privilege the latter over the former is an abuse, for which the pejorative term "speciesism" has been coined. The first statement is plain wrong; the second, the claim that animals have "rights," is sheer cant.

The biological world is a continuum. The bade biochemical mechanisms by which we tick are very similar to those in most other organisms. If they weren't, even the food we eat would poison us. Many human diseases and disorders are found in other mammals—which is why we can learn how to treat them by research on animals. Sure, there are differences, as the thalidomide case so tragically demonstrated. But given the choice between testing the toxicity of a new product on animals and not testing, there is no doubt which would be safer.

Of course, we may ask whether so many new drugs, cosmetics or other products are necessary at all, or whether such proliferation is merely the consequence of the restless innovatory needs of capitalist production. But that is not how the animal activists argue. Instead, they claim that there are alternatives to the use of animals. In some cases this is possible, and research to extend the range of such tests should have a high priority. But for many human diseases, understanding and treatment has demanded the use of animals and will continue to do so for the foreseeable future. There is no way, for instance that the biochemical causes of the lethal disease diabetes, or its treatment with insulin, could have been discovered, without experiments on mammals. And we can't use tissue cultures, or bacteria, or plants, to develop and test the treatments needed to alleviate epilepsy, Parkinsonism or manic depression. Anyone who claims otherwise is either dishonest or ignorant.

Equally, however, no biologist can or should deny the sentience of other large-brained animals. The Cartesian myth—that non-human animals are mere mechanisms, pieces of clockwork whose expressions of pain or suffering are no more than the squeak of a rusty cog—is just that, a myth. It was necessary to the generations of Christian philosophers who, following Descartes, wished to preserve the spiritual uniqueness of "Man" whilst accepting the hegemony of physics and biology over the rest of nature. And it was convenient to some 19th-century physiologists in absolving them from responsibility for the consequences of their experiments. But if I believed for one moment that my chicks were mere clockwork, I might as well stop working with them at all, and go play with computers instead.

Unless, of course. I experimented on humans. And this, the privileging of humans, is the nub of the question. Just because we are humans, any discussion of rights must begin with human rights. How far are those rights to be extended—does it even make sense to talk of extending them—to the "animal kingdom"? The animal kingdom isn't composed only of cats and dogs, mice and monkeys. It includes slugs and lice, wasps and mosquitoes. How far can the concept of right be extended—to not swatting a mosquito that is sucking your blood? To prevent your cat from hunting and killing a rat? Does an ant have as many rights as a gorilla?

Most people would say no—though I have met one activist who argued that even viruses had souls! I think most animal righters are really arguing that the closer animals are to humans, biologically speaking—that is, evolutionarily speaking—the more rights they should have. So where does the cut-off come? Primates? Mammals?

Vertebrates? The moment one concedes that question, it is clear that the decision is arbitrary—that it is *we*, as humans, who are conferring rights on animals—not the animals themselves.

Put like this, the spurious nature of the term *speciesism* becomes apparent. It was coined to make the claim that the issue of animal rights is on a par with the struggles for women's rights, or black people's rights, or civil rights. But these human struggles are those in which the oppressed themselves rise up to demand justice and equality, to insist that they are not the objects but the subjects of history.

Non-human animals cannot conceive or make such a claim, and to insist the terms are parallel is profoundly offensive, the lazy thinking of a privileged group.

Indeed, it is sometimes hard to avoid the impression that, for some among the animal rights movement, non-human animals take precedence over humans. The movement's absolutism and its seeming openness to members of extreme right-wing groups, reinforce the view that, for many of its activists, there is no automatic relationship between a concern for animal rights and one for human rights. Among others, there is an air of sanctimonious hypocrisy. They may, if they wish, refuse insulin if they are diabetic, L-dopa if they have Parkinsonism, antibiotics or surgical procedures that have been validated on animals before being used with humans—but I deny them any right to impose their personal morality on the rest of suffering humanity.

Nonetheless, it is essential to listen to the message that the movement carries. Its strength, despite its inchoate ideology, is, I believe, in part a response to the arrogant claim to the domination of nature that western scientific culture drew from its scriptural roots. The animal rights movement is part of a widespread romantic reaction to the seemingly cold rationality of science. Scientists who ignore the strength of this reaction do so at their peril—which is why this week sees the launch, by the British Association for the Advancement of Science of a "Declaration on Animals in Medical Research" signed by more than 800 doctors and scientists, defending the controlled use of animals.

The argument about how non-human animals should be treated is at root about how we as humans should behave. It is here that the biological discontinuities between humans and other animals become important. Our concern about how we treat other species springs out of our very humanness, as biologically and socially constructed creatures. We do not expect cats to debate the rights of mice. The issue is not really about animal rights at all, but about the *duties* that we have just because we are human.

And I am sure that we do have such duties, to behave kindly to other animals, with the minimum of violence and cruelty, not to damage or take their lives insofar as it can be avoided, just as we have duties to the planet's ecology in general. But those duties are limited by an overriding duty to other humans. I have a much-loved and exceedingly beautiful cat. But if I had to choose between saving her life and that of any human child, I would unhesitatingly choose the child. But I would save my cat at the expense of a fish. And so would the vast majority of people. That is species loyalty—speciesism if you like—and I am proud to be a speciesist.

# THOMAS SOWELL

# *Cold Compassion*

Depending on who you listen to, Thomas Sowell (b. 1930) is either a brilliant advocate of well-thought solutions for racial and other problems of our time, or a mindless black mouthpiece of the white establishment for preserving the status quo. He's written several controversial books on social issues, including *Black Education: Myths and Tragedies*, *Race and Economics*, and *Knowledge and Decisions*. This work led to his current position at the prestigious Hoover Institution of Stanford University, where he continues to produce books on issues of race and society. He also writes a monthly column on social issues, "Observations," for *Forbes* magazine, from which "Cold Compassion" was taken.

"COMPASSION" HAS BECOME ONE OF A GROWING NUMBER OF POLITIcized words (like "access" or "diversity") whose meaning has been corrupted beyond redemption. Nowhere is there more cruel indifference to the fate of flesh-and-blood human beings than among the hawkers of compassion when they talk about babies, born and unborn.

The very phrase "unborn babies" has been driven from the language by the intelligentsia of the media and academia, who have replaced it with the bloodless and detached word "fetus." The success of this desensitization campaign may be judged by how many of us were shocked to learn from the medical movie *The Silent Scream* that what happens in an abortion is not the surgical removal of some little blob of cells but the painful dismemberment of a struggling human being, attempting in vain to flee from the fatal instruments.

Those who most loudly proclaim "the public's right to know" are nowhere to be seen when it comes to the public's right to know that. Indeed, strenuous efforts are made to prevent this movie from being shown. In politically correct Palo Alto, home of Stanford University, a mere description of the process was edited out of a newspaper column on the subject.

It is not just that the reality of abortion is a little too strong for some stomachs. Even less emotionally taxing issues like adoption reflect a very similar vision of the world in which babies are to be dealt with according to ideology and expediency.

Perhaps the most gross form of this vision is shown in laws and policies against trans-racial adoption. These laws and policies not only keep many minority children needlessly languishing in orphanages or in a series of transient foster homes when there are couples ready to adopt them; courts and bureaucracies actually drag these children in tears from the only homes they have ever known, when those homes are with non-minority families.

Shattering the lives of little 2- and 3-year-old toddlers means nothing to the social welfare bureaucracies or to the academic and media ideologues who come up with fancy theories about the need to maintain cultural identity. Sometimes there is also a parade of speculative horrors to be feared from the adoption of minority children by white couples. Yet actual studies of children adopted across racial lines fail to turn up these horrors, and these youngsters' I.Q.'s are typically higher than those of minority children raised by their own parents.

Even aside from adoptions across racial lines, there is ideological opposition to adoption, as such. A recent issue of *National Review* details media campaigns against adoption in publications ranging from the *New York Times* to *Playboy*.

To the critics, adoption is not a "solution" because it has potential problems. Children may be abused by adoptive parents, or feel second-class, or the parents may feel ambivalent, or the original mother may find herself being tracked down, decades later, by the child she put up for adoption.

Of course adoption is not a solution. Neither is anything else in life. In the real world, there are only trade-offs.

Adoption has worked out fine for all sorts of people, from President Gerald Ford to black scientist George Washington Carver, who was raised by a white couple. But of course adoptions do not always work out fine, just as things do not always turn out fine when people are raised by their biological parents.

At the heart of the opposition to adoptions, or to anything that would tend to discourage abortions, is the notion that children are expendable when they inconvenience adults. Anyone who has ever raised children knows that inconvenience is their middle name—and anyone who can look back on his own childhood honestly knows that he was at least an inconvenience, if not a real pain, to his parents on many occasions.

All that goes with the territory—that is, with a universe we did not make, having constraints we cannot escape, and offering only trade-offs, however much the intelligentsia and the politicians proclaim "solutions."

The ultra-rationalistic world of the anointed, where traditional ties and mores have been dumped into the dustbin of history, is the real goal, whether the specific issue is sex education, euthanasia or adoption.

The problem is not that some people think this way. The problem is that other people not only take them seriously, but allow them to intimidate us with their pretense of special knowledge and insight, despite a record of failed theories that goes back at least a generation, leaving a trail of social wreckage from declining educational standards to rising rates of crime, drug usage and suicide.

Worst of all, we let them appropriate the word compassion, for use as a political lever, when so many of their actions betray their utter lack of it.

# ЌᴀᴛӉᴀ ᴘᴏʟʟɪᴛᴛ

# *A Dangerous Game on Abortion*

Editor, poet, and columnist for *The Nation* magazine, Katha Pollitt is known for adeptly expressing her left-of-center viewpoint on topics such as feminism, popular culture, and politics. Her column, "Subject to Debate" appears in *The Nation* every other week and is frequently reprinted in newspapers nationwide. Her essays have been collected in *Reasonable Creatures: Essays on Women and Feminism* (1994). In "A Dangerous Game on Abortion," Pollitt argues that the common ground that many see between the pro-life and pro-choice camps may not be as large as it seems.

CAN THERE BE A TRUCE IN THE ABORTION WARS? A LOT OF PEOPLE would like to think so. Bob Dole hopes that adding a rider on tolerance will take the sting out of the plank in the Republican platform that calls for a ban on all abortion. The feminist writer Naomi Wolf wants pro-choicers to acknowledge abortion as a "sin" and "moral iniquity" that is sometimes necessary, but sometimes a selfish indulgence. The Common Ground Network for Life and Choice tries to get activists on both sides to lower the decibel level, so that they can work together to lower the rate of unwanted pregnancies.

Calming the waters is a goal that plainly appeals to those who are tired of the abortion debate: Common Ground's tiny following (300 active members) received plenty of rapturous press for its conference in Madison, Wis., earlier this month.

Who can quarrel with civility? Respectful talk is always good, even if it means that pro-choicers agree to call abortion opponents by the misleading term "pro-lifers" (a Common Ground convention that I'll follow here with some misgivings). But when talking together becomes working together, the pro-choice people play a dangerous game, lending support to proposals that are both ineffectual and contrary to their own values.

Adoption is a big item on the Common Ground agenda: It should be made easier, more respectable, less racially fraught, less expensive.

Maybe so. But in its position paper on the subject, Common Ground goes so far as to suggest that states subsidize adoption with family planning funds—hardly a recipe for fewer unwanted pregnancies. Will pro-adoption campaigns result, as Hillary Rodham Clinton claimed in a letter to Common Ground, in "far fewer abortions"? Not likely.

Adoption is an enormously complicated issue all by itself. Involving the rights of at least four separate people (birth mother, birth father, baby and adoptive parent) and raising many delicate questions of class, race and religion. It may be the perfect choice for some pregnant girls and women, but it's not a one-size-fits-all solution to reducing the 1.3 million abortions in the United States each year.

When pro-choicers agree to promote adoption as "an abortion alternative," they are accepting, perhaps without realizing it, the anti-choice view: that the fetus has a right to life, that abortion is "selfish" and that girls and women should undergo pregnancy and childbirth, at whatever personal cost to provide babies for childless couples. These costs not only include the physical pain and risks of childbearing, but also the possibility of disrupted adolescence, lost schooling, social shame, family ostracism and, as women who gave up their babies in the 1950's and 1960's have testified, permanent sorrow.

Sex education is another area in which a well-intentioned search for common ground leads, in practice, to pro-life turf. In the chapter of Common Ground in Norfolk, Va., pro-choicers are working with pro-lifers to bring a program called "Better Beginnings" to the local schools. Aimed at 10- to 14-year-olds, it is essentially an advertising campaign to promote sexual abstinence.

This is a laudable goal, but do such programs lower teen-age pregnancy rates? Not according to two respected research groups, the Alan Guttmacher Institute and the Sex Information and Education Council. Their research shows that abstinence-only programs don't work. To prevent teen-age pregnancy, sex education has to include information about birth control, preferably well before students start having sex.

So why did pro-choicers, who support education about contraceptives, agree to support an abstinence-only program? Opponents of abortion rights were also against birth control. Abstinence was common ground. "At least we get a half a loaf," said Lisa Persikoff, executive director of Planned Parenthood of Southeastern Virginia.

This may look like coalition politics, but it isn't a coalition when one side simply adopts the other's agenda. Abstinence-based sex education isn't half of an abstinence- and contraception-based sex education. It's a wholly different program, one that denies young people life-saving information in the false belief that knowledge of birth control encourages sex.

Adoption? Abstinence? Abortion as moral iniquity? Those who support a woman's right to choose have nothing to gain by taking on either the programs or the language of their opponents. It's the pro-lifers who stand to gain. They give up nothing, while looking ever so reasonable and flexible, and their marginal ideas become accepted as mainstream solutions.

What would a real coalition of pro-life and pro-choice activists look like? Opponents of legal abortion would call for large increases in public financing for contraception and frank, age-appropriate sex education. People who support a woman's right to an abortion would fight so that no woman felt forced to abort a wanted pregnancy because of poverty or lack of support.

Actually, though, pro-choicers are already active on behalf of poor women. But how many pro-lifers are campaigning for more birth control and sex education? The truth is, the Common Ground model mistakes the real relation between the pro-life and pro-choice camps. Only pro-lifers want to impose their views on others. Pro-choicers wish only to let each woman choose for herself. For pro-lifers, a woman who carries to term is always a success story, because whatever the cost to her, a life has been saved. For pro-choicers, what's important is that women decide for themselves what's best.

Logically, then, the pro-life philosophy forbids a pro-choice position. The pro-choice philosophy includes pro-life views. Thus, pro-choicers already occupy the common ground, along with the majority of Americans, who, as Bob Dole has been forced to recognize, do not want the pro-life vision to be the law of the land, whatever their private feelings about abortion are.

It wouldn't hurt pro-choicers to act as if they understood that.

## ROY BOWEN WARD

# Is the Fetus a Person? The Bible's View

Typically, we think of the abortion battle as a fight between the "religious" pro-life position and the "non-religious" pro-choice position. However, there are significant numbers of religious people whose opinions fall on the pro-choice side of the abortion debate. But doesn't the Bible forbid abortion? Not according to Roy Bowen Ward, a preacher and biblical scholar who argues that, according to the Bible, the fetus is *not* a person, and so abortion is not forbidden in the Bible. This essay originally appeared on the World Wide Web page of the Religious Coalition for Reproductive Choice (http://www.rcrc.org).

I GREW UP IN THE DEEP SOUTH, WHERE THE SEGREGATION OF THE races was a burning issue. Racial segregation was a political question, an economic question, and, of course, a moral question. But the questioning came to an abrupt halt for me and many others when we were taught that racial segregation was the will of God. Once the issue was formulated as a matter of God's will—with appropriate texts from the Bible (e.g., Gen. 9:25) presented as proof—there were no longer any gray areas. Segregation became merely a matter of doing God's will, no matter what the consequences might be for black people. As Peter and the apostles once said, "We must obey God rather than men" (Acts 5:29). Of course, we have come to realize that the effort to support racial segregation with quotations from the Bible was a clear misuse of the Bible.

Today the abortion debate has reached a similar point; in the media, as well as in countless churches, American people are being told that the Bible condemns abortion. This invocation of the Bible tends to simplify, for many people, what is actually a very complex issue. It becomes a matter of doing God's will, no matter what the consequences might be for women, for their potential offspring, or for society.

## The Bible Is Silent on Abortion

Before embarking on a crusade under the banner of God's will according to the Bible, one ought to know just what the Bible does and does not say about God's will in the matter. One thing the Bible does not say is "Thou shalt not abort."

Most of the antiabortion books that I can find that were written before the 1973 Supreme Court decision in *Roe v. Wade* were written by Roman Catholics, and they readily agreed that the Bible was essentially silent on the subject. John T. Noonan, an antiabortion Roman Catholic scholar writing in 1970, simply admits, "The Old Testament has nothing to say on abortion."[1] The Jesuit scholar John Connery, in his history of the abortion issue, writes: "If anyone expects to find an explicit condemnation of abortion in the New Testament, he will be disappointed—The silence of the New Testament regarding abortion surpasses even that of the Old Testament."[2] When I went to Bible dictionaries and encyclopedias, including those I used when I was a student at Abilene Christian College,[3] I could find no entries under "abortion," probably because Noonan and Connery were correct: The Bible does not deal with the subject of abortion.

The silence of the Bible is curious, and one should be careful about arguing from silence. Gleason L. Archer tries to explain this silence by claiming that abortion was not even practiced in the ancient world.[4] But Archer is clearly wrong. Israel's neighbors the ancient Assyrians had a law, dating at least from the 12th century B.C., concerning a woman's self-induced abortion.[5] And by the time of the New Testament, techniques for inducing abortion were sophisticated and widely used, as we may learn from Greek and Roman medical writers.[6] The reason neither Old nor New Testament authors condemned abortion was not that abortion had not been invented yet.

Meredith Kline attempts to explain the silence in this way: "The most significant abortion legislation in the biblical law is that there is none. It was so unthinkable that an Israelite woman should desire an abortion that there was no need to mention this offense in the criminal code."[7] But Kline's conclusion is not persuasive: it was not uncommon for authors of both Testaments to condemn the practices of their neighbors, such as idol worship, sacred prostitution, and the like, yet they did not choose to condemn abortion.

But, someone might say, both Testaments contain the commandment "Thou shalt not kill" (e.g., Exod. 20:13, Matt. 5:21). No direct object is supplied for the verb "to kill"; does the prohibition also cover feticide?

Here we must be careful to look at the commandment in context. Certainly the commandment does not indiscriminately refer to killing anything alive–the Israelites were expected to kill animals, both to eat and to sacrifice. They were also expected to kill Philistines and other enemies in war. And whoever killed his father or mother was to be killed (Exod. 21:17). The command not to kill was certainly not "pro-life" in an unqualified way.

Thoughtful people have drawn a distinction between that which is living (i.e. biological life)–which includes plants, animals, tissues, organs, and even sperm–and that which might become a person.[8] (The "pro-life" movement should really be called the "pro-person" movement.) But according to the Bible, what is a person? Is the fetus a person?

## Concept of Nephesh

The initial problem with answering this question according to the Bible is that *person* is an English word derived from the Latin *persona*, but the books of the Christian Bible were written in Hebrew, Aramaic, and Greek. Here we have to be careful not to impose our 20th-century notions of "person" on the ancient Hebrew, Aramaic, and Greek texts, for that would be to beg the question. What we need to do in a more general way is to ask about the anthropology of the Bible. How is a human being defined?

Long before the abortion debate, scholars of the Old Testament agreed that the most important Hebrew word describing a human being was *nephesh*, a word that occurs 755 times in the Hebrew Bible. As E. Jacob puts it, *nephesh* is "the usual term for man's total nature," and the defining characteristic of a *nephesh* is breath.[9] In fact, Jacob argues that the etymology of *nephesh* goes back to a root that means "to breathe."[10]

The classic text is Gen. 2:7: "Then Yahweh God formed the earth creature of dust from the earth, and breathed into its nostrils the breath of life; and the earth creature became a living *nephesh*."[11] The language suggests a potter molding a vessel of clay–the form is made from the dust of the earth. But not until the form breathes is it a *nephesh*–as Hans Walter Wolff puts it, "a living being, a living person, a living individual."[12]

Another text that makes clear the relationship between *nephesh* and breathing is the story of the son of the widow from Zarephath (1 Kings 17:17-24). The son became ill, and we are told that "there was not breath in him" (v. 17). The widow accused Elijah of bringing about her son's death (v. 18), whereupon Elijah prayed to Yahweh God, asking why He had slain her son (v. 20). Elijah beseeched, "Let this child's *nephesh* return to his inward parts" (v. 21). The prayer was answered; "the *nephesh* of the child returned to his inward parts and he lived" (v. 22). As Wolff comments, "Living creatures are in this way exactly defined in Hebrew as creatures that breathe."[13]

It is this interconnection between *nephesh* as the living person and as breath that informs the miraculous vision of Ezekiel—the vision of the dry bones: "And as I looked, there were sinews on them, and flesh had come upon them, and skin had covered them; but there was no breath in them" (Ezek. 37:8). Ezekiel calls for breath to come, and we are told that "the breath came into them and they lived . . . "(Ezek. 37: 10).

## The Fetus Is Not a Person

If *nephesh* is the fundamental term for the living being, the "person," in Hebrew thought, and if *nephesh* is basically understood as a creature that breathes, then a fetus is not a *nephesh*, not a living person.

This conclusion seems consistent with the one law in the Bible that refers to miscarriage. When men were fighting and they caused a pregnant woman to miscarry, the penalty was a fine; if the mother was harmed, it was "life for life" (Exod. 21:22-23). It is generally accepted that this passage implies that the fetus did not have the same status as the mother in ancient Hebrew law.

Since the 1973 Supreme Court *Roe v. Wade* decision, conservative Protestant scholars, attempting to support an antiabortion position, have called into question the long-standing interpretation that Exod. 21:22-23 refers to miscarriage. They argue that it refers instead to premature birth. According to this line of interpretation, if both the premature child and the mother are unharmed, a fine is levied, but if either the premature child or the mother is harmed, the penalty is life for life, eye for eye, and so forth.

But this new interpretation is not plausible. The law in Exod. 21:22-23 is worded quite similarly to that in the Code of Hammurabi, 209 and 210:

> If a seignior struck a[nother] seignior's daughter and has caused her to have a miscarriage [literally, caused her to drop that of her womb], he shall pay ten shekels of silver for her fetus. If that woman had died, they shall put his daughter to death.[14]

A similar parallel is found in the Hittite Laws, 1.17: "If anyone causes a free woman to miscarry [literally, drives out the embryo]—if (it is) the 10th month, he shall give 10 shekels of silver, if (it is) the 5th month, he shall give 5 shekels of silver and pledge his estate as security."[15]

E. A. Speiser, writing in 1963—long before the abortion issue clouded the scene—commented on the Hittite phrase, "drives out . . . the embryo," and noted that the force of the Hebrew verb used in Exod. 21:22 is practically the same.[16] In other words, when scholars had no axes to grind in the abortion debate, they readily understood Exod. 21:22-23 to refer to miscarriage, paralleling other ancient Near Eastern laws.[17]

The distinction made in Jewish circles between the breathing *nephesh* and the fetus was maintained through the time that the books of the New Testament were being written and collected, as is illustrated by the rule preserved in the Mishnah concerning therapeutic abortion:

> If a woman was in hard travail, the child must be cut up while it is in the womb and brought out member by member, since the life of the mother has priority over the life of the child; but if the greater part of it [the child] was already born, it [the child] may not be touched, since the claim of one life cannot override the claim of another life.[18]

The concept of the person embodied in the word *nephesh* continued to be held, not only by the Jews, but also by those Jews we call Christians, such as the Apostle Paul. The early Christian proclamation of the resurrection of the body presupposes the holistic view of a person, that is, the *nephesh* concept. For Paul, it was the breath of God that raised Jesus from the dead, and it is the breath of God that will make us alive in the resurrection to come (Rom. 8:9-11). James 2:26 puts it succinctly: "For just as the body without breath is dead, so faith without works is dead."

Conservative Protestant writers, in their attempt to find some passages in the Bible with which to argue that the fetus is a person, turn to several texts that refer to the womb, passages such as the

139th Psalm; Isaiah, Chapter 49; and Jeremiah, Chapter 1. However, these writers fail to take into account the details of these passages.

The psalmist of the 139th Psalm has been accused by his enemies (v. 19), and he closes with a plea to God to search him to see if there is any wickedness in him (vv. 23, 24). But before making that plea, the psalmist proclaims that God already knows him and his innocence (v. 1ff.), and his words even before he speaks them (v. 4); God will always be with him, even in the grave. Then he claims:

> It is you who did form my kidneys, who did
> weave me together in my mother's womb.
> My bones were not hidden from you when I was
> being made in secret, intricately wrought in the
> depths of the earth.
> Your eyes have seen my embryo.
> In your books were written, every one of them, the
> days that were formed for me, when as yet there
> were none of them.
> (vv. 13,15,16)

This passage really says no more than that God was his creator and therefore knew him before he was born, as is also the point in Isaiah 49:5. Indeed, the psalmist refers only to the embryo (or shapeless thing) that God was weaving together. The passage no more supports the notion that the fetus is a person (nephesh) than does Jer. 1:5, in which the claim is made that Yahweh knew Jeremiah before Yahweh formed him in the womb.

If one turns the argument around and says that it is wrong to abort a fetus because God created it, then one is faced with other difficulties. Should a physician not remove or transplant a kidney? Because God created plants and living creatures, does that mean we may not kill organisms in either category?

None of the passages mentioned above provide a basis for arguing that the fetus is a person (nephesh); they provide a basis only for the faith that God is creator of all and that in His sovereignty He knows people before they exist, even as He knows words before they are uttered or days before they occur.

I have tried to show that in the Bible the basic understanding of a person is that of a breathing individual. There is no living person until there is breath; when breath departs, there is only a corpse. According to this basic concept the fetus is not a person.

The commandment "Thou shalt not kill" is not an unqualified order not to kill any biological life, and there is no evidence from the Bible that terminating the biological life of the fetus was regarded as murder. He who caused a woman to miscarry was fined, but if he killed the mother, he was a murderer and his own life was forfeit (Exod. 21:22-25).

In the final analysis, the Bible is silent on the subject of abortion. As I was taught as a youth, "Speak where the Bible speaks. Be silent where the Bible is silent."

## Notes

1. John T. Noonan, "An Almost Absolute Value in History," in *The Morality of Abortion: Legal and Historical Perspectives.* John T. Noonan, ed., (Cambridge: Harvard UP, 1970), p. 6.

2. John Connery, S.J. *Abortion: The Development of the Roman Catholic Perspective* (Chicago: Loyola UP, 1977), p. 34.

3. For example, James Orr, ed., *The International Standard Bible Encyclopaedia* (Grand Rapids, Mich.: Wm. B. Eerdmans Publishing Company, 1939).

4. "Surgical abortion was hardly possible until the development of modern techniques in the operating room; in ancient times the babies were killed in the womb only when their mother was also slain." G. L. Archer, *Encyclopedia of Bible Difficulties* (Grand Rapids, Mich.: Zondervan Publishing House, 1982), p. 246.

5. "The Middle Assyrian Laws," no. 53, trans. by T. J. Meek, in *The Ancient Near Eastern Texts.* J. B. Pritchard, ed., (Princeton: Princeton UP, 1955).

6. See, among others, Soranus, *Gynecology,* trans. by O. Temkin (Baltimore: Johns Hopkins UP, 1956). A good summary of methods is supplied by M. J. Gorman, *Abortion and the Early Church* (Downers Grove, Ill.: InterVarsity Press, 1982), pp. 15-18.

7. Meredith Kline, "Lex Talionis and the Human Fetus," *Journal of the Evangelical Theological Society* 20 (1977), 193-202.

8. For example, see H. T. Englehart, Jr., "Medicine and the Concept of Person," in *Ethical Issues in Death and Dying.* T. L. Beauchamp and S. Perlin, eds., (Englewood Cliffs, N.J.: Prentice Hall Inc., 1978), p. 271ff.

9. E. Jacob, *"psuche, ktl,"* in *Theological Dictionary of the New Testament*, vol. 9. Gerhard Freiderich, ed., (Grand Rapids, Mich.: Wm. B. Eerdmans Publishing Company, ET 1974), p. 620 and throughout.

10. The basic meaning might have been "throat," but as Hans Walter Wolff notes, "This controversy is probably to no purpose, since for Semitic peoples eating, drinking, and breathing all took place in the throat; so it was the seat of the elemental vital needs in general." *Anthropology of the Old Testament* (Philadelphia: Fortress Press, ET 1974), p. 14.

11. Translation by Phyllis Trible, in *God and the Rhetoric of Sexuality* (Philadelphia: Fortress Press, 1978), p. 75.

12. Wolff, p. 22.

13. Wolff, p. 59

14. Code of Hammurabi, trans. by T. J. Meek, in *The Ancient Near Eastern Texts*. J. B. Pritchard, ed., (Princeton: Princeton UP, 1955).

15. Hittite Laws, trans. by A. Goetze, in Pritchard, ed.

16. E. A. Speiser, "The Stem PLL in Hebrew," *Journal of Biblical Literature* 82 (1963), 303.

17. Even the pro-life Gorman admits that Exod. 21: 22-23 refers to "accidental abortion"; Gorman, p. 107, note 1; cf. pp. 40-44.

18. M. Oholoth 7:6, trans. by Herbert Danby, *The Mishnah* (Oxford: Oxford UP, 1933). Cf. J. Neusner, *A History of the Mishnaic Law of Purities: Part Four: Ohalot: Commentary* (Leiden: E. J. Brill, 1974), p. 187.

*Student Essay*

# SARAH PENNINGTON DOUD

---

# Changing Kyle

This essay puts a different spin on the abortion debate presented in this chapter by describing one of the realities of raising a child. You might be a bit shocked by the blunt, to-the-point, but completely accurate description of changing a diaper in this essay, but you shouldn't be—it's something everyone needs to know how to do.

FIRST, I HAVE TO CATCH HIM. KYLE RUNS WITH THE DISCOMbobulated gait of a paraplegic wearing artificial limbs for the first time. On the Rosslyn Children's Center playground, Kyle weaves between tricycles and hides in spaces my left leg couldn't fit through, let alone my entire body. Our game of chase is played out daily; providing primary day care for Kyle means changing his dirty diapers even if I have to drag him off the Hippity Hop.

At twenty months of age, Kyle knows when he has had a bowel movement, but he is not self-conscious about the portable toilet smell that wafts around him like Pigpen's dust cloud. He would rather ride in the Cozy Coupe or go down the Little Tikes slide—anything but have his diaper changed. When I have him cornered, I scoop him up in my arms and promise I'll be as quick as I can.

Changing Kyle's diaper can be more exciting than Monday night football and a bag of chips: he is my "talker." Kyle started to speak in two-word phrases at fourteen months and adds at least three new words to his vocabulary every day. Once, upon hearing a caregiver remark that he'd been spoiled by my constant doting, Kyle responded, "I'm not spoiled. I'm *handsome.*" Kyle's delightfully healthy self-image results in part from the phenomenon Russell Baker describes: "When you're the only pea in the pod, your parents are likely to get you confused with the Hope Diamond."

Kyle's mother, Angela, a Dubliner, is genetically responsible for

Kyle's red hair and his Irish forehead (thin skin, thick skull). Angela blames her husband, Paul, a Polish-Italian, for Kyle's fiery temper. Kyle's temper tantrums on the changing table are insufferable—a caregiver's version of Chinese water torture.

The diapering procedure at a licensed day care center has more steps than the pre-flight check for the Space Shuttle. When fifteen children share the same Formica changing table, every bacterial infection within fifty feet comes looking for a host. A roll of changing paper rests at one end of the table, and pulling it down creates a protective layer between the table and Kyle's bottom. For huge bowel movements, "BM's," I wear two rubber gloves on each hand. I lay Kyle on the table, perpendicular to me, and give him something to hold in his hands. In my experience, boys *need* something to occupy their hands while I play with their favorite toy. During a blizzard last winter, I filled soda bottles with colored water, vegetable oil, and confetti, then glued the caps on. Now my staff stores the bottles in the changing room to keep their babies' idle hands busy. Toys are essential to the success of changing Kyle's diaper. He is *always* poopy.

I change Kyle's disposable diapers with wanton disregard for the environment. I use antibacterial wipes, three or four at a time, and when my gloves get dirty, I rip them off and put on new ones. Thank God for trash cans with step-on lids, and further thanks to the genius who left a window in the door to the changing room. When the smell becomes so bad I can't breathe, I put a hand on Kyle's stomach to keep him from rolling over and I lean out the window, sucking in fresh air.

Kyle's skin is so sensitive that sometimes I avoid using diaper wipes; instead, I moisten a handful of paper towels with warm water and use those to clean him. Kyle's blessed with a pharmacist father; Paul keeps his son's diaper shelf stocked with Nystatin, Desitin, A&D ointment, and sulfa oxide creams. Nystatin is our favorite—when Kyle's bottom bleeds with open sores and I still have to change him every hour, we spread the Nystatin over every inch of his rear end. Kyle understands that the "keem," as he calls it, is going to make his diaper rash "all better."

Kyle is a difficult child to change—in keeping with common European practice, Angela refused to let Kyle be circumcised, calling the surgery "barbaric" and "insensitive." I pull the foreskin back, exposing the tip of the penis, and wipe it clean. Bacteria thrive in unclean, uncircumcised penises. Regularly spraying the table with bleach solution reduces the risk of infection from Coxsackie (better known as hand, foot, and mouth disease), streptococcus, Fifth's Disease, and a host of other predatory viruses.

The rule for wiping is front to back for girls, back to front for boys. I pry open the folds of wrinkled pink skin over Kyle's testicles, his scrotum, which can trap stray flecks of excrement. I check his upper thighs, double-check his bottom, and apply diaper cream.

Putting the fresh diaper on is the easiest step: bottom up, diaper under, bottom down, the front of the diaper comes up and over his genitals and fastens to the back with adhesive tape. After changing sixty diapers a week for fourteen months, I can complete the process in less than two minutes. It's simple, if not easy. Difficult, but worth it. Like a red-haired toddler I know.

*Student Essay*

# KATHERINE CRANE

# *Handling Room 15*

Another side of the abortion debate is the issue of abortions for fetuses with brain damage or other diseases. While this essay doesn't address that issue specifically, it does offer a very realistic glimpse into the world of mentally retarded children.

"ARE YOU SURE YOU ARE INTERESTED IN THIS, KATIE?" MR. BECKER asked. "Not everyone can handle what you are going to witness this afternoon." My math teacher's tone matched his expression: precise, pointed, cold and pensive. Years of right triangles and permutations made him a calculating man, confident in his assessment of students and their potential. When he wasn't solving equations or summing up students, Mr. Becker took volunteers to the Hattie Larlham Foundation, a home for severely retarded children, a place especially significant to him. I didn't understand why he cared about HLF until I heard his daughter spent the short five years of her life there, fluttering between life and death, stricken with a rare brain-deteriorating condition. Seeing my name on the volunteer list obviously surprised him. He knew I wasn't a mathematician or a "visually minded student," and I knew I only took his class to pass it, so we were not especially close.

I grimaced. I took offense at his doubts about my ability to "handle" the children at the Hattie Larlham Foundation. My impeccable self-confidence as a "spring senior" prohibited me from envisioning myself as weak and vulnerable to a bunch of kids, no matter what their condition. I effectively "handled" the school newspaper, AP European History, a boyfriend, the college application process, my worried mother, fickle friends, and the Moore Street Mens' Shelter, so the prospect of baby-sitting a retarded child did not seem like a daunting task, much less one I would be incapable of handling.

I did not see any patients, or "special children," as they called them, when I entered the warm lobby, which smelled of the tangible "Band-Aid" stench of health care. Four of us stood there, I the only female, chatting idly until a male nurse, dressed in street clothes, welcomed us to the Foundation. He thanked us in advance for volunteering to work with a "special child" two days a week. He explained that the rest of our experience would come naturally, that there was not anything he could really instruct us to do. "Love them," he politely asked, or maybe he instructed, and he pointed at me to follow. I do not know now what I expected then to see behind Room 15, but I was fairly confident that my job would be to rock a small, sickly infant until he fell asleep.

"His name is Daniel," the nurse explained before we entered, "we don't make it practice to reveal any information about our children, but I will tell you that Daniel is an exception at HLF. He's been here the longest of anyone, including staff. He's exceeded our age limitation by two years and we're not sure if Medicare will cover him next after he turns twenty-one. He likes girls, hates his diaper, so if he tries to take it off, hold his hands. I'm going to let you go in alone."

I opened the door slowly, wishing there was an observation window like the ones in asylums so I could prepare myself for Daniel.

A glance from a window would allow me to see without detection, experience without contact. I entered. His massive body had curled itself into fetal position on a large blue mat in the center of the room, between his crib, stuffed animals and television which played a "Barney" video. His face tucked itself away from me, so I gingerly circled his body to view him face to face, half out of curiosity, half out of respect. A foul odor emanated from him, a putrid combination of teenage body odor, feces, and the palpable, decrepit smell of my great-grandmother. A puddle of mucus and phlegm had gathered under his mouth and heaving, stuffy nose, and my disgust caused me to take a jerking step backwards into a neatly sorted pile of *Curious George* books. The sudden movement woke the man, and his crusted brown eyes stared at my disbelieving face, yet his head did not move from the blue mat. His features were grossly distorted, his brown hair matted and tangled, his mouth gaping and groping for words he had never spoken.

"I'm Katie," I said stupidly, "what's your name?"

Daniel let out a sickening grunt.

Not knowing whether to run or stay, speak or remain silent, I did nothing. I tried to suppress feelings of sympathy in order to shield myself from despair, sensing, yet not knowing for sure whether pity would help or harm the situation. I crouched down to the floor, held his chaffed, cold hand which reflexively held mine and started tell him about my day; how I lost my keys that morning; how Mr. Becker's class bored me more than usual; how Jessie kissed another boy, making him the third of the week. He smiled, showing his tremendously stained, yellow, crooked teeth. Certain topics seemed funny to him, especially those which made my voice inflect and those which were appropriate to teenagers. He laughed and snorted while I spoke, still clutching my hand until I broke away during the end of the session. As I tried to disengage my hand from his, he held on tighter, and I had to use my other hand to pry his grip apart. Freed, I started to stand up when he let out a horrifying bellow and tears began streaming down his face. I ran towards the door expecting him to lash out at me physically, but all his body did was futilely attempt to swivel around to see me as I closed the door to Room 15.

Later the nurse would tell me the scientific name for Daniel's reaction, how he established some sort of bond with me they had never witnessed before in him. The nurse said he might have fallen in love on some basic, incomprehensible level, and he encouraged me to come back and see him if I wished. He congratulated me for handling the situation well, for making the effort to communicate with Daniel and effectively doing so.

"Please come back," he said, and I politely smiled, nodded my head, put on my coat, and left. Mr. Becker picked us up and asked how our experiences were; everyone told him about the sick babies they rocked to sleep. I said nothing. The next Thursday I "missed the bus." Tuesday I had "homework." The next week, the roads were "too icy." And the next week I just stayed home. Sometimes I wonder if he remembers me or if he's moved from the blue mat. And I worry.

# 7

# COMING

# OF

# AGE

# ZORA NEALE HURSTON

# *I Get Born*

Zora Neale Hurston (1901–1961) was born in Eatonville, Florida, the "first incorporated Negro town in America." Zora's early education was sporadic, but she was eventually able to finish high school and go to college. Hurston, like her native town, was uniquely independent. She studied anthropology in college, and was said to be the only woman able to measure the heads of Harlem men with a pair of calipers without getting "bawled out." Hurston's interest in anthropology adds a depth to her fiction, so that when we read we don't just read a story, we explore with her an entire culture. Like her other novels, *Their Eyes Were Watching God* and *Moses, Man of the Mountain*, "I Get Born" from *Dust Tracks on a Road* immediately engages the reader with Hurston's honesty, sense of humor, and gift for storytelling.

THIS IS ALL HEAR-SAY. MAYBE SOME OF THE DETAILS OF MY BIRTH AS told me might be a little inaccurate, but it is pretty well established that I really did get born.

The saying goes like this. My mother's time had come and my father was not there. Being a carpenter, successful enough to have other helpers on some jobs, he was away often on building business, as well as preaching. It seems that my father was away from home for months this time. I have never been told why. But I did hear that he threatened to cut his throat when he got the news. It seems that one daughter was all that he figured he could stand. My sister, Sarah, was his favorite child, but that one girl was enough. Plenty more sons, but no more girl babies to wear out shoes and bring in nothing. I don't think he ever got over the trick he felt that I played on him by getting born a girl, and while he was off from home at that. A little of my sugar used to sweeten his coffee right now. That is a Negro way of saying his patience was short with me. Let me change a few words with him—and I am of the word changing kind—and he was ready to change ends. Still and all, I looked more like him than any child in the house. Of course, by the time I got born, it was too late to make any suggestions, so the old man had to put up with me. He was nice about it in a way. He didn't tie me in a sack and drop me in the lake, as he probably felt like doing.

People were digging sweet potatoes, and then it was hog-killing time. Not at our house, but it was going on in general over the country like, being January and a bit cool. Most people were either butchering for themselves, or off helping other folks do their butchering, which was almost just as good. It is a gay time. A big pot of hasslits cooking with plenty of seasoning, lean slabs of fresh-killed pork frying for the helpers to refresh themselves after the work is done. Over and above being neighborly and giving aid, there is the food, the drinks and the fun of getting together.

So there was no grown folks close around when Mama's water broke. She sent one of the smaller children to fetch Aunt Judy, the mid-wife, but she was gone to Woodbridge, a mile and a half away, to eat at a hog-killing. The child was told to go over there and tell Aunt Judy to come. But nature, being indifferent to human arrangements, was impatient. My mother had to make it alone. She was too weak after I rushed out to do anything for herself, so she just was lying there, sick in the body, and worried in mind, wondering what would become of her, as well as me. She was so weak, she couldn't even reach down to where I was. She had one consolation. She knew I wasn't dead, because I was crying strong.

Help came from where she never would have thought to look for it. A white man of many acres and things, who knew the family well, had butchered the day before. Knowing that Papa was not at home, and that consequently there would be no fresh meat in our house, he decided to drive the five miles and bring a half of a shoat, sweet potatoes, and other garden stuff along. He was there a few minutes after I was born. Seeing the front door standing open, he came on in, and hollered, "Hello, there! Call your dogs!" That is the regular way to call in the country because nearly everybody who has anything to watch has biting dogs.

Nobody answered, but he claimed later that he heard me spreading my lungs all over Orange County, so he shoved the door open and bolted on into the house.

He followed the noise and then he saw how things were, and, being the kind of a man he was, he took out his Barlow Knife and cut the navel cord, then he did the best he could about other things. When the mid-wife, locally known as a granny, arrived about an hour later, there was a fire in the stove and plenty of hot water on. I had been sponged off in some sort of a way, and Mama was holding me in her arms.

As soon as the old woman got there, the white man unloaded what he had brought, and drove off cussing about some blankety-blank people never being where you could put your hands on them when they were needed. He got no thanks from Aunt Judy. She grumbled for years about it. She complained that the cord had not been cut just right, and the bellyband had not been put on tight enough. She was mighty scared I was going to have a weak back, and that I would have trouble holding my water until I reached puberty. I did.

The next day or so a Mrs. Neale, a friend of Mama's, came in and reminded her that she had promised to let her name the baby in case it was a girl. She had picked up a name somewhere which she thought was very pretty. Perhaps she had read it somewhere, or somebody back in those woods was smoking Turkish cigarettes. So I became Zora Neale Hurston.

There is nothing to make you like other human beings so much as doing things for them. Therefore, the man who grannied me was back next day to see how I was coming along. Maybe it was a pride in his own handiwork, and his resourcefulness in a pinch, that made him want to see it through. He remarked that I was a God-damned fine baby, fat and plenty of lung-power. As time went on, he came infrequently, but somehow kept a pinch of interest in my welfare. It seemed that I was spying noble, growing like a gourd vine, and yelling bass like a gator. He was the kind of man that had no use for puny things, so I was all to the good with him. He thought my mother was justified in keeping me.

But nine months rolled around, and I just would not get on with the walking business. I was strong, crawling well, but showed no inclination to use my feet. I might remark in passing, that I still don't like to walk. Then I was over a year old, but still I would not walk. They made allowances for my weight, but yet, that was no real reason for my not trying.

They tell me that an old sow-hog taught me how to walk. That is, she didn't instruct me in detail, but she convinced me that I really ought to try. It was like this. My mother was going to have collard greens for dinner, so she took the dishpan and went down to the spring to wash the greens. She left me sitting on the floor, and gave me a hunk of cornbread to keep me quiet. Everything was going along all right, until the sow with her litter of pigs in convoy came abreast of the door. She must have smelled the cornbread I was messing with and scattering crumbs about the floor. So, she came right on in, and began to nuzzle around.

My mother heard my screams and came running. Her heart must have stood still when she saw the sow in there, because hogs have been known to eat human flesh.

But I was not taking this thing sitting down. I had been placed by a chair, and when my mother got inside the door, I had pulled myself up by that chair and was getting around it right smart.

As for the sow, poor misunderstood lady, she had no interest in me except my bread. I lost that in scrambling to my feet and she was eating it. She had much less intention of eating Mama's baby, than Mama had of eating hers. With no more suggestions from the sow or anybody else, it seems that I just took to walking and kept the thing a-going. The strangest thing about it was that once I found the use of my feet, they took to wandering. I always wanted to go. I would wander off in the woods all alone, following some inside urge to go places. This alarmed my mother a great deal. She used to say that she believed a woman who was an enemy of hers had sprinkled "travel dust" around the doorstep the day I was born. That was the only explanation she could find. I don't know why it never occurred to her to connect my tendency with my father, who didn't have a thing on his mind but this town and the next one. That should have given her a sort of hint. Some children are just bound to take after their fathers in spite of women's prayers.

## EDITH WHARTON

# The Valley of Childish Things

Edith Wharton (1862–1937) began her life as the daughter of wealthy New York socialites, who expected her to become one herself. She performed as required for a time, but became bored with social obligations. Around the turn of the century, she disappointed her family by becoming a writer. Her first novel, *The House of Mirth* (1905), established her as one of America's finest writers. She went on to write a succession of novels, essays, and short stories. Several of her novels, including *Ethan Frome* and *The Age of Innocence,* have been made into successful films.

ONCE UPON A TIME A NUMBER OF CHILDREN LIVED TOGETHER IN THE Valley of Childish Things, playing all manner of delightful games, and studying the same lesson books. But one day a little girl, one of their number, decided that it was time to see something of the world about which the lesson books had taught her; and as none of the other children cared to leave their games, she set out alone to climb the pass which led out of the valley.

It was a hard climb, but at length she reached a cold, bleak table-land beyond the mountains. Here she saw cities and men, and learned many useful arts, and in so doing grew to be a woman. But the tableland was bleak and cold, and when she had served her apprenticeship she decided to return to her old companions in the Valley of Childish Things, and work with them instead of with strangers.

It was a weary way back, and her feet were bruised by the stones, and her face was beaten by the weather; but halfway down the pass she met a man, who kindly helped her over the roughest places. Like herself, he was lame and weather-beaten; but as soon as he spoke she recognized him as one of her old playmates. He too had been out in the world, and was going back to the valley; and on the way they talked together of the work they meant to do there. He had been a dull boy, and she had never taken much notice of him; but as she listened to his plans for building bridges and draining swamps and cutting roads through the jungle, she thought to herself, "Since he has grown into such a fine fellow, what splendid men and women my other playmates must have become!"

But what was her surprise to find, on reaching the valley, that her former companions, instead of growing into men and women, had all remained little children. Most of them were playing the same old games, and the few who affected to be working were engaged in such strenuous occupations as building mudpies and sailing paper boats in basins. As for the lad who had been the favorite companion of her studies, he was playing marbles with all the youngest boys in the valley.

At first the children seemed glad to have her back, but soon she saw that her presence interfered with their games; and when she tried to tell them of the great things that were being done on the tableland beyond the mountains, they picked up their toys and went farther down the valley to play.

Then she turned to her fellow traveler, who was the only grown man in the valley; but he was on his knees before a dear little girl with blue eyes and a coral necklace, for whom he was making a garden out of cockleshells and bits of glass and broken flowers stuck in sand.

The little girl was clapping her hands and crowing (she was too young to speak articulately); and when she who had grown to be a woman laid her hand on the man's shoulder, and asked him if he did not want to set to work with her building bridges, draining swamps, and cutting roads through the jungle, he replied that at that particular moment he was too busy.

And as she turned away, he added in the kindest possible way, "Really, my dear, you ought to have taken better care of your complexion."

# ANNIE DILLARD

# from *An American Childhood*

Annie Dillard (b. 1945) is probably best known for writing that grapples with her relationshp with God and the natural world in such books as *Holy the Firm* and *Pilgrim at Tinker Creek,* which won a Pulitzer Prize in 1975. Although written with the same intense emotion, her book *An American Childhood* takes a different direction from her earlier works, drawing on her memories of growing up in a middle-class neighborhood in Pittsburgh, Pennsylvania. In this selection, Dillard describes one of the adventures of her childhood—writing from a child's perspective, with a little adult wisdom seeping through.

SOME BOYS TAUGHT ME TO PLAY FOOTBALL. THIS WAS FINE SPORT. You thought up a new strategy for every play and whispered it to the others. You went out for a pass, fooling everyone. Best, you got to throw yourself mightily at someone's running legs. Either you brought him down or you hit the ground flat out on your chin, with your arms empty before you. It was all or nothing. If you hesitated in fear, you would miss and get hurt: you would take a hard fall while the kid got away, or you would get kicked in the face while the kid got away. But if you flung yourself wholeheartedly at the back of his knees—if you gathered and joined body and soul and pointed them diving fearlessly—then you likely wouldn't get hurt, and you'd stop the ball. Your fate, and your team's score, depended on your concentration and courage. Nothing girls did could compare with it. Boys welcomed me at baseball, too, for I had, through enthusiastic practice, what was weirdly known as a boy's arm. In winter, in the snow, there was neither baseball nor football, so the boys and I threw snowballs at passing cars. I got in trouble throwing snowballs, and have seldom been happier since.

On one weekday morning after Christmas, six inches of new snow had just fallen. We were standing up to our boot tops in snow on a front yard on trafficked Reynolds Street, waiting for cars. The cars traveled Reynolds Street slowly and evenly; they were targets all but wrapped in red ribbons, cream puffs. We couldn't miss. I was seven; the boys were eight, nine, and ten. The oldest two Fahey boys were there—Mikey and Peter—polite blond boys who lived near me on Lloyd Street, and who already had four brothers and sisters. My parents approved of Mikey and Peter Fahey. Chickie McBride was there, a tough kid, and Billy Paul and Mackie Kean too, from across Reynolds, where the boys grew up dark and furious, grew up skinny, knowing, and skilled. We had all drifted from our houses that morning looking for action, and had found it here on Reynolds Street.

It was cloudy but cold. The cars' tires laid behind them on the snowy street a complex trail of beige chunks like crenellated castle walls. I had stepped on some earlier; they squeaked. We could have wished for more traffic. When a car came, we all popped it one. In the intervals between cars we reverted to the natural solitude of children.

I started making an iceball—a perfect iceball, from perfectly white snow, perfectly spherical, and squeezed perfectly translucent so no snow remained all the way through. (The Fahey boys and I considered it unfair actually to throw an iceball at somebody, but it had been known to happen.) I had just embarked on the iceball project when we heard tire chains come clanking from afar. A black Buick was moving toward us down the street. We all spread out, banged together some regular snowballs, took aim, and, when the Buick drew nigh, fired.

A soft snowball hit the driver's windshield right before the driver's face. It made a smashed star with a hump in the middle.

Often, of course, we hit our target, but this time, the only time in all of life, the car pulled over and stopped. Its wide black door opened; a man got out of it, running. He didn't even close the car door.

He ran after us, and we ran away from him, up the snowy Reynolds sidewalk. At the corner, I looked back; incredibly, he was still after us. He was in city clothes: a suit and tie, street shoes. Any normal adult would have quit, having sprung us into flight and made his point. This man was gaining on us. He was a thin man, all action. All of a sudden, we were running for our lives.

Wordless, we split up. We were on our turf; we could lose ourselves in the neighborhood backyards, everyone for himself. I paused and considered. Everyone had vanished except Mikey Fahey, who was just rounding the corner of a yellow brick house.

Poor Mikey, I trailed him. The driver of the Buick sensibly picked the two of us to follow. The man apparently had all day. He chased Mikey and me around the yellow house and up a backyard path we knew by heart: under a low tree, up a bank, through a hedge, down some snowy steps, and across the grocery store's delivery driveway. We smashed through a gap in another hedge, entered a scruffy backyard and ran around its back porch and tight between houses to Edgerton Avenue; we ran across Edgerton to an alley and up our own sliding woodpile to the Halls' front yard; he kept coming. We ran up Lloyd Street and wound through mazy backyards toward the steep hilltop at Willard and Lang.

He chased us silently, block after block. He chased us silently over picket fences, through thorny hedges, between houses, around garbage cans, and across streets. Every time I glanced back, choking for breath, I expected he would have quit. He must have been as breathless as we were. His jacket strained over his body. It was an immense discovery, pounding into my hot head with every sliding, joyous step, that this ordinary adult evidently knew what I thought only children who trained at football knew: that you have to fling yourself at what you're doing, you have to point yourself, forget yourself, aim, dive.

Mikey and I had nowhere to go, in our own neighborhood or out of it, but away from this man who was chasing us. He impelled us forward; we compelled him to follow our route. The air was cold; every breath tore my throat. We kept running, block after block; we kept improvising, backyard after backyard, running a frantic course and choosing it simultaneously, failing always to find small places or hard places to slow him down, and discovering always, exhilarated, dismayed, that only bare speed could save us—for he would never give up, this man—and we were losing speed. He chased us through the backyard labyrinths of ten blocks before he caught us by our jackets. He caught us and we all stopped.

We three stood staggering, half blinded, coughing, in an obscure hilltop backyard: a man in his twenties, a boy, a girl. He had released our jackets, our pursuer, our captor, our hero: he knew we weren't going anywhere. We all played by the rules. Mikey and I unzipped our jackets. I pulled off my sopping mittens. Our tracks multiplied in the backyard's new snow. We had been breaking new snow all morning. We didn't look at each other. I was cherishing my excitement. The man's lower pants legs were wet; his cuffs were full of snow, and there was a prow of snow beneath them on his shoes and socks. Some trees bordered the little flat backyard, some messy winter trees. There was no one around: a clearing in a grove, and we the only players.

It was a long time before he could speak. I had some difficulty at first recalling why we were there. My lips felt swollen; I couldn't see out of the sides of my eyes; I kept coughing.

"You stupid kids," he began perfunctorily.

We listened perfunctorily indeed, if we listened at all, for the chewing out was redundant, a mere formality, and beside the point. The point was that he had chased us passionately without giving up, and so he had caught us. Now he came down to earth. I wanted the glory to last forever.

But how could the glory have lasted forever? We could have run through every backyard in North America until we got to Panama. But when he trapped us at the lip of the Panama Canal, what precisely could he have done to prolong the drama of the chase and cap its glory? I brooded about this for the next few years. He could only have fried Mikey Fahey and me in boiling oil, say, or dismembered us piecemeal, or staked us to anthills. None of which I really wanted, and none of which any adult was likely to do, even in the spirit of fun. He could only chew us out there in the Panamanian jungle, after months or years of exalting pursuit. He could only begin, "You stupid kids," and continue in his ordinary Pittsburgh accent with his normal righteous anger and the usual common sense.

If in that snowy backyard the driver of the black Buick had cut off our heads, Mikey's and mine, I would have died happy, for nothing has required so much of me since as being chased all over Pittsburgh in the middle of winter—running terrified, exhausted—by this sainted, skinny, furious redheaded man who wished to have a word with us. I don't know how he found his way back to his car.

*Student Essay*

# ASHLEY WAGNER

# *The Third Row*

In this essay, Ashley Wagner gives a different perspective on childhood from that of Dillard. Where Dillard speaks of familiarity, Wagner's childhood included an encounter with the unfamiliar. In this essay, Wagner describes being forced to adapt to another country's language and culture—and succeeding.

THE FIRST DAY OF FOURTH GRADE. NO BIG DEAL, YOU'RE THINKING, every nine-year-old does it: a little math, a little reading, maybe even some social studies or art to add color. No, this was different: this year I would sit in a desk on the *other* side of the Atlantic braving a new school as well as a new language.

I found out in the end of the third grade that my father had been offered a promotion. Great, I thought, except that this job would require that the family move. No problem, I rationalized, we've moved before and it wasn't that bad. Where to? France . . . France can you believe it? I'm moving to that country where all they do is eat bread and cheese, drink wine, wear berets, and do romantic stuff. Well, I was underage for both wine and romance, bread and cheese didn't sound like much of a meal, and, to be perfectly honest, berets never really fit my style.

Despite these initial reservations, I began to look forward to "the big move." My parents sent my brother and me to a tutor who taught us some basics in French to prepare us for our arrival. When our plane touched down in Paris, I could count up to six in French and my new vocabulary consisted of the words: "chat," "balon," "avion," "aeroport," "s'il vous plaît," "merci," "de rien," and, although I'm not sure if I even knew what it meant, I could say "Polly voo fron say?" I felt confident with my grasp on the new language and my ability to learn more, but nothing could have prepared me for what I would encounter when I entered the fourth grade that fall.

I would have been terrified to walk into any classroom in a new school, but I was terrified even more when I saw the fear-inflicting dictator of the fourth grade. In the past, I had always been blessed with the epitome of elementary teachers: women who liked apples, who wore bows and conservative dresses, who had pleasant faces, and who were kind, patient, good-natured. When I walked through the doors of my new classroom, I found Madame Mirlicourtois, with a horrific mane of hair dyed blonde and sprayed until it stood on end, a leather jacket, skin-tight pants, hot red lipstick, and her blouse unbuttoned below the point of decency, but not low enough to get herself kicked out of the school system. (Remember this is France we're talking about, where topless beaches are the norm. I suppose a little cleavage shouldn't cause too much uproar, but it sure shocked me!) This woman had less patience than a woman in labor and couldn't feign benevolence no matter how hard she might try. I soon discovered that she could scream as loud as I wanted to the moment I stepped into that room.

Alienated and afraid, I took a seat and listened to what sounded like the unintelligible screeching of an enraged vulture. Then, miraculously, the principal whisked me away to a French-as-a-Second-Language class. Here I met Monsieur Galley. As far as I could tell, this man had never brushed his teeth, or even experimented with the miraculous power of deodorant. He welcomed the class in broken English and we began our studies. Without much delay, I realized that, along with personal hygiene, Monsieur Galley lacked a certain amount of intelligence as he took two weeks to teach material that should have taken only two days to cover. Resenting his teaching as an insult to my academic potential, I was almost happy to return to the regular class.

When I did return, the class was seated neatly in three distinct rows. Madame Mirlicourtois had arranged the seating assignments according to scholastic aptitude. Much to my surprise, Madame led me to a seat in the last desk of the third row. Had she not received my records that showed how I had previously excelled in school? There must be some mistake; I panicked. No mistake. According to Madame Mirlicourtois, I was incapable of performing at the same level as the natives. Ashamed and humiliated, I sunk into my chair barely able to hold back the tears.

During the next few months, I alternated between the two classes, reading and writing with Monsieur Galley, and math, poetry, and art with Madame Mirlicourtois. In the regular class seated in the third row, I watched as Madame Mirlicourtois praised students from the first row and ridiculed and abused those of us in the third. I once witnessed as Madame in fit of fury picked up my deskmate by the ear and hauled her up to the front of the class screaming because she had made a mistake copying the notes from the board. This incident made me extremely uneasy, partly because I really had to go to the bathroom but was too afraid of her wrath and the humiliation I would face if I asked in imperfect French, but also because I knew that it could have been me. Most of all, I just wanted out of that row.

In Monsieur Galley's class, I was becoming more and more exasperated. I knew I would never make it to the first row at the rate he was teaching. Determined to do what ever it took, I made a plan to get out of that row of shame and degradation. I got a tutor outside of class, worked harder than I thought possible for a nine-year-old, tested out of the French-as-a-Second-Language class, and soon enough my improvement caught the eye of that evil woman who taught the fourth grade. Just before Christmas break, I left my seat in the third row, bypassed the second, and landed the last available seat in the first row. There I sat and smiled. The world was at my feet.

# RICHARD WRIGHT

# The Library Card

Richard Wright (1908–1960) started his life on a plantation in Mississippi. He lived in the South as a youth and was a voracious reader. The books he read—by authors like Stephen Crane, H. L. Mencken, and Sinclair Lewis—made a strong impression on the young Wright. His formal schooling finished by age fifteen, Wright worked his way through menial jobs, moving to Chicago in the late 1920s. He continued to read, and in 1932 became a member of the Communist party. His first success as a writer was in left-wing publications like *New Masses* and *Left Front.* In 1938 he published his first book, *Uncle Tom's Children,* which was well received. From that point, Wright was able to support himself through his writing, publishing the dozens of essays, short stories, and books, including *Native Son, Black Boy,* and *The Outsider,* that made him one of our nation's greatest writers. In this selection, from his autobiography, *Black Boy,* Wright becomes transformed through reading H. L. Mencken.

ONE MORNING I ARRIVED EARLY AT WORK AND WENT INTO THE BANK lobby where the Negro porter was mopping. I stood at a counter and picked up the Memphis *Commercial Appeal* and began my free reading of the press. I came finally to the editorial page and saw an article dealing with one H. L. Mencken. I knew by hearsay that he was the editor of the *American Mercury,* but aside from that I knew nothing about him. The article was a furious denunciation of Mencken, concluding with one, hot, short sentence: Mencken is a fool.

I wondered what on earth this Mencken had done to call down upon him the scorn of the South. The only people I had ever heard denounced in the South were Negroes, and this man was not a Negro. Then what ideas did Mencken hold that made a newspaper like the *Commercial Appeal* castigate him publicly? Undoubtedly he must be advocating ideas that the South did not like. Were there, then, people other than Negroes who criticized the South? I knew that during the Civil War the South had hated northern whites, but I had not encountered such hate during my life. Knowing no more of Mencken than I did at that moment, I felt a vague sympathy for him. Had not the South, which had assigned me the role of a non-man, cast at him its hardest words?

Now, how could I find out about this Mencken? There was a huge library near the riverfront, but I knew that Negroes were not allowed to patronize its shelves any more than they were the parks and playgrounds of the city. I had gone into the library several times to get books for the white men on the job. Which of them would now help me to get books? And how could I read them without causing concern to the white men with whom I worked? I had so far been successful in hiding my thoughts and feelings from them, but I knew that I would create hostility if I went about the business of reading in a clumsy way.

I weighed the personalities of the men on the job. There was Don, a Jew; but I distrusted him. His position was not much better than mine and I knew that he was uneasy and insecure; he had always treated me in an offhand, bantering way that barely concealed his contempt. I was afraid to ask him to help me get books; his frantic desire to demonstrate a racial solidarity with the whites against Negroes might make him betray me.

Then how about the boss? No, he was a Baptist and I had the suspicion that he would not be quite able to comprehend why a black boy would want to read Mencken. There were other white men on the job whose attitudes showed clearly that they were Kluxers or sympathizers, and they were out of the question.

There remained only one man whose attitude did not fit into an anti-Negro category, for I had heard the white men refer to him as a "Pope lover." He was an Irish Catholic and was hated by the white Southerners. I knew that he read books, because I had got him volumes from the library several times. Since he, too, was an object of hatred, I felt that he might refuse me but would hardly betray me. I hesitated, weighing and balancing the imponderable realities.

One morning I paused before the Catholic fellow's desk.

"I want to ask you a favor," I whispered to him.

"What is it?"

"I want to read. I can't get books from the library. I wonder if you'd let me use your card?"

He looked at me suspiciously.

"My card is full most of the time," he said.

"I see," I said and waited, posing my question silently.

"You're not trying to get me into trouble, are you, boy?" he asked, staring at me.

"Oh, no, sir."

"What book do you want?"

"A book by H. L. Mencken."

"Which one?"

"I don't know. Has he written more than one?"

"He has written several."

"I didn't know that."

"What makes you want to read Mencken?"

"Oh, I just saw his name in the newspaper," I said.

"It's good of you to want to read," he said. "But you ought to read the right things."

I said nothing. Would he want to supervise my reading?

"Let me think," he said. "I'll figure out something."

I turned from him and he called me back. He stared at me quizzically.

"Richard, don't mention this to the other white men," he said.

"I understand," I said. "I won't say a word."

A few days later he called me to him.

"I've got a card in my wife's name," he said. "Here's mine."

"Thank you, sir."

"Do you think you can manage it?"

"I'll manage fine," I said.

"If they suspect you, you'll get in trouble," he said.

"I'll write the same kind of notes to the library that you wrote when you sent me for books," I told him. "I'll sign your name."

He laughed.

"Go ahead. Let me see what you get," he said.

That afternoon I addressed myself to forging a note. Now, what were the names of books written by H. L. Mencken? I did not know any of them. I finally wrote what I thought would be a foolproof note: *Dear Madam: Will you please let this nigger boy*—I used the word "nigger" to make the librarian feel that I could not possibly be the author of the note—*have some books by H. L. Mencken?*—I forged the white man's name.

I entered the library as I had always done when on errands for whites, but I felt that I would somehow slip up and betray myself. I doffed my hat, stood a respectful distance from the desk, looked as unbookish as possible, and waited for the white patrons to be taken care of. When the desk was clear of people, I still waited. The white librarian looked at me.

"What do you want, boy?"

As though I did not possess the power of speech, I stepped forward and simply handed her the forged note, not parting my lips.

"What books by Mencken does he want?" she asked.

"I don't know, ma'am," I said, avoiding her eyes.

"Who gave you this card?"

"Mr. Falk," I said.

"Where is he?"

"He's at work, at the M—— Optical Company," I said. "I've been in here for him before."

"I remember," the woman said. "But he never wrote notes like this."

Oh, God, she's suspicious. Perhaps she would not let me have the books? If she had turned her back at that moment, I would have ducked out the door and never gone back. Then I thought of a bold idea.

"You can call him up, ma'am," I said, my heart pounding.

"You're not using these books, are you?" she asked pointedly.

"Oh, no, ma'am. I can't read."

"I don't know what he wants by Mencken," she said under her breath.

I knew now that I had won; she was thinking of other things and the race question had gone out of her mind. She went to the shelves. Once or twice she looked over her shoulder at me, as though she was still doubtful. Finally she came forward with two books in her hand.

"I'm sending him two books," she said. "But tell Mr. Falk to come in next time, or send me the names of the books he wants. I don't know what he wants to read."

I said nothing. She stamped the card and handed me the books. Not daring to glance at them, I went out of the library, fearing that the woman would call me back for further questioning. A block away from the library I opened one of the books and read a title: *A Book of Prefaces*. I was nearing my nineteenth birthday and I did not know how to pronounce the word "preface." I thumbed the pages and saw strange words and strange names. I shook my head, disappointed. I looked at the other book; it was called *Prejudices*. I knew what that word meant; I had heard it all my life. And right off I was on guard against Mencken's books. Why would a man want to call a book Prejudices? The word was so stained with all my memories of racial hate that I could not conceive of anybody using it for a title. Perhaps I had made a mistake about Mencken? A man who had prejudices must be wrong.

When I showed the books to Mr. Falk, he looked at me and frowned.

"That librarian might telephone you," I warned him.

"That's all right," he said. "But when you're through reading those books, I want you to tell me what you get out of them."

That night in my rented room, while letting the hot water run over my can of pork and beans in the sink, I opened *A Book of Prefaces* and began to read. I was jarred and shocked by the style, the clear, clean sweeping sentences. Why did he write like that? And how did one write like that? I pictured the man as a raging demon, slashing with his pen, consumed with hate, denouncing everything

American, extolling everything European or German, laughing at the weaknesses of people, mocking God, authority. What was this? I stood up, trying to realize what reality lay behind the meaning of the words. . . . Yes, this man was fighting, fighting with words. He was using words as a weapon, using them as one would use a club. Could words be weapons? Well, yes, for here they were. Then, maybe, perhaps, I could use them as a weapon? No. It frightened me. I read on and what amazed me was not what he said, but how on earth anybody had the courage to say it.

Occasionally I glanced up to reassure myself that I was alone in the room. Who were these men about whom Mencken was talking so passionately? Who was Anatole France? Joseph Conrad? Sinclair Lewis, Sherwood Anderson, Dostoevski, George Moore, Gustave Flaubert, Maupassant, Tolstoy, Frank Harris, Mark Twain, Thomas Hardy, Arnold Bennett, Stephen Crane, Zola, Norris, Gorky, Bergson, Ibsen, Balzac, Bernard Shaw, Dumas, Poe, Thomas Mann, O. Henry, Dreiser, H. G. Wells, Gogol, T. S. Eliot, Gide, Baudelaire, Edgar Lee Masters, Stendhal, Turgenev, Huneker, Nietzsche, and scores of others? Were these men real? Did they exist or had they existed? And how did one pronounce their names?

I ran across many words whose meanings I did not know, and I either looked them up in a dictionary or, before I had a chance to do that, encountered the word in a context that made its meaning clear. But what strange world was this? I concluded the book with the conviction that I had somehow overlooked something terribly important in life. I had once tried to write, had once reveled in feeling, had let my crude imagination roam, but the impulse to dream had been slowly beaten out of me by experience. Now it surged up again and I hungered for books, new ways of looking and seeing. It was not a matter of believing or disbelieving what I read, but of feeling something new, of being affected by something that made the look of the world different.

As dawn broke I ate my pork and beans, feeling dopey, sleepy. I went to work, but the mood of the book would not die; it lingered, coloring everything I saw, heard, did. I now felt that I knew what the white men were feeling. Merely because I had read a book that had spoken of how they lived and thought, I identified myself with that book. I felt vaguely guilty. Would I, filled with bookish notions, act in a manner that would make the whites dislike me?

I forged more notes and my trips to the library became frequent.

Reading grew into a passion. My first serious novel was Sinclair Lewis's *Main Street*. It made me see my boss, Mr. Gerald, and identify him as an American type. I would smile when I saw him lugging his golf bags into the office. I had always felt a vast distance separating me from the boss, and now I felt closer to him, though still distant. I felt now that I knew him, that I could feel the very limits of his narrow life. And this had happened because I had read a novel about a mythical man called George F. Babbitt.

The plots and stories in the novels did not interest me so much as the point of view revealed. I gave myself over to each novel without reserve, without trying to criticize it; it was enough for me to see and feel something different. And for me, everything was something different. Reading was like a drug, a dope. The novels created moods in which I lived for days. But I could not conquer my sense of guilt, my feeling that the white men around me knew that I was changing, that I had begun to regard them differently.

Whenever I brought a book to the job, I wrapped it in newspaper—a habit that was to persist for years in other cities and under other circumstances. But some of the white men pried into my packages when I was absent and they questioned me.

"Boy, what are you reading those books for?"

"Oh, I don't know, sir."

"That's deep stuff you're reading, boy."

"I'm just killing time, sir."

"You'll addle your brains if you don't watch out."

I read Dreiser's *Jennie Gerhardt* and *Sister Carrie* and they revived in me a vivid sense of my mother's suffering; I was overwhelmed. I grew silent, wondering about the life around me. It would have been impossible for me to have told anyone what I derived from these novels, for it was nothing less than a sense of life itself. All my life had shaped me for the realism, the naturalism of the modern novel, and I could not read enough of them.

Steeped in new moods and ideas, I bought a ream of paper and tried to write; but nothing would come, or what did come was flat beyond telling. I discovered that more than desire and feeling were necessary to write and I dropped the idea. Yet I still wondered how it was possible to know people sufficiently to write about them? Could I ever learn about life and people? To me, with my vast ignorance, my Jim Crow station in life, it seemed a task impossible of achievement. I now knew what being a Negro meant. I could endure the hunger. I had learned to live with hate. But to feel that there were feelings denied me, that the very breadth of life itself was beyond my reach, that more than anything else hurt, wounded me. I had a new hunger.

In buoying me up, reading also cast me down, made me see what was possible, what I had missed. My tension returned, new, terrible, bitter, surging, almost too great to be contained. I no longer *felt* that the world about me was hostile, killing; I *knew* it. A million times I asked myself what I could do to save myself, and there were no answers. I seemed forever condemned, ringed by walls.

I did not discuss my reading with Mr. Falk, who had lent me his library card; it would have meant talking about myself and that would have been too painful. I smiled each day, fighting desperately to maintain my old behavior, to keep my disposition seemingly sunny. But some of the white men discerned that I had begun to brood.

"Wake up there, boy!" Mr. Olin said one day.

"Sir!" I answered for the lack of a better word.

"You act like you've stolen something," he said.

I laughed in the way I knew he expected me to laugh, but I resolved to be more conscious of myself, to watch my every act, to guard and hide the new knowledge that was dawning within me.

If I went north, would it be possible for me to build a new life then? But how could a man build a life upon vague, unformed yearnings? I wanted to write and I did not even know the English language. I bought English grammars and found them dull. I felt that I was getting a better sense of the language from novels than from grammars. I read hard, discarding a writer as soon as I felt that I had grasped his point of view. At night the printed page stood before my eyes in sleep.

Mrs. Moss, my landlady, asked me one Sunday morning:

"Son, what is this you keep on reading?"

"Oh, nothing. Just novels."

"What you get out of 'em?"

"I'm just killing time," I said.

"I hope you know your own mind," she said in a tone which implied that she doubted if I had a mind.

I knew of no Negroes who read the books I liked and I wondered if any Negroes ever thought of them. I knew that there were

Negro doctors, lawyers, newspapermen, but I never saw any of them. When I read a Negro newspaper I never caught the faintest echo of my preoccupation in its pages. I felt trapped and occasionally, for a few days, I would stop reading. But a vague hunger would come over me for books, books that opened up new avenues of feeling and seeing, and again I would forge another note to the white librarian. Again I would read and wonder as only the naïve and unlettered can read and wonder, feeling that I carried a secret, criminal burden about with me each day.

That winter my mother and brother came and we set up housekeeping, buying furniture on the installment plan, being cheated and yet knowing no way to avoid it. I began to eat warm food and to my surprise found that regular meals enabled me to read faster. I may have lived through many illnesses and survived them, never suspecting that I was ill. My brother obtained a job and we began to save toward the trip north, plotting our time, setting tentative dates for departure. I told none of the white men on the job that I was planning to go north; I knew that the moment they felt I was thinking of the North they would change toward me. It would have made them feel that I did not like the life I was living, and because my life was completely conditioned by what they said or did, it would have been tantamount to challenging them.

I could calculate my chances for life in the South as a Negro fairly clearly now.

I could fight the Southern whites by organizing with other Negroes, as my grandfather had done. But I knew that I could never win that way; there were many whites and there were but few blacks. They were strong and we were weak. Outright black rebellion could never win. If I fought openly I would die and I did not want to die. News of lynchings were frequent.

I could submit and live the life of a genial slave, but that was impossible. All my life had shaped me to live by my own feelings and thoughts. I could make up to Bess and marry her and inherit the house. But that, too, would be the life of a slave; if I did that, I would crush to death something within me, and I would hate myself as much as I knew the whites already hated those who had submitted. Neither could I ever willingly present myself to be kicked, as Shorty had done. I would rather have died than do that.

I could drain off my restlessness by fighting with Shorty and Harrison. I had seen many Negroes solve the problem of being black by transferring their hatred of themselves to others with a black skin and fighting them. I would have to be cold to do that, and I was not cold and I could never be.

I could, of course, forget what I had read, thrust the whites out of my mind, forget them; and find release from anxiety and longing in sex and alcohol. But the memory of how my father had conducted himself made that course repugnant. If I did not want others to violate my life, how could I voluntarily violate it myself?

I had no hope whatever of being a professional man. Not only had I been so conditioned that I did not desire it, but the fulfillment of such an ambition was beyond my capabilities. Well-to-do Negroes lived in a world that was almost as alien to me as the world inhabited by whites.

What, then, was there? I held my life in my mind, in my consciousness each day, feeling at times that I would stumble and drop it, spill it forever. My reading had created a vast sense of distance between me and the world in which I lived and tried to make a living, and that sense of distance was increasing each day. My days and nights were one long, quiet, continuously contained dream of terror, tension, and anxiety. I wondered how long I could bear it.

*Student Essay*

# AALIYAH EL-AMIN

# *Milestones*

Our societal notions of "growing up" are not fixed in stone. They change, based on time, social status, gender, and race. In this essay, Aaliyah El-Amin explores what it means to be grown up in the context of these ever-changing societal norms.

*I WALKED SLOWLY DOWN THE BRICK PATH, TRYING TO UNDERSTAND* *all that was around me. Decisions, I had so many decisions to make. Each one was so important now. It was as if someone handed me a piece of paper and said here, please write your life plans down. The day was not at all helpful as the clouds emitted a terrible roar and drops fell endlessly on the once dry path. I stared at the puddle forming at my feet, thinking.*

"I am not drunk."

The giggling girl screamed and lost her balance like a deck of cards. Her eyes were bright red and her mouth stuck in a permanent smile. I had been wandering down my hall, procrastinating as usual, when I heard her extremely loud voice.

"It is Monday night," I said, half out loud and half to myself.

She looked up at me wide-eyed and sparkling.

"Yeah, but I am twenty years old and I do not have class tomorrow."

The ten-year-old boy watched me as I walked to my car. We had been working together for months now.

"You know, I like you right," he said. I only smiled.

"No, I did not know."

It all seemed so perfectly normal then, to have the utmost respect for your elders . . . until his comments became increasingly sexual and every day he would make a sexual advance. I walked briskly, realizing that his eyes were planning something. He walked over to me, his face containing something no ten-year-old's should. Without a word he placed his fingers on my bottom and ran away giggling, whispering to those around, how he had gotten a piece of me.

The woman walked timidly into the shelter. She looked so worn out. On her shoulders she bore the burdens of not only herself but the two children she held delicately under each arm.

"Hi," she said, "I am Betty Fisher."

Beaten and abused by her husband, she had come here for refuge and love. The two eyes looked up at me. In the background the pictures they had drawn the last week caught mine.

"Abuse is not Love."

In each picture there was a picture of their families . . . or something like that.

My mother sat hunched over the kitchen table, bills spread out all over, spilling onto the floor. She sat there for two hours figuring and refiguring, *trying to work out everything she could. I picked up one of the envelopes and stared at the task that was one of her many responsibilities . . .*

All of the above scenes have a common thread. They in one way or another depict the thought of, or the occurrence of the same inevitable event . . . growing up or coming of age. Growing up is comprised of a multitude of different aspects; however, the main components seem to be the loss of innocence and the acceptance of responsibility. For some, the thought of coming of age is looking forward to the frivolous things in life such as the freedom to drink or get into clubs. Others, however, do not have the time to think about these trivial elements, because they are forced to grow up prematurely. Coming of age is not only the loss of innocence, but also the gradual process through life. All of the people above have made the transformation from the pure beings we are at the beginning of our lives to the ones that the world around us makes us become.

When I was younger I yearned to grow up. I was sick of the rules and regulations that governed me as a child. I wanted to be free to make my own decisions and handle my life. Funny how, as I looked at the future, I only saw the advantages. Only the things I would gain that I was then deprived of. You know, like when you turn eighteen and you officially become adult, you have also come of age.

I remember when most of my friends were turning eighteen. The time when society deems you capable of handling yourself and gives you most of the rights you longed for as a child. The first thing that most of them did was go out and buy a pack of cigarettes. Turning eighteen did not symbolize getting older because there was more responsibility to take on, more wisdom learned. Rather, the age symbolized the privilege of partaking in freedoms that were not always granted . . . the ability to indulge in frivolous activities that are not essential to living.

For example, the drunk girl on my hall made a conscious decision to lose her innocence. By abusing her freedom, she directly proved that she was not capable of handling that freedom. In the choosing to end her innocence, she has refused to take responsibility for herself. The notion that because she is now old enough to be considered an adult causes her to believe that she has come of age. Similar to how I believed I would also come of age when I was old enough to do whatever I wanted. It is logical to assume that she believes she has now reached the point in her life that almost every child longs for. I asked this girl what she thought gave her the right to drink on a weeknight.

"It's that time Aaliyah, I am old enough."

Some people are given more time than others, more time to be pure and simplistic. The ten-year-old and the two battered children were robbed of their innocence, forced to come of age earlier than they should have. The ten-year-old boy was only granted a mere ten years, maybe less. He had learned from those who had already come of age and they deprived him of his precious time. He hasn't the time to long for freedom to drink and smoke; he has already experienced more than he should have.

In the same respect, the two children with their battered mother had also been deprived of their right to be young. They are, however, different from the ten-year-old, in that they learned not about sex too early but of hate and hurting. Though everyone learns about hurt at a fairly little age, they had been subject to constant abuse from one who should have given them nothing but unconditional love. It was in their tired and drawn faces: they were not mature but rather broken.

Our world has managed to corrupt our youth before they even have time to decide if they want to be corrupted. Before they are even capable of understanding what it is they should filter out and what it is that they should keep. We do not give them that decision; they are forced to give up those invaluable youth years which they can never regain, unaware of what is happening to them.

I am fairly familiar with domestic abuse as both of my parents had abusive parents. My father was more directly hurt by the incidents that took place in his home. He struggled throughout life and about two years ago he decided to seek counseling. One day he came home with balloons and he was wearing a little birthday hat. I could barely suppress my giggles.

"Um, dad, what is this about?" He looked at me with eyes I had never seen before.

"We had a party tonight with the group."

I asked my mom later why my forty-two-year-old father was having a party with Barney hats during a group that was supposed to help him.

"Aaliyah," she said, "you have to understand that your father did not get to be a child. He was forced to grow up before his time and he can not move on if he does not get a chance to experience what all too many of us take for granted . . . the thing is it can never ever be the same."

How great mothers are for words of wisdom. The ten-year-old, the two kids, and my father were forced to come of age, they have not spent their young years yearning to experience all the frivolous things that I did. These children do not long to grow up because they already have.

*I stood staring at the puddle for what seemed like hours. The drops fell from my now soaked hair and joined the already fallen rain; it was if my youth was slowly draining and I was becoming a part of the real world. How silly we are when we are young . . . yearning for something that we do not completely understand. How silly we are when we grow, forcing others to join us when they are not ready. In that rain I grew anxious for the years to come, and longed for the ones that passed.*

# RUSSELL BAKER

# from Growing Up

Russell Baker is a journalist whose ideas were shaped as he grew up in a poor family during the Great Depression. He spent his adolescent years in Baltimore, and after college landed a job as a reporter for the *Baltimore Sun*. Eventually he moved to the *New York Times*, where in 1962, he began writing his famous "Observer" column, which he continues to write today. His wry, incisive commentary in "Observer" earned him the Pulitzer Prize in 1979. Shortly thereafter, he began work on his own autobiography, conducting exhaustive interviews with family members in order to create a more accurate picture of depression-era America. The result, in 1983, was the Pulitzer Prize-winning *Growing Up*, which covers Baker's childhood, followed in 1989 by *The Good Times,* which describes the early years of Baker's career in journalism. In this excerpt from *Growing Up*, he recounts the shame of "going on relief" and contrasts it with the joy of Chrismas.

[MY] PAPER ROUTE EARNED ME THREE DOLLARS A WEEK, SOMETIMES four, and my mother, in addition to her commissions on magazine sales, also had her monthly check coming from Uncle Willie, but we'd been in Baltimore a year before I knew how desperate things were for her. One Saturday morning she told me she'd need Doris and me to go with her to pick up some food. I had a small wagon she'd bought me to make it easier to move the Sunday papers, and she said I'd better bring it along. The three of us set off eastward, passing the grocery stores we usually shopped at, and kept walking until we came to Fremont Avenue, a grim street of dilapidation and poverty in the heart of the West Baltimore black belt.

"This is where we go," she said when we reached the corner of Fremont and Fayette Street. It looked like a grocery, with big plate-glass windows and people lugging out cardboard cartons and bulging bags, but it wasn't. I knew very well what it was.

"Are we going on relief?" I asked her.

"Don't ask questions about things you don't know anything about," she said. "Bring that wagon inside."

I did, and watched with a mixture of shame and greed while men filled it with food. None of it was food I liked. There were huge cans of grapefruit juice, big paper sacks of cornmeal, cellophane bags of rice and prunes. It was hard to believe all this was ours for no money at all, even though none of it was very appetizing. My wonder at this free bounty quickly changed to embarrassment as we headed home with it. Being on relief was a shameful thing. People who accepted the government's handouts were scorned by everyone I knew as idle no-accounts without enough self-respect to pay their own way in the world. I'd often heard my mother say the same thing of families in the neighborhood suspected of being on relief. These, I'd been taught to believe, were people beyond hope. Now we were as low as they were.

Pulling the wagon back toward Lombard Street, with Doris following behind to keep the edible proof of our disgrace from falling off, I knew my mother was far worse off than I'd suspected. She'd never have accepted such shame otherwise. I studied her as she walked along beside me, head high as always, not a bit bowed in disgrace, moving at her usual quick, hurry-up pace. If she'd given up on life, she didn't show it, but on the other hand she was unhappy about something. I dared to mention the dreaded words only once on that trip home.

"Are we on relief now, Mom?"

"Let me worry about that," she said.

What worried me most as we neared home was the possibility we'd be seen with the incriminating food by somebody we knew. There was no mistaking government-surplus food. The grapefruit-juice cans, the prunes and rice, the cornmeal—all were ostentatiously unlabeled, thus advertising themselves as "government handouts." Everybody in the neighborhood could read them easily enough, and our humiliation would be gossiped through every parlor by sundown. I had an inspiration.

"It's hot pulling this wagon," I said. "I'm going to take my sweater off."

It wasn't hot, it was on the cool side, but after removing the sweater I laid it across the groceries in the wagon. It wasn't a very effective cover, but my mother was suddenly affected by the heat too.

"It is warm, isn't it, Buddy?" she said. Removing her topcoat, she draped it over the groceries, providing total concealment. "You want to take your coat off, Doris?" asked my mother.

"I'm not hot, I'm chilly," Doris said.

It didn't matter. My mother's coat was enough to get us home without being exposed as three of life's failures.

From then on I assumed we were paupers. . . .

[My mother] was a magician at stretching a dollar. That December, with Christmas approaching, she was out at work and Doris was in the kitchen when I barged into her bedroom one afternoon in search of a safety pin. Since her bedroom opened onto a community hallway, she kept the door locked, but needing the pin, I took the key from its hiding place, unlocked the door, and stepped in. Standing against the wall was a big, black bicycle with balloon tires. I recognized it instantly. It was the same second-hand bike I'd been admiring in a Baltimore Street shop window. I'd even asked about the price. It was horrendous. Something like $15. Somehow my mother had scraped together enough for a down payment and meant to surprise me with the bicycle on Christmas morning.

I was overwhelmed by the discovery that she had squandered such money on me and sickened by the knowledge that, bursting into her room like this, I had robbed her of the pleasure of seeing me astonished and delighted on Christmas day. I hadn't wanted to know her lovely secret; still, stumbling upon it like this made me feel as though I'd struck a blow against her happiness. I backed out, put the key back in its hiding place, and brooded privately.

I resolved that between now and Christmas I must do nothing, absolutely nothing, to reveal the slightest hint of my terrible knowledge. I must avoid the least word, the faintest intonation, the weakest gesture that might reveal my possession of her secret. Nothing must deny her the happiness of seeing me stunned with amazement on Christmas day.

In the privacy of my bedroom I began composing and testing exclamations of delight: "Wow!" "A bike with balloon tires! I don't believe it!" "I'm the luckiest boy alive!" And so on. They all owed a lot to movies in which boys like Mickey Rooney had seen their wildest dreams come true, and I realized that, with my lack of acting talent, all of them were going to sound false at the critical moment when I wanted to cry out my love spontaneously from the heart. Maybe it would be better to say nothing but appear to be shocked into such deep pleasure that speech had escaped me. I wasn't sure, though. I'd seen speechless gratitude in the movie too, and it never really worked until the actors managed to cry a few quiet tears. I doubted I could cry on cue, so I began thinking about other expressions of speechless amazement. In front of a hand-held mirror in my bedroom I tried the whole range of expressions: mouth agape and eyes wide; hands slapped firmly against both cheeks to keep the jaw from falling off; ear-to-ear grin with all teeth fully exposed while hugging the torso with both arms. These and more I practiced for several days without acquiring confidence in any of them. I decided to wait until Christmas morning and see if anything came naturally. . . .

That Christmas morning she roused us early, "to see what Santa Claus brought," she said with just the right tone of irony to indicate we were all old enough to know who Santa Claus was. I came out of my bedroom with my presents for her and Doris, and Doris came with hers. My mother's had been placed under the tree during the night. There were a few small glittering packages, a big doll for Doris, but no bicycle. I must have looked disappointed.

"It looks like Santa Claus didn't do too well by you this year, Buddy," she said, as I opened packages. A shirt. A necktie. I said something halfhearted like, "It's the thought that counts," but what I felt was bitter disappointment. I supposed she'd found the bike intolerably expensive and sent it back.

"Wait a minute!" she cried, snapping her fingers. "There's something in my bedroom I forgot all about."

She beckoned to Doris, the two of them went out, and a moment later came back wheeling between them the big black two-wheeler with balloon tires. I didn't have to fake my delight, after all. The three of us—Doris, my mother, and I—were people bred to repress the emotional expressions of love, but I did something that startled both my mother and me. I threw my arms around her spontaneously and kissed her.

"All right now, don't carry on about it. It's only a bicycle," she said.

Still, I knew that she was as happy as I was to see her so happy.

*Student Essay*

# ΜΛRΚ GΕRRΛRD

# *Bozo Revisited*

Mark's story could be that of any child learning the truth—about Santa Claus, the Easter Bunny, or Superman. In this case, it happened to be Bozo the Clown. What makes this story so effective is precisely that it *is* something we have all experienced in one way or another. Note how Mark uses the perspective of a child to effectively build dramatic tension in the story.

I DO NOT REMEMBER VERY MUCH OF KENNY WEINGUARD. THE MEMory I have of him is hazy, and the face my mind connects with the name could very well be wrong. However, I do remember his birthdays. Mrs. Weinguard, Kenny's mother, was a fierce, talkative and overbearing woman who was sickeningly attached to her son. The birthday parties she threw for him were the envy of the entire neighborhood.

My memory of her is quite vivid. She was an artist and fancied herself to be the Auntie Mame type. She wore long colorful gowns with baubles, beads and bangles of every shape and color imaginable hanging everywhere. I was very frightened of her, thinking she was some sort of Gypsy sorceress. I always had the feeling she never liked me much. But her "events," as she liked to call them, were above reproach. For Kenny's fifth birthday she rented a movie theater and showed us "The Man Who Would Be King." For Kenny's sixth birthday she took us to a Cubs game. But on Kenny's seventh birthday she outdid even herself; she managed to get hold of a birthday party's worth of tickets to the taping of Bozo's Circus. This was quite a feat at the time. The waiting list for tickets was just under seven years. I have visions of her recovering in the maternity ward dictating a letter for tickets.

When I received my invitation, though I knew it was sent only as a favor to my mother, I was thrilled. I was an avid Bozo watcher, and I knew every aspect of the show. I thought of Bozo, Cookie, and Mr. Ned as my own personal friends. The circus acts amazed me. I was enraptured by the cartoons. The most exciting thought, however, was the chance to be chosen out of the studio audience to play the Bozo Bucket game. Even at the young age of seven I was a television addict. My sister and I spent endless hours pretending to do our own television shows. The thought of being a TV star, even for just a moment, fulfilled my every fantasy.

After what seemed to be years of waiting, the big day finally arrived. I bounded out of bed that morning and rushed to my mother. I was astounded to find her still in bed sleeping. I rushed and woke her up, imploring her to wake up and get me ready. She informed me, in that "I wish I never had a child" voice that parents take in the early hours of the morning, that it was six thirty, and as the show was not until two in the afternoon, I should leave her alone and find something else to occupy my time. I was heartbroken at this rebuke. How could my mother be so unconcerned on this, the most important day of my life? After what seemed to be another decade, my mother took my best clothes and got me dressed. She drove me over to the Weinguard's house and dropped me off.

As I walked to the door a strange sense of foreboding overtook me. I looked at the gradually darkening sky and realized a big storm was on its way. I ran to the door and rang the bell. Mrs. Weinguard opened it. The door creaked ominously. I felt like I was in the middle of a *Munsters* episode. I tried to shake thoughts of disaster out of my mind, but they persisted even as Mrs. Weinguard herded us out of the house and into her station wagon.

The ride to the studio was a nightmare. The rain by the middle of the car ride became so heavy that it was impossible to see out any of the windows. I was terrified. The car was crowded with eight other screaming seven-year-olds. I was hot in my rain gear but too cramped to manage to get out of it. Mrs. Weinguard led us in a round of "Row, Row, Row Your Boat" as she maneuvered the car blindly at death-defying speeds. I was never so happy in my life as when we finally arrived and I again put my young feet on solid ground.

We ran for cover in the main entrance of the WGN building. Before I had time to dry, I was standing in the Bozo studio. My original feeling of excitement crept back, and the horrors of the car ride faded into the background. We were ushered up to the top row of a set of bleachers, and the usher made a point of sitting Kenny on the aisle. I was squeezed between Kenny and his mother. I looked around and was astounded at how small the studio looked. What appeared to be a huge circus tent at home was actually the size of a small gymnasium. I mentioned this to Mrs. Weinguard. She looked down at me, straightened my tie, and told me I didn't know how to dress myself.

Then the music started and my heart jumped. Mr. Ned, the ringmaster, appeared. He greeted us, and excitedly told us to turn our heads to the center ring to watch some performing poodles. I eagerly turned my head and saw nothing. The music in the background came to a halt. An announcement was made that the poodles had been pre-recorded and that if we wished to see them we could look at the monitors. I searched for a monitor. The closest one was so far away I could see and hear nothing. After five minutes the poodles stopped and commercials appeared on the distant monitor. During this break, another announcement was made. We were told that Bozo was sick and would not be performing. A gasp went through the audience. I was devastated. Before I could gather my thoughts the show resumed. Mr. Ned announced a clown act. This time it was live. I was so angry that the clowns didn't strike me as the least bit funny. After the clown act had come to a conclusion, Cookie, one of the clowns, introduced a cartoon. The cartoon, like the poodles, was pre-recorded. I could hardly contain myself. I looked around, bewildered, and noticed the audience felt the same as I did. My anger gradually turned to self-pity. I resigned myself to the fact that Bozo was all a great hoax.

Eventually the Bozo Bucket Game, the climax of the show, arrived. The magic arrows began flashing across the distant TV monitor. My self-pity vanished as I intently watched the screen. Would I be the one picked? Would I have the chance to be seen by millions of people across the world? Would I win all those fabulous prizes? I watched as the magic arrows landed. I gasped as they landed on me. I jumped up. I was screaming and carrying on. My thoughts began to move in slow motion. I could imagine my mother sitting at home, beaming with parental pride, watching as her son became a television superstar. I started to move sideways, only to see Kenny half way down the bleachers already. Mrs. Weinguard turned to me, smiled, and informed me that the arrows had landed on Kenny because it was his birthday. I stopped dead in my tracks. I sat down completely dumbfounded. They had sat Kenny down at the aisle because he was chosen beforehand. The magic arrows were a fraud. Bozo's circus was a fraud. I watched silently as Kenny loused up the game.

The ride home seemed like an eternity. I told Mrs. Weinguard that I was sick and didn't wish to go back to her house for the party portion of the "event." Mrs. Weinguard pleasantly agreed. When I got home, I ran upstairs and collapsed crying in my mother's arms. I was too incoherent to tell her what had happened. She assumed I had gotten into a fight with someone. I felt oddly comforted by my mother's inappropriate comforting words. At the very least my mother was not pre-recorded.

# ANNE FRANK

# *Diary*

Anne Frank (1929–1945) was a young girl in Amsterdam who went into hiding with her family during World War II to avoid the horrors of the Holocaust. Her diary ("Kitty") is her personal record of their hiding—a hiding which ended in her own internment and death. It was published by her family after the war, and was adopted by children and adults around the world as the honest, innocent story of an average girl trapped in extraordinary circumstances. In this excerpt, she recounts the changes she has gone through since her family went into hiding.

Tuesday, 7 March 1944

DEAR KITTY,

IF I THINK NOW OF MY LIFE IN 1942, IT ALL SEEMS SO UNREAL. IT WAS quite a different Anne who enjoyed that heavenly existence from the Anne who has grown wise within these walls. Yes, it was a heavenly life. Boy friends at every turn, about twenty friends and acquaintances of my own age, the darling of nearly all the teachers, spoiled from top to toe by Mummy and Daddy, lots of sweets, enough pocket money, what more could one want? You will certainly wonder by what means I got around all these people. Peter's word "attractiveness" is not altogether true. All the teachers were entertained by my cute answers, my amusing remarks, my smiling face, and my questioning looks. That is all I was—a terrible flirt, coquettish and amusing. I had one or two advantages, which kept me rather in favor. I was industrious, honest, and frank. I would never have dreamed of cribbing from anyone else [I would never have refused anyone who wanted to crib from me]. I shared my sweets generously, and I wasn't conceited.

Wouldn't I have become rather forward with so much admiration? It was a good thing that in the midst of, at the height of, all this gaiety, I suddenly had to face reality and it took me at least a year to get used to the fact that there was no more admiration forthcoming.

How did I appear at school? The one who thought of new jokes and pranks, always "king of the castle," never in a bad mood, never a crybaby. No wonder everyone liked to cycle with me, and I got their attentions.

Now I look back at that Anne as an amusing, but very superficial girl, who has nothing to do with the Anne of today. Peter said quite rightly about me: "If ever I saw you, you were always surrounded by two or more boys and a whole troupe of girls. You were always laughing and always the center of everything!"

What is left of this girl? Oh, don't worry, I haven't forgotten how to laugh or to answer back readily. I'm just as good, if not better, at criticizing people, and I can still flirt if . . . I wish. That's not it though, I'd like that sort of life again for an evening, a few days, or even a week; the life which seems so carefree and gay. But at the end of that week, I should be dead beat and would be only too thankful to listen to anyone who began to talk about something sensible.

I don't want followers, but friends, admirers who fall not for a flattering smile but for what one does and for one's character. I know quite well that the circle around me would be much smaller. But what does that matter, as long as one still keeps a few sincere friends? Yet I wasn't entirely happy in 1942 in spite of everything; I often felt deserted, but because I was on the go the whole day long, I didn't think about it and enjoyed myself as much as I could. Consciously or unconsciously, I tried to drive away the emptiness I felt with jokes and pranks. Now I think seriously about life and what I have to do. One period of my life is over forever. The carefree school days are gone, never to return. I don't even long for them any more; I have outgrown them, I can't just only enjoy myself as my serious side is always there.

I look upon my life up till the New Year, as it were, through a powerful magnifying glass. The sunny life at home, then coming here in 1942, the sudden change, the quarrels, the bickerings, I couldn't understand it, I was taken by surprise, and the only way I could keep up some bearing was by being impertinent.

The first half of 1943: my fits of crying, the loneliness, how I slowly began to see all my faults and shortcomings, which are so great and which seemed much greater then. During the day I deliberately talked about anything and everything that was farthest from my thoughts, tried to draw Pim to me; but couldn't. Alone, I had to face the difficult task of changing myself, to stop the everlasting reproaches, which were so oppressive and which reduced me to such terrible despondency.

Things improved slightly in the second half of the year, I became a young woman and was treated more like a grownup. I started to think, and write stories, and came to the conclusion that the others no longer had the right to throw me about like an india-rubber ball. I wanted to change in accordance with my own desires. But one thing that struck me even more was when I realized that even Daddy would never become my confidant over everything. I didn't want to trust anyone but myself any more. At the beginning of the New Year: the second great change, my dream. . . . And with it I discovered my longing, not for a girl friend, but for a boy friend. I also discovered my inward happiness and my defensive armor of superficiality and gaiety. In due time I quieted down and discovered my boundless desire for all that is beautiful and good.

And in the evening, when I lie in bed and end my prayers with the words, "I thank you, God, for all that is good and dear and beautiful," I am filled with joy. Then I think about "the good" of going into hiding, of my health and with my whole being of the "dearness" of Peter, of that which is still embryonic and impressionable and which we neither of us dare to name or touch, of that which will come sometime; love, the future, happiness and of "the beauty" which exists in the world; the world, nature, beauty and all, all that is exquisite and fine.

I don't think then of all the misery, but of the beauty that still remains. This is one of the things that Mummy and I are so entirely different about. Her counsel when one feels melancholy is: "Think of all the misery in the world and be thankful that you are not sharing in it!" My advice is: "Go outside, to the fields, enjoy nature and the sunshine, go out and try to recapture happiness in yourself and in God. Think of all the beauty that's still left in and around you and be happy!"

I don't see how Mummy's idea can be right, because then how are you supposed to behave if you go through the misery yourself? Then you are lost. On the contrary, I've found that there is always some beauty left—in nature, sunshine, freedom, in yourself; these can all help you. Look at these things, then you find yourself again, and God, and then you regain your balance.

And whoever is happy will make others happy too. He who has courage and faith will never perish in misery!

Yours, ANNE

# E. B. WHITE

# Once More to the Lake

For such a "simple" man, E. B. (Elwyn Brooks) White the writer exhibited remarkable complexity. There is E. B. White the grammarian, who popularized and revised the remarkably brief but profound *Elements of Style* written by his teacher, William Strunk, Jr. There is E. B. White the beloved author of children's books, of which he wrote just three, all classics: *Stuart Little, Charlotte's Web,* and *The Trumpet of the Swan.* There is E. B. White the stylist, who wrote mostly unsigned but uniformly cherished essays for *The New Yorker* for over forty years. But mostly, E. B. White was a quiet man, who kept a few animals on his small farm in Maine, and occasionally wrote about his seemingly insubstantial life in a most eloquently substantial way.

ONE SUMMER, ALONG ABOUT 1904, MY FATHER RENTED A CAMP ON A lake in Maine and took us all there for the month of August. We all got ringworm from some kittens and had to rub Pond's Extract on our arms and legs night and morning, and my father rolled over in a canoe with all his clothes on; but outside of that the vacation was a success and from then on none of us ever thought there was any place in the world like that lake in Maine. We returned summer after summer—always on August 1st for one month. I have since become a salt-water man, but sometimes in summer there are days when the restlessness of the tides and the fearful cold of the sea water and the incessant wind that blows across the afternoon and into the evening make me wish for the placidity of a lake in the woods. A few weeks ago this feeling got so strong I bought myself a couple of bass hooks and a spinner and returned to the lake where we used to go, for a week's fishing and to revisit old haunts.

I took along my son, who had never had any fresh water up his nose and who had seen lily pads only from train windows. On the journey over to the lake I began to wonder what it would be like. I wondered how time would have marred this unique, this holy spot—the coves and streams, the hills that the sun set behind, the camps and the paths behind the camps. I was sure that the tarred road would have found it out and I wondered in what other ways it would be desolated. It is strange how much you can remember about places like that once you allow your mind to return into the grooves that lead back. You remember one thing, and that suddenly reminds you of another thing. I guess I remembered clearest of all the early mornings, when the lake was cool and motionless, remembered how the bedroom smelled of the lumber it was made of and of the wet woods whose scent entered through the screen. The partitions in the camp were thin and did not extend clear to the top of the rooms, and as I was always the first up I would dress softly so as not to wake the others, and sneak out into the sweet outdoors and start out in the canoe, keeping close along the shore in the long shadows of the pines. I remembered being very careful never to rub my paddle against the gunwale for fear of disturbing the stillness of the cathedral.

The lake had never been what you would call a wild lake. There were cottages sprinkled around the shores, and it was in farming country although the shores of the lake were quite heavily wooded. Some of the cottages were owned by nearby farmers, and you would live at the shore and eat your meals at the farmhouse. That's what our family did. But although it wasn't wild, it was a fairly large and undisturbed lake and there were places in it which, to a child at least, seemed infinitely remote and primeval.

I was right about the tar: it led to within half a mile of the shore. But when I got back there, with my boy, and we settled into a camp near a farmhouse and into the kind of summertime I had known, I could tell that it was going to be pretty much the same as it had been before—I knew it, lying in bed the first morning, smelling the bedroom, and hearing the boy sneak quietly out and go off along the shore in a boat. I began to sustain the illusion that he was I, and therefore, by simple transposition, that I was my father. This sensation persisted, kept cropping up all the time we were there. It was not an entirely new feeling, but in this setting it grew much stronger. I seemed to be living a dual existence. I would be in the middle of some simple act, I would be picking up a bait box or laying down a table fork, or I would be saying something, and suddenly it would be not I but my father who was saying the words or making the gesture. It gave me a creepy sensation.

We went fishing the first morning. I felt the same damp moss covering the worms in the bait can, and saw the dragonfly alight on the tip of my rod as it hovered a few inches from the surface of the water. It was the arrival of this fly that convinced me beyond any doubt that everything was as it always had been, that the years were a mirage and there had been no years. The small waves were the same, chucking the rowboat under the chin as we fished at anchor, and the boat was the same boat, the same color green and the ribs broken in the same places, and under the floor-boards the same fresh-water leavings and débris—the dead hellgrammite, the wisps of moss, the rusty discarded fishhook, the dried blood from yesterday's catch. We stared silently at the tips of our rods, at the dragonflies that came and went. I lowered the tip of mine into the water, tentatively, pensively dislodging the fly, which darted two feet away, poised, darted two feet back, and came to rest again a little farther up the rod. There had been no years between the ducking of this dragonfly and the other one—the one that was part of memory. I looked at the boy, who was silently watching his fly, and it was my hands that held his rod, my eyes watching. I felt dizzy and didn't know which rod I was at the end of.

We caught two bass, hauling them in briskly as though they were mackerel, pulling them over the side of the boat in a businesslike manner without any landing net, and stunning them with a blow on the back of the head. When we got back for a swim before lunch, the lake was exactly where we had left it, the same number of inches from the dock, and there was only the merest suggestion of a breeze. This seemed an utterly enchanted sea, this lake you could leave to its own devices for a few hours and come back to, and find that it had not stirred, this constant and trustworthy body of water. In the shallows, the dark, water-soaked sticks and twigs, smooth and old, were undulating in clusters on the bottom against the clean ribbed sand, and the track of the mussel was plain. A school of minnows swam by, each minnow with its small individual shadow, doubling the attendance, so clear and sharp in the sunlight. Some of the other campers were in swimming, along the shore, one of them with a cake of soap, and the water felt thin and clear and unsubstantial. Over the years there had been this person with the cake of soap, this cultist, and here he was. There had been no years.

Up to the farmhouse to dinner through the teeming, dusty field, the road under our sneakers was only a two-track road. The middle track was missing, the one with the marks of the hooves and splotches of dried, flaky manure. There had always been three tracks to choose from in choosing which track to walk in; now the choice was narrowed down to two. For a moment I missed terribly the middle alternative. But the way led past the tennis court, and something about the way it lay there in the sun reassured me; the tape had loosened along the backline, the alleys were green with plantains and other weeds, and the net (installed in June and removed in September) sagged in the dry noon, and the whole place steamed with midday heat and hunger and emptiness. There was a choice of pie for dessert, and one was blueberry and one was apple, and the waitresses were the same country girls, there having been no passage of time, only the illusion of it as in a dropped curtain—the waitresses were still fifteen; their hair had been washed, that was the only difference—they had been to the movies and seen the pretty girls with the clean hair.

Summertime, oh summertime, pattern of life indelible, the fade-proof lake, the woods unshatterable, the pasture with the sweetfern and the juniper forever and ever, summer without end; this was the background, and the life along the shore was the design, the cottages with their innocent and tranquil design, their tiny docks with the flagpole and the American flag floating against the white clouds in the blue sky, the little paths over the roots of the trees leading from camp to camp and the paths leading back to the outhouses and the can of lime for sprinkling, and at the souvenir counters at the store the miniature birch-bark canoes and the post cards that showed things looking a little better than they looked. This was the American family at play, escaping the city heat, wondering whether the newcomers in the camp at the head of the cove were "common" or "nice," wondering whether it was true that the people who drove up for Sunday dinner at the farmhouse were turned away because there wasn't enough chicken.

It seemed to me, as I kept remembering all this, that those times and those summers had been infinitely precious and worth saving. There had been jollity and peace and goodness. The arriving (at the beginning of August) had been so big a business in itself, at the railway station the farm wagon drawn up, the first smell of the pine-laden air, the first glimpse of the smiling farmer, and the great importance of the trunks and your father's enormous authority in such matters, and the feel of the wagon under you for the long ten-mile haul, and at the top of the last long hill catching the first view of the lake after eleven months of not seeing this cherished body of water. The shouts and cries of the other campers when they saw you, and the trunks to be unpacked, to give up their rich burden. (Arriving was less exciting nowadays, when you sneaked up in your car and parked it under a tree near the camp and took out the bags and in five minutes it was all over, no fuss, no loud wonderful fuss about trunks.)

Peace and goodness and jollity. The only thing that was wrong now, really, was the sound of the place, an unfamiliar nervous sound of the outboard motors. This was the note that jarred, the one thing that would sometimes break the illusion and set the years moving. In those other summertimes all motors were inboard; and when they were at a little distance, the noise they made was a sedative, an ingredient of summer sleep. They were one-cylinder and two-cylinder engines, and some were make-and-break and some were jump-spark, but they all made a sleepy sound across the lake. The one-lungers throbbed and fluttered, and the twin-cylinder ones purred and purred and that was a quiet sound too. But now the campers all had outboards. In the daytime, in the hot mornings, these motors made a petulant, irritable sound; at night, in the still evening when the after-glow lit the water, they whined about one's ears like mosquitoes. My boy loved our rented outboard, and his great desire was to achieve singlehanded mastery over it, and authority, and he soon learned the trick of choking it a little (but not too much), and the adjustment of the needle valve. Watching him I would remember the things you could do with the old one-cylinder engine with the heavy flywheel, how you could have it eating out of your hand if you got really close to it spiritually. Motor boats in those days didn't have clutches, and you would make a landing by shutting off the motor at the proper time and coasting in with a dead rudder. But there was a way of reversing them, if you learned the trick, by cutting the switch and putting it on again exactly on the final dying revolution of the flywheel, so that it would kick back against compression and begin reversing. Approaching a dock in a strong following breeze, it was difficult to slow up sufficiently by the ordinary coasting method, and if a boy felt he had complete mastery over his motor, he was tempted to keep it running beyond its time and then reverse it a few feet from the dock. It took a cool nerve, because if you threw the switch a twentieth of a second too soon you could catch the flywheel when it still had speed enough to go up past center, and the boat would leap ahead, charging bull-fashion at the dock.

We had a good week at the camp. The bass were biting well and the sun shone endlessly, day after day. We would be tired at night and lie down in the accumulated heat of the little bedrooms after the long hot day and the breeze would stir almost imperceptibly outside and the smell of the swamp drift in through the rusty screens. Sleep would come easily and in the morning the red squirrel would be on the roof, tapping out his gay routine. I kept remembering everything, lying in bed in the mornings—the small steamboat that had a long rounded stern like the lip of a Ubangi, and how quietly she ran on the moonlight sails, when the older boys played their mandolins and the girls sang and we ate doughnuts dipped in sugar, and how sweet the music was on the water in the shining light, and what it had felt like to think about girls then. After breakfast we would go up to the store and the things were in the same place—the minnows in a bottle, the plugs and spinners disarranged and pawed over by the youngsters from the boys' camp, the fig newtons and the Beeman's gum. Outside, the road was tarred and cars stood in front of the store. Inside, all was just as it had always been, except there was more Coca-Cola and not so much Moxie and root beer and birch beer and sarsaparilla. We would walk out with a bottle of pop apiece and sometimes the pop would backfire up our noses and hurt. We explored the streams, quietly, where the turtles slid off the sunny logs and dug their way into the soft bottom; and we lay on the town wharf and fed worms to the tame bass. Everywhere we went I had trouble making out which was I, the one walking at my side, the one walking in my pants.

One afternoon while we were there at that lake a thunderstorm came up. It was like the revival of an old melodrama that I had seen long ago with childish awe. The second-act climax of the drama of the electrical disturbance over a lake in America had not changed in any important respect. This was the big scene, still the big scene. The whole thing was so familiar, the first feeling of oppression and heat and a general air around camp of not wanting to go very far away. In midafternoon (it was all the same) a curious darkening of the sky, and a lull in everything that had made life tick; and then the way the boats suddenly swung the other way at their moorings with the coming of a breeze out of the new quarter, and the premonitory rumble. Then the kettle drum, then the snare, then the bass drum and cymbals, then crackling light against the dark, and the gods grinning and licking their chops in the hills. Afterward the calm, the rain steadily rustling in the calm lake, the return of light and hope and spirits, and the campers running out in joy and relief to go swimming in the rain, their bright cries perpetuating the deathless joke about how they were getting simply drenched, and the children screaming with delight at the new sensation of bathing in the rain, and the joke about getting drenched linking the generations in a strong indestructible chain. And the comedian who waded in carrying an umbrella.

When the others went swimming my son said he was going in too. He pulled his dripping trunks from the line where they had hung all through the shower, and wrung them out. Languidly, and with no thought of going in, I watched him, his hard little body, skinny and bare, saw him wince slightly as he pulled up around his vitals the small, soggy, icy garment. As he buckled the swollen belt suddenly my groin felt the chill of death.

*Student Essay*

# PEARL KLEIN

# Once More to the Pool

Pearl's essay follows the pattern of White's, but since her reflection comes at a younger age, the conclusion is different.

FROM THE TIME I COULD SWIM UNTIL I WAS NINE YEARS OLD, I SPENT every summer underwater. All summer long, from the moment the municipal pool opened, my family and I would be there for a full day of fun in the concrete, three different-sized pools, gloriously sticky snack foods at breaks for grown-up swims, and home again to sweat underneath a fan and the Indiana moon.

When we first arrived, if the pool was just opening, the dressing room would be almost dry, with the only light a murky grey natural light that leaked through transomlike windows near the ceiling. You were required to take a shower before entering the pool, but getting your hair wet counted. The shower didn't have knobs for the water, just a space-age round button, the size of a baby's fist, which we'd punch as hard as we could; when the button came back out, automatically, the water would stop and the sentence was up.

The next two steps that impeded our progress to the pool were the footbath and the basket. Early in the day, like during the summer when I took swim lessons at eight-thirty in the morning, the footbath would be almost empty, just a little trickle of water covering a rubber mat. By the time we left, it would be ankle-deep, or knee-deep for tots. The water would be either freezing and fresh or warmly overused, and if I hadn't been in a hurry, I might have enjoyed the massage of the rubber mat. But all I could think of was getting to the pool.

The last step was to exchange a clothing basket for a pin with a number on it. Nothing was locked up but I knew everything would be safe in the locker room, full of sullen teenagers hiding behind a clutch door and a sign that said "Authorized Personnel Only." I felt sorry for those people, trapped without visitors, but they seemed to enjoy their authority, or at least, their authorization. They gave you a numbered metal tag attached to a safety pin, you pinned it to your bathing suit, and you were off!

Not so fast, kids! No running on the concrete! No roughhousing by the pool! First, we put our towels down. Then we took off our rubber thongs. We had to make sure Mom could see us. Only accompanied children allowed in the medium pool—come on, Mom!

I couldn't dive without noseplugs and I never liked the breathing they taught for the crawlstroke, so most of the time I did somersaults or handstands, swam in endless rotation with my friend Jessica: between her legs, she between mine, or sat on the steps that gradually got deeper in gradually colder water. Sometimes I would rescue ladybugs from drowning or being sucked into the mysterious water-cleaning system, but they were all so dumb they just went right back in. On my toughest days I'd plow down the waterslide face forward on my belly, screaming all the way.

Other days I preferred the calm warmth of the tot pool to more visceral thrills, and I'd daydream while water bubbled out of the center of this shallow fountain, sometimes getting bumped into by a floating toddler. But the best times I ever had were in the medium pool. We were allowed to take inflatable toys in this pool, and until it popped, we had a yellow dolphin that would dive and leap as you tried to gain a seat on its slippery back. Sometimes we'd be there when the clouds coated the sky but before lightning cleared and closed the pool. It would just be me and my brother and sister in our chlorinated blue heaven, riding a yellow dolphin, waiting until the last alarm.

My underwater years ended abruptly when my family moved from sunny Indiana to moist Seattle, land of the indoor pool. Pools were serious places there, with divided lanes, rectangles with ladders but no stairs, no slides, no lost ladybugs. Pools without fences or wading depths, no clouds above and no room for a dolphin or a dreamer. I left the water within the walls and, unable to adapt to graceful, boring laps, have rarely returned.

*Student Essay*

# JONATHAN MUIR

# *Bottom of the Ninth*

It is probably more illuminating to describe a single, seemingly unimportant event in rigorous detail than to try to make a sweeping generalization about something more substantial. That's how Jonathan Muir attempts to address the subject of "growing up"—instead of trying to tackle the issue all at once, he describes a single incident from his childhood, and tries to give it significance in the larger context of his life.

THERE WAS A TIME WHEN MY LIFE SEEMED SO SIMPLE TO ME. I HAD it planned. I didn't put it down in writing, but I had been over it thousands of times in my head. Each time it was the same, never wavering. I had dreams but they were more than mere aspirations, because I knew something that everyone else did not. I knew how to make my dreams realities. As far as I was concerned it was only a matter of time until mine came true. I was twelve.

My dearest friend and mentor, Dutch Schroeder, fostered this perspective in me at an early age. I cannot remember the day we first met, but my earliest memories are of Dutch.

I was always mesmerized by his hands. Powerful. Weathered. Delicate. His were the hands so skilled that they were asked to help craft the first atomic bomb. His were the hands so quick and nimble that they were granted the honor of playing baseball with Babe Ruth. His were the hands so tender and nurturing that they helped cultivate over fifty years of marriage. Yet his hands still longed to hoist one last trophy, to grasp one last dream: to catch a foul ball. It was Dutch who taught me why we dream.

I can trace the greatest lesson Dutch ever taught me to one spring evening when we attended a University of Texas baseball game at Disch-Falk Field. My dad, Dutch, and myself had made this trip at least a hundred times before.

We missed church more often than we missed a baseball game. Baseball was our religion: our seats the pew, the game's program our Bible, and the Longhorns' legendary coach, Cliff Gustafson, our God. Every game my dad and I, Dutch's disciples, would follow him up the steps to our seats, arms full of Coke, popcorn, and hot dogs. Once we sat down we didn't leave our seats until the game was over. My dad filled out his scorecard before each game. As he did Dutch would slowly turn his head to him and in his warm, gentle voice preach his sermon: "You know that if a ball ever comes up here, don't worry about catching it. Just lean aside and I'll take care of it." And then he'd smile so that all that remained of his eyes were two little slivers. And so it was, every game.

It was Dutch's pre-game sermon that made our trip to the ballpark a pilgrimage. Dutch attended game after game in an attempt to achieve his last childhood dream, to catch a foul ball at a baseball game. Dutch's pursuit of his dream taught us that we had to follow our hearts. If we truly believe in our dreams we must see them through until the end, we must not lose faith. My dad and I went to all of those games not out of a love for baseball, or a loyalty to our team, but out of a love for Dutch. We wanted to believe as he did. We wanted to share his passion. If we saw Dutch catch that ball, and actually be a part of mission, maybe, just maybe, his joy of living, his zest for life might rub off on us, so that we, too, might be blessed.

As season after season gave way to fall, a weaker man might have given up on his quest. But even as his once strong body became tired with age and his health deteriorated, Dutch persisted, never missing a game, never losing hope. And it was on a date that I can't remember against a team I can't recall that I came to understand Dutch's message. I was twelve.

It was late in the game and Texas was just about to wrap up another victory. My dad sat recording the results of the previous at bat, looking down at his score sheet as the batter fouled off a pitch. I could see it coming, advancing towards us ever so slowly, so slowly that I could count its stitches, attempting to prolong destiny. As the ball approached us, my dad, not bothering to even look up or lift his pencil, leaned towards me as Dutch reached over and cradled the ball into his hands, hands created for this moment.

Dutch opened up his hands to take a look at that which he most coveted. There was no wonderment or disbelief scrawled on his face. Dutch had known that someday it would happen. He just smiled. And as Dutch smiled, the crowd erupted in a tremendous roar, applauding more than his spectacular catch, they applauded his perseverance. As Dutch stood to accept his applause he raised his prize high in the air for all to see.

Dutch is gone now, but the memory of that sticky Austin spring night to this day moistens my palms and brow with sweat. The roasting of peanuts still lingers fresh in my nose. The crisp smack of the ball striking a mitt still rings clear in my ears. My eyes still water and my heart still aches. But as his memory is and always will be vivid in my memory, now that he is gone I find it increasingly more difficult to dream. Plans that I thought would become realities are now tossed aside, forgotten. I've lost my direction. Now I have but one remaining dream: To be twelve again.

# Acknowledgments

ABBEY: "Polemic: Industrial Tourism and the National Parks" from *Desert Solitaire* by Edward Abbey. Copyright © 1968 by Edward Abbey. Reprinted by permission of Don Congdon and Associates, Inc.

ATWOOD: "Pornography" by Margaret Atwood. Copyright © 1983 by Margaret Atwood. Reprinted by permission of Phoebe Larmore.

BAKER: Reprinted from *Growing Up* by Russell Baker. Copyright © 1982. Published by Contemporary Books, Inc.

BLAIR: "Shattering the Myth of the Glass Ceiling" by Anita K. Blair, from *The Los Angeles Times*, May 7, 1996. Copyright © 1996, Los Angeles Times. Reprinted by permission.

CROCKETT: "'Haven't We Met . . .?' The Pickup Line Just Goes On and On" by Stephanie A. Crockett. Copyright © 1995 by the Washington Post Writers Group. Reprinted by permission of the author.

DIDION: "On Keeping a Notebook" from *Slouching Toward Bethlehem* by Joan Didion. Copyright © 1966, 1968 by Joan Didion. Reprinted by permission of Farrar, Straus, and Giroux, Inc.

DILLARD: Excerpt from *An American Childhood* by Annie Dillard. Copyright © 1987 by Annie Dillard. Reprinted by permission of HarperCollins Publishers, Inc.

DOHENY: "Desperately Seeking Anyone" by Kathleen Doheny, from *The Los Angeles Times*, November 14, 1994. Copyright © 1994, Los Angeles Times. Reprinted by permission.

EBELING: "The Failure of Feminism," by Kay Ebeling. Copyright © 1990 by *Newsweek*.

FRANK: "Diary" from *The Diary of Anne Frank: The Critical Edition* by Anne Frank. Copyright © 1986 by Anne Frank. Fonds, Basle/Switzerland, for all texts of Anne Frank. Used by permission of Doubleday, a division of Bantam Doubleday Dell Publishing Group, Inc.

GERZON: "Manhood: The Elusive Goal" from *A Choice of Heroes* by Mark Gerzon. Copyright © 1982 by Mark Gerzon. Reprinted by permission of Houghton Mifflin Company. All rights reserved.

HASSELSTROM: "The Cow Versus the Animal Rights Activist"

*New Statesman & Society*. Reprinted by permission of Guardian/ Observer News Services.

SAFIRE: "The Perfect Paragraph" by William Safire, from *The New York Times*, January 15, 1995. Copyright © 1995, New York Times. Reprinted by permission.

SOWELL: "Cold Compassion" by Thomas Sowell. First published in *Forbes* magazine, August 2, 1993. Reprinted by Permission of Forbes Magazine Copyright © Forbes Inc., 1993.

SUZUKI: "What is Zen?" by D. T. Suzuki. Copyright © 1959 by Princeton University Press. Renewed 1987 by Princeton University Press. Reprinted by permission of Princeton University Press.

THEROUX: "Being a Man," from *Sunrise with Seamonsters* by Paul Theroux. Copyright © 1985 by Cape Cod Scriveners Co. Reprinted by permission of Houghton Mifflin Co. All rights reserved.

THUROW: "Why Women are Paid Less Than Men" by Lester C. Thurow, from the *New York Times*, March 8, 1991. Copyright © 1991, New York Times. Reprinted by permission.

VONNEGUT: "How to Write with Style" by Kurt Vonnegut. Copyright © 1982, International Paper Company. Reprinted by permission.

WARD: "Is the Fetus a Person?" by Dr. Roy Bowen Ward. Copyright © 1996, Religious Coalition for Reproductive Choice. Reprinted by permission of the author.

WHITE: "Once More to the Lake" from *One Man's Meat* by E. B. White. Copyright © 1941 by E. B. White. Reprinted by permission of HarperCollins Publishers, Inc.

WOOLF: "If Shakespeare Had Had a Sister," from *A Room of One's Own* by Virginia Woolf. copyright © 1929 by Harcourt Brace Jovanovich, Inc., and the Author's literary estate. Reprinted by permission.

WRIGHT: "The Library Card" from Chapter 13 of *Black Boy* by Richard Wright. Copyright © 1937, 1942, 1944, 1945 by Richard Wright. Copyright renewed 1973 by Ellen Wright. Reprinted by permission of HarperCollins Publishers, Inc.